The Politics of Ephemeral Digital Media

T0384821

In the age of "complex TV," of social networking and massive consumption of transmedia narratives, myriad short-lived phenomena surround films and TV programs raising questions about the endurance of a fictional world and other mediatized discourse over a long arc of time. The life of media products can change direction depending on the variability of paratextual materials and activities such as online commentaries and forums, promos and trailers, disposable merchandise and gadgets, grassroots video production, archives, and gaming. This book examines the tension between permanence and obsolescence in the production and experience of media by-products, analyzing the affections and meanings they convey and uncovering the machineries of their persistence or disposal. Paratexts, which have long been considered only ancillary to a central text, interfere instead with textual politics by influencing the viewers' fidelity (or infidelity) to a product and affecting a fictional world's "life expectancy." Scholars in the fields of film studies, media studies, memory and cultural studies are here called to observe these by-products' temporalities (their short form and/or long temporal extension, their nostalgic politics or future projections) and assess their increasing influence on our use of the past and present, on our temporal experience, and, consequently, on our social and political self-positioning through the media.

Sara Pesce teaches Film History and Performance Studies at the University of Bologna. She has published works on the historical roots of Hollywood, cultural memory, and performance. Among the subjects of her books are Hollywood Jewish founders (*Dietro lo schermo*, 2005), World War II memory in Italian film (*Memoria e Immaginario*, 2008), and Laurence Olivier (*Laurence Olivier nei film*, 2012).

Paolo Noto is Lecturer in film history at the University of Bologna. He is one of the editors in chief of *L'avventura. Internation Journal of Italian Film and Media Landscapes* and the secretary of the open access journal *SERIES* (series.unibo.it). He has authored two books, dedicated to the Italian neorealism (*Il cinema neorealista*, with Francesco Pitassio, 2010) and to the application of genre theory to the Italian post-war cinema (*Dal bozzetto ai generi*, 2011).

Routledge Studies in New Media and Cyberculture

For a full list of titles in this series, please visit www.routledge.com.

The Politics of Ephemeral Digital Media

Permanence and Obsolescence in Paratexts

Edited by Sara Pesce and Paolo Noto

LONDON AND NEW YORK

First published 2016
by Routledge

2 Park Square, Milton Park, Abingdon, Oxfordshire OX14 4RN
711 Third Avenue, New York, NY 10017

Routledge is an imprint of the Taylor & Francis Group, an informa business

First issued in paperback 2018

Library of Congress Cataloging-in-Publication Data

Names: Pesce, Sara, editor. | Noto, Paolo, 1978– editor.
Title: The politics of ephemeral digital media: permanence and obsolescence in paratexts / edited by Sara Pesce and Paolo Noto.
Description: New York; London: Routledge, 2016. |
Series: Routledge studies in new media and cyberculture; 34 |
Includes bibliographical references and index.
Identifiers: LCCN 2016001399
Subjects: LCSH: Digital media—Technological innovations. |
Mass media and culture. | Paratext.
Classification: LCC P96.T42 P74 2016 | DDC 302.23/1—dc23
LC record available at http://lccn.loc.gov/2016001399

ISBN: 978-1-138-85792-6 (hbk)
ISBN: 978-1-138-31974-5 (pbk)

Typeset in Sabon
by codeMantra

Contents

     and an Archaeology of Presence   110
     FABRICE LYCZBA

  8 Sound Memories: "Talker Remakes," Paratexts,
     and the Cinematic Past   123
     KATHLEEN LOOCK

  9 Paratexts from Cinephilia to Mediaphilia
     (through Ludification Culture)   138
     ROY MENARINI AND LUCIA TRALLI

PART III
Mutant Paratexts: Interactivity, Promotion, Gameplay, Fandom

 10 Interactivity and the Modalities of Textual-Hacking:
     From the Bible to Algorithmically Generated Stories   155
     WILLIAM URICCHIO

 11 One Does Not Simply Walk Away from the Past.
     The Van Der Memes and the Dynamics of
     Memory and Spreadability   170
     PAOLA BREMBILLA

 12 "You Had to Be There": Alternate Reality Games and
     Multiple Durational Temporalities   183
     STEPHANIE JANES

 13 The TV Recap: Knowledge, Memory, and
     Complex Narrative Orientation   198
     CLAUDIO BISONI

 14 *The Girl with the Dragon Tattoo*: Paratexts
     in a Flexible World   213
     MARTA BONI

 15 TV Series, Convergence Culture, and
     the Davy Crockett Hat   228
     VERONICA INNOCENTI AND GUGLIELMO PESCATORE

     List of Contributors   241
     Index   247

Acknowledgments

This book is one of the outcomes of a wider project led by Guglielmo Pescatore called Media Mutations, a series of international events based in the Department of Arts of the University of Bologna, Italy, which started in 2008 with Corto circuito, a conference organized by Michele Fadda and dedicated to cinema in the age of convergence. Since then, Media Mutations has been gathering scholars to investigate those textual forms and artifacts that reveal the transformations occurring in the contemporary mediascape (the latest editions have covered themes including TV series, ephemeralia, and games). Several of the contributors of this volume presented their papers at the fifth edition, Ephemeral Media. Time, Persistence and Transience in Contemporary Screen Culture (Bologna, 21–22 May 2013), organized by Sara Pesce, Paul Grainge, and Roberta Pearson. On this occasion we want to express our gratitude to the conference organizers, to all the conference's speakers (and especially to Stephanie Janes, for her invaluable help in proofing the manuscript) to those who joined this editorial project later, and to the Department of Arts for supporting Media Mutations.

The Politics of Ephemeral Digital Media
Permanence and Obsolescence in Paratexts

Sara Pesce and Paolo Noto

The idea of this book was born out of the necessity to better understand and assess a number of paratextual forms (from memes to animated Graphics Interchange Formats [GIFs]; from digital promotional materials to interactive games; from fan videos to cinephiliac blogging) populating the contemporary realm of entertainment and affecting it in ways that interfere not only with textual meaning, but also with the viewers' fidelity (or infidelity) to a product, or with a fictional world's "life expectancy." This need is felt, we believe, by the scientific community, as well as by the media industry and by consumers of transmedia narratives and "complex TV."[1] What this work questions is not so much the permanence or evanescence of these by-products, as the effects of durability or ephemerality that their production and consumption have on a large scale within the mediascape.

The myriad short-lived phenomena surrounding films, TV programs, and news raises questions concerning the endurance of an imaginary world over a long arc of time. The life of a film or a TV series—based on the affections it produces and the meanings it conveys—can change direction depending on the variability and ephemerality of the materials surrounding it, including pop-up ads, online commentaries, short-lived announcements, and replaceable merchandise. Real-time tweeting, for example, can influence the fortune of a TV show by inducing unexpected attention peaks or by expanding its meaning beyond the momentary borders of the broadcast and activating encounters with previous or current media artifacts.

This book aims at grasping the involvement of these phenomena in our temporal experience, in terms of retrieval of the past or projection in the future, perception of time flow, sense of continuity or discontinuity, lifespan, and memory. It also aims to further clarify their roles in our consequent social and political self-positioning through the media in a society where all sorts of retro trends exist and fragments "threaten" to become hegemonic.[2]

Film and media scholars (especially Jonathan Gray, whose recent work is further expanded in this book)[3] have acknowledged the importance of paratexts and ephemeralia as elements that help to situate texts in society. They have questioned the discursive role of textual by-products and cross-media derivatives, their constructive or disruptive connection to a primary text, and their function as agents of remediation.[4] In doing so, they have uncovered elusive textualities, especially when dealing with natively digital texts (hypertexts, videogames, immersive 3D, augmented reality, and web-docs). In other words, the extraordinary growth and easy use of ancillary forms has brought attention to textual expansions and to the dynamics between what is supposedly central (an ur-text, as William Uricchio intriguingly suggests in Chapter 10) and what is apparently peripheral, such as quotes generated by the extraction and migration of textual materials, promotional games that create bridges between the textual temporal dimension and the real-life user experience, or teasers that induce future expectations.

Moreover, as Paul Grainge's edited book on "ephemeral media" has underlined,[5] paratextual phenomena participate in a sociocultural quest—an increasing concern for changes in time regimes dictated by the advent of new television, portable electronic devices, and social media.[6] Media temporality is connected to the length of each product they convey, often involving a divergence between what is extremely short or compressed and what is extremely long or expanded. On the one hand, the contemporary mediascape is permeated by the extraordinary abundance of short form, as the logic of digital media (based on modularity and recombination) favors the creation of short texts.[7] On the other hand, paratexts are especially capable of supporting "vast narratives" by expanding their lifespan and durability, but also by helping viewers to orient themselves in narrative ecosystems, such as those established by contemporary TV series, whose content is often distributed over time and space.[8] A dialectic between permanence and obsolescence is apparent in the production and experience of these products. The interest in paratextual temporality may stem, as Gray maintains in Chapter 2 in this volume, from "the realization that media still disappears from us all the time. Consider, for instance, a bus shelter that over its lifetime may host hundreds of posters for movies, but each for no more than a week or two."

On the basis of these premises, we suggest that these paratextual materials should be observed in the overarching context of a changing epistemology of time and a changing culture of memory. This involves the need to provide interpretations of the contemporary "culture of time" by observing specific phenomena taking place within a digital culture dealing with the "threat" of perishability, or, on the contrary, embodying a utopia of permanence. Thus, our discussion seeks to trigger a dialogue between film/media studies and memory studies.

Academic research on "digital memory"[9] and on what Andrew Hoskins has called "the end of decay time"[10] has stimulated a widespread awareness of the changes investing knowledge and its transmission in the digital age. Firstly, paratextual consumption is based on the action of being networked, of creating or using links and associations based on personal experience. It therefore embodies what has been defined as "connective memory"[11]; that is, a practice of remembering based on multiple interactive trajectories supported by the abundance and accessibility of communication networks. Connective memory emphasizes process and connection over information retrieval and participates in the tension between ephemera and permanence characterizing media digital content.

Secondly, issues of popular memory, heritage, and patrimony are markedly at stake, as some of our authors highlight. Heritage is continuously questioned by paratextual interactions with a text. Persistence of shared contents can be influenced by digital procedures leading web navigators to a particular item: Google's search algorithm replaces the machineries of popular memory favoring the majority interest.

Thirdly, the archival drives and nostalgic motives inhabiting certain complex mechanisms of interaction between film promotion and consumers can be seen as participating in a contemporary 'memory boom' culture, grown increasingly concerned with the capacity for forgetting.[12]

The contributions collected in this book address these issues by adopting different points of view. The first section of the volume (*Understanding "Short Shelf-Life" Media*) responds to the need to give a theoretical framework to our questions on problematic length, ephemerality, and paratextuality in the digital age. This part is dedicated to the definition of the political, social, epistemological, and theoretical problems at stake by delving into case studies and comparative analysis.

Sara Pesce's cultural approach in Chapter 1 situates the phenomena of creation, circulation, and storage of extemporary and short products in the context of the contemporary fear of oblivion and preoccupation for integrity and survival (personal, political and planetary). Her chapter tackles the extraordinary quantity of paratextual materials circulating on- and offline, bringing into focus the issue of ecology, preservation of goods and contents versus their disposal. It uses the metaphor of "short shelf-life media" to discuss how the abundance and scarce life expectancy of media paratexts are rooted in a chain of production and a culture of remembering that can be better understood in the context of "post-scarcity" citizenship and of the "traumatic culture" of the new millennium, permeated by an imaginary of perennial emergence.

In Chapter 2, Jonathan Gray brings to the fore the political aspect of paratextual media. He argues that, besides working as devices for accessing and taking control of primary texts, "paratexts matter" as long as they can drive the political interpretation of TV shows such as *Mad Men* (AMC, 2007–2015). Their disappearance, Gray adds, given the difficulties of collecting and, most of all, properly archiving ephemeralia, can bring about the misunderstanding of the social and political meaning of media artifacts for the audiences that concretely used them.

According to Giulio Lughi's epistemological approach in Chapter 3, "the world of digital media forces us to rethink the relationship between space and time in the organization of textuality" in the digital age. In particular, it demands that we acknowledge that, for example, systems of geotagging using textual elements such as metadata, can be assimilated into paratexts, causing texts to become spaces (viable, inhabitable), while spaces may become texts (readable, writable).

Valentina Re's theoretical approach in Chapter 4 defends the use of the conceptual tools developed by French theorist Gérard Genette and proposes to complement the notion of paratext with the more recent Genettian works on *immanence* and *transcendence* by considering transmedia franchises and vast narratives, like *Lost* (ABC 2004–2010) or *Supernatural* (The WB 2005–2006, The CW 2006–), as works with "plural immanence." In this perspectivem ephemeral tools can be used to prevent and even resist the ephemerality of works that have "fragmentary manifestations."

An explicit historical outlook questioning how contemporary media are entrenched in the past is necessary to understand the meaning and the future directions of the phenomena under scrutiny. How far does digital paratextuality diverge from off-screen phenomena belonging to the past, including early cinema? Is the blurring or extinction of a "source text" being made the object of nostalgia? Questions like these express a chronological viewpoint that is offered especially from the standpoint of visual culture and "screen culture," which adds perspective to Gray's pivotal work on paratexts, while also expanding the important suggestions about the temporality of short forms posed by Paul Grainge's book on transitory screen culture. Many of our contributors explain paratextual phenomena against the background of the media history: of cinema and television, film culture, games and critical discourse, of technologies and marketing strategies. Part II of this volume (*Screen Time and Memory*) brings this effort to the fore.

The encounter between a "classical" content and a present-day form of fruition is the theme of Roberta Pearson's challenging chapter, Chapter 5: what are the shared memories of actors playing Sherlock Holmes that a contemporary user can retrieve on the Internet? What do they reveal about all the elements involved (Holmes, Internet, the users) and about the "current configurations of popular memory"? Pearson finds that different platforms provide the scholar with similar results: Google Images, Facebook, and Flickr "favor the popular and the contemporary." We might say they work less as repositories of archival images than as "flow diagrams" revealing the construction of changing shared memories.

Nostalgia, and the way it can be shaped by ephemeral contents, is the object of Kim Walden's chapter, Chapter 6, which focuses on the promotional campaign for *TRON: Legacy* (Joseph Kosinski, 2010). The author addresses the tension between permanence and obsolescence in the context of communities of gamers and fans of the original *TRON* and uses the distinction—outlined by Svetlana Boym[13]—between restorative and reflective nostalgia to argue that "forms of remembering/misremembering have had the effect of creating an edited, idealized version of the early days of the games arcades and, more broadly, of our cultural past."

In Chapter 7, which is dedicated to 1920s ballyhoo, Fabrice Lyczba explains that the performance of early cinema's stunts has something in common with contemporary forms of film and media marketing. Ballyhoo stunts performed not only a transitional function (that is, they helped viewers to enter the fictional universe) but also a transactional role (they helped users to establish a communicative pact with the text). Ballyhoos were often performed in "essentially playful, self-reflexive, and participatory" ways by the involved audience. Media, Lyczba concludes, "do not vanish" in the path that leads viewers from playful paratexts to texts, but stand as the environment in which that game can be played.

Traditional feature films could themselves be ephemeral objects, Kathleen Loock contends in Chapter 8, and so they were in the early years of Hollywood's golden age. During the transition from silent to sound between 1927 and 1931, however, a sense of historicity was added to these otherwise short-lived artifacts by their "talker remakes." Paratextual sources like fan letters and articles on trade press surrounded these remakes in a way that "kept the memory of silent film versions alive" and "served archival and mnemonic functions that contributed to Hollywood's processes of self-historicization."

In Chapter 9, Roy Menarini and Lucia Tralli maintain that cinephilia, a form of consumption and attachment to media products that may appear confined to a certain idea of modernity, can be affected by the changes brought on by the digital era. A new temporality of consumption emerges, which allows fans to simultaneously watch and discuss films. New cinephilia, according to the authors, has the seemingly paradoxical effect of multiplying paratextual discourses on film (reviews, lists, discussions, live tweets, and so on), while at the same time encouraging permanence through the re-aestheticizing of media culture, for example by promoting the canonization of certain films, or a "sort of desire for individual texts."

The world surrounding a text calls attention particularly to the consumption of entertainment—be it creative, active, or conditioned. The theme of the third section of this volume (*Mutant Paratexts. Communication, Promotion, Gameplay, Fandom*) is the way in which short-lived forms are used by actual audiences. The authors in this section tackle forms of media artifacts that they find particularly emblematic of the present era, either too long to be contained in the traditional dimensions of text (such as transmedia franchises, TV series, and alternative reality games [ARGs]) or too short to be treated as autonomously worthy of analysis (such as Internet memes and recaps).

Part III opens with William Uricchio's chapter, Chapter 10, which intriguingly puts a diverse selection of case studies into a diachronic perspective, simultaneously offering a methodological frame of reference. Uricchio addresses the issue of permanence and obsolescence by inviting us to reconsider the interconnected notions of stability and interactivity, and then the underlying concepts of agency and temporality. Against a thought-provoking array of examples (the Bible, nineteenth-century literature, games, contemporary participatory documentaries, algorithm-generated narratives), the author invites us to trace "generative practices": how does the work of communities of readers that deal with preexisting texts create new textual variations?

Paola Brembilla in Chapter 11 shows that ephemeral user-generated content, such as the Internet memes series known as *Crying Dawson* (originally meant as parodies of the actor James Van Der Beek's performances) can be turned into a promotional vehicle for the actor himself and prove to be particularly persistent. In this process, which also puts into tension audience behaviors and corporate branding strategies, users have an active role in re-shaping memories and meanings. However, as Brembilla shows, the online popularity of the meme is not automatically converted into a "source of profit for the traditional TV industry."

Alternate reality games expressly created for the promotion of films, Stephanie Janes contends in Chapter 12, are often addressed as ancillary artifacts leading to their primary texts, or as sites for user empowerment, but they are rarely analyzed in a temporal perspective. This can be done, according to the author, in three intertwined ways. The first way is to consider the different temporalities that ARGs create in reference to their users. They are not exactly short forms, as they can last months or even years, but their existence is conditional on their marketing function. Second is the way those regimes of time are used by film marketers, and third are "the ways ARG audiences construct and maintain mediated memories of such experiences," for example, documenting the games and creating grassroots archives for otherwise hyper-ephemeral experiences.

A quintessentially ancillary form such as recaps—brief segments used in TV series to condense the storyline of previous episodes for the benefit of forgetful or inexperienced viewers—is considered by Claudio Bisoni in Chapter 13 as much more meaningful than a mere summary. Expanding on Jason Mittell's discourse on the experience of the consumption of new serials as a selective navigation inside an expansive media space, Bisoni sees the recap as "a map" allowing spectators to orient themselves within the complexity of serial narratives. It appears as a textual device that can help viewers to construct and preserve memories of long serial forms.

In a transmedia franchise such as that drawn from Stieg Larsson's *The Girl with the Dragon Tattoo*, Marta Boni in Chapter 14 argues that paratexts are "sites of negotiation of meaning and translation across worlds, parts of a semiotic process through which an ecosystem adapts to the environment during its lifetime." Single fragments of the primary texts (like the GIFs produced by users) may become ephemeral and spreadable, but that makes them extremely important in keeping the balance and adaptability of the entire ecosystem. Their function is to help users to orient themselves in ever-changing narrative environments, but also to allow them to actively participate in the construction of vast narratives generated by "the interaction, at a global level and in different spaces, of all its elements and the production of meaning created by all users."

The book closes with Veronica Innocenti and Guglielmo Pescatore's chapter, Chapter 15, which allows for a summary of a few pivotal issues treated in the volume: the interaction between digital technology and individual experience in users' engagement with the complex narrative forms; the tension between short-form and extended narratives; and the dubious ephemerality of the extremely various forms of textual extraction. The authors revisit the long-debated question of intertextuality in audiovisual artifacts in light of the convergence/divergence paradigm. According to the authors, fragments extracted from and integrated into TV series are necessarily ephemeral. Being spreadable objects, they "are comparable to items of the world of fashion that suddenly are everywhere at a given time and are forgotten [a] few weeks later, only to return again after 10 years." From this point of view, permanence, as well as transience, "is not due to the action of a subject that convenes a primary text and reworks it, making it present again, but to a media and social practice that does not need the presence of a subject agent."

Notes

1. Jason Mittell, *Complex TV. The Poetics of Contemporary Television Storytelling* (New York: New York University Press, 2015).
2. Thomas Hylland Eriksen, "Stacking and Continuity. On Temporal Regimes in Popular Culture," in *24/7. Time and Temporality in the Network Society*, ed. Robert Hassan and Ronald E. Purser (Stanford, CA: Stanford Business Books, 2007), 151; Derek Kompare, "The Benefits of Banality: Domestic Syndication in the Post-Network Era," in *Beyond Prime Time: Television Programming in the Post-Network Era*, ed. Amanda D. Lotz (New York: Routledge, 2009), 55–74.
3. Jonathan Gray, *Show Sold Separately: Promos, Spoilers and Other Media Paratexts* (New York: New York University Press, 2010).
4. Jason Mittell, "Serial Orientations. Paratexts and Contemporary Complex Television," in *(Dis)Orienting Media and Narrative Mazes*, eds. Julia Eckel, Bernd Leiendecker, Daniela Olek, and Chrisine Piepiorka (Bielefield, Germany: Transcript Verlag, 2013), 165–182.
5. Paul Grainge, ed., *Ephemeral Media: Transitory Screen Culture from Television to YouTube* (London: BFI and Palgrave Macmillan, 2011).
6. Robert Hassan and Ronald E. Purser, eds., *24/7. Time and Temporality in the Network Society* (Stanford, CA: Stanford Business Books, 2007); Emily Keighley, ed., *Time Media and Modernity* (London: Palgrave Macmillan, 2012); Sarah Sharma, *In the Meantime: Temporality and Cultural Politics* (Durham, NC: Duke University Press, 2014).
7. Gudrun Held and Sabine Schwarze, *Testi brevi: Teoria e pratica della testualità nell'era multimediale* (Frankfurt am Main: Peter Lang, 2011).
8. Veronica Innocenti and Guglielmo Pescatore. "Information Architecture in Contemporary Television Series," *Journal of Information Architecture* 4.1–2 (2012): 57–72, accessed 20 July 2015, *http://journalofia.org/volume4/issue2/05-pescatore*.
9. A vast bibliography testifies to the research on memory in the context of the digital age. We may draw here a few titles in three main areas that can be connected to the theme of paratextuality. One is the research on the politics and technologies of saving and archiving—such as Joanne Garde-Hansen,

Andrew Hoskins, and Anna Reading, *Save as ... Digital Memories* (London: Palgrave Macmillan, 2009) or Wolfgang Ernst, *Digital Memory and the Archive* (Minneapolis: University of Minnesota Press, 2013). The second is the topic of meditating memory—Josè van Dijck, *Mediated Memories in the Digital Age* (Stanford, CA: Stanford University Press, 2007), or Oren Meyers, Motti Neiger, and Eyal Zandberg, *On Media Memory. Collective Memory in a New Media Age* (London: Palgrave Macmillan, 2011). The third is the crucial issue of forgetting—such as Alessia Ghezzi, Ângela Pereira, and Lucia Vesnić-Alujević, *The Ethics of Memory in a Digital Age: Interrogating the Right to be Forgotten* (London: Palgrave Macmillan, 2014).

10. Andrew Hoskins, "The End of Decay Time," *Memory Studies* 6.4 (2013): 387–389.

11. Andrew Hoskins, "7/7 and Connective Memory. Interactional Trajectories of Remembering in Post-Scarcity Culture," *Memory Studies* 4.3 (2011): 269–280; Akil N. Awan, Andrew Hoskins, and Ben O'Loughlin, *Radicalisation and Media: Connectivity and Terrorism in the New Media Ecology* (London: Routledge, 2011).

12. See Aleida Assman's extensive work on the state of cultural memory in contemporary and past culture. For the latest updates on her work on the issue of forgetting, see her lecture titled "Forms of forgetting": *https://electure-ms. studiumdigitale.unifrankfurt.de/vod/clips/xkAbEqaHKV/flash.html*, accessed 9 November 2015.

13. Svetlana Boym. *The Future of Nostalgia* (New York: Basic Books, 2001).

References

Awan, A. N., Hoskins, A. and O'Loughlin, B., *Radicalisation and Media: Connectivity and Terrorism in the New Media Ecology*. London: Routledge, 2011.

Boym, Svetlana. *The Future of Nostalgia*. New York: Basic Books, 2001.

Ernst, Wolfgang. *Digital Memory and the Archive*. Minneapolis: University of Minnesota Press, 2013.

Garde-Hansen, Joanne, Andrew Hoskins, and Anna Reading. *Save as ... Digital Memories*. London: Palgrave Macmillan, 2009.

Ghezzi, Alessia, Ângela Pereira, and Lucia Vesnić-Alujević, *The Ethics of Memory in a Digital Age: Interrogating the Right to be Forgotten*. London: Palgrave Macmillan, 2014.

Grainge, Paul, ed. *Ephemeral Media: Transitory Screen Culture from Television to YouTube*. London: BFI and Palgrave Macmillan, 2011.

Gray, Jonathan. *Show Sold Separately: Promos, Spoilers and Other Media Paratexts*. New York: New York University Press, 2010.

Hassan, Robert, and Roland E. Purser, eds. *24/7. Time and Temporality in the Network Society*. Stanford, CA: Stanford University Press, 2007.

Held, Gudrun, and Sabine Schwarze. *Testi brevi. Teoria e pratica della testualità nell'era multimediale*. Frankfurt am Main: Peter Lang, 2011.

Hoskins, Andrew. "7/7 and Connective Memory. Interactional Trajectories of Remembering in Post-Scarcity Culture," *Memory Studies* 4.3 (2011): 269–280.

———. "The End of Decay Time." *Memory Studies* 6.4 (2013): 387–389.

Hylland Eriksen, Thomas. "Stacking and Continuity. On Temporal Regimes in Popular Culture." In *24/7. Time and Temporality in the Network Society*, eds. Robert Hassan and Ronald E. Purser. Stanford, CA: Stanford Business Books, 2007.

Innocenti, Veronica, and Guglielmo Pescatore. "Information Architecture in Contemporary Television Series." *Journal of Information Architecture* 4.1–2 (2012): 57–72. Accessed 20 July 2015. *http://journalofia.org/volume4/issue2/05-pescatore.*

Keightley, Emily, ed. *Time Media and Modernity.* Basingstoke, UK: Palgrave MacMillan, 2012.

Kompare, Derek. "The Benefits of Banality: Domestic Syndication in the Post-Network Era," in *Beyond Prime Time: Television Programming in the Post-Network Era,* ed. Amanda D. Lotz. New York: Routledge, 2009.

Lessig, Lawrence. *Remix: Making Art and Commerce Thrive in the Hybrid Economy.* New York: Penguin Press, 2008.

Meyers, Oren, Motti Neiger, and Eyal Zandberg, eds. *On Media Memory. Collective Memory in a New Media Age,* London: Palgrave Macmillan, 2011.

Mittell, Jason. "Serial Orientations. Paratexts and Contemporary Complex Television." In *(Dis)Orienting Media and Narrative Mazes,* eds. Julia Eckel et al., 165–182. Bielefield: Transcript Verlag, 2013.

———. *Complex TV. The Poetics of Contemporary Television Storytelling.* New York: New York University Press, 2015.

Sharma, Sarah. *In the Meantime. Temporality and Cultural Politics.* Durham, NC: Duke University Press, 2014.

van Dijck, Josè. *Mediated Memories in the Digital Age.* Stanford, CA: Stanford University Press, 2007.

Part I

Understanding "Short Shelf-Life" Media

1 Short Shelf-Life Media

Ephemeral Digital Practices and the Contemporary Dream of Permanence

Sara Pesce

Introduction

In the contemporary culture of compulsive digitization and connectivity, the *short-lived* and the *surplus* emerge in many forms. The purpose of this chapter is to show how the enormous amount of extemporary and short products created, stored, and circulated online disguises concerns for decay that intersect with the overabundance of materials, therefore reflecting contemporary politics and discourse on the food supply, ecology, and recycling. I describe these media production practices and media use as "short-shelf life media."

In the field of entertainment and information, a few examples of the short-lived and the surplus are: cell phone news and news on the web broadcast as cascades of content (placeless, without clear priorities, and updated every 30 minutes, as in the case of Wireless Application Protocol (WAP) news;[1] bonus materials mushrooming around a film (extra film footage, commentary tracks, interactive games—included on DVDs and conceived as ancillary or spare); promos, hypes, and synergies activated by the industry before or during the projection of a film[2] (conceived as fleeting, although their reiterated impact might be found on the web); the cluster of merchandise branding surrounding a show or a fictional character (challenging the notion of peripheral and superfluous); a number of secondary screen artifacts, including videogames and impromptu user-generated products such as fan videos, fake trailers, and mash-ups[3] that can reactivate and enormously expand the primary text's meaning and value; finally, forms of reproduction and use of items derived from the diegesis: "textual pieces" such as costumes, clothing, and objects imitated or bought and used to reenact and transform the fictional world, as in the case of cosplay—costumed role-playing inspired by a fictional character. Although not all of these phenomena appear in a strictly textual form—as in the case of toys and gadgets—they might all be included in the wide category of paratextual media. Their common denominator is the fact that they raise interest, excitement, or concern because of their modes of connecting to an epicenter or to a foundational entity: a core text—the film, TV show, serial episode, commercial, or piece of news.

The purpose of my analysis is not to discover what the paratexts do to the text, as Jonathan Gray does in his successful attempt to problematize what is to be considered primary and what is secondary and peripheral. Nor is it my primary concern to consider the durational and circulatory temporalities characterizing the "fugitive" nature of media viewing, as in Paul Grainge's edited collection.[4] It is, rather, to highlight the meaningful link between the workings of paratexts and certain collective behaviors that emerge "in a world marked by deepening political, economic, cultural and environmental insecurity."[5] There is a connection, I believe, between the use and production of media paratexts and specific hopes or anxieties connected to the individual's sense of power or powerlessness when confronted with: 1. long arches of time and broad narrative architectures, 2. models of the performance of citizenship and ethos in the complex globalized geopolitical environment. All these concerns and behaviors revolve around a problematic temporality. They reveal a preoccupation for "short shelf life" that interlaces citizenship and media architectures, disclosing historical ambivalences regarding time consumption, future projections, and the preservation of past and present moments.

Responses to "short-shelf life" emerge in the daily use of digital media. The cases I have in mind are selected from the massive and varied repositories of user-generated film content, like those found on YouTube. I will analyze how these responses are embedded in the dissemination of cryptic or overt procedures of online film archiving, self-archiving, and video sharing, including amateur filmed documentation of catastrophic events. Scale and volume are crucial motors (not merely an effect) of these procedures. Storage, heritage, and patrimony are always, although not overtly, issues at stake. This, moreover, crucially constitutes a practice of memory emphasizing process and connection over information retrieval. In fact, metaphors of memory work as a process of morphing have inhabited recent popular cinema.[6] Likewise, the popular conceptualization of the way we use the web emphasizes feeling, reexperiencing, and rewriting over data managing. The enormous number of practices, from which I draw examples, originate in the fabrication and consumption of cinema, television, and web industry products: films, TV series and shows, web series, commercials and other non-narrative content. These activities always involve the extraction of fragments and the treasuring of certain parts of texts. This is not only a grassroots phenomenon, but also an industrial, commercial, and institutional one: indeed, it reveals a "chain of production," of maintenance and continuous reactivation of archival material, all of which involve a variety of agents.

The most revealing traits of these paratextual phenomena are a self-conscious contribution to the saturation of the media environment, as well as of experience,[7] and a textual recoding—along this "chain of production"—that calls into question the experience of time and history. I suggest that these traits ought to be observed from the perspective of a changing epistemology of time and a changing culture of memory. I pose the questions of how the digitalized process of expansion, dissemination and anticipation of the text displace the predictability and the logic of the clock. And I also examine how brevity and extractability contribute to the fact that a single memorial object or a single memory practice dissolves with the use of digital media.

Therefore, my discussion of short-form and ephemeral media seeks to trigger a dialogue between film/media studies and memory studies, although it recognizes that economic, political, and strictly sociological viewpoints are also involved: especially those concerning consumerism in the global market, new forms of liberal citizenship, community, status, and affluence. The abundance and the scarce life expectancy of media paratexts are rooted in films' chains of production and in a culture of remembering films—in particular in the pleasure produced by reactivativating excerpts of filmed materials. This "mushrooming" of film extraction practices needs to be placed in the context of a contemporary "memory boom" culture, which began in the last decades of the millennium,[8] and furthermore in the context of the "traumatic culture" of the new century, permeated by an imaginary of perennial emergence.[9]

My perspective on short shelf-life media aims not solely to reveal the workings of paratexts as cultural performances that concern the projection into the future and treasuring of the past. I also wish to explain short-media against the background of a cultural concern for stability, where decomposition is a crucial value: an ecological value. The decomposition of organic matter is an important ecosystem process in many natural environments, to the same extent as innovative responses to resource variability in biodiverse ecosystems. Similarly, paratextual media are resources. Their resourcefulness entails renewal rates, detritus, and diversity, which benefit the survival not only of fictional environments, but also—the real object of my focus—of the consumer's integrity.

Mediated Personal Memory Objects: Souvenirs, Collections, Compulsive Accumulation

Let us consider the numerous amateurish, professional, or semiprofessional forms of reuse of digitalized audiovisual content, such as (fan) vidding and fake trailers, mash-ups, remixes, and video essays, gag dubbings, demo reels, or animated Graphics Interchange Formats (GIFs). These objects are circulated on personal blogs (and facilitated by mobile apps such as Vine and Snapchat) through platforms of video-sharing including Youtube, Vimeo, Tumblr,[10] Veoh, or Metacafe, or displayed on websites created by video content producers and publishers, as in the case of WatchMojo—which manufactures paratextual videos ranking, among other things, cinema and television shows.[11] Part of this content is increasingly being incorporated into websites like Flickr[12] or Pinterest, hosting not only images but also videos that are specifically conceived to allow for personal collections and act as personalized media catalogues. Moreover, some forms of reuse are disseminated and scored by fandom-oriented "meta-blogs" such as those dedicated to film series (e.g., *Castlefanvideos*, or *The Best Lost Fan Videos*). They can also be treasured by amateur archives like *The Archive of Our Own* or fan video archives like *TV Fanvids Live Journal*. These are all examples of paratextual media activities: they hint at a text, they comment on a text, they remember and treasure a text, but the text in its entirety is elsewhere. In short, we can note a circularity of paratextual media production, paratextual media archiving enabled by major video sharing platforms,[13] and their re-archiviation according to personal, mnemonic criteria.

The "cultural drive" of these specific activities of online recirculation of audiovisual short materials has a lot to do with the "reinvention of government" and the "survivalism" characterizing new liberal citizenship, as mentioned above. It also includes a drive to monetize forms of archiving, albeit often indirectly. The valorization of individual resourcefulness is crucial for new liberal forms of citizenship, which include the appropriation of a variety of technologies for the management of the self. Television and digital hyperconnectivity are the technologies that play a role on a mass scale: reality TV, for example, has an agenda of advice, rules, demonstrations, games, experiments and tests that empower the citizen through the management of conduct and behavior.[14] The use of appropriate technologies is effective for containing the perils of a globalized socioeconomic system, like the threat of deterioration—be it cultural, material, or environmental—and for keeping the rigors of the market under control.[15] This can be explained via the context of a trauma culture induced by extremely mediatized natural cataclysms and terroristic attacks. As I will discuss later, this culture of trauma and vulnerability focuses on the issue of survival, implying the mobilization of private resources (skills, money, volunteerism) in order to manage and protect both the natural environment and ourselves. In all this, the citizen's worth is enhanced by the active subject's connective role, by the awareness of an agency working in a supranational governmental regime, and by an acknowledgment of the subject's global reach.

In many senses, the cultural drive of recirculation described so far is shared by the agenda of other sources for the reuse of film content. Film industry archives, for example, make available short reels and discarded or neglected materials. This is the case of *Paramount Stock Footage Collections*, an online archive containing clips available for purchase, taken from contemporary or vintage cinematic footage—including material from classic films—that is sorted thematically. Governmental or educational archives like those of the Library of Congress or UCLA also preserve and circulate audiovisual material. Although these institutions are not involved in paratextual phenomena (since their scope is preserving integral texts), they are pushed by the same wide-ranging motivation I am describing here: the appeal, the interest, the worth of giving new life to past contents. Other examples include amateur web archives, like the *British TV Ark*—an online television museum, conceived as a tribute to historical television containing cult shows, advertisements, news and weather forecasts, series, game and quiz shows or soaps. Moreover, a number of hybrids between cultural institutions and community sites, like *The American Internet Archive*,[16] aim at preventing digital-born material from disappearing. They feature preview reels, compilations of classic TV footage, and a variety of materials surrounding TV shows that are available for download and are often accompanied by nostalgic comments, sometimes devaluing contemporary television.

All these forms of recirculation participate in a cultural machinery that runs along two main trajectories, both of which are connected to a changing culture of remembering. The first trajectory is a widespread "compulsive" accumulation of images—also problematized by recent cinema.[17] This accumulation is clearly related to what has been described as the democratization of archives[18] and is associated with brevity and instantaneity, but also with fluctuating personal chronopolitics.[19] Pleasure and value derive, among other things, from the fulfillment of a desire to dominate a potentially infinite amount of content through the use and selection of materials. The ever-increasing size of personal visual digital collections normally outpaces people's capacity to keep track of their content.[20] It outpaces even the normal capacity to enjoy these contents in their entirety. Unless the "collector" indulges in bingeing, which is often connoted as a form of resistance or anarchy, "paratextual consumption"—brief, partial, indexical—normally surpasses the viewing of film texts in their entirety. As a matter of fact, this drive towards accumulation reveals a fear of forgetting.[21] It unveils a connection between the boom in memory and the boom in forgetting.[22] However, the challenge posed to remembering is not only brought on by oversupply. In a world of hyperconnections, it is rather "the 'spreadability', virality and contagion of the living archive that holds future memory hostage to the vagaries of the digital."[23]

In fact, the second trajectory is the collapse of *collective* memory and the concomitant rise of a personal, *connective* memory, where the moment of connection is the moment of recollection,[24] and the single object or single memory practice dissolves in the use of digital media. Based on the prominence of online autobiographical practices in the era of post-scarcity (where the archive is driven inward and subjectivity is archival and archived), connective memory is commanded by the dynamics of the node or nexus.[25] The make-up of connective memory is antimonumental and disrupts the idea of recollection as immutable and inerasable. Multiple interactive trajectories, intersecting with each other, colliding into each other, and transforming one another, work in cycles within new media and old media, enabling continuous countermemories that pour from institutions to individuals and vice versa.

This fact is inextricable, I would argue, from the mushrooming of paratextual media: there is no ending online, no closure.

The "circulatory activities" of the paratextual media so far mentioned share a principle of appraisal. Quantity of information, as mentioned before, is not the only issue at stake in this appraisal. In many cases, audio-visual materials are also perceived as "patrimony." This fact is explicit in the agenda of full-fledged archives. Television archives like the Paley Centers for Media in New York and Los Angeles, for example, have "historically been founded on attempts to arrest TV from the everyday flows of ephemeral time and lived space and to make it into a document." They are connected to an idea of saving the past and are therefore "tied to a fundamental loss, to destruction, and even to a 'radical evil.'"[26]

Instead, the idea of patrimony is more implicit in the "collective archival bricolage"[27] activated on YouTube and other video-sharing platforms. Appraisal sustained by a sense of loss can be addressed to a single artifact and can be expressed in verbal form, for example, in the commentaries included below posts: situational memories resulting from dialogues on the site, nostalgia for original broadcast transmissions of a TV show or for a particular movie theatre. Moreover, appraisal can be nonverbal. The very fact that materials are reusable makes them worthy, and therefore appreciation also brings to the foreground abundance, a wide choice.

The variety of activities surrounding the reuse of filmed material gives meaning to content and content use alike. It reveals an attention to the role of individual work motivated by pleasure, gain, or educational purposes. Individual work, and therefore *memory work*,[28] are crucial in giving meaning to details, errors, personal appreciations and hyperreactions. Differently from the phenomena of close-knit fan communities in the 1990s, which Henry Jenkins discussed on his blog (the "remix communities" in which interpretative context was provided by fandom), in the new millennium creating, circulating, and storing paratextual media are imbued with the idea of recycling. This recycling involves media contents that are primarily perceived as material, even personal, "edible" objects.

A drive toward re-consumption embraces numerous forms of content remediation, from transmedia narration to merchandizing, and includes the input of fictional objects into the real world, as in the case of cosplay. The notion of "mediated personal memory objects" suggested by Van Dijck foregrounds the importance of the material artifact that invokes memory. The changing materiality of the artifact is relevant in the mental processes of those who perceive and use it.[29] More than that, the feeling of personal power and creativity plays a crucial role. Empowerment occurs decisively through the accumulation and manipulation processes connected to the new type of materiality inherent in digital objects. Yet this materiality is undeniably ambivalent: on the one hand, the digital is commonly equated with the immaterial. On the other hand, digital technology is perceived as vulnerable to decay: softwares become obsolete, hardwares are perceived as not robust.

Recycling constitutes a pervasive need for the overabundant film production that today populates big and small screens. It consists mainly in the practice of reprocessing narratives by means of adaptation.[30] With paratextual phenomena, though, recycling has to do with the dynamic between the loss of transitory content and the retrieval and storage of that content. That is to say, a sense of evanescence and easy forgetfulness, which has long permeated the consumption of television products, was largely overcome by the post-broadcast era. Television content can be retrieved and downloaded online; its consumption can be postponed or rescheduled; historical content can be salvaged.[31] The sense of ephemerality is transformed into an inflation of mediated personal objects, which is demonstrated by new forms of cinephilia online, or new archival forms, ranging from the digitalization of institutional film archives[32] to the digital recording of life-stories, such as *Story Corps*.[33]

Reuses are performances of memory that allow for exploring successions of links between personal meaning, experience, context, extracted film contents, and "broader aspects of shared, social, memory and national identity."[34] In the North American and European context, they involve an ecologic mindset that engages the individual and his or her agency as a consumer.

Film Culture, Trauma, Survivalism

Let us take a few excerpts of cinematic and televisual material, such as fan tributes to actors or characters,[35] animated GIFs found on Tumblr, or mash-ups mixing classic film fragments and using a self-composed musical score.[36] Can we consider these to be souvenirs? Structurally, their foregrounding of formal devices and their rapid drifts of setting and point of view "feed into the characteristically collagist, fragmentary, timeless, even the 'musical' quality of the memory text."[37] Indeed, these materials exploit film's exclusive ability to transport viewers across space and time, therefore showing "structural affinities to memory."[38] Moreover, paratextual engagement can be viewed as a way to keep records of one's life. It can be included in the kind of video-making activities associated with social networks and messaging. It belongs to the range of diffused connections that are, as Susan Aasman maintains, "home moviemaking in a new way: they produce what we now call digital memories."[39] In fact, numerous forms of audiovisual reuse participate in a changing film culture that combines the pleasure of watching and involving oneself in filmed narratives with a personal activity of digital data management, which in turn aims to preserve what is perceived simultaneously as accessible, usable, and ephemeral: film.

This calls into question a concern for content disposal, behind which lies a disposal economy and its technologies. Personal manipulation of fragments, conservation of pieces, sharing: these actions rescue precious objects, salvaging them from an extraordinary volume of available material.

Consider, for example, videos that edit classical film endings published on Vimeo. It is a performance of the personal capacity to choose and preserve what is worthy. Value is produced when a meaningful future is activated by an audiovisual object, even if that object is overtly acknowledged as a surplus and potential waste.

In her analysis of "knowledge and transmission in the age of digital technologies," Diana Taylor maintains that the current era is dominated by a structural uncertainty due to an epistemological turn, comparable to the "world before the invention of the printing press in the early 1400s, or after the spread of print culture in the late 1500s."[40] My main thesis in this chapter is that short, paratextual media *shape* cultural processes as much as they *reflect* a culture struggling with the contradictions of a utopia of unlimited capacity and a dystopia of unsustainable growth in a "post-scarcity" world. With this in mind, I address the question of the influence of a changing film culture—and its recycling and reiterative mechanisms (devices of retrieval, fascination with a moment in time, and reactivation of that moment through successive viewings)—on the problematic management of personal digital data. All of this is interlaced with the new challenge of personal impact on pivotal collective events and on the environment.

Reality television, expanded seriality, and transmedia storytelling have changed film culture as much as digital cinema and a pervasive culture of nostalgia. This mutating film culture has influenced the individual impact on memory ever since the advent of the home recording technologies like VHS. Home recording, though, stemmed from the will to interact not so much with the film text as with the televisual flux. The capacity to interfere with the flow of broadcasted information and leisure materials has expanded ever since, extending it to daily activities of self-broadcasting and social networking. This expansion, this dissemination, seems to be an ever-increasing phenomenon. It has been facilitated, for example, by systemic Facebook updates. In 2011, Facebook introduced a timeline in users' profiles, allowing for a valorization of the time manipulation of images and videos.[41] The massive colonization of video content on social networks contributes to the extensive migratory process from cinema to online digital media, as analyzed by Bolter and Grusin[42] and Francesco Casetti.[43]

This changing film culture actively participates in the contemporary culture of uncertainty, as revealed, surprisingly, by the recent upsurge of variegated user-generated film content. The massive spread of this kind of content started in the new millennium with the documentation, via cell phones and other electronic devices, of cataclysms and devastations such as the tsunami in Sumatra in 2005 or the attack on the World Trade Center in 2001. It has functioned as a mediator between a pervasive sense of the vulnerability of prosperous societies (the liability of our material culture; the fragility of our daily personal stability and that of stately governance; the perishability of our technology and technological products) and the urge for personal agency with respect to this wide range of uncertainties. All this has fostered a survivalist mindset.

Catastrophe videos show tragedies as they are taking place. Their large quantity offers multiple points of view, competing with each other for the primary position in the capacity to approach the tragedy. Similarly, trauma cinema, whose resurgence is clearly bound to the survivalist issues presented by acts of terrorism or environmental crises, incorporates self-reflexive techniques that translate the fragility of the audiovisual means. Its textual fragmentation hints at the subject's psychic condition: a dissociative relationship between present consciousness and past event. The traumatic text is characterized by the instability of representation and the instability of the subject.[44] On closer examination, the instability of representation is constitutive of amateur videos of catastrophes (consider, for example, the videos of the World Trade Center "jumpers" on 9/11), which set a crucial disparity between the experience of events and an official, broadcast, and often monopunctual mediation. Moreover, their virality spreads a new, skeptical view of the ideal of the ever-increasing capacity to control and discipline the political and natural environment, particularly for technologically advanced societies. In the last decade and a half, video remixing and fanvidding have been indebted to this kind of traumatic video production and diffusion online, marking a memorial media boom, dominated by obsessive re-consumption of past conflicts and catastrophes. In a context dominated by an imagined, perennial state of emergency,[45] paratextual phenomena and catastrophe videos share a fundamental civic impulse: articulating a personal stance, giving a contribution, counteracting an injustice or a tendency perceived as harmful, participating and sharing a crucial collective event. Confronted with the instabilities and ever-present potential for trauma, this connective, viral, and plural mechanism reveals the compelling emergence of a skilled, informed, engaged, and far-reaching citizenship. A new utopia of personal control is revealed, one that is based on the circulation of information and sustained by the materiality of films as mediated personal memory objects.

Permanence, Resilience, and Sustainable Growth in a Post-Scarcity World

Being agents of the recirculation, anticipation, and displacement of experience, most of the phenomena under scrutiny here problematize time regimes. They challenge projections into a perfectionable future, reveal the contradictions of the nostalgia for an idealized past, and bring to the fore individual chronopolitics.

The pleasure factor behind these phenomena is rooted in a temporal stance that implies the creation of value. Value in these cases can be associated with brevity or speed (a very problematic value itself)[46]; it is linked to instantaneity and synchronicity, or it is related to time retrieval. Countervalues can also be involved: the luxury of wasting time (applauded by fan sites),[47] the interference with the broadcast flux, the leisure of extemporaneity (a time dimension that is not rooted), and the empowering feeling of controlling repetition. Therefore, paratexts implicitly treasure multiple temporalities and the micropolitics of temporal coordination. They imply that temporal practices are not uniform but rather specific to the labor—that is, the contingent circumstances and managements of living bodies—that produces each experience.

Moreover, as stated before, the temporal regimes of paratextuality are inherent in what has been called digital memory culture: "keeping track, recording, retrieving, stockpiling, archiving, backing-up and saving." These are actions that defer one of our greatest fears of this century: information loss.[48] This fear is pervasive and can be found in many forms of digitalized content: "online mementos, photographs taken with digital cameras or camera phones, memorial web pages, digital shrines, text messages, digital archives (institutional and personal), online museums, online condolence message boards, virtual candles, souvenirs and memorabilia traded on eBay, social networking and alumni websites."[49]

The concern for persistence, the need for—and lack of—future envisioning, and the fear of loss are all involved. In the 1990s, memory emerged as a key concern in Western societies due to the disappearance of living witnesses to crucial historical events like Shoah. A turning toward the past took place, which contradicted the founding principle of modernity that envisioned a promising future based on productivity and progress.[50] It introduced a new principle of preservation based on a persistent sense of loss. A pervasive emphasis on collecting and preserving life stories has bared evidence to this sentiment. Therefore, a memory boom society has grown increasingly concerned with the capacity for forgetting and at the same time has become largely aware of the capacity of digital technologies to capture, seize, and manipulate the past. In fact, the abundance and vast circulation of short, ephemeral, and parceled textual remediations not only indirectly participate in the contemporary taboo of forgetfulness. It also contributes to what Robert Hassan has defined as the network society's "new time," a practice of time that displaces the logic of predictability and regularity in the clock and calendar. The temporal regime that dominated society and politics until the advent of networked neoliberalism has come to an end. This mirrors a society that cannot be narrated as a project.

> Within the growing domain of network time, stability (such as it was) has become much less tenable in social life; a centre that would hold (more or less) as a fulcrum around which social life could be narrated as a project, begins to shake free of its moorings; and a society (and state) that once saw planning and regulation and the projection of a political future for its citizens as its central raison d'être, begins to turn toward market forces for meaning and inspiration.[51]

Paratextual temporality touches on the important issues of impermanence and the lack of projectuality; but more than anything else it involves a cultural dream of permanence. This permanence–loss duality finds parallels in contemporary societies' abundance of commemorative forms, in the anxiety of source extinction, and in the proliferating forms of archiving oral culture. A survivalist impulse pervades different realms of contemporary life—information, education, civic sense, leisure—and includes extremist manifestations: an emphasis on military resistance, renowned forms of personal training in autarchic subsistence in the case of emergency, and numerous aberrant behaviors deriving from a "wound culture." The pervasive fear of loss and obsolescence, its related survivalist impulses, and the catastrophic mentality diffused by the trauma culture of the new millennium are at least partially managed by the process of archiving and its implications of permanence (i.e., of assuring appropriate and valuable survival of certain artifacts from the past).

Most importantly, it is precisely because media paratextuality is characterized by brief consumption, repeatability, and easy forgetfulness versus concern for storage that it can be read in terms of an ecological utopia. This ecological paradigm is inherent in paratexts' saturation of the media landscape and is expressed by the dynamics between permanence, decay, and residue that they activate. Such processes are strongly dominated by the conflict and coexistence between the drive to stability and the ecological value of decomposition or recycling. As Aleida Assmann maintains:

> In a consumerist culture and with an economy that combines an ever increasing production of goods with an ever shorter cycle of renewal and disposal, the accumulation of discarded objects has become a major problem; the vast amount of highly toxic, non-biodegradable materials makes this problem into one of ecological survival. ... A growing ecological awareness now insists that material products be designed in such a way that after use they no longer survive as relics but instead conform to the pattern of organic decay and renewal, or technological obsolescence and recycling. While in the field of culture men dream of permanence, in the field of waste disposal the dream is of total disappearance. ... What in one field (e.g., that of toxic materials) is a cause of the utmost concern is regarded in the field of culture as the ultimate aim, and art's longing for eternity finds its deadly fulfillment in nuclear waste. Poisonous materials of industry and the aesthetic materials of art are linked in a paradoxical structural homology.[52]

Ecology pursues the goal of sustainability, balance within an ecosystem, and therefore stability and permanence. In the realm of media, this ecological paradigm describes not only user behavior, but also a tendency of the industries, which conceive their product as "an ongoing and renewable generator of value—whether it be exchange, symbolic, or sentimental—rather than merely as a one-time commodity."[53] Survival, sustainability, as well as individual and communal coherence granting the maintenance of a unspoiled ecosystem, are all concerns that develop in the context of an environmental crisis and of a growing trend toward offloading welfare and social services.

This ecological plea is intrinsically tied to a sense of "the global" in a post-scarcity world and involves resilience. When applied to the contemporary social sphere, resilient behaviors involve the notion—and painful perception—of geopolitical globality. Postindustrial societies are threatened by the economic and social consequences of the continuous growth of goods and services.[54] The possibility for poorer countries to enjoy the fruits of this increasing abundance might be a crucial consequence—involving the risks of this system's change—as well as the collapse of natural ecosystems and the world's climate. For the citizens of developed countries, where abundance has produced a shift of emphasis from managing production to managing consumption, global awareness implies the fear of the unsustainability of a post-scarcity world. Therefore, abundant supply at extremely low cost implies an anxiety over the global system's capacity to sustain itself and over strategies of resilience that call attention to the temporal limits of the current geopolitical system.

In contemporary technological societies, resilience emerges forcefully in two principal territories: the fight against terrorism and the effort for environmental preservation. Vulnerability and insecurity are always involved in both, which are also perceived as issues to be resolved by means of individual effort. The main forces involved in the make-up of resilience come from institutions and people. Consider the use of the term *resilience* in relation to the terrorist attacks on New York on 9/11 and on London on 7/7 2001. "Authorities diagnose resilience in terms of whether populations suffer post-traumatic stress disorders … following an attack." On the contrary, resilience can emerge as the capacity to adapt[55]: social resilience, when it is at a grassroots level, is based on extemporary, expanded collaboration.

Conclusion

The metaphor of "short shelf-life media" encompasses different challenges concerning decay, abundance, and sustainability in a globalized world. These challenges are entailed in media paratextuality. The notion of short shelf-life media draws on that of a lifespan and hints at the users' self-perception through time, highlighting their personal life expectancy and their capacity to control it. This lifespan includes viewers' past film-viewing experiences, and the envisioning of future effects of accumulation implied in their paratextual activities. Short shelf-life media interlace the fragility of the human life duration with the realm of film life, at the same time evoking the solidity achieved by motion pictures due to their length.[56] Finally, this metaphor draws on the availability of goods on shop shelves, their consumption and, moreover, their perishability. The temporality of media use has an economic worth in the digital context—a category rooted in the industrial mentality.

Moreover, the digital has the potential to make an enormous impact on world economies of abundance, because consumption of an informational item does not imply having one item less on the market. Unlike tangible items, "when you consume an informational item—like downloads of applications, or mp3—you copy it and there is now one more of that good, not one less."[57]

In a sense, this metaphor intersects recent arguments posed by memory studies. It reinforces the idea that digitalized mediations of memory fuel a connection between memory and consumerism.[58] At the same time, it draws from a biologic mind-set, sharing its premises with the growing domain of ecological and naturalistic viewpoints on media: media-ecology and the idea of narrative ecosystems.[59] In their definition of digital memory, Garde-Hansen, Hoskins, and Reading[60] underline memory's engagement with difference and describe it as an "active, subjective, organic, emotional, virtual and uncertain production."[61] The authors invoke a Darwinian ecology, applying it to an information ecology based on the idea of "diversity, continual evolution, change and differentiation."[62]

We may push the biological notion further and focus on paratextuality as a system of micro phenomena, or viral phenomena, therefore introducing a microbiologic point of view that emphasizes the paratextual workings of decomposition. On the one hand, we have the minuscule organic causes of decomposition and decay: consider the example given by Paul Booth's recent work on horror fans making video trailers for *Saw* (James Wan, 2004).[63] These are instances of trailers that are judged to have pegged a film incorrectly; as such, they show how active paratexts are in setting alternative ground rules for viewing. Other cases also call into question the notion of *textual performer*[64] through their active use of the text as a social resource. They unveil surveillance practices, creative responses to the guilt for being passive voyeurs, and an interventionist ethos. On the other hand, the biological notion implies conservational components: the archival impulses so far described.

Therefore, since paratextual media indicate and contribute to the dissolving of texts—or, when seen from a different perspective, participate in a perennial textual expansion and dissemination that spreads beyond the confines of film narratives and film viewing—they also appear as markers of a complex culture of challenged sustainability continuously seeking and generating resources for survival. Decomposition and the dream of permanence are the opposite poles of the paratextual life cycle. Because paratexts are never conceived as long-term artifacts, the moment they are imagined, their status as discarded objects is implicit. But this expected organic decay implies a principle of resilience. It triggers a chain of experiences that sustain an ongoing and renewable generation of value. This translates into leisure the crucial issues of survival, sustainability, and welfare: of ecological citizenship.

Notes

1. Thomas Hilland Eriksen, "Stacking and Continuity: On Temporal Regimes in Popular Culture," in *24/7. Time and Temporality in the Network Society*, ed. Robert Hassan and Ronald E. Purser (Stanford, CA: Stanford Business Books, 2007), 152.
2. Jonathan Gray, *Show Sold Separately. Promos, Spoilers, and Other Media Paratexts* (New York: New York University Press, 2010); John Thorton Caldwell, *Production Culture: Industrial Reflexivity and Critical Practice in Film and Television* (Durham, NC: Duke University Press, 2008).
3. Barbara Klinger, *Beyond the Multiplex: Cinema, New Technologies and the Home* (Berkeley: University of California Press, 2006), 191–238; Chuck Tryon, *Reinventing Cinema: Movies in the Age of Media Convergence* (New Brunswick, NJ: Rutgers University Press, 2010).
4. Paul Grainge, ed., *Ephemeral Media. Transitory Screen Culture from Television to YouTube* (London: Palgrave Macmillan, 2011).
5. Alison Hearn, "Insecure: Narratives and Economies of the Branded Self in Transformation Television," *Continuum: Journal of Media and Cultural Studies* 22.4 (2008): 495.
6. Josè van Dijck, *Mediated Memories in the Digital Age* (Stanford, CA: Stanford University Press, 2007).
7. Take, for example, a TV show like *Biggest Loser* (NBC, 2004–) conceived as an integrated system consisting of an interactive website, tie-in merchandise, networking facilities, and informative podcasts. Laurie Ouellette and James Hay, *Better Living through Reality TV. Television and Post-Welfare Citizenship* (Malden, MA: Blackwell, 2008), 87.
8. Aleida Assmann, *Erinnerungsräume: Formen und Wandlungen des kulturellen Gedächtnisses* (München: C. H. Beck, 1999). Elena Agazzi and Vita Fortunati eds., *Memoria e Saperi* (Rome: Meltemi, 2007).
9. Mark Seltzer, "Wound Culture. Trauma in the Pathological Public Sphere," *October* 80 (1997): 3–26. Richard Crownshaw, *The Afterlife of Holocaust Memory in Contemporary Literature and Culture* (London: Palgrave Macmillan, 2010).
10. Tumblr is particularly interesting, as it shows the most popular content at a given moment. Tumblr serves as a depository, albeit a continuously changing one. By selecting and publicizing the contents that are mostly shared, it mediates a communal memory.
11. WatchMojo.com does not feature amateur content, nor does it allow users to upload videos. Its 'Top Ten' videos and other materials summarizing specific niche topics are professionally produced and change periodically.
12. Since 2008, Flickr has allowed paid subscribers to upload videos limited to 90 seconds in length and 150 MB in size. In 2009, Flickr added high-definition videos.
13. For a discussion on YouTube as unintentional archive, see Lynn Spiegel, "Housing Television. Architectures of the Archive," *The Communication Review* 13 (2010): 63.
14. Oulette and Hay, *Better Living through Reality TV*, 7.
15. Barry Hindess, "Neo-liberal Citizenship," *Citizenship Studies* 6.2 (2002): 127–143.

16. The American Internet Archive collaborates with institutions including the Library of Congress and the Smithsonian.

17. Federica Muzzarelli, "Memorie cinematografiche. La sindrome archiviale della modernità," *Fata Morgana* 25 (2015): 122.

18. Joanne Garde-Hansen, "Digital Memories. The Democratization of Archives," in *Media and Memory*, ed. Joanne Garde-Hansen (Edinburgh: Edinburgh University Press, 2011), 70–87; Ernst Wolfgang "The Archive as Metaphor," *Open* 7 (2004): 46–43.

19. Sarah Sharma, *In the Meantime. Temporality and Cultural Politics* (Durham, NC: Duke University Press, 2014).

20. Van Djike, *Mediated Memories in the Digital Age*, 145.

21. Paul Connerton, "Seven Types of Forgetting," *Memory Studies* 1 (2008): 59–71.

22. Andreas Huyssen, *Present Pasts: Urban Palimpsests and the Politics of Memory* (Palo Alto, CA: Stanford University Press, 2003).

23. Andrew Hoskins, "The End of Decay Time," *Memory Studies* 6.4 (2013): 388.

24. Andrew Hoskins, "7/7 and Connective Memory. Interactional Trajectories of Remembering in Post-Scarcity Culture," *Memory Studies* 4.3 (2011): 269–280; José Van Dijk "Memory Matters in the Digital Age," in *Mediated Memories in the Digital Age*, ed. José Van Dijk (Stanford, CA: Stanford University Press, 2007), 27–52.

25. Hoskins, "The End of Decay Time." On the role of media texts' circulation in the construction of autobiographical narrative selves, see Emily Keighley, "Introduction," in *Time Media and Modernity* ed. Emily Keighley (London: Palgrave MacMillan, 2012). See also Federica Villa, "Autobiografiche. Scritture del tempo sullo sconcerto," *AAM-TAC: Arts and Artifacts in Movie. Technology, Aesthetics, Communication* 7 (2010): 60.

26. Lynn Spiegel, "Housing Television: Architectures of the Archive," *The Communication Review* 13.1 (2010): 55.

27. Ibid., 65.

28. Annette Kuhn, "Memory Texts and Memory Work. Performances of Memory in and with Visual Media," *Memory Studies* 3.3 (2010): 298–313.

29. Van Dijck, "Memory Matters in the Digital Age," 35.

30. Christine Thomson, *Storytelling in Film and Television* (Cambridge, MA: Harvard University Press, 2003).

31. Grainge, "Introduction."

32. Mary Ann Doane, *The Emergence of Cinematic Time. Modernity, Contingency, the Archive* (Cambridge, MA: Harvard University Press, 2002).

33. StoryCorps is one of the largest oral history projects recording, sharing, and preserving American life stories. Since 2003, each conversation has been recorded on a CD to share and is preserved at the American Folklife Center at the Library of Congress.

34. Annette Kuhn, "Memory Texts and Memory Work. Performances of Memory in and with Visual Media," *Memory Studies* 3.4 (2010): 304.

35. See, for example, "Martha Jones Tribute—Shakespeare's Sonnet18 (Doctor Who MV)," accessed 1 July 2015, *https://www.youtube.com/watch?v=EYWx8SD7BbA*.

36. See, for example, "Clip Cinnamon Girl (Dunkelbunt)," accessed 1 July 2015, *https://vimeo.com/album/2056855/video/12452415*.

37. Kuhn, "Memory Texts and Memory Work," 299.

38. Alison Landsberg, "Cinematic Temporality: Modernity, Memory and the Nearness of the Past," in Keightley, *Time, Media and Modernity*, 88.
39. "Just like home movie practices, these new media practices all share the basic function of keeping a record of our lives." Susan Aasman, "Saving Private Reels. Archival Practices and Digital Memories (Formerly Known as Home Movies) in the Digital Age, in Amateur Filmmaking," in *The Home Movie: The Archive, the Web*, ed. Laura Rascaroli, Gwenda Young, and Barry Monan (London: Bloomsbury, 2014), 253.
40. Diana Taylor, "Save As … Knowledge and Transmission in the Age of Digital Technologies," *Imagining America, Paper* 7 (2010), accessed 15 June 2015, *http://surface.syr.edu/ia/7*.
41. Angela Maiello, "Dalla memoria archivio alla memoria funzionale." *Fata Morgana* 25 (2015): 72.
42. Jay David Bolter and Richard Grusin, *Remediation. Understanding New Media* (Cambridge, MA: MIT Press, 1998).
43. Francesco Casetti, "L'esperienza filmica e la ri-locazione del cinema." *Fata Morgana* 4 (2008): 23–40.
44. Janet Walker, *Trauma Cinema. Documenting Incest and the Holocaust* (Berkeley, CA: University of California Press, 2005).
45. Mark Seltzer, "Wound Culture. Trauma in the Pathologic Public Sphere." *October* 80 (1997): 3–26.
46. Sarah Sharma (cit.) disputes a line of critical inquiry that she calls "speed theory," initiated by Paul Virilio. She sets it against the background of contingent practices of time consumption and of the recent cultural turn to slowness. Sharma fosters an understanding of how social experiences of time are multiple and uneven, and recognizes the temporal dimensions of power in a way that allows us to comprehend the ideological value attached to personal, particular ways of being in time.
47. The Fanvid page of Tvtropes.org states: "It's not the most productive activity in the world, but for the most dedicated, it is one of the most time-consuming." Accessed 15 June 2015, *http://tvtropes.org/pmwiki/pmwiki.php/Main/Fanvid*.
48. Joanne Garde-Hansen, Andrew Hoskins, and Anna Reading, eds., *Save as … Digital Memories* (London: Palgrave Macmillan, 2009), 5.
49. Ibid., 4.
50. Barbara Adam, *Time* (Cambridge, MA: Polity Press, 2004).
51. Robert Hassan, "Networked Time and the 'Common Ruin of the Contending Classes,'" *TripleC* 11.2 (2013): 362.
52. Assmann, *Cultural Memory and Western Civilization. Functions, Media, Archives* (Cambridge, UK: Cambridge University Press, 2011), 335.
53. Jenkins, Ford, and Green, *Spreadable Media*, 133.
54. Philip Sadler, *Sustainable Growth in a Post-Scarcity World. Consumption, Demand, and the Poverty Penalty* (Farnham, UK: Gower, 2010).
55. Akil N. Awan, Andrew Hoskins, Ben O'Loughlin, *Radicalisation and Media. Connectivity and Terrorism in the New Media Ecology* (London: Routledge, 2011), 11.
56. Paul Grainge, "Introduction: Ephemeral Media," in *Ephemeral Media: Transitory Screen Culture from Television to YouTube*, ed. Paul Grainge (London: BFI, 2011), 5.
57. Sadler, *Sustainable Growth in a Post-Scarcity World*, 60.

58. See, for example, Marika Sturken, *Tourists of History: Memory, Kitsch, and Consumerism from Oklahoma City to Ground Zero* (Durham, NC: Duke University Press, 2007), 9. Sturken talks about American contemporary experiences of the past as "tourism of history," exemplified by purchasing a World Trade Center memento on eBay, by which a sense of the past is conveyed "through consumerism, media images, souvenirs, popular culture, and museum and architectural reenactments."

59. Veronica Innocenti and Guglielmo Pescatore, "Information Architecture in Contemporary Television Series," *Journal of Information Architecture* 4: 1–2 (Fall 2012), accessed 25 October 2015, *http://journalofia.org/volume4/issue2/05-pescatore*; Claudio Bisoni and Veronica Innocenti, eds., *Media mutations. Gli ecosistemi narrativi nello scenario mediale contemporaneo: spazi, modelli, usi sociali* (Modena: Mucchi, 2013); Veronica Innocenti, Guglielmo Pescatore and Luca Rosati, "Converging Universes and Media Niches in Serial Narratives. An Approach through Information Architecture," in Artur Lugmayr and Cinzia Dal Zotto, ed., *Media Convergence Handbook—Vol. 2 Firms and User Perspectives* (XXX: Springer, 2015): 122–131.

60. Garde-Hansen, Hoskins, Reading, *Save As … Digital Memories*, 7.

61. Ibid.

62. Ibid., 9. The authors draw on Nardi and O'Day's idea of information ecologies. Bonnie Nardi and Vicki O'Day, *Information Ecologies: Using Technology with Heart* (Cambridge, MA: MIT Press, 1999).

63. These fans have a high level of "cineliteracy," which turns out to be a means to normalize the excesses characterizing the *Saw* franchise. Paul Booth, "*Saw* Fandom and the Transgression of Fan Excess," in David Gunkle and Ted Gournelos, eds., *Transgression 2.0: Media, Culture and the Politics of a Digital Age* (New York: Continuum, 2011).

64. Kurt Lancaster, *Interacting with Babylon 5* (Austin: University of Texas Press, 2001). Lancaster argues that the constellation of texts, products, and paratexts that surround the series *Babylon 5* allows fans to immerse themselves in a world of role-playing and in a mutual process of performance. This role-playing does not simply express meanings and identities, but moreover forges them.

References

Aasman, Susan. "Saving Private Reels. Archival Practices and Digital Memories (Formerly Known as Home Movies) in the Digital Age, in Amateur Filmmaking." In *The Home Movie, the Archive, the Web*, eds. Laura Rascaroli, Gwenda Young, Barry Monan, 245–256. London: Bloomsbury, 2014.

Adam, Barbara. *Time*. Cambridge, MA: Polity Press, 2004.

Agazzi, Elena, and Vita Fortunati, eds. *Memoria e Saperi*. Rome: Meltemi, 2007.

Assmann, Aleida. *Erinnerungsräume: Formen und Wandlungen des kulturellen Gedächtnisses* (München: C. H. Beck, 1999).

———. *Cultural Memory and Western Civilization. Functions, Media, Archives*. Transl. Aleida Assmann and David Henry Wilson. Cambridge, UK: Cambridge University Press, 2011.

Awan, Akil N., Andrew Hoskins, and Ben O'Loughlin. *Radicalisation and Media. Connectivity and Terrorism in the New Media Ecology*. London: Routledge, 2011.

Bolter, Jay David, and Richard Grusin. *Remediation. Understanding New Media.* Cambridge, MA: MIT Press, 1998.

Booth, Paul. "Saw fandom and the Transgression of Fan Excess." In *Transgression 2.0: Media, Culture and the Politics of a Digital Age*, eds. David Gunkle and Ted Gournelos, 69–84. New York: Continuum, 2011.

Caldwell, John Thornton. *Production Culture: Industrial Reflexivity and Critical Practice in Film and Television.* Durham, NC: Duke University Press, 2008.

Casetti, Francesco. "L'esperienza filmica e la ri-locazione del cinema." *Fata Morgana* 4 (2008): 23–40.

Connerton, Paul. "Seven Types of Forgetting." *Memory Studies* 1 (2008): 59–71.

Crownshaw, Richard. *The Afterlife of Holocaust Memory in Contemporary Literature and Culture.* London: Palgrave Macmillan, 2010.

Doane, Mary Ann. *The Emergence of Cinematic Time. Modernity, Contingency, the Archive.* Cambridge, MA: Harvard University Press, 2002.

Eriksen, Thomas Hylland. "Stacking and Continuity. On Temporal Regimes in Popular Culture." In *24/7. Time and Temporality in the Network Society*, eds. Robert Hassan and Ronald E.Purser, 141–160. Stanford, CA: Stanford University Press, 2007.

Ernst, Wolfgang. "The Archive as Metaphor." *Open* 7 (2004): 46–43.

Garde-Hansen, Joanne, Andrew Hoskins, and Anna Reading. *Save as ... Digital Memories.* London: Palgrave Macmillan, 2009.

Grainge, Paul, ed. *Ephemeral Media. Transitory Screen Culture from Television to YouTube* London: Palgrave Macmillan, 2011.

Gray, Jonathan. *Show Sold Separately. Promos, Spoilers, and Other Media Paratexts.* New York: New York University Press, 2010.

Gunkle David, and Ted Gournelos, eds. *Transgression 2.0: Media, Culture and the Politics of a Digital Age.* New York: Continuum, 2011.

Hassan, Robert. "Networked Time and the 'Common Ruin of the Contending Classes.'" *TripleC* 11.2 (2013): 359–374.

———, and Roland E. Purser, eds. *24/7. Time and Temporality in the Network Society.* Stanford, CA: Stanford University Press, 2007.

Hearn, Alison. "Insecure: Narratives and Economies of the Branded Self in Transformation Television." *Continuum: Journal of Media & Cultural Studies* 22.4 (2008): 495–504.

Hindess, Barry. "Neo-liberal Citizenship." *Citizenship Studies* 6.2 (2002): 127–143.

Hoskins, Andrew. "7/7 and Connective Memory. Interactional Trajectories of Remembering in Post-Scarcity Culture." *Memory Studies* 4.3 (2011): 269–280.

———. "The End of Decay Time." *Memory Studies* 6.4 (2013): 387–389.

Huyssen, Andreas. *Present Pasts: Urban Palimpsests and the Politics of Memory.* Palo Alto, CA: Stanford University Press, 2003.

Jenkins, Henry, Sam Ford, and Joshua Green. *Spreadable Media. Creating Value and Meaning in a Networked Culture.* New York: New York University Press, 2013.

Keightley, Emily, ed. *Time Media and Modernity.* London: Palgrave Macmillan, 2012.

Klinger, Barbara. *Beyond the Multiplex: Cinema, New Technologies and the Home.* Berkeley: University of California Press, 2006.

Kuhn, Annette, "Memory Texts and Memory Work. Performances of Memory in and with Visual Media." *Memory Studies* 3.4 (2010): 298–313.

Lancaster, Kurt. *Interacting with Babylon 5.* Austin: University of Texas Press, 2001.

Landsberg, Alison. "Cinematic Temporality. Modernity, Memory and the Nearness of the Past." In *Time Media and Modernity*, ed. Keightley Emily, 85–101, London: Palgrave Macmillan, 2012.

Maiello, Angela. "Dalla memoria archivio alla memoria funzionale." *Fata Morgana* 25 (2015): 65–76.

Muzzarelli, Federica. "Memorie cinematografiche. La sindrome archiviale della modernità." *Fata Morgana* 25 (2015): 115–126.

Nardi, Bonnie, and Vicki O'Day, *Information Ecologies: Using Technology with Heart*. Cambridge, MA: MIT Press, 1999.

Ouellette, Laurie, and James Hay. *Better Living through Reality TV. Television and Post-Welfare Citizenship*. Malden, MA: Blackwell, 2008.

Rascaroli, Laura, Gwenda Young, and Barry Monan, eds. *The Home Movie, the Archive, the Web*. London: Bloomsbury, 2014.

Sadler, Philip. *Sustainable Growth in a Post-Scarcity World. Consumption, Demand, and the Poverty Penalty*. Farnham, UK: Gower, 2010.

Seltzer, Mark. "Wound culture. Trauma in the Pathologic Public Sphere." *October* 80 (1997): 3–26.

Sharma, Sarah. *In the Meantime. Temporality and Cultural Politics*. Durham, NC: Duke University Press, 2014.

Spigel, Lynn. "Housing Television. Architectures of the Archive." *The Communication Review* 13 (2010): 52–74.

Thomson, Christine. *Storytelling in Film and Television*. Cambridge, MA: Harvard University Press, 2003.

Tryon, Chuck. *Reinventing Cinema: Movies in the Age of Media Convergence*. New Brunswick, NJ: Rutgers University Press, 2010.

van Dijck, Josè. *Mediated Memories in the Digital Age*. Stanford, CA: Stanford University Press, 2007.

———. "Memory Matters in the Digital Age." In *Mediated Memories in the Digital Age*, 27–52. Stanford, CA: Stanford University Press, 2007.

Villa, Federica. "Autobiografiche. Scritture del tempo sullo sconcerto." *AAM-TAC. Arts and Artifacts in Movie. Technology, Aesthetics, Communication* 7 (2010): 57–63.

Walker, Janet. *Trauma Cinema. Documenting Incest and the Holocaust*. Berkeley: University of California Press, 2005.

2 The Politics of Paratextual Ephemeralia

Jonathan Gray

When hearing senior scholars of television reflect on the challenges of doing textual analysis of television in the 1970s, I have often been both charmed and frightened by the prospect of studying television before the VCR, when the medium was ephemeral. Countering my nostalgic encounter with an era in which watching live and together mattered (for I now watch almost everything via DVR, DVD, On Demand, or off an app) was my horror at the idea of how to capture, hold onto, and examine television when it was forever slipping away from one. How would I do my job well? How could I not falter in such an era? Immediately challenging my belief, though, was, on one hand, the realization that much television is still ephemeral—soaps, talk shows, and quiz shows, for instance, rarely make it to DVD, On Demand, or apps. On the other hand, though, came the realization that media still disappear from us all the time. Consider, for instance, a bus shelter that over its lifetime may host hundreds of posters for movies but each for no more than a week or two. With the majority of almost any media product's budget allocated to promotion, media is announced from all sorts of similar locales and perches, only to disappear from them in a few days. And while the movie, television show, or other media product may be available thereafter on DVD, via network apps, on Netflix, and in various other commercial, academic, or public venues and/or archives, much of its paratextual trace vanishes. Each paratext that vanishes, however, represents yet more meaning, or paths to meaning that similarly disappears and that is lost to us as media analysts.

To some, the disappearance of ads, trailers, toys, merchandise, press coverage, and more may seem wholly unproblematic. After all, textual analysis as a technique regularly fetishizes a solitary engagement with "the thing itself," excluding the static and noise introduced by paratexts. Paratextual ephemerality, therefore, may to some be a blessing in disguise, a clearing of the way that makes our job as analysts easier. But as I will argue here, paratexts matter. The ads that graced my hypothetical bus shelter did not just gesture at films: they created meaning for them. They set up expectations; they introduced commuters to their genres, characters, plots, environments, styles, and tones. They offered interpretive strategies, and they aimed to shut down or hide others. They spoke to specific commuters and shunned others.

And importantly, they did so not just for those commuters who eventually watched the films in question but also for those who did not. The latter group are of course still part of society, and thus when discussions about what a film was, what it meant, what it "did" occurred, all manner of participants in that discussion could have had opinions and meanings formed by those posters, or by the articles in the magazines they'd read, the licensed merchandise that glared at them as they walked through shopping malls or high streets, the pop-up ads, reviews, and commentary they encountered online, and so forth.

If, as analysts, we seek only to know what a film was as an aesthetic object entirely divorced from and irrelevant to society, then admittedly none of that information is needed. But if instead we want to situate texts in society, to inquire into their discursive roles and functions, each bus shelter ad or its kin that is taken down is one less point of meaning creation to which we have access. Even if that poster reappears, scanned, or digitized online, it likely does not tell us where it was, who it spoke to, and what it sat next to. This chapter takes this disappearance seriously, asking what it is that paratexts do to and for a text, why it matters that we hold onto them, and what happens when we lose them. Moreover, in asking what a paratext does to and for a text, I aim to situate it as a creator of *meaning and ideology*, and I insist that paratexts can play potentially decisive roles in determining the political, ideological life of a text and, moreover, that this life can change directions repeatedly owing in large part to the ephemerality of paratexts and hence to the variability of what version of the text presents itself.

Why Paratexts Matter

Paratexts matter. I have made this argument elsewhere[1] and thus do not wish simply to restate the case here, but suffice it to say that paratexts regularly play a constitutive role in the construction of meaning. In Gérard Genette's terms, the paratext is a text's threshold,[2] a spatial metaphor that is helpful inasmuch as it suggests that the first part of a text that we encounter will always be the paratext. At the "outskirts" of the text, these paratexts will either greet us, encouraging us to come in, or they will turn us away, insisting that we are not welcome, that the text exists for others instead. But far from simply pointing us inward or away, paratexts introduce us to the text in the process, and they start to tell us about the text, allowing us to experience the text for the first time. Thus, regardless of whether we move onward and away, or journey further into the text, we will have a sense of what that text is.

Paratexts can tell us a great deal about a text, about its central characters, its tone, its world, and that world's logic, its genre, its style, what it is all about, its politics, and what it is as an affective entity. We might consider trailers as iconic paratexts here and think of all the times that trailers have variously excited us about a text, thereby tantalizingly bringing the text to life, albeit briefly, or allow us immediately to decide that we will never watch this film, having decided unequivocally that this text is not for us. We might also think of instances when trailers are judged to have pegged a film incorrectly, suggesting it is one genre when a later viewing suggests it is another genre, inviting us to view the film one way when the film itself later seems to demand a different viewing. Or we might think of moments when trailers clash with other paratexts, when, for instance, a trailer suggests that a film is one thing, while an interview in *Entertainment Weekly* suggests it is another thing. Taken together, all of these possibilities illustrate how active paratexts are in setting the ground rules for viewing, and in initiating and *authoring* a text at the point(s) of entry.

Genette's spatial metaphor, though, does not adequately capture a second key role of paratexts, which is to later insist upon or change those ground rules. Paratexts, after all, do not only exist at a text's outskirts. DVD bonus materials are likely watched more often after watching the film or television show itself; posters are seen not just before viewing but after too; many interviews and reviews regularly address themselves to an audience that is presumed to have seen the film or television show already; and fan productions and commentary similarly hail audiences that have already seen the film or show (or other item of media). Spinoff and collectible merchandise, meanwhile, is more usually marketed at past viewers, not at would-be viewers. In these instances, the paratext is no less operative than when it is first on the scene. Rather, in these instances, we should expect paratexts to play a key role in the re-authoring of a text. They will subtly or explicitly insist that certain readings and interpretations are normative, "correct," and preferred, while abnormalizing and problematizing others. They will focus on certain aspects of a text, ignoring others completely, in ways that may recalibrate how we are invited to make sense of that text. They will add depth to some elements of a text, complicate other elements, and skip over others. They are also more than capable of adding substantively to a text, as in the case of transmedia extensions that might add characters, worlds, history, and breadth to a fictional world, or as in the case of some fan productions that crack a text open, add more to it, then reassemble it in a new form.

In *Show Sold Separately*, I argued as much, focusing on the role that paratexts play in changing and creating meaning. But it is worth highlighting here some of the knock-on effects of paratexts changing and creating meaning. One is to say that paratexts play a key role in authoring texts, or, more precisely, paratextual creators are textual authors. Though we have long reserved the title of "author" for a single nominated figure associated with the film, television show, book, videogame, or other media product, authorship is multiple, and when paratexts can change meanings, at times profoundly, then we must acknowledge how trailer editors, poster designers, book cover artists, fan producers, DVD producers, and so forth are all authors in their own right.[3] And to acknowledge them fairly as authors is to acknowledge that authorship is a fractured process, spread out over time, not simply preceding the work or product in question. Anything authored can be re-authored, and paratexts will be the primary means of re-authoring.

From this observation about authorship follow a series of other observations about textual power. Authorship, after all, is about power, about determining who has the ability and the right to speak for the text, and who gets to speak with the text. Authorship is authority, a position of power over a text, meaning, and culture. Hence, paratextual re-authoring assures that this power to speak is shared among many, and it disallows any text the ability to speak in one way continuously, unabated. Hopefully, we might note the degree to which this situation denies any text too much power, for with smart and careful paratextual engagement, we can always re-author texts, negating past meanings and uses. Practically, though, this situation should invite us to realize how content producers have regularly aimed to control the paratextual field precisely to shut down alternate readings and to maintain authorship, authority, and power. Indeed, if following Umberto Eco, all texts are "open,"[4] paratexts are key tools for managing what any given text is at a specific moment in time, and it is through paratexts that various stakeholders may work to limit how open a text can truly be at specific moments.

We should realize, too, that as academics and analysts we risk simply falling into a convenient trap if we romantically insist on directors and showrunners being the true authors, fetishizing their relationship to the work itself in the process, when most directors and showrunners are single agents in a large network of authorship, where the media corporation that owns their property controls much of the rest of that network. In other words, when we as analysts focus primarily on directors and showrunners, we regularly take our eye off the coordinating practices of the many paratextual authors as acts of power, authorship, and management, and we thereby fail properly to understand corporate authorship and the many ways in which it might work against, or otherwise delimit, the director's or showrunner's authorship and the openness of a text. By way of illustrating this process, I will now offer an example of paratextual authorship where the politics of a text are at stake, before turning explicitly to a discussion of its temporality and the ephemerality of some of those paratexts.

Mad Men's Paratextual Antifeminism

Mad Men (AMC, 2007–2015) has been a critical darling since its early days, winning countless nominations and awards for acting, writing, and directing, and attracting academic attention far and wide. While a great deal of this attention has been directed at it as "quality television," arguably just as many articles have focused on it as a feminist text,[5] and indeed at the level of the television show, *Mad Men* regularly engages in feminist critique, most notably of business culture, and of national myths about the mid-twentieth century nuclear family. This feminist voice is supported paratextually too, at times, most prominently by the choice to add a documentary on *The Birth of the Independent Woman* on the Season 2 DVD: interspliced with scenes from the show are talking head segments from prominent feminist critics and archival footage about the place of women in 1950s and 1960s America that situate *Mad Men* as working hand in hand with this documentary, repopulating history with a female perspective, and interrogating past accounts.[6] But elsewhere in the textual universe, a great many paratexts are disassembling its feminism, and it is to these that I now turn.

Some of the paratexts reduce the show's feminist figures, story arcs, and interests to style alone. Precisely because *Mad Men* is also popularly known as a highly stylized show, its feminism regularly teeters on the edge of being forgotten by accounts that flatten that feminism and roll it back up as only so much style. Such a strategy is most clearly, and strategically, on show in *Mad Men*'s relationship with Banana Republic. For several years now, the show and the clothing retailer have worked together to create a Mad Men clothing line. The clothing line and its ads reduce *Mad Men* solely to being something stylized, fashionable, and chic. Betty Draper may be known to audiences of the show as an unhappy housewife, whose challenge to the picture-perfect nostalgic rendering of the 1950s that looms largely in the United States' cultural imaginary and memory is often the vanguard of the show's feminist criticism. But in ads that ask "Are You Betty?", picturing a demure-looking blond model who shares a petite build with Draper's actress January Jones, Betty is reduced to a cold, distant style. The television show's Betty is often pitiable, certainly not enviable (no viewer should want to be Betty), as opposed to countless sitcom depictions to the contrary. But the ad's Betty is a style and a commodity to be purchased, rendered the object of desire. Clearly, Banana Republic does not want an advertising campaign that suggests women who feel unloved, disempowered, and emotionally abused by their husbands will love their clothes. So they re-author Betty to be none of those things, and instead simply to be coldly aloof, in a supposedly sexy way, with a practiced and deliberately empty expression designed to gain her attention, not to be read as a sign of inner turmoil. The ad engages a semiotic reprogramming and re-authoring, therefore, transforming signs of misery, abuse, and disempowerment into signs of sexual control and desirability. Betty is either evacuated entirely as a site of feminist critique and made instead into style that can be purchased, or may retain vestiges of feminist critique, but vestiges that are re-purposed as markers of style and cool, with feminism as little more than pose.

Banana Republic would also seem to be especially interested in *Mad Men* because of its relationship to the past, offering an older, "classic" style of dress as contemporary and "now." *Mad Men* helps here, since it is a show about the past that enjoys significant buzz for being new, fresh, and at television's cutting edge. But the show's relationship to the past is again more contested and fractured than the Banana Republic ads' constructed relationship to the past. *Mad Men* often invokes nostalgia to criticize and undercut it. For instance, in "The Wheel," Don pitches an ad campaign to Kodak that is wrapped in nostalgia and that sees him ponder the nature of nostalgia to the Kodak execs. As he does so, he shows slides from his wedding and of his wife and family, using them to depict a happy family, while elsewhere in the episode we see Betty admit to a therapist and to her daughter's young friend Glenn that she is desperately alone and that Glenn might be her only friend, and we see her leave for the holidays with the children yet without Don.

In short, the episode acutely attacks mediated nostalgic spectacle, providing something of a key to understanding what the show is trying to do, namely, to expose nostalgia of the 1950s and early 1960s as built on lies constructed to sell things. But when Banana Republic gets involved, it offers a different relationship to the past, where the past is something to be loved, embraced, and idolized *as* style and spectacle, before being renewed in the present. Admittedly, *Mad Men* regularly risks suggesting a similar relationship to the past in other scenes and episodes when the past is very much a style and spectacle, so Banana Republic is not making up such a meaning out of whole cloth. Rather, what we see here are paratexts shifting the text away from its more feminist and critical meanings, and amplifying its more superficial meanings.

The show's feminism is further challenged, or outright destroyed, in many articles in the entertainment press featuring the show's main actresses. January Jones and Christina Hendricks in particular, but more recently Elisabeth Moss, too, are regularly delivered to magazine readers solely as women to be looked at as objects of sexual desire. Thus, Jones has appeared naked in *GQ*, with the November 2009 cover title "Mad Men's January Jones Unzips," and was billed as "Hollywood's Ice-Hot Blonde" on the May 2011 cover of *W*, the large-print font announcing her as "Mad Sexy," while she appears wearing only stiletto heels and a bustier. Hendricks's shoot with *Esquire* is hypersexualized, with her crawling around in leather on all fours, eating a watermelon, and so forth; an ad for London Fog features her in a jacket but focuses on her exposed bra; and one of AMC's own advertising images for *Mad Men* depicts her being stared at by various men. Even beyond images, she is regularly translated into text as a sexual object alone, as when *The Daily Mail* dubs her "The Queen of Curves," writing further that "Christina Hendricks is about to drive men everywhere mad again. The buxom beauty explodes on the cover of the May 2013 issue of Canada's Flare Magazine."[7] Elisabeth Moss, meanwhile, appears on the 8 March 2012 cover of *Page Six Magazine* as "Mad Men's Elisabeth Moss," lifting up a coat to reveal black silk stockings and garter belt. The cover print offers a quote from her that "Sometimes you just want to be a bad girl," with "bad girl" in huge yellow print. Thus, when the women of *Mad Men* appear in magazines—regularly coded, no less as stars of *Mad Men*—they regularly appear in "lad mags" aimed at men, as little more than eye candy.

While it is the actresses who appear this way, not the characters, inevitably these images hold the potential to upset and sour the feminist potential of those characters by casting doubts upon the authenticity or legitimacy of that feminism. Certainly, some articles seem to relish the act of thwarting their characters' feminism. *The New York Daily News*, for example, writes that "Sultry actress Christina Hendricks loves playing 'Mad Men' character Joan Holloway, but says she's only like her in one way: pleasing her husband."[8] In such instances, paratexts unite to question the characters' and show's feminist intentions and commentary. Meanwhile, when *Mad Men*'s men are featured in men's magazines, they are regularly depicted unironically as emblems of masculine power, thereby again leaving the show's feminism in jeopardy. Interviews with creator Matthew Weiner may help to restore a sense of the feminist voice,[9] but these are hardly as plentiful or accessible as the parade of actors and actresses on covers of magazines that many people may not even buy, but will see on magazine shelves peppered throughout everyday life or advertised online.

What I hope to have illustrated is that *at the point of writing this chapter*, the somewhat feminist television show *Mad Men* has a decisively unfeminist, and sometimes antifeminist, public (paratextual) face: magazines, their related Internet versions, Banana Republic ads, and many interviews with the cast disassemble its feminism. The writers' own efforts are regularly rebuffed or deflected by other paratextual authors. Admittedly, I have not focused on other paratexts that extend or hold in place *Mad Men*'s feminism, and there are some—from some critics' reviews to the aforementioned DVD set, for instance. But at worst they might fail, and at most they might leave the status of the text's feminism heavily contested.

Paratexts (Not) in the Archive

However, this is a book about ephemerality, so I now wish to inquire into the staying power of any of these paratexts and to ask what *Mad Men* will look like in, say, two decades. In doing so, I hope to shine light upon how paratextual archiving, or the lack thereof, matters to the ways in which we as analysts do our jobs. With few exceptions, if we are writing about television shows, films, and other media products years later, we still have access to those products. In this case, for instance, my department's Instructional Media Center owns the *Mad Men* DVDs, and I can access those easily. DVD and digital wear and tear notwithstanding, moreover, twenty years from now someone else could access those same DVDs. The episodes themselves, and anything appended to those DVDs, could in theory enjoy a long life. By contrast, many of the other paratexts I have discussed in this chapter will likely have disappeared, or will only exist in archives that no future scholar of *Mad Men* may think to examine. Twenty years from now, Banana Republic's ads will have long gone, or their remnants will not likely tell us where these ads could be found, details on who they were directed at will likely have vanished, and thus their status will be in question. Few libraries, too, are actively archiving lad mags, so presumably their own trace will die out relatively quickly. How then should we examine and make sense of *Mad Men*?

The aforementioned documentary appended to Season Two will doubtlessly help situate and frame *Mad Men* as feminist, as critically engaged with history, and as aspiring to be culturally and socially important in its own way. By being included on the official *Mad Men* DVD, it has seemingly won the paratextual posterity sweepstakes. Yet even then, its place is tenuous. AMC did not translate it into every language in which *Mad Men* is sold, which means that the documentary is nowhere to be seen in many foreign language versions of the show. AMC might also re-release the DVD at any time, reconfigured with new paratexts or with old ones removed. And we are naïve if we believe that all regular viewers' and even academics' encounters with *Mad Men* will be with its DVD. As streaming companies such as Netflix, Amazon, and Hulu gain greater market share and power, DVDs may disappear outright, tossed from many a popular or academic library as readily as many VHS tapes have been tossed in the previous decade. And with them will go the documentary. Or many others will experience the show, or re-experience it, via "illegal" means, torrenting it, for example, or buying a pirated DVD. Again, these informal economies are unlikely to pass on the documentary. Thus, even a paratext whose place in the canon seems enshrined for now may soon disappear from sight.

What will be lost when these paratexts disappear? Analysts who wish to make sense of what a text *was* and what it *did* in social, cultural terms will henceforth be working at a significant disadvantage. Consequently, we should cast the reliability of their analyses into doubt. This is the future for *Mad Men*, but it is the present for many other texts, as we might flatter ourselves with knowing what a text was and what it did because we have watched the show, film, or product itself ... but we have not seen much of its paratexts. Take the case of *I Love Lucy* (CBS, 1951–1957), for instance, another text whose feminism is questionable. One might see Lucy's never-ending antics and plots to escape the domestic space as feminist, or one might see the ultimate failure of each of those antics and plots as a patriarchal swatting of the feminist fly.[10] The show, I would argue, is frustratingly unclear as to its politics, at times leaning one way, at times another. But what did its paratexts do and say? How were *Lucy* and Lucille Ball framed in ways that may have precluded or favored its politics? Clearly, some records exist that allow us to answer these questions, but too few, in too few places, while the show is still regularly featured in broadcasting history classes and analyzed without any of those paratexts at hand.

Paratextual ephemerality, therefore, poses a clear and ever-present danger to the quality of our analysis. We need not even wait several decades for the danger to announce itself, as regularly just a month or two later, many paratexts have disappeared. By and large, they are not being saved either, as most libraries and archives hold on to the product itself, not the paratexts.

An interesting, albeit limited, exception here can be found in the George Foster Peabody Archives in Athens, Georgia. The archives are attached to the George Foster Peabody Awards and hence draw from and collect all submissions to the awards, one of the very oldest of their type. Located at the University of Georgia, the Archives exist primarily to house the Peabody Awards' extensive audiovisual holdings, but occasionally submissions include a paratext or more. The Peabody Archives have held on to these and boxed them (resulting in approximately one hundred boxes worth of material), and though they remain a barely utilized resource, they are well catalogued and available through the University's Special Collections, and a small selection is often publicly exhibited there too. The collection is wonderfully eclectic: for instance, one can find glossy booklets produced by television networks specifically for award-granting bodies or critics, but also *Nurse Jackie* (Showtime, 2009–) first-aid kits, a range of *American Idol* (Fox, 2002–) hats and scorecards, alongside a huge binder full of photocopied reviews and press clippings about the show, a *Friday Night Lights* (NBC, 2006–2011) blanket, and a host of educational materials and binders documenting various children's shows' activities in the community. In addition to holding a remarkably impressive archive of radio and television from the last few decades, therefore, the Peabody Archives also include T-shirts, posters, lunchboxes, aprons, evidence bags, blood slides, a shirt with lipstick on it (from *Mad Men*), stickers and buttons, index cards designed for testing material in shows, large metal or wooden briefcases, nerf swords, fake gold coins, slides, postcards, medical clipboards and scrubs, a miniature prison door, binders documenting synergistic events at local community centers and baseball stadiums, pirate chests, magazines and newspapers, comics, baseball caps, pictures of billboards and bus shelters containing ads for the shows, and more. It is a treasure trove of paratexts, even though nobody set out with that goal in mind, and even though its contents rely entirely on the whims of what broadcasters will submit alongside their television, radio, or web program.

At times, these paratexts tell us little about a text and its cultural life. At other times, however, they tell us more. *The Simpsons* (Fox, 1989–), for instance, has nominated itself many years and regularly sends a bevy of *Simpsons*-related merchandise and materials. Of particular interest to me as I looked at these were a series of magazines and newspapers that included *Simpsons* artwork on their covers, even when the stories were not about *The Simpsons*. For example, the archive includes a copy of the 10 November 2005 *LA Weekly*, with a cover story, "Green to the Core: How I Learned to Stop Worrying and Love Nuclear Power." When one flips to the article, *The Simpsons* is not mentioned a single time, but the characters adorn its cover in total, with Springfield's nuclear power plant emitting green fumes as Lisa picks flowers, the rest of the family enjoys a picnic, and a three-eyed fish swims past them in a river leading outward from the plant. Or a copy of the 25 December 2001, *Village Voice* similarly uses *Simpsons* artwork on the cover, depicting Homer gorging on donuts in the control room of the nuclear power plant while flames consume his coworkers, and with the title, "Who Insures Nuclear Power Plants? You Do." Once again, though, *The Simpsons'* presence is restricted solely to artwork—not even to accompanying text—on the cover, with no references at all in the article itself. Taken together, these paratexts tell us about how *The Simpsons* has been used to talk about nuclear power, what it threatens, how poorly it is regulated, and a connection to environmental politics.

Both newspapers used *Simpsons* images presumably to garner attention, perhaps to build on associations we already have with the show and its characters, and the newspapers would have had to pay for these images to be drawn especially for them. Therefore, the covers color *The Simpsons'* politics by association as environmentally concerned, as critical of nuclear power. Together, they subtly remind us that very little else in popular culture is critical of nuclear power, such that each magazine references *The Simpsons*, not anything else. And few if any researchers would find these with even exhaustive searches for all-things-Simpsons outside the Peabody Archives, precisely because the show's name is never uttered on either the covers or in the articles, thereby rendering it invisible to the word searches that dominate journalistic archive databases. Cases such as these gesture at what is at stake in preserving and archiving paratexts, as we can extend their lives, hold onto them, and then use them to better inform cultural analyses of media.

Yet even Peabody's reach is limited. The archive saves only what is sent to it, from a self-selecting group of (predominately American) shows and producers who surely are interested in sharing only paratexts that flatter. *American Idol*'s massive binder of reviews and press clippings unsurprisingly does not include anything that makes the show look bad: all the reviews glow; all the clippings announce the show as important. *The Simpsons*, meanwhile, may send more than anyone else, but they aren't sending unlicensed merchandise, and even what they do send is but a tiny selection of the significant whole. So very much is still missing, in other words. Moreover, the path is set for the archive's paratextual collection to dwindle. Whereas submissions were long required to take physical form, thereby making it easy to slip something else in the package, as the Peabody Awards attempt to manage ever-increasing submission numbers by moving toward greater digitization, submissions may soon take digital form alone, submitted as single files, with room for digital attachments but not for physical extras.

In this respect, we might consider how the paratext's fate in the Peabody Archives echoes that of its likely fate in many other archives, as a push toward digitization (complete with the promise of saving space) could vastly reduce many archives' interest in saving physical remnants and paratexts. Admittedly, other digital paratexts may be saved in greater numbers, but this will only happen if concerted attention is placed on underlining and highlighting the importance of saving paratexts. Paratexts already risk being excluded by archivists since they don't enjoy the aura and public adoration that films, television shows, books, and other media products do, so we must work hard to ensure that their value is made clear, so that they are saved.

Textual Decay: A Conclusion

Throughout this chapter, I have argued for the importance of paratexts in situating what a text is, what it does, what role and status it has politically, and, thus, in short, why and how it matters to us as analysts and citizens. Given the importance of paratexts, moreover, I have suggested that their ephemerality should trouble and worry us. Decay threatens all archives, but decay is often thought of in terms of the strength of book spines, the lifespan of microform, DVDs, or other recording devices, and digital decay. The text itself, though, risks constant decay if we are not archiving it: just as we would be alarmed to see that pages of a book had crumbled over time or that entire files had become corrupted and unopenable, so too should we be alarmed to consider the decay of texts in our memories and archives when their paratexts disappear.

To conclude this chapter, then, the message for the future should be clear: we must endeavor to save more. Conclusions regarding past and present practice stem from this observation as well, for we should at the least be aware of the absences, lacks, gaps, and decay in the texts that we study. We might also be bolder and more creative in looking for long shadows, footprints, and other evidence of a paratext's former presence. Certainly, there is a self-replication of the myth of the solitary genius work at play here: if we look for textual meaning and seek to understand the roles that a text held and holds in society, yet we do not have paratexts at hand to help us better situate those roles, we might convince ourselves that a film, television show, or other media product can speak itself, and that its audiences interact only with that product. Alternatively, to acknowledge the importance of paratexts dictates that we acknowledge a necessity to involve them in our analyses, or to tiptoe carefully when we do not have them at hand. The point is not falsely to offer hopes of an authentic, perfectly comprehensive textual analysis: this is not possible. Rather, we must realize the ephemerality of textuality due to the appearances and disappearances of paratexts, and we must be more careful, on one hand, to situate our readings within an awareness of the text's shifting borders, and, on the other hand, to save and archive paratexts that allow us to chart a text's ebbs and flows more convincingly.

Notes

1. Jonathan Gray, *Show Sold Separately: Promos, Spoilers, and Other Media Paratexts* (New York: New York University Press, 2010).
2. Gérard Genette, *Paratexts: The Thresholds of Interpretation*, trans. Jane E. Lewin (Cambridge, UK: Cambridge University Press, 1997).

3. For more, see Jonathan Gray, "When Is the Author?" in *The Companion to Media Authorship*, eds. Jonathan Gray and Derek Johnson (Malden, MA: Wiley-Blackwell, 2013), 88–111.
4. Umberto Eco, *The Open Work*, trans. Anna Cancogni (Cambridge, MA: Harvard University Press, 1989).
5. See, for instance, Stephanie Coontz, "Why 'Mad Men' Is TV's Most Feminist Show," *The Washington Post*, 10 October 2010, accessed 15 December 2014, *http://www.washingtonpost.com/wp-dyn/content/article/2010/10/08/AR2010100802662.html*.
6. See Mary Celeste Kearney, "When *Mad Men* Pitches Feminism: Popular Education and Historical Witnessing Through DVD Special Features," *Memory Connection* 1.1 (2001): 420–435, accessed 15 December 2014, *http://www.memoryconnection.org/wp-content/uploads/2011/12/MaryCelesteKearney1.pdf*.
7. *Daily Mail*, "'I've Been Rejected a Million Times': Christina Hendricks The Queen of Curves on Her Struggle to Make it in Hollywood," 5 April 2013, accessed 15 December 2014, *http://www.dailymail.co.uk/usshowbiz/article-2304737/Christina-Hendricks-queen-curves-struggle-make-Hollywood.html*.
8. Chiderah Monde, "Christina Hendricks of 'Mad Men': I Dress Up for My Husband at Home," *The New York Daily News*, 24 May 2013, accessed 15 December 2014, *http://www.nydailynews.com/entertainment/gossip/christina-hendricks-dress-husband-article-1.1343297#ixzz2YVtafY5F*.
9. See Tom Matlack, "Is *Mad Men* a Feminist Show?", *The Huffington Post*, 13 August 2009, accessed 15 December 2014, *http://www.huffingtonpost.com/tom-matlack/is-imad-meni-a-feminist-s_b_230097.html*.
10. See Patricia Mellencamp, "Situation Comedy, Feminism, and Freud: Discourses of Gracie and Lucy," in *Studies in Entertainment: Critical Approaches to Mass Culture*, ed. Tania Modleski (Bloomington: Indiana University Press, 1986), 80–95.

References

Anonymous. "'I've Been Rejected a Million Times': Christina Hendricks The Queen of Curves on Her Struggle to Make It in Hollywood." *Daily Mail*, 5 April 2013. Accessed 15 December 2014. *http://www.dailymail.co.uk/usshowbiz/article-2304737/Christina-Hendricks-queen-curves-struggle-make-Hollywood.html*.
Coontz, Stephanie. "Why 'Mad Men' Is TV's Most Feminist Show." *The Washington Post*, 10 October 2010. Accessed 15 December 2014. *http://www.washingtonpost.com/wp-dyn/content/article/2010/10/08/AR2010100802662.html*.
Eco, Umberto. *The Open Work*. Trans. Anna Cancogni. Cambridge, MA: Harvard University Press, 1989.
Genette, Gérard. *Paratexts: The Thresholds of Interpretation*. Trans. Jane E. Lewin. Cambridge, UK: Cambridge University Press, 1997.
Gray, Jonathan. *Show Sold Separately: Promos, Spoilers, and Other Media Paratexts*. New York: New York University Press, 2010.
———. "When Is the Author?" In *The Companion to Media Authorship*, eds. Jonathan Gray and Derek Johnson, 88–111. Malden, MA: Wiley-Blackwell, 2013.
Kearney, Mary Celeste. "When *Mad Men* Pitches Feminism: Popular Education and Historical Witnessing Through DVD Special Features." *Memory Connection* 1.1 (2001): 420–435. Accessed 15 December 2014. *http://www.memoryconnection.org/wp-content/uploads/2011/12/MaryCelesteKearney1.pdf*.

Matlack, Tom. "Is *Mad Men* a Feminist Show?" *The Huffington Post*, 13 August 2009. Accessed 15 December 2014. *http://www.huffingtonpost.com/tom-matlack/is-imad-meni-a-feminist-s_b_230097.html.*

Mellencamp, Patricia. "Situation Comedy, Feminism, and Freud: Discourses of Gracie and Lucy." In *Studies in Entertainment: Critical Approaches to Mass Culture*, ed. Tania Modleski, 80–95 (Bloomington: Indiana University Press, 1986).

Monde, Chiderah. "Christina Hendricks of 'Mad Men': I Dress Up for My Husband at Home." *The New York Daily News*, 24 May 2013. Accessed 15 December 2014. *http://www.nydailynews.com/entertainment/gossip/christina-hendricks-dress-husband-article-1.1343297#ixzz2YVtafY5F.*

3 Paratext between Time and Space in Digital Media

Giulio Lughi

Introduction

This chapter proposes to review the current concept of the paratext, taking into account how the technocultural peculiarities of digital media force us to consider new aspects of textuality, particularly the relationship between space and time. The basic paradigms used in this analysis stem from classic digital media studies (such as those of Castells, Landow, Bolter and Grusin, and Manovich),[1] the key concepts of which have been refocused on paratext and the relationship between space and time.

In the contemporary cultural landscape, the great variety of paratextual materials that surround the world of mass media (literature, film, television) is extremely evident: commercials, trailers, "making of", merchandising, and so on. This proliferation creates a suggestion of ephemerality, it forces us to reconsider the temporality of cultural values, and it introduces a world of liquid and elusive textuality. But when we shift the focus from traditional media (old media, mass media) to the world of digital media, besides the parameter of time it is also necessary to pay attention to the parameter of space. More precisely, the world of digital media forces us to rethink the relationship between space and time in the organization of textuality.

Many of the innovative aspects that distinguish digital media are in fact strictly tied to the dimension of space: what Manovich calls the database culture,[2] in which information is stored using a spatial organization; the free availability of large amounts of data,[3] seen as lands to be traveled over; various forms of dynamic visualization, like the geographic explorations offered by Google Earth; social narratives, such as fan fiction or other forms of collaborative writing by authors all over the world; the peculiar characteristics of mobile devices, where moving in space is implicit; hypertextuality,[4] in the terms of Landow, a form of textuality that is strictly connected to the idea of explorable maps; transmedia storytelling, the organization of complex narrative forms based on the production of different but interrelated contents, disseminated across multiple communication forms (e.g., books, cinema, television, games, merchandising).[5]

Consequently, in order to examine how the concept of the paratext is changing in digital media, we have to start from a consideration concerning space. In digital texts, it is not easy to distinguish the boundaries that separate the main text from the paratextual elements. Traditionally, the concept of paratext implies—as a premise and in opposition—the existence of a text and the fact that this text is closed and autonomous. In the world of print there is a clear distinction (also as it relates to layout and type set) between the text and the paratextual elements: footnotes, comments, and reviews. In mass media there is a clear distinction between text (a film, for example) and trailer, or review, or behind the scenes. In digital media text uniformity falls apart, and the edges of the text are weakened: for instance, while surfing the net, the constant movement from one link to the next dissolves the sense of main text. Alternatively, in the more advanced forms of web-docs[6] there is no single common thread because the different informational materials are combined by several logical connections.

Of course, this is not true when referring to texts that have been simply digitized (books, movies, music, images, videos, etc., transferred onto a digital support). In these cases, the text retains its compactness, and the difference between it and the paratext is very clear. We can say the same about phenomena related to the social dimension of the Internet, such as fan fiction or comments on blogs, where it is quite clear what is text and what is paratext.

But when we are dealing with natively digital texts (hypertexts, videogames, immersive 3D, augmented reality, etc.: the horizon toward which textuality is slowly evolving), the relationship between text and paratext becomes more complex (see the later section in this chapter, "The Deep/Surface Structure Opposition").

In the same way, in digital media there are complex relationships between space and time. Digital media are in fact characterized in many ways by "short time". Technological innovation causes the obsolescence of hardware devices; software evolution constantly pushes toward new text, image, sound, and video formats; the evanescence of text—appearing on the screen but not anchored to any physical media—undermines the concept of cultural life and renders the notion of cultural assets problematic. The endless dynamics of production and consumption lead us more and more to the creation of new products, formats, and series.

At the same time, closely connected with the temporal concept of "short time" is the spatial concept of "short form". The logic of digital media, based on modularity and recombination, leads to the creation of short texts,[7] which must be assembled by procedures of textual editing, as was the case with hypertexts in the 1990s. This same thing is happening now—in more general terms—in the "remix culture,"[8] where existing materials are modified and/or recombined to create new original works, in line with that "deep remixability" that according to Manovich develops and overtakes the old concept of "multimedia".[9]

This convergence between "short time" and "short form" seems to lead to a kind of short circuit between space and time, which is emphasized by the increasing spread of mobile communication devices (see the section "The

Mobile/Locative Paradigm"). Beyond their current technological declinations in digital media, the relationships between space and time—and their cultural implications—are also topics of great interest in industrial modernity theories. According to Schivelbusch,[10] the evolution of transport modes in the industrial age has conditioned not only the physical geography of the areas involved, but also the "mental geography" of the people involved, and consequently the way space and time are perceived. This originates from the general phenomenon of space–time contraction, which not only increases the speed of transports, but also produces a general globalization and acceleration of communication, technologies, and markets.[11] Let's not forget that Marcel Proust's *Recherche*, written around the 1920s, is interspersed with interesting observations on how much the railway, the car, and the telephone modified social and cultural relationships between people and places.

Therefore, it is worth tracking down some elements in the recent past that may be useful in defining the concept of paratext from this point of view.

Between Time and Space

The complexity of the relationship between space and time is already clear in the distinction between time and duration developed by Henri Bergson (1859–1941) in 1889,[12] where the philosopher keeps his distance from the concepts of scientific and geometric time and opens his reflections to the social and psychological dimensions of time in the mental space of experience.

Even in literature, at the end of the nineteenth century we find the first signs of a crisis destined to affect the parameters of textuality. The compositional technique of the *feuilleton*, in fact, causes a sort of break in the linearity of space–time in the organization of the novel, which will later be the characteristic of the classic hypertext. The reading experience, which in classic tales provides an immersive experience of continuity, in the *feuilleton* forces the reader to make space–time leaps to switch from one episode to another.

In some fundamental semiotic theories, we already find a vision of the text as a territory, made up of several interconnected elements, which stands alongside the vision of the text as a fabric, which requires instead a pathway of linear, sequential continuity.[13] As can be seen, the parameters of space and time start to mingle at this point: the text fabric unfolds over time (weaving is a process of time), it requires a strong authorial identity, and it presents a consistent succession of events. The text-territory instead unfolds in space, is polycentric by nature, and opens the way to paratextual interventions from the outside (as with the readers of the feuilleton, who intervened in the plot, and as is now happening in the practice of collaborative writing, which is typical of digital media).

In 1937, the Russian scholar Mikhail Bakhtin (1895–1975) had already coined the term *chronotope*[14] to define the unit of analysis used to study the temporal and spatial categories represented in the communication processes of a narrative—a methodological approach needed to tackle precisely the polyphonic complexity that, according to the Russian scholar, characterizes the whole historical development of the novel.

The narrative complexity that results from the combination of space and time is also the theme of Jorge Luis Borges's (1899–1986) reflections on the possibility of building what he defines as an "infinite book," a book that can be transmitted across generations by allowing individual reader–writers to add pages or edit what was written in the past.[15] Very often Borges was seen as the forerunner of the hypertextual narrative model: a model that is certainly not attributable to the world of print, where the edges of the text are defined once and for all, but rather to the world of handwriting, to the cultural tradition of the manuscripts that grew through the glosses and were modified by the paratextual practice of the scribes. Or even further back, the model may be attributable to the world of orality, where the text is always open to endless additions and modifications. In Ts'ui Pên's projects (the fictional character of *The Garden of Forking Paths* to which Borges entrusts the task of developing this hypothetical model), the "infinite book" should realize the presence of time (the writing) and space (the labyrinth), making an infinite return back in time, which becomes an infinite return back in space.

Thus, the evident dissolution of linear and sequential time in hypertext fiction is compensated by a strong emphasis on space. Visualization becomes predominant if compared to reading, and the representation takes over the narration,[16] as in videogames or interactive novels. In hypertext fiction, the flowing of time is replaced by the spatial exploration of the maze-text, creating a sense of disorientation, which results from the excess of information and from the uncertainty as to which path to follow. The linear time of the traditional tale is replaced by a cyclical, recursive time, basically static and strongly related to the spatial dimension.

It is also important to note that the definition of paratext formulated by Gérard Genette is closely related to a spatial definition. Both the term *paratext* and those terms connected to it, such as epitext and peritext, derive from the use of prepositional prefixes (para-, peri-, epi-), which in the ancient Greek language have a predominantly spatial meaning.[17] According to Ellen McCracken, who extends Genette's theories about paratext to the digital world, the act of reading (time-determined activity) on e-book devices produces a cognitive modification that leads the digital reader to continuous spatial movements, approaching ("centripetal") or distancing ("centrifugal") with respect to the central core of the narrative.[18]

For example, the experience of buying and reading a text for the Kindle through Amazon changes the criteria for defining the text in this direction. As I read the text on the Kindle, in fact, I can write some comments that refer to specific passages in the text. I can also choose that my comments be made public and then be viewed by other readers who have purchased the same text. But this means that the future buyer of that text will also buy my comments. From his point of view, in some way, my comments are already a part of the text. For instance, in an academic essay, the future reader will probably have the opportunity to purchase the text already accompanied by all the comments that represent the various critical positions aroused by the text within the scientific community: a text that has integrated its para-texts, although it is still possible to distinguish them, as was the case for the glosses written in the margin of ancient manuscripts.

More generally, in addition to the comments added to the text, we must consider that all actions taken by the e-book reader contribute to composing a great paratext, investigated with statistical methods by the data mining systems. For example, the behavior of exploration preceding a purchase; the time and manner of reading; the chapters, or characters, on which the digital reader focused; the quotations shared on social networks—all of these items are recorded in an identity profile and represent a real hidden paratext (see the later section "The Deep/Surface Structure Opposition"). In this way the act of reading, which is naturally placed on the axis of time, produces an extension of the text size, which is located on the axis of space.

This interweaving of space and time has always marked the most reliable theories about mass media communication. In the work of John B. Thompson, there is clearly an awareness that the global spread of communication tends to cancel out both spatial and temporal distances, compressing them into a generalized space–time dimension. This is typical, for instance, of live broadcasting, where events are placed in a nondescript place and an ever-lasting present.[19] Delocalization and detemporalization are the key words that explain the deep change that the world of mass media introduces into the perceptual and cognitive habits of the media user.

In Castells's theory, one of the key points is what the scholar defines as "informationalism"[20]: the new global economy based on the production of value through the generation, processing, management, and application of knowledge. This global economy is realized in a new operational space, the space of flows, as opposed to the traditional static space of places. The space of places is found, for example, in relationships between neighbors, in close and confined spaces, between people who actually know each other. In contrast, the space of flows is the virtual space represented by the extension given by the net, connecting people via digital communication and not face to face.

More recently, in the context of digital culture, Bruce Sterling coined the definition of "spime"[21] (a contraction of space and time) in order to define the textual "meta-objects" increasingly present in everyday life, such as RFID (Radio-Frequency IDentification) microchips that can locate a book catalogued in a library at any given moment; or smartphones, which have the common characteristic of being "conscious" of their spatial coor-dinates (space) and of the moment in which they are operating (time). In other words, digital devices, especially mobile ones, seem to fully realize the meaning of the Latin expression *hic et nunc*, which indicates the position of the subject in a defined spatiotemporal situation.

These brief considerations show how the superimposition of space and time has often been present in the cultural and communicative phenomena of modernity. In digital media, this combination is even more pronounced. In the next paragraphs, there is a proposal to reconsider the current concept of the paratext, taking into account how the technocultural peculiarities of digital media force us to consider new aspects of textuality due to the relationship between time and space. Particularly, we will consider two factors of change: the opposition between surface structure and deep structure, and the mobile/locative paradigm.

The Deep/Surface Structure Opposition

Digital media are the transposition of the technical, professional, emotional, and cultural world of mass media into the new technological environment offered by the rise of information communication technology (ICT). In this transposition, the key element that characterizes digital media is the distinction between two different levels:

- *The surface structure*: the place—on a computer or tablet screens—that offers a display apparently similar to what we are used to seeing on paper, film, and television screens;
- *The deep structure*: the place—consisting of hardware and software—where the digital information is processed. The deep structure is a logic engine, based on the underlying database and algorithms, which performs calculations on abstract entities, but which is able to generate everything that appears in the surface structure and render it perceivable to the human senses.[22]

These two layers are engaged in a dynamic process that is something like the vertical model of generative-transformational grammar that Noam Chomsky (1928–) formulated to explain the functioning of language, by basing it on the distinction between deep structure and surface structure. The central idea of generative-transformational grammar is that the two structures are different and that the surface structure is determined by repeated application of certain formal operations, called "grammatical transformations."[23] In this way, the component of the syntactic grammar must generate, for each phrase, deep structures and surface structures, and must link them.

Similarly, in digital media the paratextual elements are not directly observable by the user, but they lie (and work) at a deeper level. While in pre-digital media the paratext is visible on the same horizontal plane of the text (for instance: the footnotes are on the same page as the text), in digital media the paratext is not visible to the reader, but it determines the structure of the visible text, as, for example, in HTML instructions, hidden to the reader but fundamental to build the text that appears on the surface.

Given the difference between deep and surface structure, the main characteristic of digital media is interactivity. That means the text becomes able to receive an input, perform calculations, and return an output. In other words, the text—which used to be only visible—in the last quarter of the twentieth century becomes practicable and accessible. This transformation of the textual space from visible space to a viable, playable space represents the decisive turning point in opposition to the previous mass media age and is due to the fact that the paratextual elements, which guide the dynamic behavior of the text, are placed in the deep structure.

One area where this phenomenon is most visible is the new graphic, aesthetic, and communicative design of digital texts. The use of advanced technologies at the deep paratextual level (HTML 5, Cascading Style Sheets, JavaScript, server side programming, etc.) allows us to abandon the traditional paper-based graphical settings. For instance, the source code of an HTML page includes (a) the content elements that will appear at the superficial level of the text; (b) the formatting elements that will remain invisible but that are crucial for the global definition of the text because they work as an organizational tool for viewing, understanding, and contextualizing the text. In other words, they play a paratextual role. The question is even more complex when we consider a third category: (c) the semantic elements:

- *metadata*—paratextual elements par excellence, with the task of guiding and clarifying the interpretation of data: a typical example are key words that enable the user to search for specific information within the text;
- *ontologies*—logical patterns used to describe the semantic relationships between the various elements of the deep structure and able to guide the work of intelligent agents. Examples are the logical relations used by the recommendation systems that guide us in our purchases or in our online booking, or algorithmic problem solving;
- more generally, *the Semantic Web*—the transformation of the web from a simple stock of texts into a complex structure where—by means of metadata and ontologies—the semantic interactions between documents can also be identified. Examples include "derived from ...," "connected to ...," and "contemporary to ...," establishing a true network of meanings.

This way, dynamic pages are produced using a multiplicity of layers and the automatic reconfiguration of the graphic elements that compose the page, in conjunction with semantic metadata that provide the reader with a complex experience. This change can be seen increasingly in all communicative contexts and products: economic, institutional, and artistic.

A particularly strong feature of the digital text, where we can easily understand the relationship between deep and surface structure, is the introduction in markup languages—such as HTML, the universal language for web pages—of Cascading Style Sheets [CSS], a programming technique that incorporates some functionalities already known to advanced users of writing programs and to those who deal with editorial composition in the professional field.

Style Sheets allow authors to specify the instructions for presentation of the text only once, rather than insert them individually into the tag for each item. Style Sheets are sets of instructions (which may be contained within the text itself or in a separate file) that tell the browser how to graphically display the different parts of the text. Of course, the browser must be able to recognize the "different parts of the text," and it does so thanks to the fact that these are marked with tags. For example, paragraphs are preceded by the <p> tag and followed by </p>; headers are preceded by the <H1> tag and followed by </H1>; and so on. This means that when the browser finds a pair of tags, instead of displaying the text between them in a standard way, it goes on to read the instructions in the Style Sheet and applies them to the tagged text (e.g., the font to be used, the color, and the spacing). This results in a greater versatility of the text and a remarkable ease of management. If we want to change the font size of all the sections of a site, we only need to modify the statement contained in the Style Sheet and not all occurrences in the text. The process may seem complex, but it is emblematic of how the text in digital media is no longer located on a single level but is the result of the sum of instructions placed on several paratextual levels.[24]

Faced with a digital text, it is therefore always necessary to assess the two levels: the surface one, which shows objects, colors, and shapes that appear on the page; and the deep one, which acts on a level below and determines how the page is built. Unlike reading on paper (where the page exists before reading and the reader's task is just to place himself or herself in the best condition for reading), in computer-mediated communication the page does not exist physically but is built by an algorithm that carries out the instructions placed in the paratext when the player comes into action. In this sense, a text on the computer is always virtual: the reader never has direct access to the medium on which the information is filed, as with books, paintings, posters, and the like, but sees only, on the surface, the result of operations that take place at the deep level of the paratext.

The Mobile/Locative Paradigm

The "mobile/locative" paradigm means that the fruition of cultural contents, in mobility situations and in exactly localized geocultural environments, is deeply changing the relationship between experience, information, visualization, and spectacularization. The position of the user in both space and time, equipped with a smartphone, becomes the paratextual element that determines the particular text that the user "writes" while walking in the urban space.

Mobile communication is a revolution not only because it relates to the consumption of telephone devices (today mobile phones have a higher worldwide diffusion than fixed connections) but also because it changes the cultural setting of networking. The scenario is still evolving, as mobile phones have not yet found that stability of form and function needed to launch a phase of standardization in production and consumption. In this sector, the proprietary temptations of consumer electronics manufacturers, telephone operators, and major players in the communication business are still strong. Overall, however, the process of domestication has begun, which represents the threshold required for a stable placement of mobile communication in the social and cultural horizon of people.

Mobile devices are certainly objects through which we can communicate, but they are also objects through which our physical position can be determined. This applies not only to satellite tracking systems like GPS (Global Positioning System), but also to all devices that incorporate cellular telephone systems, which allow full traceability in geographic space and the recognition of the user. The applications of these tracking systems are now widespread in promotion. For example, in 2008 special billboards were prepared for the launch of a Coldplay album. They were equipped with a microprocessor that was able to get in touch with the mobile phones of passers-by and allowed them to download the video clips of the songs. They are developing hypotheses akin to science fiction, very similar to those presented in the movie *Minority Report* (Steven Spielberg, 2002) where the main character is recognized by billboards that automatically address him with personalized commercial offers.

Interactivity, targeted distribution of media content, tracking of user mobility in the urban environment: these are the elements that now form the basis of the processes—ever more widespread and increasingly important from an economic point of view—that require us to see real spaces as texts. Consciously or unconsciously, the modern *flâneur*, equipped with a phone, moves in the urban space continuously, leaving digital footprints of her or his passage, that represent the paratext according to which data mining systems will propose tailor-made entertainment and special offers. In this sense, mobility is now closely associated with location, that is, with the communication and media paradigm where the physical location of the user becomes a parameter of the utmost importance. "Where are you?" is the opening phrase of a cell phone conversation, but "Where are you?" is also the question that—thanks to geolocalization—the big players of media can immediately answer, in order to profile, with increasing precision, their commercial offers.

We are witnessing what might be called a relocation of communication, in partial contrast—or at least in countertendency—to the interpretive tradition that insisted, as in the case of Joshua Meyrowitz, on the concept of delocalization (with its related forms of deterritorialization, detemporalization, etc.) as a fundamental characteristic of media cultures.[25] In digital media, as I have noted elsewhere, texts become spaces as they become viable (e.g., in hypertexts and videogames). In contrast, spaces become texts as they become readable and writable (e.g., in media walls and geotagging).[26]

In this particular moment of cultural evolution, from mass media to digital media, the space factor is gaining considerable relevance. A scenario emerges in which spaces and technologies are interrelated and where the perspective of what Dourish and Bell label ubicomp (ubiquitous computing) is becoming a part of our daily life and culture.[27] The technology extends more and more into all fields of experience, and at the same time becomes more and more miniaturized, thin, mobile, pervasive, and invisible. It impacts on interpersonal relationships, but also on the interaction design of augmented reality, on the input processes resulting from the multiplication of context-aware sensors, on the management of big data that is collected by sensors, and on the infinite forms of visualization with which these processes are returned to the sensitivity of "human" users.

Mobile/locative media extend the cultural revolution of the network into physical environments, where they release the ability to hypermediate social relationships through new differentiated, perhaps adventurous, unpredictable practices. This is a new territory to explore, where digital creativity can give rise to forms of locative art that bring together the so far disconnected experiences of pervasive computing, site-specific installations, place-based storytelling, geotagging, and urban interaction.[28]

There are several areas of contemporary cultural communication where this specular relationship between text and paratext is evident, for example:

- *Location-based games*—one of the most important forms in which we can find this specular relationship between text and paratext. A location-based game somehow evolves and progresses via the player's location; it needs localization technologies (for instance, satellite positioning like GPS) to use positional data as paratextual elements that guide and determine the macrotext of the game in play.[29]
- *Augmented reality*—some experiments in this field are also proposing attractive situations in which a new mix between text and paratext is able to build innovative forms of mediated emotion and real/virtual involvement. An example of this hybrid approach to the urban experience, characterized by a textual fragmentation seeking new forms of aggregation, is Komplex.28.[30] This is an integrated project, a multimedia experience that mixes participatory technologies such as augmented reality with literary and filmic references that constantly evoke the nomadic uncertainty of the urban experience. The real and imagined city overlap into a synthetic experience, where the city itself with its mediated forms and metascreens, used as paratexts, gives life to the emotional interface of the project. Nomadism becomes the key to interpreting these forms of urban art games, where the aesthetic experience merges with forms of gaming activities placed within an urban space, which is historically full of social, political, and emotional significance.
- *Geotagging*—these are forms of participation where the physical presence and socio-spatial-temporal location of people during the communication processes are of the utmost importance. In geotagging, people

use mobile devices while they explore urban spaces, signaling their position but also commenting on the historical, geographical, cultural, and artistic places they visit. In this way, at a deep level, a paratextual network of references is formed that is superimposed on the geographical territory. It also generates a network of micro-textual, modular, elements that form a coherent collective experiential macrotext, as in the case of the "walk show" organized in Rome in the context of the Urban Experience initiative.[31]

- *User's movement tracking*—these are systems that are increasingly embedded in the most important social networks, such as Foursquare or Google, in order to keep track of people's movements in space and time, using paratextual metadata to reconfigure the textuality of the live experience in spectacular forms of interactive visualization.

Conclusions: Cultural Heritage between Ephemerality and Resilience

Walter Ong has taught us that the great transformations in communication systems force us to completely reconfigure our cognitive and cultural framework, although this change is often slow and always has some elements that recall the past.[32] At the time, Marshall McLuhan pointed out that often the true extent of technocultural change is not felt by the people who are surrounded by it. For example, the car, at its appearance, was regarded as a sort of "horseless carriage" because its actual innovative power was not seen in terms of a cultural and social paradigm shift, or in terms of a reorganization of the space and time experience that the new means of transport necessarily brought with it.[33]

Resuming the reasoning of McLuhan, today we have to face the problem of how digital media are radically reorganizing our textual and extratextual experiences, in particular the mental and social configurations related to space and time. Ephemerality and resilience should not be seen in the light of the print culture, or of the mass media, as if they were "horseless carriages." As Yehuda Kalay observed, today we run the risk—when considering the contemporary culture—of looking at digital media as mere instruments of reproduction and renewal of the past, losing sight of their inherent principles.[34]

In this chapter, we have attempted to identify—condensed around the theme of the paratext—the most important features that characterize the textual culture of digital media. The most challenging reflections in this field lead us today to the definition of a remix culture, a conceptual embrace where the significance of deep structure (where "software takes command" says Manovich[35]) is essential and where—through modularity—social actors elaborate concerted practices to take possession of the textual complexity that digital media offer them, taking on the challenge to better understand these new shapes of knowledge.

Notes

1. See Manuel Castells, *The Rise of the Network Society* (Oxford, UK: Blackwell, 1996), George Landow, *Hypertext 2.0. The Convergence of Contemporary Critical Theory and Technology* (Baltimore, MD: Johns Hopkins University Press, 1997); Jay David Bolter and Richard Grusin, *Remediation. Understanding New Media* (Cambridge, MA: MIT Press, 1999); Lev Manovich, *The Language of New Media* (Cambridge, MA: MIT Press, 2001) and *Software Takes Command* (London: Bloomsbury, 2013); Henry Jenkins, *Convergence Culture. Where Old and New Media Collide* (New York: New York University Press, 2006).
2. "After the novel, and subsequently cinema, privileged narrative as the key form of cultural expression of the modern age, the computer age introduces its correlate—the database," Manovich, *The Language of New Media*, 218.
3. See Henry Jenkins, Sam Ford, and Joshua Green, *Spreadable Media. Creating Value and Meaning in a Networked Culture* (New York: New York University Press, 2013).
4. See Landow, *Hypertext 2.0.*
5. See Andrea Phillips, *A Creator's Guide to Transmedia Storytelling* (New York: McGraw-Hill, 2012).
6. See *http://lasthijack.submarinechannel.com/?_ga=1.31164284.2121843823.14 24192569*, accessed 19 October 2015.
7. Gudrun Held and Sabine Schwarze, *Testi brevi: Teoria e pratica della testualità nell'era multimediale* (Frankfurt am Main: Peter Lang, 2011).
8. Lawrence Lessig, *Remix: Making Art and Commerce Thrive in the Hybrid Economy* (New York: Penguin Press, 2008).
9. Manovich, *Software Takes Command*, 110.
10. Wolfgang Schivelbusch, *Geschichte der Eisenbahnreise: Zur Industrialisierung von Raum und Zeit im 19. Jahrhundert* (München-Wien: Hanser, 1977).
11. This aspect has been investigated, for example, in the works of historians such as Geoffrey Barraclough, *An Introduction to Contemporary History* (London: Watts, 1964) and contemporary philosophers such as Diego Fusaro, *Essere senza tempo. Accelerazione della storia e della vita* (Milan: Bompiani, 2010).
12. Henri Bergson, *Time and Free Will: An Essay on the Immediate Data of Consciousness* (Mineola, NY: Dover Publications, 2001).
13. See Andrea Valle, "Osservazioni preliminari sulla teoria dei modi di produzione segnica". *E|C Rivista dell'Associazione Italiana Studi Semiotici*, 20 March 2007, accessed 15 July 2015, *http://www.ec-aiss.it/includes/tng/pub/tNG_download4. php?KT_download1=0c591285c790b8ea9648cf485c475f7c.*
14. Mikhail M. Bakhtin, "Forms of Time and of the Chronotope in the Novel", in *The Dialogic Imagination*, trans. Caryl Emerson and Michael Holquist (Austin: University of Texas Press, 1981), 84–258.
15. Jorge Luis Borges, "El jardín de los senderos que se bifurcan", in *Ficciones* (Buenos Aires: Sur, 1944).
16. Jean Clément, "Afternoon, a Story: du narratif au poétique dans l'oeuvre hypertextuelle", *A:\LITTÉRATURE*, numéro spécial des Cahiers du CIRCAV, Actes du colloque Nord Poésie et Ordinateur (Roubaix: CIRCAV-GERICO, 1994).
17. Gérard Genette, *Paratexts: Thresholds of Interpretation*, trans. Jane E. Lewin (Cambridge, UK: Cambridge University Press, 1997).

18. Ellen McCracken, "Expanding Genette's Epitext/Peritext Model for Transitional Electronic Literature. Centrifugal and Centripetal Vectors on Kindles and iPads". *Narrative* 21.1 (2013): 105–124.
19. John B. Thompson, *The Media and Modernity: A Social Theory of the Media* (Cambridge, MA: Polity Press, 1995).
20. Castells, *Rise of the Network Society*.
21. Bruce Sterling, *Shaping Things* (Cambridge, MA: MIT Press, 2005).
22. For these points, see also Giulio Lughi, *Cultura dei nuovi media* (Milan: Guerini, 2006), 110–30.
23. Noam Chomsky, *Aspects of the Theory of Syntax* (Cambridge, MA: MIT Press, 1965).
24. An interesting example of creative use of CCS is visible to the URL *http://www.csszengarden.com*, where we see how the same text can have completely different layouts, simply by applying different style sheets.
25. See Joshua Meyrowitz, *No Sense of Place* (Oxford, UK: Oxford University Press, 1985).
26. Giulio Lughi, "Text-space dynamics" (NUL–New Urban Languages, Milan 19–21 June 2013 Conference Proceedings), *Planum. The Journal of Urbanism* 28.2 (2013): 1–6.
27. Paul Dourish and Genevieve Bell, *Divining a Digital Future: Mess and Mythology in Ubiquitous Computing* (Cambridge, MA: MIT Press, 2011).
28. This is the theme of a collection edited by Erik Ekman, *Throughout. Art and Culture Emerging with Ubiquitous Computing* (Cambridge, MA: MIT Press, 2012).
29. Borries et al., *Space Time Play. Computer Games, Architecture and Uranism: The Next Level* (Berlin: Birkhäuser, 2007).
30. *http://www.lebfilm.com/28film.html*, accessed 19 October 2015.
31. *http://www.urbanexperience.it/eventi/walkabout-camminare-parlando-di-roma*.
32. Walter Ong, *Orality and Literacy. The Technologizing of the Word* (London: Methuen, 1982).
33. Marshall McLuhan, *Understanding Media* (New York: New American Library, 1964).
34. Yehuda E. Kalay, "Preserving Cultural Heritage through Digital Media", in Yehuda E. Kalay, Thomas Kvan, and Janice Affleck, eds., *New Heritage: New Media and Cultural Heritage* (London: Routledge, 2008), 1–10.
35. Manovich, *Software Takes Command*.

References

Bakhtin, Mikhail. M. "Forms of Time and of the Chronotope in the Novel". In *The Dialogic Imagination: Four Essays*, 84–258. Trans. Caryl Emerson and Michael Holquist. Austin: University of Texas Press, 1981.
Barraclough, Geoffrey. *An Introduction to Contemporary History*. London: Watts, 1964.
Bergson, Henri. *Time and Free Will: An Essay on the Immediate Data of Consciousness*. Trans. F. L. Pogson. Mineola, NY: Dover Publications, 2001.
Bolter, J. David, and Richard Grusin. *Remediation. Understanding New Media*. Cambridge, MA: MIT Press, 1999.

Borges, Jorge Luis. "El jardín de los senderos que se bifurcan". In *Ficciones*. Buenos Aires: Sur, 1944.

Borries von, Friedrich, Steffen P. Walz, Matthias Boettger, eds., *Space Time Play. Computer Games, Architecture and Urbanism: The Next Level*. Berlin: Birkhäuser, 2007.

Castells, Manuel. *The Rise of the Network Society*. Oxford, UK: Blackwell, 1996.

Chomsky, Noam. *Aspects of the Theory of Syntax*. Cambridge, MA: MIT Press, 1965.

Clément, Jean. "Afternoon, a Story: du narratif au poétique dans l'oeuvre hypertextuelle", *A:\LITTÉRATURE*, numéro spécial des *Cahiers du CIRCAV, Actes du colloque Nord Poésie et Ordinateur*, Roubaix: CIRCAV-GERICO, 1994. Accessed 15 July 2015. *http://hypermedia.univ-paris8.fr/jean/articles/Afternoon.htm*.

Dourish, Paul, and Genevieve Bell. *Divining a Digital Future: Mess and Mythology in Ubiquitous Computing*. Cambridge, MA: MIT Press, 2011.

Ekman, Ulrik, ed. *Throughout. Art and Culture Emerging with Ubiquitous Computing*. Cambridge, MA: MIT Press, 2012.

Fusaro, Diego. *Essere senza tempo. Accelerazione della storia e della vita*. Milan: Bompiani, 2010.

Genette, Gérard. *Paratexts: Thresholds of Interpretation*. Trans. Jane E. Lewin. Cambridge, UK: Cambridge University Press, 1997.

Held, Gudrun, and Sabine Schwarze. *Testi brevi:Teoria e pratica della testualità nell'era multimediale*. Frankfurt am Main: Peter Lang, 2011.

Jenkins, Henry. *Convergence Culture. Where Old and New Media Collide*. New York: New York University Press, 2006.

———, Sam Ford, and Joshua Green. *Spreadable Media: Creating Value and Meaning in a Networked Culture*. New York: New York University Press, 2013.

Kalay, Yehuda E. "Preserving Cultural Heritage through Digital Media". In *New Heritage: New Media and Cultural Heritage*, eds. Yehuda E. Kalay, Thomas Kvan, and Janice Affleck, 1–10. London: Routledge, 2008.

Landow, George P., *Hypertext 2.0. The Convergence of Contemporary Critical Theory and Technology*. Baltimore, MD: Johns Hopkins University Press, 1997.

Lessig, Lawrence. *Remix: Making Art and Commerce Thrive in the Hybrid Economy*. New York: Penguin Press, 2008.

Lughi, Giulio. *Cultura dei nuovi media*. Milan: Guerini, 2006.

———. "Text-space dynamics" (NUL–New Urban Languages, Milan, 19–21 June 2013 Conference Proceedings). *Planum. The Journal of Urbanism* 28.2 (2013): 1–6.

Manovich, Lev. *The Language of New Media*. Cambridge MA: MIT Press, 2001.

———. *Software Takes Command*. London: Bloomsbury, 2013.

McCracken, Ellen. "Expanding Genette's Epitext/Peritext Model for Transitional Electronic Literature. Centrifugal and Centripetal Vectors on Kindles and iPads". *Narrative* 21.1 (2013): 105–124.

McLuhan, Marshall. *Understanding Media*, New York: New American Library, 1964.

Meyrowitz, Joshua. *No Sense of Place*. Oxford, UK: Oxford University Press, 1985.

Ong, Walter. *Orality and Literacy. The Technologizing of the Word*. London: Methuen, 1982.

Phillips, Andrea. *A Creator's Guide to Transmedia Storytelling*. New York: McGraw-Hill, 2012.

Schivelbusch, Wolfgang. *Geschichte der Eisenbahnreise: Zur Industrialisierung von Raum und Zeit im 19. Jahrhundert*. München-Wien: Hanser, 1977.

Sterling, Bruce. *Shaping Things*. Cambridge, MA: MIT Press, 2005.

Thompson, John B. *The Media and Modernity: A Social Theory of the Media*. Cambridge, MA: Polity Press, 1995.

Valle, Andrea. "Osservazioni preliminari sulla teoria dei modi di produzione segnica". *E|C Rivista dell'Associazione Italiana Studi Semiotici*, 20 March 2007. Accessed 15 July 2015. *http://www.ecaiss.it/includes/tng/pub/tNG_download4. php?KT_download1=0c591285c790b8ea9648cf485c475f7c.*

4 Beyond the Threshold

Paratext, Transcendence, and Time in the Contemporary Media Landscape

Valentina Re

Introduction

In the past few decades, complex narrative experiences such as *The Blair Witch Project* (Daniel Myrick, Eduardo Sanchez 1999), *The Matrix* (The Wachowskis, 1999–2003), or *Lost* (ABC, 2004–2010) have increasingly undermined the conventional audiovisual text, namely, the movie (or the TV show) considered as a *text-object*, culturally (conventionally) perceived as *closed* and complete. These films or TV series are no longer collectively and easily conceived as autonomous, key products of the film industry. Rather, they compel us to perform an activity of interpretation and consumption that transcends the *film-as-object* and extends the storyworld as well as the scope of viewers' participation.

Among the labels that describe these new forms of narrative, Henry Jenkins's category of "transmedia storytelling,"[1] which becomes "hard transmedia"[2] in Geoffrey Long's definition and "balanced transmedia"[3] in Jason Mittell's, definitely had a strong impact on film and media studies. Starting from Jenkins's definition and throughout its subsequent developments, the notion of transmedia storytelling has inevitably addressed, more or less explicitly, Gérard Genette's long-standing research on textual transcendence or "transtextuality," considered as "all that sets the text in a relationship, whether obvious or concealed, with other texts."[4] While contemporary scholarly literature on transmedia storytelling features various, if problematic, references to Genette's best known publications about transtextuality (especially *Palimpsests* and *Paratexts*[5]), almost no reference can be found to Genette's last works, in which the concept of transcendence seems to be expanded, re-articulated, and fully theorized.[6]

In the first two parts of this chapter,[7] I will discuss both the advantages and disadvantages of studying contemporary transmedia narratives in light of Genette's theoretical framework. In particular, I will demonstrate the advantage of reconsidering Genette's best known concepts *through* his recent categories of "immanence" and "transcendence." In the third section I will discuss why the heuristic value of reconsidering Genette's classical theoretical framework on the basis of a broader concept of transcendence emerges in particular when we refer to the dimension of time. More precisely, I will explore how studying the modes of transcendence can provide us with suitable tools to investigate the temporal dimension of transmedia narratives, regardless of whether we have a unique date of appearance for a unique, main (or primary) text. Furthermore, we will see how Genette's forms of transcendence prove to be particularly useful in relation to one of the main features of the contemporary media landscape, namely, the tension between ephemerality and permanence, "the relation between stability and impermanence, the substantial and the evanescent, the monumental and the momentary."[8]

Paratexts and the Contemporary Media Landscape

Recent studies such as Gray's *Show Sold Separately*[9] or Grainge's *Ephemeral Media*[10] indicate a kind of *paratextual proliferation* in the contemporary mediascape, with a dissemination of secondary (top-down) and tertiary (bottom-up) paratexts such as ads, making-ofs, alternate reality games (ARGs), mash-ups, and other fan creations: these studies drive our attention to the renewed role of paratexts in shaping media production and reception, as well as to the multifaceted forms in which media content produces meaning. However, at the same time, contemporary notions of transmedia storytelling or narrative ecosystem[11] seem to undermine the very concept of paratext and of a hierarchical organization of texts. In order to unpack this apparent contradiction, I would like to start with Jenkins's *Convergence Culture*, in particular the chapter devoted to *The Matrix* franchise: "This is probably where *The Matrix* fell out of favor with the film critics, who were used to reviewing the film and not the *surrounding apparatus*. Few of them consumed the games or comics or animated shorts, and, as a consequence, few absorbed the essential information they contained."[12]

The term *surrounding* implicitly refers to the specific location of paratextual elements, which indeed surround and extend the text. However, despite the fact that this apparatus surrounds the film, Jenkins does not and could not use the term *paratext* because of the specific relation between films, shorts, comics, and games in *The Matrix* franchise.

Indeed, as Gérard Genette states, the relationship between paratext and text is based on functionality and dependence, that is, on subordination. Genette expresses this idea very clearly:

> The paratext in all its forms is a discourse that is fundamentally heteronomous, auxiliary, and dedicated to the service of something other than itself that constitutes its raison d'être. This something is the text. ... The paratextual element is always subordinate to "its" text, and this functionality determines the essence of its appeal and its existence.[13]

It is exactly this notion of functionality that prevents Jenkins from using the term *paratext*.[14] According to Jenkins, the problem with the reception of *The Matrix* is that games, comics, or animated shorts could traditionally and conventionally be considered as paratexts of a film, and most critics have therefore automatically considered them as such. Contrary to these expectations, *The Matrix*'s peculiarity consists in "integrating multiple texts to create a narrative so large that it cannot be contained within a single medium"[15] and in proposing a "transmedia story" that "unfolds across multiple media platforms, with each new text making a distinctive and valuable contribution to the whole."[16] From Jenkins's perspective, all the elements that actively and synergistically work together with the film in order to create a larger narrative called *The Matrix* are not paratexts. At most, they could be considered as parallel texts, since the movie has lost that centrality which, in the past, had placed its surrounding elements in a functional and subordinate position. Thus, more generally speaking, the notion of paratext appears inappropriate to describe the contemporary mediascape.

This seems to be confirmed by Jason Mittell in his study, *Complex TV*: "The definition of transmedia storytelling problematizes the hierarchy between text and paratext, for in the most ideally balanced example all texts would be equally weighted, rather than one being privileged as 'text' while others serve as supporting 'paratexts.'" However, according to Mittell, this kind of problematization does not concern all forms of transmedia storytelling, but only "balanced transmedia." As Mittell puts it:

> It is useful to distinguish between Jenkins' proposed ideal of balanced transmedia, with no one medium or text serving a primary role over others, with the more commonplace model of unbalanced transmedia, with a clearly identifiable core text and a number of peripheral transmedia extensions that might be more or less integrated into the narrative whole.[17]

Thus, we can conclude that, in addition to balanced transmedia, there are also unbalanced transmedia in which a hierarchical (rather than equal) relationship among different texts is reestablished and in which the concept of paratext is still meaningful—as happens, for instance, in many television-based transmedia that "must always support and strengthen the core television experience."[18]

In face of the threat represented by balanced transmedia, scholars such as Jonathan Gray have tried to maintain a broader acceptance of the concept of paratext in the era of convergence cinema and transmedia storytelling. Gray takes into account Jenkins's idea of "multi-platformed media text" or "convergent text"[19] in the chapter devoted to *in medias res* paratexts, "that inflect or redirect the text following initial interaction."[20] "For texts that destabilize any one media platform as central," specifies Gray, "each platform serves as a paratext for the others."[21] The claim that any text can assume a paratextual function in relation to another—or, to put it another way, that any text can determine, shape, and affect the access and the experience of another text—is certainly true, but it might sound too unspecific. Functionality, in Genette's definition, is the fundamental trait that characterizes paratexts, which are explicitly conceived as auxiliary texts. Thus, there is no reason to preserve Genette's terminology, or to talk about paratexts, to describe what appears to me as a general and common condition of cultural consumption, in which any text can mediate the access, interpretation, and use of another text.

Another classical work by Genette that is often implicitly evoked when discussing the creation of multi-platformed texts is *Palimpsests*. For instance, with respect to the franchise *24* (Fox, 2001–2010), Carlos Alberto Scolari identifies four kinds of expansion of a storyworld: interstitial microstories, parallel stories, peripheral stories, and user-generated content platforms such as blogs and wikis.[22] Although Scolari never mentions *Palimpsests*, these strategies can be related to the field of "continuations" and "sequels," which, in Genette's theoretical framework, are texts "in the second degree" ("hypertexts"), "derived from another preexistent text" ("hypotext") through a process of transformation.[23] More precisely, "interstitial microstories" are very similar to "*elleptic* continuation[s], meant to fill in a median gap or ellipsis." In addition, "parallel stories" closely resemble "*paraleptic* continuation[s], designed to bridge paralipses or lateral ellipses ('Meanwhile, back at the ranch …')". As for "peripheral stories," they seem to coincide with two of Genette's categories: "*proleptic* continuation[s]"—a "forward continuation (i.e., what will come *after*)," and, most importantly, the "*analeptic* or backward continuation (i.e., what came *before*), meant to work its way upstream, from cause to cause, to a more radical or at least a more satisfactory starting point."[24]

Although *Palimpsests* can still provide useful tools to analyze transmedia narratives, a few objections can be raised. As mentioned earlier, when we deal with parallel rather than hierarchically ordered texts (we can again think of *The Matrix*), we cannot identify a primary text ("hypotext") upon which a secondary text ("hypertext") is grafted. Moreover, when he distinguishes between hypertexts and hypotexts, Genette clearly refers to texts produced by different authors in different times, rather than to a unique narrative project conceived by one single author or team (as in the case of transmedia storytelling). Yet, we also need to keep in mind that it is precisely in *Palimpsests* that Genette mentions the case of "*several texts* that refer in some way to one another—several texts, even if signed by the same name. This 'autotextuality' or 'intratextuality' is a specific form of transtextuality, which ought perhaps to be considered in itself—but no hurry."[25] Twelve years would pass before Genette would return to the issue by investigating the concept of "plural immanence" in his *Work of Art. Immanence and Transcendence* (*Palimpsests* was originally published in 1982, *Work of Art*, in 1994).

The main aim of this chapter is to reconsider the notion of paratext in light of Genette's latter research. In order to do this, I need to better define the concept of "text" implied by "paratext," and discuss the role played by the couple text/paratext in the contemporary mediascape. Then, I will consider the relationship between the couple text/paratext and the couple immanence/transcendence, as well as the potential role of the latter in the contemporary media ecosystem.

The Matrix in Transcendence

Only a narrow definition of the concept of text ("a more or less long sequence of verbal statements that are more or less endowed with significance")[26] allows us to address the status, belonging, and function of elements such as book covers, titles, intertitles, notes, and prefaces—in other words, of paratexts. Yet, if we accept (as Genette does) an extension of the concept of paratext to areas where "the work does not consist of a text" (or, in other words, the work does not consist of a sequence of verbal statements), how can we move forward?[27]

I think we can find a point of reference in the specification "a more or less long sequence": in any case, we are dealing with a series that is marked by a given and preestablished length, at least in a certain cultural context—a series that is culturally and collectively perceived as stable, closed and complete. Or, to put it another way: "For some people the text is an object, a book, a thing, a 'work' ... that is considered as unified in a certain cultural context. This work has an author and a reader, a context of production and a context of reception."[28] Therefore, the notion of paratext makes sense if we regard the text as an object that is culturally (conventionally) conceived as closed and complete.

This is one of the definitions of text (but not the only one) that we can find in *Paratexts*. With respect to this narrow definition, the paratext plays an ambivalent role insofar as it both implies and undermines the text. It is an "'undefined zone' between the inside and the outside"[29] that challenges those textual (and cultural) boundaries upon which it entirely depends.[30] Thus, the concept of paratext is able to 'expose' the cultural construction of that idea of text-as-object to which, in any case, it is inextricably tied (through a relation of subordination, as we have seen). Yet, what happens when the relation is missing, as in the case of transmedia storytelling? Do the notions of paratext and text-as-object become useless?

Far from being inadequate to the understanding of the contemporary media landscape, the concepts of text/paratext allow us to better define the innovative quality of a transmedia phenomenon such as *The Matrix*: we understand how *The Matrix* undermines the conventional filmic text (the text-as-object) exactly because of the change in the conventional relationship between text and paratext, which compels us to problematize textual limits. This is precisely the point: the concepts are still operational, while their "traditional" objectifications no longer function.

The *Matrix*-film is no longer collectively perceived as a text or a complete product, and compels us to a narrative experience that transcends the film-as-object. Again, it is all about the limits of the text-as-object, and it appears that we can imagine an "undefined zone between the inside and the outside" (that is, a paratextual zone) only if the inside and the outside are clearly distinguishable.[31]

I should add that the crisis of the text-as-object is not necessarily due to the difficulty of establishing its size. More probably, such a crisis concerns the idea of size itself. As the idea of narrative ecosystem seems to suggest, the problem is therefore not that of identifying new dimensions, but of abandoning the idea of preestablished dimensions ("a more or less long sequence"). Innocenti and Pescatore write:

> The forms of consumption are more and more connected to forms of serial and transmedia concatenation: rather than the cinematic experience, it is a new experience of *continuity and permanence*, as well as *partiality and incompleteness* of any single audiovisual product, which nowadays ensures the audiences' cohesion and continuity in consumption.[32]

Therefore, in the narrative ecosystem, the simultaneous permanence and partiality of every single element (in other words, the impression of inhabiting a rich and long-lasting world that, however, cannot be grasped as a whole from within a unique text) ensures cohesive and long-lasting consumption. Every element, or text, seems to represent a sort of *partial manifestation* of something larger, unmarked by any stable or preestablished size, and yet clearly distinguished and perceived as a whole: an environment in which we can live and interact for a long period of time.

As I mentioned earlier, *The Matrix* invites us to perform activities of interpretation and consumption that *transcend* the film-as-object and extend the storyworld as well as viewers' participation. What do these activities of interpretation and consumption entail? What is *The Matrix* telling us, when we observe it *in transcendence*? In my opinion, to answer this question we need to extend the scope of the discussion beyond Genette's *Palimpsests* and *Paratexts*, and include the final outcomes of his research about the general phenomenon of 'textual transcendence' in *The Work of Art. Immanence and Transcendence*.[33]

In this book, Genette explains that artworks consist in an immanence (i.e., in an object that can be physical or ideal) and in a transcendence: that is to say, a work "can obscure or else surpass the relation it maintains with the material or ideal object it basically 'consists in.'"[34] Of course, there are many different ways in which a work can obscure or surpass the relation with its own object of immanence. I am particularly interested in the case in which "a work immanates, not in one object … but in several non-identical, concurrent objects. This mode of transcendence is called plurality of immanence (or plural immanence) and is described by the symbolic formula 'n objects of immanence for 1 work.'"[35]

This kind of plurality, of course, has no quantitative limits (or preestablished dimensions), and the *work effect* (i.e., the effect of cohesion, the perception of *operal identity*) is determined by several criteria, always flexible and variable, including an underlying authorial intention or creative project (a unified design is an essential condition of transmedia storytelling),[36] and cultural conventions.[37] Based on the criterion of authorial or unified project, the content produced (more or less independently) by users could not be considered as a form of plurality of immanence, although it represents an essential component of transmedia storytelling. However, we should also note that none of the criteria of *operal identity*

> has anything of the absolute about it, and even less (so to speak) of the absolutely legitimate. They are eminently gradualistic and elastic. … They are also highly susceptible to modification and evolution: we have seen to what extent changes in aesthetic paradigm have influenced the public's *operal tolerance*, by which I mean the capacity of one generation to treat as a version of a work what the preceding generation would perhaps have regarded as a mere genetic document, or even simply tossed into the waste basket.[38]

The key role of reception in determining the operal identity clearly emerges here, making it possible, at least in principle, to extend the scope of the plurality of immanence to User Generated Content (UGC).

As already noted, the film and any other element of a narrative ecosystem, just like any object of immanence of a plural work, seem to represent a sort of 'partial manifestation' of something larger. This specific situation can be described thanks to a second form of transcendence, namely, the "partiality of immanence." This form of transcendence "occurs whenever a work is manifested in a fragmentary or indirect manner, according to the formula '1/n objects of immanence for 1 work.'"[39] By connecting plurality and partiality of immanence, we can reach a key issue. As Genette explains, "works with plural immanence [such as transmedia narratives or narrative ecosystems] are, so to speak, all destined (if to varying degrees) to have dissociated and, therefore, incomplete manifestations in every occurrence."[40] However, the criteria for determining the operal identity are eminently relative. This can explain why a crossmedia narrative, in transcendence, can have, or be experienced through, different degrees of completeness—although completeness should be regarded as a vanishing point rather than as an objectively determinable fact. In other words, the tension between plurality and partiality of immanence drives consumers to extend their narrative experiences, while also allowing them to perceive different degrees of narrative completeness. Furthermore, the idea of plural immanence allows us to conceive textual relationships in a "plural work" irrespective of the ideas of derivation and functionality that, while strongly marking hypertextual and paratextual relations, do not seem appropriate for transmedia narratives.

Paratextuality, Transcendence, and Time

The heuristic value of reconsidering the notion of paratext in light of the broader concept of transcendence emerges in particular when we refer to the dimension of time. According to Genette, and on the basis of the functional dimension, "the *temporal* situation of the paratext … can be defined in relation to that of the text."[41] Thus, by adopting as a "point of reference the date of the text's appearance," we can identify four types of paratext:

> Certain paratextual elements are of prior (public) production: for example, prospectuses [and] announcements of forthcoming publications. ... These are therefore *prior* paratexts. Other paratextual elements—the most common ones—appear at the same time as the text: this is the *original* paratext. ... Finally, other paratextual elements appear later than the text, perhaps thanks to a second edition ... or to a more remote new edition. ... Here we have grounds for differentiating between the merely *later* paratext ... and the *delayed* paratext.[42]

One can immediately see the problem of applying such a classification to transmedia storytelling. For instance, in the cases of Jenkins's balanced transmedia and of Long's hard transmedia, all the elements composing the narrative are "designed as such from the outset."[43] In other words, they are all *original*. To put it more radically, there is no such thing as a date of the text's appearance, by which we could determine the temporal situation of ancillary paratexts.

Conversely, by removing the functional aspect and by emphasizing plurality, the overall study of the modes of transcendence can provide us with more suitable tools to investigate the temporal dimension of transmedia narratives (and of any artwork in general), regardless of whether we have a unique date of appearance for a unique, primary text. The notion of partiality of immanence, for instance, seems to include the passing of time in its very definition. As Genette writes,

> This mode is characteristic of all the situations in which one, several, or even all the members of a work's audience are confronted, knowingly or not, with an incomplete and, as it were, deficient manifestation of the work, some parts or aspects of which are *momentarily or definitively inaccessible to them*. ... In that situation, reception is partial, not because of a subjective lack of attention, but rather because of the objective fact that *absence or occultation has rendered one part or aspect of the object of immanence imperceptible*. ... In all these cases, I am dealing with an incomplete manifestation of an object of immanence that may either itself be (or have become) incomplete ..., or else may exceed this manifestation in one way or another ..., and so merely be incomplete for me and other who, like me, *have only limited ... access to the object for the time being*.[44]

Paratextuality is essentially connected to ephemerality by virtue of its intermittent nature: "If... a paratextual element may appear at any time," Genette writes, "it may also disappear, definitively or not."[45] Differently, the interconnection between plurality and partiality of immanence and, more precisely, the dissociated manifestations that works with plural immanence tend to have, seem to better highlight the tension between ephemerality and resilience that characterizes the contemporary media landscape and the related experiences of "continuity and permanence, as well as partiality and incompleteness of any single audiovisual product."[46]

This tension between permanence and partiality can also be productively compared to the tension between permanence and impermanence recently discussed by Paul Grainge in his Introduction to *Ephemeral Media*. According to Grainge, ephemerality needs to be understood within the frame of a "communicational culture of rapid delivery and ubiquitous availability"[47] and marks the relationship of screen and other media forms to "regimes of time (duration, shortness, speed)" and "regimes of transmission (circulation, storage, value)."[48] The tension between ephemerality and permanence becomes more evident when, for instance, we consider video-hosting sites such as YouTube. On the one hand, YouTube hosts a wide array of content (from trailers to making-ofs, opening title sequences, commercials, fan vids and mash-ups) and grants it greater stability. On the other hand, this huge number of clips tends to make content more ephemeral. In other words, availability does not necessarily imply accessibility and, as Michael Gubbins underlines, "the irony is that the sheer volume of content has made discovering that content more difficult."[49] More generally speaking, the web is ephemeral in its abundance—in addition to the "constant threat of materials disappearing as specific links rot and pages are taken down"[50]—and, similarly, various online video-on-demand services are at the same time more ubiquitous and more dispersed.

This same tension between evanescence and stability, in addition to characterizing transmedia narratives in the form of a dialectic between partiality and plurality of immanence, depends on the different modes of existence of all the texts that compose them. In fact, when a work (or a narrative) immanates in several objects and media, distinct technologies and patterns of distribution and consumption affect the duration of all the objects forming the work. In addition, more traditional cultural forms (such as TV episodes compared, for instance, to mobisodes), delivered through more traditional distribution platforms (such as theatrical compared to nontheatrical forms), tend to provide some texts, in terms of availability, with longer durations.[51] Moreover, transmedia or extended narratives are composed of texts that imply different qualities of "user time": many websites or games, for instance, tend to determine a single and punctual use (ephemerality), whereas a movie or a book may encourage repeated viewings and readings (permanence).

We have seen that, far from being inadequate for the comprehension of the contemporary media landscape, the couple text/paratext allows us to better define the innovative quality of transmedia phenomena. But how does the paratext fit in the relations connecting contemporary textual forms and consumption practices to time? To discuss the current validity of the notion, we can refer to Jason Mittell's "orienting paratexts," an idea strictly related to complex serial forms and transmedia franchises.

Orienting paratexts exist in both official and unofficial (frequently fan-made) forms. They are mainly meant to help the viewers make sense of a complex narrative, particularly in relation to time, events, characters, and space. In his analysis, Mittell focuses on the encyclopedic wiki and addresses the famous case of *Lostpedia*, the wiki dedicated to the TV show *Lost*. In Mittell's perspective, orienting "paratexts are distinct from transmedia paratexts[52] that explicitly strive to continue their storyworlds across platforms. ... Instead, these orienting practices exist outside the diegetic storyworld."[53]

While the very notion of transmedia storytelling, as we have seen, seems to be to some extent incompatible with the use of a term such as transmedia paratexts, the notion of orienting paratext can be very helpful to understand how the concept of paratext is still operational and productive in the contemporary media system. Orienting paratexts, and especially fan-made paratexts such as wikis, can merge several interesting aspects of paratext, transcendence, and time within a visual culture characterized by both ephemerality and permanence.

I propose to briefly consider a few examples taken from the wiki dedicated to the TV series *Supernatural* (The WB-The CW, 2005–).[54] The *SuperWiki* is basically organized into four categories: "canon," "fandom," "library" and "production." Typical information provided by orienting paratexts are concentrated in the categories "canon" and "library," which provide a great amount of details about characters, events, time, and space. Yet, in the category "canon," as well as in "fandom" and "production," we can easily detect the effort to record and document all those transmedia expansions (both official and unofficial) that, if compared to the core product of the franchise (the TV series), are more inclined to ephemerality.

For instance, the main category "canon" includes a subcategory "official tie-ins" that offers a detailed record of the Anime series, including episode information, promos, related interviews and links; the comics and the novels, with images, all the covers and detailed summaries; the magazine, with a detailed record of all the twenty-six issues published from 2007 to 2011; the official companion books, the role-playing games, and other kinds of media, such as Dean's phone number with the record of the messages one could hear by calling the number during season one. Moreover, in the categories "production" and "fandom," both official and unofficial merchandising is accurately recorded, and the latter category also offers a detailed list of unofficial tie-ins and, above all, fan initiatives, where the risk of ephemerality is of course stronger: conventions are meticulously documented with pictures, videos, and reports; fan projects (such as challenges, petitions, charity projects, online fanzines, blogs or sites, cosplay competitions, and events) and fan works (fan fictions, fan vids, fan art, and fan music) are accurately reported; finally, the entire fandom history is extensively reviewed, with precise chronicles from 2005 to 2009. What clearly emerges is the need not only to map the franchise in all its transmedia expansions, providing a wealth of orienting clues, but also to create an archive in which transmedia

expansions and fans' works (both online and offline) are accurately catalogued and documented, so that they can *resist* the passing of time and
remain accessible after the first appearance, though in a partial, mediated,
or indirect form.

Concluding Remarks: Orienting Paratexts and Time

Orienting paratexts, besides providing information to improve narrative
comprehension, can also be considered as a way fans manage to *resist
ephemerality* through the very use of *ephemeral tools* such as the wikis,
which are "potentially always in flux."[55] Orienting paratexts have both
a spatial (they operate as maps and provide clues to help in orientation)
and temporal dimension, since they provide timelines (of the storyworld
as well as of the fandom) and preserve transmedia expansions, increasing
their duration even in partial or mediated forms. While emphasizing that
"*Lostpedia*'s core function is a shared archive of data,"[56] Mittell does not
specifically address the wiki with respect to the tension between ephemerality and permanence. And yet, as we have seen in relation to the *SuperWiki*,
the need to manage this tension, with particular reference to transmedia
expansions, is a very important feature of fan wikis.

In conclusion, we can maintain that the idea of paratext is still very useful
to understand the dynamics of the contemporary mediascape, especially if
considered in light of the modes of transcendence. First, as we have seen, the
notion of paratext helps us to understand how the cultural definition of the
text-as-object is changing as transmedia franchises gradually push media
production and consumption toward a dialectic between plurality and
partiality of immanence, continuity and incompleteness, permanence and
ephemerality. Second, since works with plural immanence (such as transmedia narratives) are all variously destined to have fragmentary manifestations, paratexts also become a place to negotiate ephemerality. It is clear
that many of us are not able to access the entire *Supernatural* world in all
its official and unofficial, online and offline expansions, from the novels to
the conventions, from the comics to fan vids. Yet, thanks to orienting paratexts such as the fan wiki, we can obtain information, pictures, videos, and
reports, and manage this new experience "of *continuity and permanence*, as
well as *partiality and incompleteness* of any single audiovisual product,"[57]
that seems to profoundly characterize our everyday relationship to transmedia narrative environments.

Notes

1. Henry Jenkins, *Convergence Culture* (New York: New York University Press, 2006).
2. Geoffrey Long, *Transmedia Storytelling. Business, Aesthetics and Production
   at the Jim Henson Company*, Degree of Master of Science in Comparative
   Media Studies at the Massachusetts Institute of Technology (2007), 20, accessed
   6 March 2015. *http://dspace.mit.edu/handle/1721.1/39152*.

3. Jason Mittell, *Complex TV* (prepublication edition, MediaCommons Press, 2012–2013), accessed 9 March 2015, *http://mediacommons.futureofthebook. org/mcpress/complextelevision*.

4. Gérard Genette, *Palimpsests*, transl. Channa Newman, Claude Dubinsky (Lincoln: University of Nebraska Press, 1997), 1.

5. Gérard Genette, *Palimpsests*; Genette, *Paratexts*, transl. Jane E. Lewin (Cambridge, MA: Cambridge University Press, 1997).

6. See in particular Genette, *The Work of Art. Immanence and Transcendence*, transl. G. M. Goshgarian (Ithaca, NY: Cornell University Press, 1997).

7. In these sections, I discuss some issues that I have previously addressed in Valentina Re, *Cominciare dalla fine. Studi su Genette e il cinema* (Milan: Mimesis, 2012).

8. Paul Grainge, "Introduction: Ephemeral Media," in *Ephemeral Media*, ed. Paul Grainge (London: BFI/Palgrave, 2011), 13.

9. Jonathan Gray, *Show Sold Separately* (New York: New York University Press, 2010).

10. Grainge, ed., *Ephemeral Media*.

11. See, for instance: Veronica Innocenti and Guglielmo Pescatore, "Dalla cross-medialità all'ecosistema narrativo," in *Il cinema della convergenza*, ed. Federico Zecca (Milan: Mimesis, 2012), 127–138; Claudio Bisoni, Veronica Innocenti, and Guglielmo Pescatore, "Il concetto di ecosistema e i media studies: un'introduzione," in *Media Mutations. Gli ecosistemi narrativi nello scenario mediale contemporaneo*, eds. Claudio Bisoni, Veronica Innocenti (Modena: Mucchi, 2013), 11–26; Guglielmo Pescatore, Veronica Innocenti, and Paola Brembilla, "Selection and Evolution in Narrative Ecosystems," Multimedia and Expo Workshops (ICMEW), IEEE International Conference, 2014, 1–6, accessed 6 March 2015, *http://ieeexplore.ieee.org/stamp/stamp. jsp?tp=&arnumber=6890658&isnumber=6890528*.

12. Jenkins, *Convergence Culture*, 104. My emphasis.

13. Genette, *Paratexts*, 12.

14. This kind of ancillarity does not imply irrelevance, just as the study of a para- text does not imply the denial of its fundamental auxiliary aspect. While often suggesting a sort of aesthetic preeminence of the text, Genette undertakes his analysis from an idea of marginality that is both literal (paratexts surround the text) and metaphorical (the importance of paratexts has been extensively over- looked), with the precise aim of discussing it and, in the case of metaphorical marginality, challenging it.

15. Jenkins, *Convergence Culture*, 95.

16. Ibid., 96.

17. Mittell, *Complex TV*.

18. Ibid.

19. Gray, *Show Sold Separately*, 41.

20. Ibid., 35.

21. Ibid., 42.

22. Carlos Alberto Scolari, "Transmedia Storytelling: Implicit Consumers, Narrative Worlds, and Branding in Contemporary Media Production," *International Journal of Communication* 3 (2009): 586–606.

23. Genette, *Palimpsests*, 6.

24. For all the definitions, see ibid., 177.

25. Ibid., 207.

26. Genette, *Paratexts*, 1.

27. Ibid., 407.

28. Gianfranco Marrone, "L'invenzione del testo," *Versus*, 103–105 (2007): 239. Unless otherwise indicated, all translations from Italian are my own.

29. Genette, *Paratexts*, 2.

30. Consider, for instance, the case of a paratextual element such as the title. Genette writes: "The title as we understand it today is actually (and this is true at least of ancient and classical titles) an artificial object, an artifact of reception or of commentary, that readers, the public, critics, booksellers, bibliographers, ... and titologists (which all of us are, at least sometimes) have arbitrarily separated out from the graphic and possibly iconographic mass of a 'title page' or a cover. This mass includes, or may include, many appended bits of information that the author, the publisher, and their public did not use to distinguish as clearly as we do now. After much of that was set aside—the names of the author, the dedicatee, and the publisher; the address of the publisher; the date of printing; and other introductory information—it gradually became customary to retain a more limited whole as the title." Ibid., 55–56.

31. The same is true if we try to analyze transmedia based on hypertextual, rather than paratextual, relationships. How can we distinguish the hypotext from the hypertext, if the "size" of the text-as-object is no longer determinable and the relationships between texts are based on interdependence rather than derivation?.

32. Innocenti and Pescatore, "Dalla cross-medialità all'ecosistema narrativo," 130. My emphasis.

33. In *The Work of Art*, Genette outlines the relationship between immanence and transcendence on the basis and in the function of "traditional" arts. Although it would therefore make no sense to claim that this relationship can perfectly describe and be applied to contemporary narrative ecosystems, or transmedia storytelling, I am persuaded that this relationship can provide useful tools, even if this may seem a little forced.

34. Genette, *The Work of Art*, 161.

35. Ibid., 161. Plural immanences of this type are, for instance, replicas in painting, adaptations or revisions in literature and music, genetic states.

36. We can find numerous direct references to the unified strategy developed by The Wachowskis for *The Matrix*. See, for instance: "Producer Joel Silver describes a trip the filmmakers took to Japan to talk about creating an animated television series: 'I remember on the plane ride back, Larry sat down with a yellow pad and kinda mapped out this scheme we would do where we would have this movie, and these video games and these animated stories, and they would all interact together'"—Jenkins, *Convergence Culture*, 101.

37. The idea of cultural convention brings us back to the crisis of the cinema's classical textual form, the movie, which is increasingly perceived as the partial manifestation of a larger work.

38. Genette, *The Work of Art*, 204–205.

39. Ibid., 162.

40. Ibid., 212.

41. Genette, *Paratexts*, 5.

42. Ibid., 5–6.

43. Long, *Transmedia Storytelling. Business, Aesthetics and Production at the Jim Henson Company*, 20.

44. Genette, *The Work of Art*, 211–212. My emphasis. Interestingly, there is a third mode of transcendence that is even more strictly related to the passing of time. Although it cannot be discussed within the scope of this chapter, the "operal *plurality of effects*" deserves at least to be mentioned. "In this last mode of transcendence," writes Genette, "the work again exceeds its immanence; however, in this case it does so, not because its immanence has been temporarily or permanently reduced to a lacunary ... manifestation and is therefore deficient, but rather by virtue of an operal plurality of an attentional kind. Here it is the work as an object of reception and of an aesthetic relation which takes on different appearances and meanings depending on the circumstances and context." Ibid., 230.
45. Genette, *Paratexts*, 6.
46. Innocenti, Pescatore, "Dalla cross-medialità all'ecosistema narrativo," 130.
47. Grainge, "Introduction: Ephemeral Media," 3.
48. Ibid., 9.
49. Michael Gubbins, *Audience in the Mind*, report commissioned by Cine Regio, 2014, 78, accessed 6 March 2015, *http://cineregio.org/digital_revolution/digital_revolution_2014*.
50. Grainge, "Introduction: Ephemeral Media," 8.
51. With respect to the relationship between ephemerality and forms of distributions, Paul Grainge also underlines that the ephemeral is frequently associated "with non-theatrical genres such as ads, industrial films, training videos, home movies, educational pictures, religious shorts and medical hygiene films that have become critically marginalized despite their significant relation to histories of the ordinary and the everyday." Grainge, "Introduction: Ephemeral Media," 2.
52. Transmedia and orienting paratexts interatc, but do not coincide, with Jonathan Grays's *entryway* and *in medias res* paratexts. See Gray, *Show Sold Separately*.
53. Mittell, *Complex TV*.
54. See *http://www.supernaturalwiki.com/index.php?title=Main_Page*, accessed 9 March 2015. For more detailed information about the wiki, see Deborah Kaplan, "Interview with the Super-wiki admin team," *Transformative Works and Culture* 4 (2010), accessed 6 March 2015, *http://dx.doi.org/10.3983/twc.2010.0200*; Lynn Zubernis and Katherine Larsen, eds., *Fan Phenomena: Supernatural* (Bristol, UK and Chicago: Intellect Books and University of Chicago Press, 2014).
55. Mittell, *Complex TV*.
56. Ibid.
57. Innocenti and Pescatore, "Dalla cross-medialità all'ecosistema narrativo," 130. My emphasis.

References

Bisoni, Claudio, Veronica Innocenti, and Guglielmo Pescatore. "Il concetto di ecosistema e i media studies: un'introduzione." In *Media Mutations. Gli ecosistemi narrativi nello scenario mediale contemporaneo*, eds. Claudio Bisoni and Veronica Innocenti, 11–26. Modena: Mucchi, 2013.

Genette, Gérard. *Palimpsests*. Trans. Channa Newman and Claude Dubinsky. Lincoln: University of Nebraska Press, 1997.

Genette, Gérard. *Paratexts*. Trans. Jane E. Lewin. Cambridge, UK: Cambridge University Press, 1997.

————. *The Work of Art: Immanence and Transcendence*. Trans. G. M. Goshgarian. Ithaca, NY: Cornell University Press, 1997.

Grainge, Paul. "Introduction: Ephemeral Media." In *Ephemeral Media*, ed. Paul Grainge, 1–19. London: BFI and Palgrave Macmillan, 2011.

Gray, Jonathan. *Show Sold Separately*. New York: New York University Press, 2010.

Gubbins, Michael. *Audience in the Mind*. Report commissioned by Cine regio, 2014. Accessed 6 March 2015. *http://cineregio.org/digital_revolution/digital_revolution_2014*.

Innocenti, Veronica, and Guglielmo Pescatore. "Dalla cross-medialità all'ecosistema narrativo." In *Il cinema della convergenza*, ed. Federico Zecca, 127–138. Milan: Mimesis, 2012.

Jenkins, Henry. *Convergence Culture*. New York: New York University Press, 2006.

Kaplan, Deborah. "Interview with the Super-wiki admin team." *Transformative Works and Culture* 4 (2010). Accessed 6 March 2015. *http://dx.doi.org/10.3983/twc.2010.0200*.

Long, Geoffrey. *Transmedia Storytelling. Business, Aesthetics and Production at the Jim Henson Company*. Degree of Master of Science in Comparative Media Studies at the Massachusetts Institute of Technology, 2007. Accessed 6 March 2015. *http://dspace.mit.edu/handle/1721.1/39152*.

Marrone, Gianfranco. "L'invenzione del testo." *Versus*, 103–105 (2007): 237–252.

Mittell, Jason. *Complex TV*. Pre-publication edition, MediaCommons Press, 2012–2013. Accessed 9 March 2015. *http://mediacommons.futureofthebook.org/mcpress/complextelevision*.

Pescatore, Guglielmo, Veronica Innocenti, and Paola Brembilla. "Selection and Evolution in Narrative Ecosystems." Multimedia and Expo Workshops (ICMEW), IEEE International Conference, 2014, 1–6. Accessed 6 March 2015. *http://ieeexplore.ieee.org/stamp/stamp.jsp?tp=&arnumber=6890658&isnumber=6890528*.

Re, Valentina. *Cominciare dalla fine. Studi su Genette e il cinema*. Milan: Mimesis, 2012.

Scolari, Carlos Alberto. "Transmedia Storytelling: Implicit Consumers, Narrative Worlds, and Branding in Contemporary Media Production." *International Journal of Communication* 3 (2009): 586–606.

Zubernis, Lynn, and Larsen, Katherine, eds. *Fan Phenomena: Supernatural*. Bristol, UK and Chicago: Intellect Books and University of Chicago Press, 2014.

Part II
Screen Time and Memory

5 Googling Sherlock Holmes

Popular Memory, Platforms, Protocols, and Paratexts

Roberta Pearson

Wikipedia's undoubtedly incomplete list of the actors who have played Sherlock Holmes in film, television, and radio runs to over ninety entries.[1] Sherlockian cognoscenti endlessly debate the comparative merits of these actors' portrayals and their respective claims to the accolade of best Holmes ever. In 2014, *The Guardian* ran an article entitled "Sherlock Holmes: The Many Identities of the World's Favourite Detective—in Pictures."[2] The actors pictured were Benedict Cumberbatch, star of the BBC's *Sherlock* (2010 to present), Jeremy Brett, star of the four Granada television series made between 1984 and 1994, Peter Cushing, star of Hammer's *The Hound of the Baskervilles* (1959), and Vasily Livanov, star of the Soviet television series *The Adventures of Sherlock Holmes and Dr. Watson* (1979–1986). In January 2015, as an accompaniment to the exhibition, *Sherlock Holmes: The Man Who Never Lived and Will Never Die*, the Museum of London hosted a debate among four well-known Sherlockians putting forward their nominations for the best Holmes: Douglas Wilmer, featured in the 1965 BBC *Sherlock Holmes*, Jonny Lee Miller, featured in CBS's *Elementary* (2011 to present); Basil Rathbone, who starred in two Twentieth Century Fox features and the 1940s Universal film series, and Brett. A few weeks later the Sherlockian website *I Hear of Sherlock Everywhere* ran a blog claiming that Cumberbatch is "the current generation's Sherlock Holmes."[3] Others in the "handful of actors who have come to define the world's first consulting detective" are William Gillette, the American actor-manager who first played Holmes on the stage in 1899, Rathbone, and Brett.[4]

Surprisingly absent from all but Wikipedia's list was Robert Downey Jr., star of the two Warner Bros. blockbusters, *Sherlock Holmes* (2009) and *Sherlock Holmes: A Game of Shadows* (2011), with a third feature mooted at the time of writing. The cognoscenti do not deem Downey worthy of consideration as a definitive Holmes, but by some measures, such as audience numbers, revenues generated ($524 million and $545.4 million, respectively) and global reach and recognition, the actor may well be the most popular of all Holmes impersonators, past and present.[5] Google Images provides another measure of Downey's preeminent status among Holmes actors; entering the search term "Sherlock Holmes" into the search box results in a Downey-dominated screen, his numerous images interrupted only by occasional pictures of Benedict Cumberbatch, Basil Rathbone, and Jeremy Brett. Other actors, such as Wilmer and Cushing, show up only when one repeatedly clicks through for more results. Since, as explained further below, Google's search algorithm favors the majority interest, the Google Images search result suggests that Downey, rather than his contemporary competitors, Cumberbatch and Miller, or past competitors, Brett and Rathbone, may dominate popular memory, just as he dominates the first few Google Images screens.

While the Internet does not itself possess a memory, its function as a digital repository of the memories of institutions, groups, and individuals leads me to hypothesize that it may serve as an indication of the current configurations of popular memory.[6] Academics have debated the nature of group memory since the 1952 publication of Maurice Halbwachs's seminal study, *On Collective Memory*. Central to these debates is the question of terminology; should we speak of collective memory, national memory, cultural memory, social memory, generational memory, or popular memory? This chapter does not afford the space for even a brief summary of the nuanced meanings of these multiple terms that all gesture toward the group rather than the individual. I use the term *popular* in its most basic sense "of the majority," that which most people remember. As used more specifically here, popular memory refers to the patterns of memory traces found on three Internet platforms, Google Images, Facebook and Flickr; these patterns' favoring of Downey over Rathbone on the first platform suggests what most people remember. The Internet provides access to the memory of a culturally active and numerous crowd through the aggregated traces left in its digital repository; these traces provide a more granular and bottom-up representation of popular memory than was available in the analogue age.[7] This alone makes an exploratory study of the memory traces found on the three platforms a worthwhile endeavor. However, the Internet's digital repository of memory can only offer suggestions rather than conclusive evidence as to the overall configuration of popular memory, since factors such as the powerful influence of media institutions and the composition of the cohort of Internet users skew the data. But this does not negate the value of the evidence, since popular memory has always been skewed by many factors, especially those related to a society's unequal distribution of the power to shape cultural representation.

This chapter is a speculative study of the ways in which these three Internet platforms reflect the popular memory of those actors who have over the decades portrayed Sherlock Holmes. The Sherlock Holmes character constitutes an appropriate case study by which to explore the connection between the Internet and popular memory for three reasons. First, the focus on fictional texts is intended to counter the overwhelming emphasis on the "real" in academic memory studies. Scholars have had much to say about memory of the past in both analogue and digital forms but have mostly concerned themselves with conflict, genocide, and memorialization; only a few scholars have investigated pleasurable memories of media texts rather than media texts conceived of as traumatic memories of historical events. But as these few scholarly works demonstrate, memories of media are deeply interwoven with people's life narratives, as important to what Emily Keightley terms "generational experiences" or "autobiographical trajectory" as mediated memories of historical events such as wars or assassinations.[8]

Second, as opposed to similar popular heroes such as Batman, Sherlock Holmes has never been the sole property of a major media corporation. Instead, over the decades since his first appearance in 1887 in Arthur Conan Doyle's *A Study in Scarlet*, multiple authors and institutions have exploited the character, giving rise to a great diversity of textual incarnations that might potentially leave memory traces.[9] Yet the character's current most prevalent incarnations stem from three powerful media institutions, Warner Bros., the BBC, and CBS.

Third, Holmes has a large and active worldwide fan base; many of these fans have been attracted by the Warner Bros., BBC, and CBS texts, but others have allegiances to past as well as current texts, and yet others' allegiances are only to past texts. As argued below, both media institutions and fandom play a crucial role in shaping the way my three case study platforms reflect the popular memory of the character.

The Sherlock Holmes character consists of a "network of representations" comprised of a "transmedia structure" of all the books, magazines, advertising, films, radio and television programs, YouTube videos, comic books, games, toys, advertising, fan fiction, and so forth that have accumulated since 1887.[10] A particular historical era's popular memory of the character is formed of a selective sample from the available transmedia structure; "*I Hear of Sherlock Everywhere*," for example, asserts that Cumberbatch is "the current generation's Sherlock Holmes" just as Gillette, Rathbone, and Brett may have been the Sherlock Holmes of earlier generations. The memory traces of the transmedia structure found in the Internet's digital repository point toward the dominant twenty-first century popular memory of the character.

But given the countless texts that comprise the transmedia structure and the countless traces they have left on the Internet, how to narrow the search for relevant data? The chapter focuses on screen texts, since it is probable that the majority of people will have encountered the character in that medium rather than in the myriad other texts that constitute the transmedia structure, including Conan Doyle's urtext. It focuses on Holmes actors since their names serve as the primary signifiers of the memories of Sherlockian screen texts—the Rathbone *Hound of the Baskervilles* (1939) or the Cushing *Hound of the Baskervilles*, the Wilmer television series or the Brett television series. But even this initial delimitation would yield more data than I could possibly scrutinize; for example, rather than enumerating the four actors pictured in *The Guardian* article mentioned earlier, I would have to analyze the 149 comments from readers as to whom they consider the best Holmes. Therefore, the chapter restricts the data to visual paratexts that serve as signifiers of the actors and their film and television programs. These paratexts include lobby cards, posters, billboards, fan art, and screen grabs, a great deal of it user generated even if in the form of personal photos of producer-generated materials such as billboards.[11] As Renate Lachmann says, "The memory of the text is formed by the intertextuality of its references. ... Cultural memory remains the source of an intertextual play."[12]

The chapter investigates three popular and influential Internet platforms—Google Images, Facebook, and Flickr—where Holmes actor visual paratexts can be found. I investigate these three particular platforms because as Philip M. Napoli says, "Recent research examining the distribution of audience attention across different media has found that the concentration of audience attention around relatively few sources in the traditional media realm has been largely reproduced in the online realm."[13] These platforms are undoubtedly among the few sources around which audience attention concentrates. I refer to these sites as platforms because, as Tarleton Gillespie says, the word "has emerged recently as an increasingly familiar term in the description of the online services of content intermediaries, both in their self-characterizations and in the broader public discourse of users, the press and commentators." These online services, according to Gillespie, include YouTube, search engines, blogging tools, and interactive online spaces.[14] All these platforms are governed by mathematical, technological, social, and cultural protocols. According to Lisa Gitelman, media protocols "include a vast clutter of normative rules and default conditions," "express a huge variety of social, economic, and material relationships," "get imposed, by bodies like the National Institute of Standards and Technology or the International Organization for Standardization," or "effectively imposed, by corporate giants like Microsoft, because of the market share they enjoy."[15] Since it is impossible to account for all these and the many other protocols governing the three case study platforms, I discuss those particular protocols that are most salient to the deposition and retrieval of the traces of popular memory in the form of Holmes actor visual paratexts.

The fact that government, heritage, and media institutions, together with social groups and individuals, are increasingly using the Internet as a memory depository makes it vital to understand the functioning of popular and influential platforms and their associated protocols. As Nancy Van House and Elizabeth F. Churchill say, "what is remembered individually and collectively depends in part on technologies of memory and [their] associated socio-technical practices."[16] This accords with the currently accepted paradigm in memory studies scholarship, which, in the words of Keightley and Philip Schlesinger, has an "understanding of memory ... as produced in the interstitial space between individuals who remember and social groups and being communicated in and across time by media technologies and cultural forms."[17]

Google Images

Since Google is "the most used search engine in the world, far outdistancing competitors," I began my investigation with that platform.[18] Google's underlying algorithmic operations and its users' modes of interaction inflect the platform's representation of popular memory. Google searches utilize hyperlinks; among other data, the search algorithm calculates the popularity of a website by counting how many other websites link to it and then places the most popular websites at the top of the results pages.[19] James G. Webster explains further:

> Google … ranks Web sites that possess the requisite search terms according to the number and importance of their inbound links. Hence, the linking architecture of the internet, which is itself the product of thousands of more or less independent decision makers, provides the principle [*sic*] guide for navigating hyperlinked space.[20]

But while the architecture results from thousands of decision makers, Alexander Halavais says that the search engine assumes that "hyperlinks somehow transmit power or credibility" and therefore "sends more traffic to the heavily linked sites, reinforcing that position of authority and leading to even more links."[21] The search engine's assumption reflects its programmers' assumptions concerning users' modes of interaction.

Google programs the search engine to maximize the user experience and retain satisfied customers, recognizing that, as Napoli puts it, "The search-and-retrieve dynamic … is one that extracts costs from the audience member."[22] Given time costs, users seldom look past the first page of results and further than the first three pages less than 10 percent of the time. In recognition of such usage patterns, says Eric Goldman, "search engines generally tune their ranking algorithms to support majority interests" in order to "maximize searcher perceptions of search success."[23] This tuning results in accusations that the Google search engine supports the existing hegemonic order. Argues Goldman,

> Popularity-based ranking algorithms may reinforce and perpetuate existing power structures. Websites that are part of the current power elite get better search result placement, which leads to greater consideration of their messages and views. Furthermore, the increased exposure attributable to better placement means that these websites are likely to get more votes in the future, leading to a self-reinforcing process. In contrast, minority-interest and disenfranchised websites may have a difficult time cracking through the popularity contest, potentially leaving them perpetually relegated to the search results hinterlands.[24]

While this algorithmic tuning similarly valorizes the popular and the contemporary over the minority interest and the past, this privileging of the majority interest renders the platform's memory traces a measure of "real" popular memory.

Every website that Warner Bros. erects to publicize its blockbuster Sherlock Holmes films, every link that its programmers forge between these and other sites, and every further link forged by fans increase the probability of Robert Downey paratexts dominating Google Images searches. But Warner Bros. is not the sole powerful media corporation producing Sherlock Holmes texts; the BBC and CBS also need to publicize their *Sherlock* and *Elementary* through websites and links. How then does all this play out in Google Images searches for Holmes actor paratexts? As I said above, entering the search term "Sherlock Holmes" yields a screen full of Downeys. Scrolling down turns up a few Rathbone, Cumberbatch, and Brett images among the Downeys, interspersed with the odd outlier or two such as Robert Stephens (*The Private Life of Sherlock Holmes*, 1970) or Christopher Plummer (*Murder by Decree*, 1976). The further down one scrolls, the more prominent becomes the BBC's Cumberbatch; clicking "show more results" and scrolling yet further down finally produces an image or two of *Elementary*'s Jonny Lee Miller. The algorithms are clearly favoring first Warner Bros. and then the BBC, while leaving CBS out of the running. *Sherlock*'s large and active fan base most probably accounts for some of Cumberbatch's relative standing and the lack of such a fan base for Miller's relative obscurity. The more general Sherlockian fan base's websites and links may contribute to Rathbone and Brett's repeated appearances (although Granada is still promoting their series via Facebook and Twitter; see below).

A user restricting herself to the first screen would conclude that Downey constitutes the quintessential Holmes, while a user clicking through for more results would receive the impression that Rathbone, Brett, and Cumberbatch are the quintessential Holmes of their generations. However, a user deciding to invest yet more time in the search could turn to Google's suggestions at the top of the screen: Actors; BBC; Benedict Cumberbatch; Original; Book; and Robert Downey Jr. These suggestions, like the images on the first results page, reflect the power and influence of Warner Bros. and the BBC. Clicking the Actors suggestion again results in a screen full of Downeys and Cumberbatches, although with slightly greater inclusion of alternate Holmes than the term "Sherlock Holmes" alone produced. Top of the page suggestions this time include Raymond Massey, Roger Moore, and Anthony Higgins, all quite obscure Holmes impersonators: Massey played Holmes in the 1931 *Speckled Band*; Moore in the 1976 television film *Sherlock Holmes in New York*; and Higgins in the 1993 television film *Sherlock Holmes*.

If popular memory derives from the transmedia structure that constitutes the Holmes character, then the traces of that popular memory found in the aggregate results of my Google Images searches imply that Robert Downey Jr. reigns preeminent in the early twenty-first century popular memory of the character. The results indicate that Cumberbatch, Brett, and Rathbone still play a significant, if smaller, role in that popular memory, while others, such as Massey and Moore, play a much smaller role. The traces of popular memory displayed by Google Images favor the popular and the contemporary, disadvantage the minorityinterest and the past, and show the influence of Warner Bros., the BBC, and the fans on their content. The Facebook data exhibits similar patterns; it may be that the traces of popular memory found on these virtual sites correlate well with a "real" popular memory that must remain forever inaccessible.

Facebook

Anne Kaun and Frederik Stiernstedt report that Facebook is currently the most successful of all social media platforms, with US users alone spending 114 billion minutes a month on the platform.[25] Do Facebook's traces of popular memory include the minority interest and the past alongside the popular and the contemporary? Does the influence of media corporations bias the platform toward the present, as is the case with Google Images? How do the platform's protocols inflect retrieval of the traces of popular memory?

Given this chapter's focus on Holmes actor visual paratexts, I sought those Facebook pages most likely to include such images. As opposed to Google Images, however, Facebook is not optimized for instant results but instead offers several different search options. Facebook allowed me to search for "find all pages named Sherlock," which includes all individual, group, and institutional pages related to the search term and for "find all groups named Sherlock." The first search produced links to over a thousand pages (including many irrelevant ones for commercial establishments such as pubs and restaurants), while the second produced links to under a hundred. Unlike Google Images, Facebook offers neither single-screen overviews of Holmes actor paratexts nor, aside from alternative search terms, specific suggestions as to how to drill down further.[26]

The search for "find all pages named Sherlock" produced three different categories: (1) media corporations' official pages, (2) fan pages, and (3) automatically generated pages.

The end result resembles Google's—the most popular pages appear at or near the top of the list. The most popular of the official pages is for the first Downey film, *Sherlock Holmes*, with its more than 10 million "likes" greatly exceeding the *Game of Shadows* page with more than 700,000 "likes." The official BBC *Sherlock* page comes in second behind the Warner Bros. *Sherlock Holmes* page with close to 5 million "likes." The official Granada page for the Jeremy Brett series that advertises the weekly ITV3 reruns and links to Granada's Twitter feed has over 2,500 "likes." The presence of this page confirms that media corporations will use social media to promote back-catalogue Holmes texts with revenue-producing capabilities. *Sherlock*'s large and intensively devoted fan base accounts for the preponderance of the fan sites, including, among many others, Sherlockology (a semi-official fan site to which Hartswood Films, *Sherlock*'s producers, lends its support), Sherlock memes, Sherlock Holmes BBC slash fan art, and Benedict Cumberbatch–Sherlock Holmes. The Brett and Rathbone Holmes also have fan pages. Unlike the Brett series, the Rathbone films have no official Facebook page, let alone a Twitter feed, but their continued circulation via television and DVDs clearly suffices to maintain an active fan base, albeit one dwarfed by *Sherlock* and the Downey films.

This brief analysis of Facebook's official and fan sites provides yet more evidence that media corporations and fans shape the traces of popular memory. Current texts *Sherlock* and the Downey films feature at the top of the lists of both the official and the fan pages, although *Sherlock* has much greater overall prominence. Still generating ongoing revenues for their producers and distributors, the Brett series and the Rathbone films have a small but significant presence near the top. Other older texts can be discovered only by persistently scrolling down the links; it requires a determined user to uncover the past and the minority interest in the official and fan pages. Of the ninety plus actors who have impersonated Holmes over more than one hundred years only four names—Downey, Cumberbatch, Brett, and Rathbone—have a substantial presence in the official and fan Facebook pages; these actors have the same status in the Google Images search results.

The third category of automatically generated pages exhibits a different pattern. The list includes not only the Brett series but, rather surprisingly, the 1954 US series, *Sherlock Holmes*, starring Ronald Howard and the Buster Keaton film *Sherlock Junior* (1924). These pages, Facebook tells us, are "automatically generated based on what Facebook users are interested in, and not affiliated with or endorsed by anyone associated with the topic." These automatically generated pages seem to be what Facebook previously called "community pages." *Social Media Examiner* reported in 2010 that the platform established these pages to "create a clear delineation" between official pages and "all the fan pages created around an idea or topic." The community pages

> were auto-generated from users' "Likes and Interests" and "Work and Education" sections of the personal profile Info tab. Depending on the subject matter of each Community Page, content (including the Page photo) gets automatically pulled in from Wikipedia. All other content is auto-populated from wall posts and status updates made by any Facebook user containing the keywords of the Community Page.[27]

These pages indicate the Holmes-related likes, interests, and posts of Facebook users, showing that some have a memory of Holmes actors that extends beyond Downey, Cumberbatch, Brett, and Rathbone. The identity of these users cannot of course be determined, and their individual pages cannot be visited. But the sparsely populated automatically generated pages offer limited information beyond the Wikipedia entry. The *Sherlock Junior* page includes the film poster, a picture of Keaton, links to genre pages (comedy, fantasy, crime fiction, drama film, silent film), and related pages, while the Ronald Howard page has pictures of Howard, his Watson (Howard Marion Crawford), links to genre pages (mystery fiction, detective fiction, drama film), and related pages. The automatically generated pages, while not themselves a rich repository of memory traces, offer evidence that the memory of Facebook users is not entirely restricted to present or actively promoted past content. Nonetheless, Facebook's popular memory traces are definitely skewed toward Downey and Cumberbatch, indicating, according to my hypothesis, that it is these two whom the majority of the platform's users remember.

I further interrogated Facebook's traces of popular memory by looking at the publicly accessible group Sherlock Holmes Fans, which claims to be the biggest Sherlock Holmes fan group in Facebook. The group's 21,987 members do indeed make it the largest of all Facebook pages named Sherlock Holmes Fans or variants thereof. Page administrator Sir Navid Persian explains that Sherlock Holmes Fans is "an exclusive special group about Sherlock Holmes! We welcome Photos, Polls, video clips, radio snippets, new fictions, riddles and ... dedicated to Sherlock Holmes."[28] My repeated visits to the site confirmed the page's eclecticism with regard to both time and media. These visits also threw me into a methodological quandary; the large and active membership generates constant updates, with no means either to capture the current configuration or return to previous ones. My interactions with the page resonate with Kaun and Stiernstedt's description of Facebook's temporality.

> In general, Facebook users' temporal experience is one of immediacy, ephemerality, "liveness," and flow: to be immersed in an atmosphere and an interface of rapid change and forgetfulness, rather than of remembrance and preservation. Every single post, status update, link, and like in a Facebook feed is visible only for a short period of time: for the user, the experience and feel of Facebook is one of rapid change; new stories are continually appearing, pushing old stories out of sight, downward in the stream.[29]

Just as you can step into a stream only once, you can visit a Facebook page only once; upon return, the page will have flowed on. While a page's content may be temporally diverse, the page itself exists in what Van Dijck terms "the permanent stream of visual 'present.'"[30] Facebook actively favors the ephemeral over the permanent since, as Kaun and Stiernstedt say, "steady activity promotes the page's visibility among users and potential users."[31]

I compare my observations of the Sherlock Holmes Fans page made on 18 August 2014 with those made seven months later on 20 April 2015. My first visit revealed a temporally wider range of Holmes actor paratexts on one screen than I had so far encountered on either Google Images or Facebook. The contemporary and the popular were represented by the usual Cumberbatch and Downey photos, augmented by Jonny Lee Miller and

Ian McKellan, who had recently been announced as the star of the forthcoming film *Mr. Holmes* (2015). The customary Brett and Rathbone photos represented the past but were augmented by many previous impersonators of the Great Detective. In chronological order these were William Gillette; James Bragington (*A Study in Scarlet*, 1914); Hans Albers (*Der Mann, der Sherlock Holmes war*, 1937); Reginald Owen (*A Study in Scarlet*, 1933); Peter Cushing; Nicol Williamson (*The Seven Percent Solution*, 1976); Edward Woodward (*Hands of a Murderer*, 1990) and Rupert Everett (*Sherlock Holmes and the Case of the Silk Stocking*, 2004). My return visit found a relatively more presentist page, predominantly populated by Cumberbatch and Downey with the usual sprinkling of Brett. However a few past Holmes impersonators also appeared, listed again in chronological order: Cushing (again); Christopher Lee (*Sherlock Holmes and the Deadly Necklace*, 1962); Wilmer; John Wood (*A Study in Terror*, 1965), Moore and Williamson (again). In 2014, I stepped into a stream composed of more diverse memory traces than I did in 2015. It is impossible to predict whether on a future visit I would encounter a relatively more homogeneous or diverse stream of memory traces, and it is similarly impossible to determine what accounts for the differences—although new members or newly released texts or a media corporation's publicity might be contributing factors.

Despite the methodological difficulties encountered, Facebook proved a valuable source of patterns of popular memory traces that gesture toward the memories of the majority of people in the "real" world, especially since the patterns generally correlated with those found on Google Images.

Flickr

The social network photo-sharing platform Flickr was launched in 2004 and subsequently acquired by Yahoo in 2005. By 2014, it hosted over 10 billion images and 1.8 million user groups.[32] Flickr hosts a great deal of historical content, collaborating with many US and overseas heritage institutions in The Commons, which is intended to "share hidden treasures from the world's public photography archives."[33] At the date of writing, ninety-nine institutions participate in The Commons, including the Smithsonian Institution, the Library of Congress, the British Library, and the National Library of New Zealand.[34] Amateur enthusiasts also turn to Flickr to archive images of their collections, attracted to the platform because, as Melissa Terras says, "it provides an easy and intuitive hosting platform for individuals to post, share, and discuss image-based historical material."[35] Terras found many Flickr groups devoted to graphic design (e.g., paperback covers), vintage packaging and advertising (e.g., cigarette advertising), and historical ephemera (e.g., the First World War). She asserts that "Flickr's intuitive interface allows users to collect all available information regarding the object, book, item, etc. in a form that users can see and usually search."[36] Given Flickr's commitment to photographic heritage coupled with the many Flickr groups devoted to sharing historical material, I hypothesized that the platform might offer a more diverse set of Holmes actor visual paratexts than either Google Images or Facebook. But, counter my hypothesis, Van Dijck argues that "Flickr is not a logical place to nurture interpretations of the past because the site is primed by the present—a constant flow of images whose uploading is premeditated by users' motives that vary from aesthetic preference to political conviction."[37] With regard to the Sherlock Holmes character, Van Dijck would appear to be correct.

My Flickr searches did not find any institutions or enthusiastic amateurs uploading photos of Sherlock Holmes archival material to the platform. But the searches did turn up four groups relevant to this chapter's focus on Holmes actors visual paratexts: BBC's Sherlock, Moffat's Lego, Lego Sherlock Holmes, and Sherlock Holmes. The content of the first two is self-evident, while the third includes several photos of Lego characters bearing as close a resemblance to Cumberbatch or Downey as can be achieved within the constraints of the form and none bearing a resemblance to older impersonators. The fourth, Sherlock Holmes, has 458 members and 1,309 photos (all of which I looked at); hosts "Everything about the great detective!"; and exhibits relatively greater diversity than the previous three.[38] Downey and Cumberbatch predominate as usual, in forms ranging from pavement art to billboards. Brett features in a half page of photos posted by the same user, while Rathbone appears in a screen grab of *Sherlock Holmes Faces Death* (1943) and in a shot of the bank of monitors playing Holmes films that constituted part of the Museum of London's exhibit. Only Moore and Gillette stood as exemplars of older and more obscure Holmes impersonators. Despite the fact that all the Flickr content was user generated (even if in the form of photos of producer-generated paratexts), the Flickr groups conform to the patterns of memory traces found on Google Images and Facebook. Three of the four groups found have a decided bias to the present, the corporate, and *Sherlock* fandom, while the fourth nods to the past primarily through its inclusion of Brett and Rathbone.

Having investigated the content of the four groups, I then searched for all photos tagged Sherlock Holmes, which yielded 52,638 results. Flickr offered four choices for ordering these images: relevant, date uploaded, date taken, and interesting. Date uploaded and date taken are straightforward, depending solely on one piece of datum in the user's tagging, but relevant and interesting depend on the search algorithm's judgments. According to posters in the VelocityReviews Forum, the relevant criterion resembles Google's, putting those results deemed most pertinent at the top. Posters asserted that the interesting criterion remains Flickr's closely guarded secret but speculated that it measures the number of groups in which a photo appears together with the number of views, comments, and favourites it has attracted.[39] All these criteria depend upon users' interaction with the platform: relevance upon idiosyncratic user tagging, interesting on users' preferences, and date uploaded on users' current activities. As Van Dijck reminds us, "What is often called 'collective memory' or 'cultural heritage' in relation to digital photo sharing sites is largely the result of visual data and metadata linked up by means of computer code and institutional protocols."[40] I clicked on all three, in each case scrolling down to the load more results prompt for the purposes of valid comparison.

Unlike Google's algorithm, which favors Downey, Flickr's relevant algorithm identifies Rathbone as the quintessential embodiment of the Great Detective, followed closely by Brett. Rathbone is the most noticeable Holmes actor in the upper sections of the screen, with several screen grabs of the films uploaded by one user and several photos of film posters by another. Brett also features in this valuable space most likely to catch a searcher's eye. However, as I scrolled further down, Cumberbatch and Downey replaced the earlier Holmes impersonators, with only a poster for *The Private Life of Sherlock Holmes* representing the past. The interesting algorithm privileges Cumberbatch, with Downey a poor second. Brett appears first far down the screen followed by Rathbone. Cumberbatch's pole position undoubtedly reflects the activities of *Sherlock*'s fan base, many of whom are presumably viewing, commenting on, and favoriting his images. The date uploaded algorithm produces a top row including Downey and Cumberbatch. The fact that Downey wears Iron Man's costume and stands with other Avengers gives insight into one user's idiosyncratic tagging. Overall, the date uploaded algorithm offered fewer visual actor paratexts than did the other two criteria but, like the interesting algorithm, advantaged Cumberbatch. The different results produced by clicking on relevant, interesting and date uploaded evidence the ways in which users' interactions with the platform's protocols construct somewhat different versions of popular memory. Overall, however, the platform shares Google Images and Facebook's bias to the contemporary and the popular and against the past and the minority interest.

Conclusion

If, as initially hypothesized, popular memory is derived of a selection from the transmedia structure that constitutes the Holmes character, then the traces of that popular memory found in the aggregate results of my searches across Google Images, Facebook and Flickr imply that Robert Downey Jr. and Benedict Cumberbatch reign preeminent in the early twenty-first century popular memory of the character. Brett and Rathbone, whose films and television programs continue to be actively circulated and promoted, play a smaller but still significant role in contemporary popular memory, while all but a minority has forgotten the many other impersonators of the Great Detective that Wikipedia lists. Popular memory will of course shift as the transmedia structure changes with the introduction of new texts, such as the Ian McKellan *Mr. Holmes*, or the active promotion of older texts such as the Douglas Wilmer BBC series recently released on DVD by the British Film Institute. But as long as the digital age endures, popular memory will always be subject to the influence of media corporations and the activities of fans and its traces filtered through platforms and their protocols.

This has been a speculative and preliminary exploration of the ways that Internet evidence might be used to gauge popular memory. That evidence is admittedly, for all the reasons enumerated above, a rough and ready measure, but it does permit greater access to the memories of the crowd than was possible in the analogue age. The evidence has permitted me to test and largely confirm *I Hear of Sherlock Everywhere*'s assertion that Benedict Cumberbatch is the Holmes of this generation, the one whom audiences most actively remember and promote. The assertions that Brett, Rathbone, and Gillette were the Holmes of previous generations would take months, if not years, of archival endeavor to test, although Internet evidence does allow testing the assumption that they remain an active component of twenty-first century popular memory.

Notes

1. *http://en.wikipedia.org/wiki/List_of_actors_who_have_played_Sherlock_Holmes*, accessed 29 August 2015.
2. "Sherlock Holmes: The Many Identities of the World's Favourite Detective—in Pictures," *The Guardian*, 17 April 2014, accessed 29 August 2015, *http://www.theguardian.com/books/gallery/2014/apr/17/sherlock-holmes-test-of-time-detective-tv-film-in-pictures*.
3. "Benedict Cumberbatch: Gen Y's Sherlock Holmes," accessed 29 August 2015, *http://www.ihearofsherlock.com/2015/03/benedict-cumberbatch-gen-ys-sherlock.html#.VSUQY0um1Fw*.
4. Ibid.
5. Alatheia Loeb, "Sherlock Holmes 3 Release Date, News, and Spoilers," *Crossmap*, 18 May 2015, accessed 29 August 2015, *http://www.crossmap.com/news/sherlock-holmes-3-release-date-news-and-spoilers-robert-downey-jr-s-official-facebook-page-may-have-just-hinted-that-sherlock-holmes-3-is-now-in-production-18366*.
6. The phrase "digital repository of memories" may cause some to think of the oft-repeated phase "internet archive" or indeed of the Internet Archive, which, it might be mentioned in passing, hosts much Holmes-related material. However, many of the authors whom I have read in preparing to write this chapter object to labeling these digital repositories archives. Diana Taylor well sums up the objections: "The owners may or may not commit to preserving these materials long term. Further, there is no selection process for materials uploaded online. No one vouches as to its sources or veracity. Expertise is irrelevant. The materials seem free and available to anyone with Internet access—avoiding the rituals of participation governing traditional archives" (Diana Taylor, "Save As … Knowledge and Transmission in the Age of Digital Technologies," *Forseeable Futures* 10 (2010): 8, accessed 29 August 2015, *http://imaginingamerica.org/wp-content/uploads/2011/05/Foreseeable-Futures-10-Taylor.pdf.*).
7. I thank William Uricchio for his contribution to this formulation as well as for his detailed and constructively critical comments on the chapter's first draft. However, any remaining deficiencies remain my own.

8. Emily Keightley, "Introduction: Time, Media, Modernity," in *Time, Media, Modernity*, ed. Emily Keightley (Basingstoke, UK: Palgrave Macmillan, 2012), 4. On memories of popular culture, see Annette Kuhn, *Dreaming of Fred and Ginger: Cinema and Cultural Memory* (New York: New York University Press, 2002); Sarah Stubbings, "'Look Behind You!': Memories of Cinema-Going in the 'Golden Age' of Hollywood," in *Memory and Popular Film*, ed. Paul Grainge (Manchester, UK: Manchester University Press, 2003), 65–80; Lynn Spigel and Henry Jenkins, "Same Bat Channel, Different Bat Times: Mass Culture and Popular Memory," in *Many More Lives of the Batman*, eds. Roberta Pearson, William Uricchio, and Will Brooker (London: British Film Institute, 2015), 171–201; Joanne Garde-Hansen, "The Madonna Archive: Celebrity, Aging and Fan Nostalgia," in *Media and Memory*, ed. Joanne Garde-Hansen (Edinburgh: Edinburgh University Press, 2011).

9. See Roberta Pearson, "Sherlock Holmes, a De Facto Franchise?" in *Popular Media Cultures: Writing in the Margins and Reading Between the Lines*, ed. Lincoln Geraghty (London: Palgrave MacMillan, 2015), 188–201; Roberta Pearson, "World Building Logics and Copyright: The Dark Knight and the Great Detective," in *World Building: Transmedia, Fans, Industries*, ed. Marta Boni, Martin Lefebvre, and Marc Steinberg (Amsterdam: University of Amsterdam Press, forthcoming).

10. I am drawing here on the work of Debra Ramsay. See *American Media and the Memory of World War II* (London: Routledge, 2014), 7, 9. I thank Debra for a useful conversation about this chapter's central ideas.

11. Some might argue that a screen grab, taken from the text itself, does not constitute a paratext, which by definition exists outside the text. I would respond that a screen grab recontextualized into a Facebook post is a paratext in the general sense that it points toward the text.

12. Renate Lachmann, "Mnemonic and Intertextual Aspects of Literature," in *Cultural Memory Studies: An International and Interdisciplinary Handbook*, eds. Astrid Erll and Ansgar Nünning (Berlin: Walter de Gruyter: 2008), 304.

13. Philip M. Napoli, "Hyperlinking and the Forces of 'Massification,'" in *The Hyperlinked Society: Questioning Connections in the Digital Age*, eds. Joseph Turow and Lokman Tsui (Ann Arbor: University of Michigan Press, 2009), 61.

14. Tarleton Gillespie, "The Politics of 'Platforms,'" *New Media and Society* 12.3 (2010): 348. As Gillespie points out, the term platform allows a "broadly progressive sales pitch" while "eliding the tensions inherent in their service" and is thus far from a neutral term (348). It is also the case that the term is used much more broadly, so that some scholars might, for example, refer to the telephone as a platform.

15. Lisa Gitelman, *Always Already New: Media, History, and the Data of Culture* (Cambridge, MA: MIT Press, 2006), 7.

16. Nancy Van House and Elizabeth F. Churchill, "Technologies of Memory: Key Issues and Critical Oerspectives," *Memory Studies* 1.3 (2008): 296.

17. Emily Keightley and Philip Schlesinger, "Digital Media—Social Memory: Remembering in Digitally Networked Times," *Media, Culture and Society* 36.6 (2014): 745.

18. Danny Sullivan, "Google Still World's Most Popular Search Engine by Far, But Share of Unique Users Dips Slightly," *Search Engine Land*, 11 February 2013, accessed 29 August 2015, *http://searchengineland.com/google-worlds-most-popular-search-engine-148089.*

19. Joseph Turow, "Introduction: On Taking the Hyperlink for Granted," in *The Hyperlinked Society: Questioning Connections in the Digital Age*, eds. Joseph Turow and Lokman Tsui (Ann Arbor: University of Michigan Press, 2009). It should be noted that algorithms are patented and proprietary, their exact nature a closely guarded secret from both competitors and users. The calculation of popularity is one element of Google's algorithm, but there are certainly others. This leads to diverse search results related to user, country, and other factors. As José Van Dijck says: "Google's power lies not in its ability to search fixed sets of databases, but in its ability to navigate a person through a vast repository of mutant items, yielding different content depending on when and how they are retrieved, reshaping the order of its data upon each usage" (José van Dijck, *Mediated Memories in the Digital Age* [Stanford, CA: Stanford University Press, 2007, 166]).

20. James G. Webster, "Structuring a Marketplace of Attention," in *The Hyperlinked Society: Questioning Connections in the Digital Age*, eds. Joseph Turow and Lokman Tsui (Ann Arbor: University of Michigan Press, 2009), 27.

21. Alexander Halavais, "The Hyperlink as Organizing Principle," in *The Hyperlinked Society: Questioning Connections in the Digital Age*, eds. Joseph Turow and Lokman Tsui (Ann Arbor: University of Michigan Press, 2009), 44.

22. Philip M. Napoli, "Hyperlinking and the Forces of 'Massification,'" 60.

23. Eric Goldman, "Search Engine Bias and the Demise of Search Engine Utopianism," *Yale Journal of Law and Technology* 8 (Spring 2006): 193.

24. Ibid., 193–194.

25. Anne Kaun and Frederik Stiernstedt, "Facebook Time: Technological and Institutional Affordances for Media Memories," *New Media and Society* 16.7 (2014): 1155.

26. It is possible, if not intuitively straightforward, to search Facebook for images. I tried entering variations upon "photos of Sherlock Holmes" and was given the options of Movie, Fictional Character, Book, *Game of Shadows* and Sherlock Holmes-UK. As with Google Images, these single-screen collections of images were dominated by Robert Downey and Benedict Cumberbatch, the content again reflecting corporate power and presentist fan interests.

27. Mari Smith, "Facebook Community Pages: What Your Business Needs to Know," *Social Media Examiner*, 23 June 2010, accessed 29 August 2015, *http://www.socialmediaexaminer.com/facebook-community-pages-what-your-business-needs-to-know*.

28. *https://www.facebook.com/groups/369770569705925/?ref=br_rs#_=_*, accessed 29 August 2015. Real-world fan organizations such as the Baker Street Irregulars, the Sherlock Holmes Society of London, and the Baker Street Babes have their own Facebook pages, but these have fewer members and fewer likes than the virtual only group, which added 288 members between my visits of 20 April and 4 May 2015. The relative levels of membership and growth may attest to the operations of the platform's search function; the page for Sherlock Holmes Fans appears near the top of the results for "find all groups named Sherlock Holmes," while the real-world organizations appear not at all. I had to search for them by their specific names, which might be unknown to those coming to the fandom for the first time.

29. Kaun and Stiernstedt, "Facebook Time," 1161.

30. José van Dijck, "Flickr and the Culture of Connectivity: Sharing Views, Experiences, Memories," *Memory Studies* 20.10 (2010): 2.

31. Ibid., 1160.

32. Harry McCracken, "Flickr Turns 10: The Rise, Fall and Revival of a Photo-Sharing Community," *Time*, 10 February 2014, accessed 29 August 2015, *http://time.com/6855/flickr-turns-10-the-rise-fall-and-revival-of-a-photo-sharing-community.*
33. *https://www.flickr.com/commons*, accessed 29 August 2015.
34. The Sydney Opera House, not part of The Commons, also uses Flickr. See Cristina Garduño Freeman, "Photosharing on Flickr: Intangible Heritage and Emergent Publics," *International Journal of Heritage Studies* 16.4–5 (2010): 352–368.
35. Melissa Terras, "The Digital Wunderkammer: Flickr as a Platform for Amateur Cultural and Heritage Content," *Library Trends*, 59.4 (2011): 687.
36. Ibid., 696.
37. Ibid., 9.
38. *https://www.flickr.com/groups/72128806@N00*, accessed 29 August 2015.
39. *http://www.velocityreviews.com/threads/flickr-difference-between-most-relevant-and-most-interesting.539347*, accessed 29 August 2015.
40. van Dijck, "Flickr and the Culture of Connectivity," 2.

References

Anonymous. "Benedict Cumberbatch: Gen Y's Sherlock Holmes." Accessed 1 August 2015. *http://www.ihearofsherlock.com/2015/03/benedict-cumberbatch-gen-ys-sherlock.html#.VSUQY0um1Fw.*
Bausells, Marta. "Sherlock Holmes: the many identities of the world's favourite detective—in pictures." *The Guardian*, 17 April, 2014. Accessed 1 August 2015. *http://www.theguardian.com/books/gallery/2014/apr/17/sherlock-holmes-test-of-time-detective-tv-film-in-pictures.*
Garde-Hansen, Joanne. *Media and Memory.* Edinburgh: Edinburgh University Press, 2011.
Garduño Freeman, Cristina. "Photosharing on Flickr: Intangible Heritage and Emergent Publics." *International Journal of Heritage Studies* 16.4–5 (2010): 352–368.
Gillespie, Tarleton. "The Politics of 'Platforms.'" *New Media and Society* 12.3 (2010): 347–364.
Gitelman, Lisa. *Always Already New: Media, History, and the Data of Culture.* Cambridge, MA: MIT Press, 2006.
Goldman, Eric. "Search Engine Bias and the Demise of Search Engine Utopianism." *Yale Journal of Law and Technology* 8 (2006): 188–200.
Halavais, Alexander. "The Hyperlink as Organizing Principle." In *The Hyperlinked Society: Questioning Connections in the Digital Age*, eds. Joseph Turow and Lokman Tsui, 39–55. Ann Arbor: University of Michigan Press, 2009.
Halbwachs, Maurice. *On Collective Memory.* Chicago: University of Chicago Press, 1992.
Kaun, Anne, and Frederik Stiernstedt. "Facebook Time: Technological and Institutional Affordances for Media Memories." *New Media and Society* 16.7 (2014): 1–15.
Keightley, Emily. "Introduction: Time, Media, Modernity." In *Time, Media, Modernity*, ed. Emily Keightley, 1–22. Basingstoke, UK: Palgrave Macmillan, 2012.
———, and Philip Schlesinger. "Digital Media—Social Memory: Remembering in Digitally Networked Times." *Media, Culture and Society* 36.6 (2014): 745–747.

Kuhn, Annette. *Dreaming of Fred and Ginger: Cinema and Cultural Memory*. New York: New York University Press, 2002.

Lachmann, Renate. "Mnemonic and Intertextual Aspects of Literature." In *Cultural Memory Studies: An International and Interdisciplinary Handbook*, eds. Astrid Erll, and Ansgar Nünning, 301–310. Berlin: Walter de Gruyter: 2008.

Loeb, Alatheia. "Sherlock Holmes 3 Release Date, News, and Spoilers." *Crossmap*, 18 May 2015. Accessed 1 August 2015. *http://www.crossmap.com/news/sherlock-holmes-3-release-date-news-and-spoilers-robert-downey-jr-s-official-facebook-page-may-have-just-hinted-that-sherlock-holmes-3-is-now-in-production-18366*.

McCracken, Harry. "Flickr Turns 10: The Rise, Fall and Revival of a Photo-Sharing Community." *Time*, 10 February 2014. Accessed 1 August 2015. *http://time.com/6855/flickr-turns-10-the-rise-fall-and-revival-of-a-photo-sharing-community*.

Napoli, Philip M. "Hyperlinking and the Forces of 'Massification.'" In *The Hyperlinked Society: Questioning Connections in the Digital Age*, eds. Joseph Turow and Lokman Tsui, 56–69. Ann Arbor: University of Michigan Press, 2009.

Pearson, Roberta. "Sherlock Holmes, a De Facto Franchise?" In *Popular Media Cultures: Writing in the Margins and Reading Between the Lines*, ed. Lincoln Geraghty, 188–201. London: Palgrave Macmillan, 2015.

———. "World Building Logics and Copyright: The Dark Knight and the Great Detective." In *World Building: Transmedia, Fans, Industries*, eds. Marta Boni, Martin Lefebvre, and Marc Steinberg. Amsterdam: University of Amsterdam Press (forthcoming).

Ramsay, Debra. *American Media and the Memory of World War II*. London: Routledge, 2014.

Smith, Mari. "Facebook Community Pages: What Your Business Needs to Know." *Social Media Examiner*, 23 June 2010. Accessed 1 August 2015. *http://www.socialmediaexaminer.com/facebook-community-pages-what-your-business-needs-to-know*.

Spigel, Lynn, and Henry Jenkins. "Same Bat Channel, Different Bat Times: Mass Culture and Popular Memory." In *Many More Lives of the Batman*, eds. Roberta Pearson, William Uricchio, and Will Brooker, 171–201. London: British Film Institute, 2015.

Stubbings, Sarah. "'Look Behind You!': Memories of Cinema-Going in the 'Golden Age' of Hollywood." In *Memory and Popular Film*, ed. Paul Grainge, 65–80. Manchester, UK: Manchester University Press, 2003.

Sullivan, Danny. "Google Still World's Most Popular Search Engine by Far, But Share of Unique Users Dips Slightly." *Search Engine Land*, 11 February 2013. Accessed 1 August 2015. *http://searchengineland.com/google-worlds-most-popular-search-engine-148089*.

Taylor, Diana. "Save As ... Knowledge and Transmission in the Age of Digital Technologies." *Forseeable Futures* 10 (2011). Accessed 1 August 2015. *http://imaginingamerica.org/wp-content/uploads/2011/05/Foreseeable-Futures-10-Taylor.pdf*.

Terras, Melissa. "The Digital Wunderkammer: Flickr as a Platform for Amateur Cultural and Heritage Content." *Library Trends* 59. 4 (2011): 686–706.

Turow, Joseph. "Introduction: On Taking the Hyperlink for Granted." In *The Hyperlinked Society: Questioning Connections in the Digital Age*, eds. Joseph Turow and Lokman Tsui, 1–22. Ann Arbor: University of Michigan Press, 2009.

van Dijck, José. *Mediated Memories in the Digital Age*. Stanford, CA: Stanford University Press, 2007.

————. "Flickr and the Culture of Connectivity: Sharing Views, Experiences, Memories." *Memory Studies* 4.4 (2011): 401–415.

Van House, Nancy, and Churchill, Elizabeth F. "Technologies of Memory: Key Issues and Critical Perspectives." *Memory Studies* 1.3 (2008): 295–310.

Webster, James G. "Structuring a Marketplace of Attention." In *The Hyperlinked Society: Questioning Connections in the Digital Age*, eds. Joseph Turow and Lokman Tsui, 23–38. Ann Arbor: University of Michigan Press, 2009.

6   Nostalgia for the Future

How *TRON: Legacy*'s Paratexual Promotion Campaign Rebooted the Franchise

Kim Walden

An interesting feature of film trailers is their seemingly paradoxical temporal position in generating both nostalgia and anticipation for forthcoming films, Lisa Kernan characeried this feature in her book *Coming Attractions: Reading Movie Trailers*, as "nostalgia for the future," a concept derived from Vinzenz Hediger and Raymond Williams as well.[1] In light of this tendency, this chapter explores the promotional campaign surrounding the sequel to Disney's science fiction adventure film *TRON* (Steven Lisberger, 1982). A sense of nostalgia had grown up around the film over the thirty years since its release in 1982, and this sentiment was harnessed in order to sell the film's sequel to a new generation, while also revitalizing the film for its original viewers.

This chapter unpicks the distinctive kinds of narrative "work" undertaken by the promotional campaign, drawing on a conception of nostalgia that distinguishes two distinct variants of the sentiment: restorative and reflective, each embodying a different perception of time.[2] The campaign thereby arguably creates a paratextual experience that is, in many ways, as entertaining as the film itself.

The *TRON* Phenomenon

On its release, *TRON* was considered to be flawed, but over time it has entered into folk culture. Testimony to its enduring popularity are the number of spinoffs it has spawned over the years, including novelizations for adults and children as well as graphic novels, comics, and choose-your-own-adventure books. There have been television series and animated adaptations, a theme park ride in Disneyland, videogames, console games, and a manga version released in Japan in 2010. As well as adaptations, there have been several publications about the making of the film, focusing on the visual effects production, while the film itself has been re-released and reissued in every format from Betamax to Blu-ray, with additional anniversary and collector editions.

Broadly speaking, commentary circulating around the film since its release seems to indicate three reasons for its enduring popularity. First, *TRON* was one of the first films to include a sustained sequence of computer-generated imagery. Totaling nearly 17 minutes, the film famously depicts three-dimensional virtual "light cycles" competing in a high-speed race on the vector line grid of the master control program.[3] Second, in the early days of the Internet, it was a Disney film for children that presented one of the first cinematic visualizations of cyberspace, principally through the use of light to produce the lines of vector graphs signifying the electronic space inside the computer.[4] Lastly, and perhaps most interestingly for the purposes of this investigation, the film lauded the videogame culture emerging at the time.[5]

In an interview in 2013, the film's director, Steven Lisberger, suggests that one of the reasons the film has become iconic is that it captured the sense of utopianism that prevailed about digital technology in the early 1980s.[6] Lisberger went on to say that the people the Disney film seems to have had the most impact on were its young audience. This observation is borne out by the strong memory culture surrounding the film on the web to this day, now that this audience has reached adulthood.[7] Characteristically, this takes the form of filmgoers' recollections of the impact of *TRON* on their young selves. In an article on 1980s game fandom, Will Brooker describes how *TRON* "offered gamers the flattering reassurance that they were not merely teenage hobbyists but trainee warriors, learning skills that could be transferred to a galactic war, or godlike, all-controlling 'users' revered by the champions of an electronic world."[8] This account is typical of sentiments articulated on discussion boards, blogs, and wikis across the web: "It was *TRON* that made me look at those machines in a completely different way. ... Perhaps it's nostalgia. Perhaps it's the fact that I would enjoy watching 2 ½ hours of Jeff Bridges reading the phone book. Whatever it is, I don't care. I just know that I love this movie deeply."[9] So how can the strength and endurance of sentiments felt for this children's science fiction fantasy from over thirty years ago be accounted for?

TRON: Legacy's Promotional Campaign, Flynn Lives

As there was no sequel to *TRON* for thirty years, speculations and imaginings of "what happened if" and "what happened next" prevailed as part of an informal, amateur paratextuality. In the past, this may have taken place in personal conversations and private journals, but today it is made visible online through blogs, fanzines, and discussion boards. As Umberto Eco points out in his discussion of *Casablanca* (Micheal Curtiz, 1942), in *Travels in Hyperreality*, a film may be considered to be a "cult" film if it is "ramshackle, rickety, unhinged in itself" and that lack of coherence, of course, means, it is open to speculation.[10] What *TRON: Legacy*'s promotional campaign effectively set out to do was to start to fill in the incomplete text by explaining what happened next (after the original film ends) and thereby compensate for the "lack" of knowledge about the future of the story. Vinzenz Hediger explained this idea in psychoanalytic terms, and, as Kernan points out, it can also be understood through Raymond William's idea about the false conversion of audience experiences (speculations) into "finished products."[11] By converting narrative speculation into a definitive version of the future (of the story), open-endedness is converted into a fixed ending and the pleasures of anticipation and speculation are reified in *TRON: Legacy*'s promotional campaign.[12]

The campaign produced by the award-winning marketing company, 42 Entertainment, takes the form of a web-based "movement" under the banner *Flynn Lives*. Its premise is that the film's hero, Kevin Flynn disappeared in mysterious circumstances sometime after the end of the first film and the *Flynn Lives* site is dedicated to finding him. Through this narrative device, the marketing campaign set out to chart the time from the theatrical release of the original film back in the early 1980s to the release of the sequel in 2010. In the words of 42 Entertainment's company website, the site aims to bridge the gap, with "twenty eight years of connective mythology, games and interactivity" and the campaign garnered a number of awards and accolades for its innovative approach to film marketing.[13]

Clearly, the online environment has greatly expanded the scope of paratexual promotion. Before the digital era, a film's marketing campaign would typically last about six weeks, made up of posters, press releases, and trailers for cinema and TV. However, the potential of web-based promotion has changed this significantly. For Steven Spielberg's *A.I. Artificial Intelligence* (2001), Elan Lee and Jordan Weisman conceived an ARG (alternate reality game) called *The Beast* that rolled out over twelve weeks running up to the cinema release of the film. On the back of its success, they founded 42 Entertainment and went on to develop the *Why So Serious?* campaign for *Dark Knight* (Christopher Nolan) in 2008 and then in 2010 *TRON: Legacy*'s campaign—*Flynn Lives*, both of which ran for over a year.

The duration of paratextual promotion can now be significantly extended, stretching out over weeks and months to generate awareness and anticipation for a forthcoming release; by contrast, these promotional paratexts tend to be delivered in short form. The need for brevity is acute in a context where the sheer abundance of online media means audiences devote less attention to any given component.[14] Short installments of *Flynn Lives* were published online in daily and weekly episodes, taking only minutes to view or play. In this way, audience engagement aggregates and develops over time, and this mode of transmission generates an experience of "intense seriality" more familiar in TV's long-running series and soap operas.[15]

After the film's theatrical release, the paratextual promotional campaign remained available online and could be accessed in its entirety, long after the film has disappeared from cinema programmes. The "always on" nature of the online environment ensures that the promotional paratext can enjoy a far longer lease of life than conventional promotional materials. Moreover, it creates a kind of archive of the invented past of *TRON: Legacy*, which can be re-accessed and (re)consumed (although always with the proviso that it is unmonetized and unmonetizable. While forming part of the anticipatory experience, promotional content is not designed for purchase. It functions purely in relation to the film it advertises and therefore is vulnerable to erasure at any time).[16]

What we are seeing here is a form of paratexual promotion that appropriates modes conventionally associated with pre-digital media forms: the brevity of advertising; the duration of long-running TV series and soap operas; the episodic "seriality" of broadcast TV, as well as the record of archives. Form and format conventions are no longer confined to specific media platforms. The online environment has provided the conditions for changing what promotional media can look like, and, in this instance, the dimensions of the paratextual promotional campaign for *TRON: Legacy* exceed the film it promotes.

However, while paratextual promotion of film now capitalizes on the web's opportunities for audience engagement, as I suggested at the start of this chapter, it is important to remember that this campaign did not come out of nowhere. One of the fundamental strategies for rebooting the *TRON* franchise was to draw on that groundswell of nostalgia that had developed around the film over the last thirty years. The next section of the chapter will explore the different forms nostalgia can take and examine how these are put to use in the *Flynn Lives* campaign.

The Anatomy of Nostalgia

There are different theories as to why nostalgia occurs but, in essence, it can be understood as a sense of regret that the past is gone and that one can take solace from the possibility that on some level it can be recovered and experienced again. In *The Future of Nostalgia*, Svetlana Boym asserts that there are two predominant ways in which a longing for the past is articulated.[17] First, she suggests there is a "restorative" nostalgia that focuses on the *nostos* part of the word, meaning "home," and is derived from the term "re-staure" meaning reestablishment.[18] Boym argues that "restorative nostalgia" is built on a desire to create a sense of continuity with the past and places emphasis on reconstructing the thing that is longed for.[19] In film, this form of nostalgia has provided the impetus for the reconditioning and remastering of analogue film prints. For example, to mark the twentieth anniversary of *Star Wars* (George Lucas, 1977), negatives of all three films in the original trilogy were 'restored' for rerelease so audiences could buy the films all over again.

The second nostalgic tendency derives from the *algia* part of the word and is more "reflective."[20] While looking to the past, reflective nostalgia implicitly acknowledges the irrecoverable nature of the past and brings in its wake a critical distance that is able to discern the difference between past and present.[21] This form of nostalgia has become a popular trope in television through critically reflective formats such as American Cable Network's *Mad Men* (2007–2015), which is set in the past, but a past that is viewed through the perspective of the "rear view mirror" of the present, allowing for reflection on what has changed since then.[22] "Reflective" nostalgia appreciates that the past no longer exists but meditates on the passing of time and the changes it brings with it to the meaning of things. In light of this typology of nostalgia, this chapter will now explore the ways in which nostalgia was generated and capitalized upon in this paratexual promotional campaign for the release of *TRON*'s sequel.

"I have been waiting to play that game since I was 12 and I was in there!"

The *Flynn Lives* campaign was launched at the San Diego Comic Convention in 2009. At this inaugural event, delegates were invited to a mock-up of the "Flynn's Arcade" setting from the original film. On the website, QuickTime videos of the event show excited fans marveling at their first-hand encounters with old arcade game machines. The centerpiece of the experience is an encounter with a life-sized *TRON* light cycle, and we hear one man exclaim, "I have been waiting to play that game since I was twelve and I was in there!"[23]

Memories of the past that are made concrete generate a nostalgic response in its visitors. Not all the objects are "real" in the sense of being original. Some are props created for this event, while others, like the games consoles, bring an aura of authenticity to the event. In this mix of original fact and fiction, the film set prop becomes as authentically "real" as the actual games console, and willing acceptance of the veracity of the one, and all the emotions that carries, seeps into all the rest.

What is unusual about the *TRON* film series is the time that elapsed between the first film in 1982 and its sequel in 2010, which amounts to a period of nearly thirty years. As the marketing company's press statement indicated, one of the main tasks of the promotional paratexual campaign was to establish a connection between the two films, implying continuity through the intervening years. This is achieved through the narrative of the campaign in a number of ways. Emphasis is placed on establishing a chronological connection between the two films. The fictional corporation *Encom* has a website featuring a timeline of the company's history portraying the development of the business over the time period.

There is a further timeline in the website's "Media Section" where a headline poses the question, "Who is the most brilliant computer visionary ever?" Within the campaign nostalgia is encouraged through the reestablishment of familiar figures from the original film *TRON*, with actors once again taking up their character roles to promote the forthcoming film *TRON: Legacy*. The character of Kevin Flynn is featured alongside real-world figures Microsoft founder Bill Gates and Apple's Steve Jobs, and so the campaign sutures the story of TRON into a history of real-world digital culture; as it were "Forrest-Gumping" recent histories by inserting this fiction into that history. The role of Kevin Flynn is reprised by the actor Jeff Bridges, and Bruce

Boxleitner again plays the part of Alan Bradley, albeit both are 30 years older. So, taken together what we see here is the restoration of characters and stars, further validated by famous "real-life" figures deployed to create a sense of continuity with a familiar and established past, in the present, to promote the forthcoming film.

Restorative nostalgia promotes the reconstruction of the thing that is longed for and remaining true to the aspirations of its legacy audience who remember and cherish the original. But the *Flynn Lives* paratext reconditions *TRON* for its new audience, who are encountering the story for the first time. Here we see the deployment of some of the adaptive strategies that are familiar from film and television.[24] Substitution has become a standard device to refresh long–running TV programs like the BBC's *Dr Who*, whereby the actors who play the Doctor are periodically replaced, or the 007 films in which the figure of James Bond has been played by a series of actors over the fifty years of the franchise. Likewise, in the paratextual promotional campaign *Flynn Lives*, we see this transfer undertaken, with the aging Kevin Flynn (Jeff Bridges) of the original film substituted in the sequel by the figure of his "son," Sam Flynn (Garrett Hedlund). Over the weeks and months, episodes of the campaign fill audiences in on Sam's life story and, by so doing, the paratext conditions him for heroic status in the forthcoming film.

The campaign also uses the adaptive strategy of "equivalences" to refit *TRON* for the digital age.[25] In collaboration with *Disney Interactive, 42 Entertainment* produced a playable online version of the original film's arcade game *Space Paranoids*. Instead of pushing coins into an arcade machine, the game was recast in a Flash version at *www.spaceparanoidsonline.com* as a first-person shooter-style game that renders the analogue past present once again.

The adaptation strategies of substitution and equivalence function to regenerate the story and set up the conditions for the next iteration of the franchise, but the promotional paratext does not just recycle elements from the film. It undertakes narrative work and brings new elements into the story world of *TRON*. In this way, a connection with the original is made, erasing any signs of aging or decay, and the new version reinvigorates the *TRON* franchise. For audiences new to *TRON*, the promotional campaign will be a first-time encounter, but for audiences familiar with the original *TRON*, these substitutions and equivalences are experienced as the overlaying of the new version on top of the original version of the film. In *Recycled Culture in Contemporary Art and Film: Uses of Nostalgia*, Vera Dika has suggested that this superimposition of the present over the past creates a "shifting double exposure," as the viewer experiences similarities and differences simultaneously in a kind of textual imbrication.[26] Together, these different forms of encounter make the experience of the viewing present richer. Encounters with the past and present are aggregated, creating a sense of the past in the present, and audience complicity in the fictionalization of recent history, in turn, creates the conditions in which the paratextual promotional campaign has created an "invented tradition."[27]

"Live" Events

The *Flynn Lives* campaign fuels nostalgia too. It does not just refer to the memory of what has taken place in the past but generates "live" events that establish the object of nostalgic sensibilities in the here and now and inter-polate new audiences into the nostalgic campaign. In the year leading up to the release of the film, a number of "live" publicity events were coordinated by 42 Entertainment as well as the website. The campaign at Comic Con may have started in a re-creation of "Flynn's Arcade" from the original film, but it ended at *TRON: Legacy*'s own signature location—the "End of the Line" nightclub, giving them a foretaste of the new film and enabling audiences to literally "step into the new fiction."[28]

Later, an ARG event was staged in San Francisco to celebrate the creation of an online version of *Space Paranoids*. At an open-air rally attended by hundreds of fans, the Alan Bradley character played by Bruce Boxleitner takes to the podium microphone to address the audience. This ARG event is filmed and reported as a news event on the film's website. Unlike conventional film promotionals such as trailers and posters, which propose the sequel as a future event to anticipate, events like this ARG role play codify time: first by fleshing out the franchise's narrative's back story; second by generating a sense of "event-ness" in the present, and third by setting up anticipation for the film in the future.

Fans were not just invited to spectate; they were also invited to partic-ipate in these events taking on roles themselves and becoming "actors" in the *TRON: Legacy* campaign. At an earlier briefing meeting, fans were primed to take the part of a group of "protesters" and hijack the open-air rally. They sported placards and T-shirts emblazoned with the slogan "Flynn Lives," protesting the theft of Kevin Flynn's intellectual property by *Encom* and the supposed failure of *Encom* to properly investigate Flynn's mysterious "disappearance." By taking up this invitation, audiences were urged to break with the traditional convention of screen-based storytelling in which the fictional world is separated from the real world and they were beckoned through the "fourth wall" into the fictional diegesis of the *TRON* storyworld. Participating fans were referred to as "Flynn's foot soldiers" or "field operatives," and those who were unable to attend in person were dubbed "online warriors" to encourage a sense of involvement, even at a distance from the live event itself. These staged events were then recorded and became news items within the campaign. The tropes of factual report-age were layered onto fictional foundations, and in this way these events are aggregated into the TRON mythology. As a consequence, nostalgia provided an "interpretive frame" through which audiences encountering the story for the first time approached this new franchise installment.[29]

Social Media

The promotional campaign also extended its activities through social media in order to galvanize audiences into participation. Scavenger hunts were held in cities across America and Europe, and the *Flynn Lives* Facebook page enabled fans to find out about events taking place in their locality and join in. Typical of such engagements was the fan who blogged of her participating in a scavenger hunt in Paris and linked it to the film's Facebook site. Her story was entitled A *la recherché de Kevin Flynn ou comment je me suis retrouvée á participer au jeu de pistes de TRON: Legacy (Or How I became the TRON: Legacy field operative in Paris)* and was accompanied by photographs documenting the experience from first learning about the scavenger hunt online to finding the "treasure" in the real world and reporting her findings on the *Flynn Lives* website. See Figure 6.1.

In turn, this post garnered comments and congratulations from online watchers and Facebook's "like" icon also provided online audiences with the

Figure 6.1 TRON: Legacy's Paris Scavenger Hunt. 'A la recherche de Kevin Flynn. ... Ou comment je me suis retrouvée à participer au jeu de pistes de Tron Legacy' *Miss Selector* (2010), accessed 7 March 2013. *http:// www.yasni.info/ext.php?url=http%3A%2F%2Fwww.miss-selector. com%2F2010%2F02%2Fla-recherche-de-kevin-flynn-ou-comment.html &name=Kevin+Flynn&showads=1&lc=en-us&lg=en&rg=fr&rip=gb.*

opportunity for vicarious participation. When the "like" icon is clicked, a visual representation of the "liked" object appears on the recipient's Facebook profile. Here we can see *TRON: Legacy's* paratexts migrating along chains of social connectivity, and what has been dubbed the "like economy" is promulgated by the logic of recommendations.[30] Social media promotion has its own distinct temporal rhythms as the *past* activities of one Facebook user are presented to the people on their contacts list as suggestions for possible *future* activities for them. This creates the situation in which the users' contacts are encouraged to view recommended films rather than any others.[31] So, it turns out that nostalgia is not just concerned with looking back into the past, but it also looks to the future, and through social media the currency of nostalgia may be capitalized upon by the promotional campaign too.

Restorative forms of nostalgia marshalled by this promotional campaign seek to capitalize on these sentiments by making available the things that were thought to be gone. Over the days, weeks, and months of the campaign through repeated encounters with *TRON* tropes and themes, both through live events and online, the film's canonization is cultivated. The cumulative effect of these encounters is that a clear connection is drawn between the original film and the forthcoming film, which brings into being a paradox: the manufacturing of nostalgic sensibilities for a film we have not yet seen that has been characterized as "nostalgia for the future."[32]

Games Nostalgia

Not only has *TRON* become emblematic of, and almost cultural shorthand for, the beginnings of the digital age, it has also become the focal point of nostalgia for the gaming culture because it represents the time when games first entered the zeitgeist. Videogame historian Sean Fenty has observed that the potency of this cultural memory has grown over the years, as it is not just gamers from the 1980s who experience a sense of nostalgia about the game playing of their youth.[33] Indeed, Fenty suggests that nostalgia has become a generalized experience for successive generations of gamers. Gaming technologies are changing all the time, and so all who play games may feel nostalgia as iterations of games supersede one another and older games and their platforms are consigned to obsolescence.[34] One consequence of this has been the burgeoning restorative nostalgic culture of games online.[35] Games archives, museums, and emulators have fueled the appetite for what has been described as "a perfect past that can be replayed, a past within which players can participate, and a past in which players can move and explore."[36]

Games Memory Culture

So, it would appear that the production of the *TRON* promotional paratext is not entirely in the hands of the franchise. Studies of media memory suggest that memory cultures do not simply repeat but actively edit the past by positioning it within new frames and contexts.[37] This observation is borne out by examining historical accounts of games culture and how they have evolved. In one of the first histories of games, *Joystick Nation*, J. C. Herz observed how the memory cultures of gamers of the early 1980s tended to erase from collective memory the recollection of the many poor games that flooded the market at the time.[38] Instead, gamers preferred to focus on their favorite games, which were played and replayed and survived to be ported onto the next platform. It is these games that are lauded and have come to represent the whole of the 1980s arcade gaming culture in popular memory.[39] In much the same way, it appears that cultural memory has erased the shortcomings of the original film *TRON* but celebrates its prescience. Over time, these forms of remembering/misremembering have had the effect of creating an edited, idealized version of the early days of the games arcades and, more broadly, of our cultural past.

Alongside this process of editing the past, the barometer of cultural memory has seen a dramatic shift in attitudes toward games. Herz has documented the low cultural esteem in which games were held in the late 1970s and early 1980s. She tells how "in the public perception, arcades smacked of moral turpitude" and were generally regarded as sites of delinquency.[40] The childhood recollections of the editor of a videogame culture fanzine *1-Up*, Raina Lee, bears this out as she recalls: "They (her parents) didn't really let me go alone to arcades, because they were seen as bad places with bad teenage boys."[41] It seems that arcades were regarded as "teenage hangouts" where young people wasted their time in bus stations and dingy dark corners of shopping malls.[42] Since then, however, attitudes toward games and games culture have undergone a transformation as the games community and wider culture have come to regard arcade games less as the locus of youthful delinquency and more as the unlikely location of the first green shoots of a nascent digital culture.

From the Margins to the Mainstream

Today a new generation of games historians are keen to establish that games are no longer marginal but have entered into the mainstream. As evidence, they point to the fact that games have grown into one of the largest entertainment industries, larger than the film industry.[43] In his book, *The Video Game Explosion*, games historian Mark J.P. Wolf describes how by the late 1990s, the generation that had grown up with games not only enjoyed playing them but had begun to write about them too. Games are now the focus of academic journals, anthologies, and conferences, and a growing number of universities now offer degree programs in Games Studies and Game Design.[44] Games have even become the focus of exhibitions in major art galleries such as *Game On* at London's Barbican in 2002 and *The Art of Video Games* at the Smithsonian American Art Museum in Washington, D.C., in 2012.

On reflection games historians now argue that during the 1970s video arcade games depicted in *TRON* were actually the first computers to be encountered by the (young) general public; their significance lies in the fact that they illustrated the proposition that computers might be used, not just for utilitarian purposes, but for play too.[45] In light of these changes in attitudes toward games, I would assert that the marketing campaign for *TRON: Legacy* became the focus for expressions of vindication and for exoneration of the games culture, and that this shift in cultural attitudes is why the promotional campaign resonated with its audience so effectively. As the Alan Bradley character exclaims into the microphone on stage at the *Encom* rally, "who could have known that those games would evolve into the indispensable programmes that guide our daily lives?"

Reflective Nostalgia

It is here that the *Flynn Lives* campaign evokes what in Boym's typology is recognizable as the second, more reflective form of nostalgia, and this nostalgic tendency takes a different perspective on the past to restorative nostalgia. As suggested earlier, reflective nostalgia contains an implicit awareness that a return to the past is neither possible nor desirable. It is therefore less concerned to preserve and fetishize remnants from bygone days, but more interested in reflecting on how far we have come in the journey to this point in the present.

The reflective nostalgia, evidenced in the character Alan Bradley's rally speech, demonstrates an acute awareness of the passage of time since the dawn of the digital age in the 1980s but with it a sense of critical distance on the difference between past, present, and indeed the future. This form of nostalgia knows that the past no longer exists and that *TRON* is best regarded fondly as a period piece today, but that is not the end of it. A more reflective nostalgia celebrates the foresight of the film *TRON* and the fact that fondness for the film is not an isolated experience, but is shared by many since then, and so can be regarded as part of the collective memory.

Indeed, by the end of the campaign, it becomes clear that *Flynn Lives* was not about *TRON* so much as it was about *TRON*'s audiences, as it both validates and vindicates *TRON* fandom. By engaging with the film's paratextual promotional campaign, the audience has rewritten its own history and validated its own game-playing by willingly participating in a rewriting of history in which the events of the original *TRON* actually happened and because of that, the world is a different place. In the words of one post on the site: "YOU ARE FLYNN LIVES!" Their nostalgia, like all nostalgia, perhaps is not for the past as it was, or even the past as it is actually remembered, but for a past as we would wish it to have been. If you recast the past, then you can look forward to a different future, one that has come from that past.

Notes

My thanks to Alan Peacock for his invaluable insights in our many discussions about the TRON phenomenon and to 'Miss Selector' for kindly allowing me to use her photographs of the Tron: Legacy Paris Scavenger Hunt.

1. Lisa Kernan, *Coming Attractions: Reading American Movie Trailers* (Austin: University of Texas Press, 2004), 16. Kernan's phrase "nostalgia for the future" is derived from two sources. First, Vinzenz Hediger's discussion of the relationship between trailers and the films they promote, in psychoanalytic terms as compensation for a lack (of knowledge of what the future entails) in *Trailer: Demnächst in diesem Theatre; Zur Mediengeschichte eines amerikanischen Filmwerbemittels*, Master's Thesis, University of Zurich, 1995. Second, Raymond William's discussion of the tendency of bourgeois ideology to articulate lived experiences as "finished products" in the past in *Marxism and Literature* (Oxford, UK: Oxford University Press, 1977), 128–129.
2. Svetlana Boym, *The Future of Nostalgia* (New York: Basic Books, 2001), 41.
3. Scott Bukatman, *Terminal Identity: The Virtual Subject in Post-Modern Science Fiction* (London: Duke University Press, 1994), 216; Isaac V. Kerlow *The Art of 3D: Computer Animation and Effects* (Hoboken, NJ: John Wiley, 2004), 19; Jessica Aldred, "All Aboard *The Polar Express*: A 'Playful' Change of Address in the Computer-Generated Blockbuster," *Animation* 1.2 (2006), accessed 16 December 2013, *http://anm.sagepub.com.ezproxy.herts.ac.uk/content/1/2/153. full.pdf+html*; Andrew Darley, *Visual Digital Culture: Surface Play and Spectacle in New Media Genre* (London: Routledge, 2000), 17.
4. Bukatman, *Terminal Identity*, 215; Vivian Sobchack, *Screening Space: The American Science Fiction Film* (New York: Ungar, 1993), 257–258.
5. Will Brooker, "Maps of Many Worlds: Remembering Computer Game Fandom in the 1980s," *Transformative Works and Cultures*, 2. 2009, accessed 12 March 2013, *http://dx.doi.org/10.3983/twc.2009.0034*; Henry Jenkins, "Talking *Tron*'s Media with Steven Lisberger," *Henry Jenkins.org*, 19 March 2010, accessed 26 February 2013, *http://henryjenkins.org/?s=Tron+Steven+lisberger# sthash.8iG9M6ZQ.dpuf*.
6. Henry Jenkins, "Talking *Tron*'s Media with Steven Lisberger," accessed 26 February 2013, *http://henryjenkins.org/?s=Tron+Steven+lisberger#sthash. 8iG9M6ZQ.dpuf*.
7. Ibid.
8. Brooker, "Maps of Many Worlds."
9. Jesus Diaz, "*Tron*: Celebrate 30 Years of This Classic Cult Movie," *Gizmodo.com*, 7 September (2012), accessed 16 December 2013, *http://gizmodo.com/5924594/ tron-celebrate-30-years-of-this-classic-cult-movie*.
10. Umberto Eco, *Travels in Hyper-Reality* (London: Picador, 1987), 198.
11. Kernan, *Coming Attractions*, 16.
12. Ibid.
13. The *Flynn Lives* campaign has won numerous awards, including the TEA (Themed Entertainment) Award in 2011; a Webby nomination in the movie and film category; finalist for a Cannes Cyberlions, and winner of several Movie Viral awards in 2010.
14. Paul Grainge, ed., *Ephemeral Media: Transitory Screen Culture from Television to YouTube* (London: Palgrave/BFI, 2011), 12.

15. Angela Ndalianis, *The Horror Sensorium: Media and the Senses* (Jefferson, NC: McFarland, 2012), 175.
16. The Flynn Lives site was taken down at the end of 2014, four years after the film's cinema release. The site www.flynnlives.com may now only be accessed via Internet Archive's Wayback Machine up to 1st September 2014.
17. Boym, *The Future of Nostalgia*, 41.
18. Ibid., 49.
19. Ibid., 41.
20. Ibid.
21. Ibid., 49.
22. Amy Holdsworth *Television, Memory, Nostalgia* (Basingstoke, UK: Palgrave Macmillan 2011), 110.
23. 'Flynn Lives Tron Legacy/Disney' 42 Entertainment, accessed 15 March 2013, *http://42entertainment.com/work/flynnlives*.
24. Linda Hutcheon, *A Theory of Adaptation* (London: Routledge, 2006), 10.
25. Ibid.
26. Vera Dika, *Recycled Culture in Contemporary Art and Film: The Uses of Nostalgia* (Cambridge, UK: Cambridge University Press 2003), 14.
27. Boym, *The Future of Nostalgia*, 42.
28. 42 Entertainment, accessed 15 March 2013, *http://www.42entertainment.com/work/flynnlives*.
29. Jonathan Gray, *Show Sold Separately: Promos, Spoilers and Other Media Paratexts* (New York: New York University Press, 2010), 10.
30. Anne Helmond and Carolin Gerlitz, "Anne Helmond and Carolin Gerlitz Explain the Like Economy," *Networkcultures.org* (2012), accessed 16 January 2014, *http://networkcultures.org/wpmu/unlikeus/2012/03/10/anne-helmond-and-carolin-gerlitz-explain-the-like-economy*.
31. Ibid.
32. Kernan, *Coming Attractions*, 16.
33. Sean Fenty, "Why Old School Is 'Cool': A Brief Analysis of Classic Video Game Nostalgia," in *Playing the Past: History and Nostalgia in Video Games*, eds. Zach Whalen and Laurie N. Taylor (Nashville, TN: Vanderbilt University Press, 2008), 23.
34. Ibid., 23.
35. Ibid.; J. C. Herz, *Joystick Nation: How Video Games Gobbled Our Money, Won Our Hearts and Rewired Our Minds* (London: Abacus, 1997), 65; James Newman *Videogames* (London: Routledge, 2004), 165–166; Jaakko Suominen, "The Past as the Future? Nostalgia and Retrogaming in Digital Culture," *Fibrecultural-Journal.org* 8.9 (2008), accessed 6 March 2013, *http://eleven.fibreculturejournal.org/fcj-075-the-past-as-the-future-nostalgia-and-retrogaming-in-digital-culture*; Mark J.P. Wolf, ed, *The Video Game Explosion: A History from PONG to Play-Station and Beyond* (Westport, CT: Greenwood Press, 2007), 29, accessed 8 March 2013, *http://www.herts.eblib.com/patron/FullRecord.aspx?p=329220&userid=her.52487100a4bbf43f&tstamp=1424432367&id=16b399531c0dc2023c967d36acf9740fc1324869&extsrc=ath-usr*.
36. Fenty, "Why Old School Is 'Cool,'" 22.
37. Holdsworth, *Television, Memory, Nostalgia*, 98.
38. Herz, *Joystick Nation*, 73–74.
39. Ibid.
40. Ibid., 50–51.

41. Raiford Guins, "Intruder Alert! Intruder Alert!" Video Games in Space," *Journal of Visual Culture* 3.2. 205 (2004), accessed 17 December 2013, *http://www.powerstrike.net/Intruder_Alert.pdf.*
42. Herz, *Joystick Nation*, 49.
43. Mark J.P.Wolf, ed., *The Video Game Explosion* 21, accessed 8 March 2013, *http://www.herts.eblib.com/patron/FullRecord.aspx?p=329220&userid=her.52487100a4bbf43f&tstamp=1424432367&id=16b399531c0dc2023c967 d36acf9740fc1324869&extsrc=ath-usr.*
44. Ibid., 22.
45. Ibid., 21.

References

Aldred, Jessica. "All aboard *The Polar Express*: A 'Playful' Change of Address in the Computer-Generated Blockbuster." *Animation* 1.2 (2006). Accessed 16 December 2013. *http://anm.sagepub.com.ezproxy.herts.ac.uk/content/1/2/153.full.pdf+html.*
Boym, Svetlana. *The Future of Nostalgia*. New York: Basic Books, 2001.
Brooker, Will. "Maps of Many Worlds: Remembering Computer Game Fandom in the 1980s." *Transformative Works and Cultures* 2 (2009). Accessed 12 March 2013. *http://dx.doi.org/10.3983/twc.2009.0034.*
Bukatman, Scott. *Terminal Identity: The Virtual Subject in Post-Modern Science Fiction*. London: Duke University Press, 1994.
Darley, Andrew. *Visual Digital Culture: Surface Play and Spectacle in New Media Genre*. London: Routledge, 2000.
Diaz, Jesus. "Tron: Celebrate 30 Years of This Classic Cult Movie." *Gizmodo.com*, 7 September 2012. Accessed 16 December 2013. *http://gizmodo.com/5924594/tron-celebrate-30-years-of-this-classic-cult-movie.*
Dika, Vera. *Recycled Culture in Contemporary Art and Film: The Uses of Nostalgia*. Cambridge, UK: Cambridge University Press, 2003.
Eco, Umberto. *Travels in Hyper-Reality*. London: Picador, 1987.
42 Entertainment. *Flynn Lives* (2010). Accessed 14 October 2012. *http://www.flynnlives.com.*
42 Entertainment. 'Flynn Lives Tron Legacy/Disney' *42 Entertainment.com*. Accessed 15 March 2013. *http://42entertainment.com/work/flynnlives.*
Fenty, Sean. "Why Old School Is 'Cool': A Brief Analysis of Classic Video Game Nostalgia." In *Playing the Past: History and Nostalgia in Video Games*, eds. Zach Whalen and Laurie N. Taylor, 19–31. Nashville, TN: Vanderbilt University Press, 2008.
Grainge, Paul, ed. *Ephemeral Media: Transitory Screen Culture from Television to YouTube*, London: BFI and Palgrave Macmillan, 2011.
Gray, Jonathan. *Show Sold Separately: Promos, Spoilers and Other Media Paratexts*. New York: New York University Press, 2010.
Guins, Raiford. "'Intruder Alert! Intruder Alert!' Video Games in Space." *Journal of Visual Culture* 3.2 (2004). Accessed 17 December 2013. *http://www.powerstrike.net/Intruder_Alert.pdf.*
Helmond, Anne, and Carolin Gerlitz. "Anne Helmond and Carolin Gerlitz Explain the Like Economy." *Networkcultures.org* (2012). Accessed 16 January 2014. *http://networkcultures.org/wpmu/unlikeus/2012/03/10/anne-helmond-and-carolin-gerlitz-explain-the-like-economy.*

Herz, J. C. *Joystick Nation: How Video Games Gobbled Our Money, Won Our Hearts and Rewired Our Minds.* London: Abacus, 1997.

Holdsworth, Amy. *Television, Memory, Nostalgia.* Basingstoke, UK: Palgrave Macmillan, 2011.

Hutcheon, Linda. *A Theory of Adaptation.* London: Routledge, 2006.

Jenkins, Henry. "Talking Tron's Media with Steven Lisberger." 19 March 2010. Accessed 26 February 2013. *http://henryjenkins.org/?s=Tron+Steven+lisberger#sthash. 8iG9M6ZQ.dpuf.*

Keightley, Emily, ed. *Time, Media and Modernity.* Basingstoke, UK: Palgrave Macmillan, 2012.

Kerlow, Isaac Victor. *The Art of 3D: Computer Animation and Effects.* Hoboken, NJ: John Wiley, 2004.

Kernan, Lisa. *Coming Attractions: Reading American Movie Trailers.* Austin: University of Texas Press 2004.

Mad Men (2007–2015), AMC, Weiner Bros et al.

Mittell, Jason. "TiVoing Childhood." In *Flow TV: Television in the Age of Convergence*, eds. Michael Kackman, Marnie Binfield, Matthew Thomas Payne, Allison Perlman, and Bryan Sebok, 46–54. London: Routledge, 2011.

Newman, James. *Videogames.* London: Routledge, 2004.

Ndalianis, Angela. *The Horror Sensorium: Media and the Senses* Jefferson, NC: McFarland, 2012.

Pickering, Michael, and Emily Keightley. "Retrotyping and the Marketing of Nostalgia." In *Media and Nostalgia: Yearning for the Past, Present and Future*, ed. Katharina Niemeyer, 83–94. Basingstoke, UK: Palgrave Macmillan, 2014.

Sobchack, Vivian. *Screening Space: The American Science Fiction Film.* New York: Ungar, 1993.

Suominen, Jaakko. "The Past as the Future? Nostalgia and Retrogaming in Digital Culture." *The Fibre Culture Journal* 11 (2008). Accessed 6 March 2013. *http:// eleven.fibreculturejournal.org/fcj-075-the-past-as-the-future-nostalgia-and-retrogaming-in-digital-culture.*

Wolf, Mark J.P., ed. *The Video Game Explosion: A History from PONG to PlayStation and Beyond.* Westport, CT: Greenwood Press, 2007.

7 Hoaxing the Media

1920s Film Ballyhoo and an Archaeology of Presence

Fabrice Lyczba

This chapter proposes to illustrate the following thesis: that beyond their inherent ephemerality, media paratexts matter for the historically resilient mode of media presence that they propose. While much of what Jonathan Gray has proposed to call "off-screen studies"[1] has so far focused on exploring how media paratexts, in the words of Barbara Klinger, "produce multiple avenues of access to the text,"[2] I wish here to focus on a meta-ability of media paratexts to frame not merely the narrative or the text but the text-reading activity itself. As Gérard Genette has proposed,[3] film paratexts are best analyzed as "a zone not just of transition, but of transaction." I contend that their transactional nature is essentially playful, self-reflexive, and participatory—a mode of media reception that has opened up, and continues to open up the spaces of everyday life to the presence of media fictions. Clearly, such meta-ability to receive media as an engaging game must play a key role in a project of understanding how audiences inhabit and enjoy the spaces of "cinematic heterotopia"—"the expanded space beyond the confines of the movie theatre"[4] where media fictions may be encountered through such ephemeral marketing practices.

By their nature, such practices are disposable cultural productions that mainstream opinion has long deemed "inferior" to the texts they advertise and unworthy of serious analysis. As Phil Wickham reminds us, however, it is *because* of their very ephemerality that cinema ephemera may penetrate, unseen, deep into audiences' everyday lives, becoming this persistent surround that links movie magic with the everyday to become "a backdrop to the routines of ordinary life."[5] What follows is thus an attempt at an original contribution to the still nascent field of *historical* off-screen studies[6] by focusing on how ballyhoo promotional stunts influenced the very act of engaging with cinema fictions in the 1920s, and, beyond this decade, with media creations in general.

Ballyhoo film marketing stunts of the 1920s are unique paratexts in several respects. First, they are uniquely ephemeral. Unlike many paratexts that are mostly textual and visual (posters, written advertising, books, trailers, etc.), these are performance-based "epiphenomena"[7] that exist only during performance. "Ballyhoos" are essentially street media events, organized before or during the release of a feature film at a local theater by the theater manager. Beyond their brief moment of public display, their only relay in the 1920s comes either from local newspapers that may mention the chaos they have induced in local streets, or from national professional publications for movie theater managers that publish best-case descriptions of "successful" stunts (e.g., *Motion Picture News, Exhibitors' Herald, Motion Picture World, Film Daily*).

The range and diversity of these paratexts is in itself astonishing. First, "ballyhoo" designates simple parades of marketing material: a giant cardboard likeness of a Tyrannosaurus Rex driven around Montgomery, Alabama, for the release of *The Lost World* (Harry Hoyt, 1924).[8] Slightly more complex, the parade may be closer both to its circus origins and to the diegetic world of the films portrayed: a jazz band parading around Minneapolis followed by five race-horses for the release of the horse-themed picture *Checkers* (Richard Stanton, 1919)[9]; "a full-blooded Cherokee Indian [*sic*] as ballyhoo man" standing on his "pinto pony" for the release of the Universal western *In the Days of Buffalo Bill* (Edward Laemmle, 1922) in Brooklyn[10]; or, as late as 1926, a girl on horseback, wearing green, who "[rides] about the city [Philadelphia] and [launches] featherweight arrows bearing handbills for the theatre" for the release of Pathé's serial *The Green Archer* (Spencer Gordon Bennet, 1925) at the local family theater.[11] However, press agents such as Harry Reichenbach quickly moved on from such techniques to propose more elaborately staged events, which were rapidly imitated by exhibitors around the country. This expanded the range of ballyhoo: from merely two people "discussing loudly where they would go for the evening" and mentioning *Over the Hill to the Poorhouse* (Harry F. Millarde, 1920) playing at the Lyric Theater in New York[12] to the famous hiring of a live lion discovered in the room of a gentleman named T. R. Zann at the Belleclaire Hotel, also in New York,[13] or the fake kidnapping of star Clara Kimball Young by "Mexican" bandits that Reichenbach still in 1920 declares to newspapers he has already planned, with the full support of U.S. President Wilson.[14] Their creativity seems to know no bounds and is in no way restricted by the very short shelf-life of such stunts.

Second, despite this inherent ephemerality, their intersection with audiences' everyday lives is uniquely powerful. Ballyhoo stunts are disruptive, border on the chaotic, and veer easily into the objectionable. Their very definition implies heightened visibility: in a cluttered media environment, they are masters at engaging audiences. They pry everyday spaces wide open with their outpouring of fictional characters and situations, and they impose participation in their carnival-inspired schemes. *Motion Picture News* describes the following "effective street ballyhoo" for the 1922 release of *When the Desert Calls* (Ray C. Smallwood, 1922). The Cameo Theater sends a truck filled with "real" Sahara sand and a sign that reads: "This is Sahara Desert sand, as shown in the ... picture *When the Desert Calls* now playing at the Cameo theatre. Five dollar gold pieces and other U.S. coins—real money—are buried in this sand. You are welcome to come up and dig for the money, which is yours when you find it."[15] The sign is typical street ballyhoo: it carries vital information to see the film (where and when), it blurs the line between a (fictional) prop (the fictional Sahara) and a (real) element (real sand), and it carries with it clear potential for social mayhem. And so it proves when the cart "accidentally" falls to the side and the sand ends up blocking Times Square: "the sign on the truck ... caused pandemonium, and, with a mad rush, men and women alike dug into the sand. ... For an hour and a half, during the greatest Saturday rush period, traffic was held up at New York's most important corner, while pedestrians dug with much laughter," the magazine reports, approvingly. In a similar vein, O. D. Oakley, the manager of the Regent Theater in Ottawa, Canada, is proud to report in 1924 that for his campaign for *Little Old New York* (Sidney Olcott, 1922), his street ballyhoo—arranging with the local Fire Department to have the fire-bell rung at key intersections in the city—has landed him in court: "Summoned to appear in court for blocking traffic and ringing fire-bell on hand-pump on Main street without permission. ... Newspapers got story of arrest. ... Case thrown out of court. No fine imposed. ... Reproductions made of summons for publicity purposes with copy posted in outside lobby."[16]

In this quest for visibility, the potential for pranks in questionable taste is not left unexplored: a Ku Klux Klan-dressed figure, for instance, is arrested in Madison, Wisconsin, as he "arouses some alarm" riding through town "masked, wearing white robes": "he turned out to be an advertisement for *One Clear Call* (John Stahl, 1922), news of which was in the Sunday morning papers."[17] Just as problematic for the time is this advice, published in *Motion Picture World* at the height of the 1919 Red Scare for the exploitation of the anti-Bolshevik pamphlet *Bolshevism on Trial* (Harley Knoles, 1919):

> Run an extra show at night. Have a special showing for school children. Work all of the crowd stunts. Then put up red flags about town and hire soldiers to tear them down if necessary, and then come out with a flaming handbill explaining that the play is not an argument for anarchy. Have the bills ready printed that you may get them out quickly, or the idea may boomerang. Work out the limit on this and you will not only clean up but profit by future business.[18]

Clearly, ballyhoo stunts relish their ability to organize extraordinary events in ordinary settings and confuse participants with an onslaught of fiction into everyday spaces. And complaints and comments about the confusion induced by such fictional outpourings are rife in the 1920s. West Coast theater manager Harold Franklin, having just signed for the distribution for upscale Paramount films, finds them in 1927 inherently "distasteful"–though he mentions having "a group of Indians camped in the grounds of Central Park" for the release of *The Covered Wagon* (James Cruze, 1923) as an example of a successful and tasteful stunt.[19] For movie columnist Laura Mason, such media phenomena define singularly *modern* spaces of life: "living grows more complicated every day," she writes in 1924. "When you see an almost-murder, a near-kidnapping or a rather-real fire, don't scream or turn pale, just shrug your shoulders in a bored, sophisticated sort of a way and murmur: 'what ever will these exploitation men think of, next?'"[20]

This already (in 1924!) blasé, postmodern shrug of media indifference is precisely the issue. Film ballyhoo stunts participate in what Anne Cronin, analyzing outdoor advertising in modern cities, has called the "mediatization of public space." For Cronin, outdoor ads have transformed the experience of the city into "an experience of a dreaming city, where snatches of images, text and advert structures form a mass of non sequiturs, a clamorous semantic backdrop to people's material encounters with urban places."[21] 1920s ballyhoo stunts clearly belong to an archaeological variantology of such "mediatization" by proposing that public city-spaces be opened to playful, fictional transformations and that media imaginaries also belong there. Yet, as movie paratexts involved in the reception trajectory of a film narrative, they offer more. Their "zone of transaction" is far more continuous than the dazzling clutter of conflicting advertising messages and their ephemeral "non sequitur" approach. Through them, if the city "dreams," it is a dream to be continued inside the movie theater, a dream to be soon embodied somewhere else—on the screens of the city.

In other words, the mediatization of public spaces through film ballyhoo stunts raises yet another question: the issue of what modern media and communication studies, reflecting first on immersive virtual reality technologies, then on digital technologies in general, have proposed to call "presence" or "tele-presence," commonly defined as "the experience of media as 'real' or non-mediated."[22] Media objects derived from the immaterial ghosts of the screen, ballyhoo stunts are nonetheless loud, visible, and *concrete* presences in 1920s American city-spaces. The issue, then, is more precisely to understand what it is that is being presented to audiences through such stunts. What aspect of the film world do they embody that they indeed offer as concrete experiences?

Indeed, all across America in the 1920s, in towns large and small, fictional characters routinely appear at street corners. To fully work as ballyhoo, they need first to be surprising, and thus their fictional link remains unexplained. An old lady is thus spotted one morning in 1919 in downtown Pittsburgh, regularly stopping her car and theatrically marveling at all the wonders the city has to offer, "naturally drawing a large crowd," notes the *Motion Picture News*[23]—a character, it turns out, from a soon-to-open Universal film, *The Right to Happiness* (Tom Ricketts, 1915), about a family of Russian Jewish immigrants coming to the United States and discovering its modern wonders.

In Lichtfield, Minnesota, "a weather-beaten, aged man in tattered clothes" is found walking the streets with a sign reading "I am looking for My Boy": movie fans aware of upcoming releases may guess that he is none other than the old sea captain who, in the movie *My Boy* (Victor Heerman, 1922) distributed by First National, adopts an "orphan" played by Jackie Coogan.[24] Even more theatrical, three "Turks," "dressed," according to the description of the stunt left by its designer Harry Reichenbach,[25] "in lavish splendor from pompoms to aigrets and from sea-green trousers to gold-crescented turbans," arrive in 1920 in a New York hotel, the Hotel Majestic, claiming they are "looking for Sari, the Virgin of Stamboul," and they demand to see the former U.S. ambassador to Turkey, Henry Morgenthau—who is not amused and calls them, undiplomatically, "a fake."[26] But Morgenthau, not an avid fan of the movies, does not know that the Universal film *The Virgin of Stamboul* (Tod Browning, 1920) is, as the stunt is played, still to open at a local film theater.

On 18 July of the same year, near Central Park lake, the New York police find a hat and a bag belonging to one Miss Yuki. Investigations into what looks like a case of suicide find no trace of the body, however. But this is because Yuki Onda is a fictional character in the Universal movie *The Breath of the Gods* (Rollin S. Sturgeon, 1920) that opens near Central Park at the Astor Theater on the same day.[27] Unamused, New York authorities vow to "run down publicity fakers" and propose adoption of a new law creating criminal liability for any false information provided to the police.[28] Their efforts, if successful, fall short of stopping the practice.

In 1922 again, in nearby Newark, New Jersey, police find clothes near a canal, with a note that reads: "I entered a blind bargain with Dr. Lamb on his promise that, through an operation making use of a monkey gland, youth and health would be restored to me. He failed, and this is the result.— Robert Sandell." An investigation follows, with front-page coverage in the local papers about this mysterious "blind bargain"—until the Goldwyn film *A Blind Bargain* (Wallace Worsley, 1922, with Lon Chaney as the mad doctor) opens at the local theater.[29]

Two points seem particularly important when analyzing such practices, their mode of presence, and their narrative integration. First, it is less fiction than *fictionality* as a mode that is proposed for experience. These are no trailers, offering audiences some sort of coherent (albeit not necessarily faithful) entry into the film narrative. They are "pseudo-events"[30] through which fiction comes to town. As paratexts, they are singularly negligent in introducing audiences to the narrative worlds they hail from. This is true even when the ballyhoo is used to deploy specific characters or objects seemingly derived from the diegetic world of the film—the closest these stunts ever come to performing their paratextual function of "framing the narrative." The "old man" looking for "his boy" in Lichtfield is clearly derived from the character of the sea captain of the movie; but the ballyhoo overemphasizes the emotional connection which it foregrounds to the detriment of every other element of the narrative (the immigrant boy, the rich aunt actively looking for the boy, the immigration officers who wish to send him back to Europe). At least the Miss Yuki whom the New York City police actively seeks in July 1920 sounds Japanese and appears to have committed suicide as in the movie (though nothing in the stunt suggests the spy element so prominent in the narrative and the tensions between duty to the heart and duty to the traditions that underline the whole dramatic structure of the movie). But the Robert Sandell who also appears to have killed himself in Newark has little in common with the fictional character of *A Blind Bargain*: not only is the experiment in the film meant to turn him into a monkey and not bring him youth, but the film character escapes before any harm is done and he does not kill himself. Though ballyhoo characters appear to have slipped straight out of film narratives, they tend to slip out of character in their encounter with everyday worlds through the ballyhoo stunts: there are Turkish characters in *Sari, the Virgin of Stamboul*, but the plot never travels to New York, and the villain is looking for Sari's American husband, not her—and he certainly does not try to meet with the ambassador. And movie Tarzan will not appear in New York before MGM's 1942 *Tarzan's New York Adventure*, contrary to one T. R. Zan who brings a lion to the Belleclaire Hotel in 1920.[31]

Indeed, in most ballyhoo stunts, the link with the narrative film world is loose, if not almost coincidental. Because the film *Manslaughter* (Cecil B. DeMille, 1922) features a car accident, Paramount proposes to exhibitors that they "send for a ballyhoo an automobile through the street throttled down to the lowest possible speed. It should be bannered to read: "I drive slowly and avoid 'Manslaughter,'" or even to "get your mayor or police judge to sentence speeders to see the picture."[32] Because one of the characters of Northwest drama *I Am the Law* (Edwin Carewe, 1922) is a Canadian mounted police officer, a fake police officer is made to patrol the streets of Gadsen, Alabama: "a motorcycle was secured and the bogus Chief turned into a speed cop. He chased and stopped autoists [*sic*], took their name and number, and then summoned them to appear at the Imperial theatre to see I Am the Law."[33]

An even more dramatic stunt is organized in Kansas City for the release of *In The Name of the Law* (Emory Johnson, 1922):

> "Stop! In the Name of the Law [*sic*]!" As the sharp command rang out on the air yesterday afternoon, near Ninth and Walnut streets, pedestrians turned in alarm to see a man, revolver in hand, feeling down the street with a policeman in close pursuit. ... At the same moment an automobile filled with policemen came. ... In an instant eight policemen armed with riot guns jumped out. ... There was much excitement coupled with anxiety, as a fusillade of bullets was momentarily expected. But the only shooting that occurred was the shooting of a scene for a motion picture. ... The scene will be shown in conjunction with In the Name of the Law.[34]

Such stunts propose entry into circus-like fictional film universes, not the framing of any narrative. They offer the concrete presence of fiction—of almost *any* fiction—into the routines of everyday city life.

The second important point when analyzing ballyhoo practices is related to the first. When pushing this presence of the fictional into everyday life, these stunts play on the public's sense of what is, or is not, real. Their momentary, and playful, confusion between reality and the media fake updates Barnum's "operational aesthetics," forcing audiences to wonder, if only briefly: "is it real, or is it fake?"[35] Are recruits, for instance, *really* being enlisted by the "petty officer" whom the *Film Year Book* of 1927 suggests should be on duty to man "a temporary recruiting station in the lobby" for the showing of *any* Navy-based movie?[36] What is the nature of the ancient-looking stagecoach parked in 1926 in front of the Wigwam Theater in Reno, Nevada, during the showing of *The Iron Horse* (John Ford, 1924) and identified by a banner around it as a "famous stage-coach used in *The Iron Horse*": a real prop from the film, a historical artifact, or a fake stage-coach put together for the ballyhoo?[37]

All ballyhoos, to some level, are executions of media hoaxes: they stage extraordinary, colorful, and clearly fictional events in public spaces but mask (or ignore) the diegetic origin, and, if possible, they force the public to interact—to follow the ballyhoo to the theater, to answer or not a fake court summons, to accept to be given a fake speeding ticket. Like the literary hoaxes studied by Bryan Alexander, they enforce in their execution a "bimodal" mode of reception by distinguishing between two clear reception groups:[38] those (hopefully the majority) who will play along see through the hoax and enjoy the deployment of fictionality through their life, and others—usually, authorities—who fail to understand, or appreciate, the playfulness: a grumpy ex-ambassador, a serious New York District Attorney—or the mayor of Mattoon, Illinois, who bans any bull-fighting in his town after posters appear announcing the arrival of Juan Gallardo, "the world's paramount toreador"—when in fact Gallardo is the name of a character in the upcoming *Blood and Sand* (Fred Niblo, 1922) with Rudolph Valentino, indeed a Paramount production.[39] To be enjoyed, such stunts therefore require the faculty, in the words of Michael Leja, of "looking askance"—the ability, new by the turn of the twentieth century, "to see skeptically, … to process visual experiences with some measure of suspicion, caution, and guile."[40] Without it, audiences will remain outside the magic circle of their play-spaces.

While a full history of those most inventive of movie promotional paratexts has yet to be written, it seems that ballyhoo stunts were progressively shunted from mainstream exploitation techniques in the 1920s to lower forms of B-grade exploitation cinema in the 1950s.[41] Yet their "pervasive playfulness"[42]—the sense that they offer that "everyday life is becoming interlaced with games"—has in recent years resurfaced, thanks to new digital technologies put to use in "pervasive games" such as alternate reality games (ARGs) or in "prankvertising" promotional stunts. As such, 1920s ballyhoo stunts are of peculiar importance for an archaeology of the issue of presence that modern technologies, from virtual reality goggles to augmented reality devices, have rendered particularly acute. In short, their hoaxing of the media still haunts the media and disrupts societies. Coming from a rich tradition of play in public places that would run from children's street games to ballyhoo stunts to flash mobs, pervasive games still run riots in modern cities with their unscheduled outpouring of media-derived fictions. The high-tech treasure hunt game *NIT 2000*, run in the summer of 1999, staged a scene at the WTC Marriott Hotel in New York that turned it, in the fictional world of the game, into a terrorist headquarters. Police were alerted to the presence of suspicious-looking vials of nuclear waste discovered by hotel cleaners, though no charges were filed.[43]

Some seven years later, similar hoaxing of American public space was proving far more complicated to maneuver. "Five teenage girls from Portage County face potential criminal charges after attempting to play a real-life version of *Super Mario Brothers*," local newspapers from Ravenna, Ohio, reported in April 2006. Their crime: deploying through the city streets seventeen large yellow bricks derived from the computer game, in imitation of an art project launched by Canadian artist Posterchild.[44] In this way, the presence of media fictions remains a potentially dangerous and unreconciled zone of transactions.

Prankvertising, notably, has recently come to the foreground of communication practices as the most obvious recent evolution of media hoaxing that ballyhoo stunts made popular as early as the 1920s. For film promotion, a spectacular example would be the otherworldly telekinetic powers demonstrated by an angered customer in a New York coffee shop in October 2013, all part of a promotion campaign for the upcoming release of the movie *Carrie* (Kimberly Peirce, 2013).[45] Crucially, such stunts are now relayed via YouTube, their popularity measured in the number of views recorded. Inspired by traditional TV forms of "punking," these elaborate forms of advertising play directly on our supposed inability to visually process the increase in perceptual realism that new digital media offer. For the upcoming release of *The Last Exorcism Part II* (Ed Gass-Donnelly, 2013), customers at a beauty salon in New York were filmed as they were made to suddenly see glimpses of a dead girl in a mirror, momentarily unable, it seemed, to distinguish between the digital image and their own mirror reflection.[46]

One prankvertising stunt for LG TVs is even more explicit in putting into play the increase in perceptual realism that digital media offer. An 84-inch HD TV is made to replace a window in an office where job applicants are being interviewed; images showing a comet hitting the city beyond the "window," and the impact approaching the building, are projected on the TV; the applicants, possibly actors, mistake this for real images and panic. This video, posted on YouTube on 2 September 2013, has so far been seen by more than 17 million people—thus ensuring dramatic brand exposure.[47] In its mix of media magic and more traditional hoaxing, lying and manipulative though it may be, such prankvertising explicitly proposes that audiences play with the possibility of a sudden expansion of media imaginaries into real everyday life, and requires that we still rehearse our skills at "looking askance."

As these modern variants show, an understanding of 1920s ballyhoo stunts still matters to the study of media paratexts, for they introduce a key dimension in the audience's relationship to media worlds: the hoaxing of the media. The contemporary media literature on presence has so far insisted on defining it as the illusion of non-mediation in the experience of digital and/or fictional objects—defining presence, essentially, as illusion. What this research on film paratexts shows is that presence should be approached through the exact reverse prism as audiences work their way from paratexts to textual encounter—not as an illusionary psychological state where media vanishes, but as the concrete experience of media as a game. Media do not vanish but trace the magic circle where the game will be played. In the end, it is the nature of the presence that 1920s ballyhoo stunts propose that still matters today: the presence of playful fictionality within every-day spaces—a presence that modern media still deploy, from movie-inspired prankvertising stunts to transmedia film world expansions through ARGs. Media fictions, this study suggests, are, through ephemeral paratexts, made present in our everyday life in a rather distinctive and historically resilient way: neither fully virtual nor fully real, they are a sort of embodied fictionality that transforms objects, buildings, streets, and people into active characters in the elaboration of modern spaces of heterotopia.

Notes

1. Jonathan Gray, *Show Sold Separately: Promos, Spoilers, and Other Media Paratexts* (New York: New York University Press, 2010), 4.
2. Barbara Klinger, "Digressions at the Cinema: Reception and Mass Culture," *Cinema Journal* 28.4 (1989): 9.
3. Gérard Genette, *Seuils* (Paris: éditions du Seuil, 1987), 8.
4. As Victor Burgin has proposed in *The Remembered Film* (London: Reaktion, 2004), 9–10.
5. Phil Wickham, "Scrapbooks, Soap Dishes and Screen Dreams: Ephemera, Everyday Life and Cinema History," *New Review of Film and Television Studies* 8.3 (2010): 319.
6. For other examples of off-screen studies dealing with 1920s cinema, see: Vincenz Hediger, "Putting the Spectators in a Receptive Mood" in *Limina/Le soglie del film/Film's Thresholds/X Convegno internazionale di studi sul cinema/X International Film Studies Conference, University of Udine*, eds. Veronica Innocenti and Valentina Re (Udine, Italy: Forum, 2004), 291–309; Gwendolyn Waltz, "Confounding! Sense Deception and 'Film to Life' Effects" in *XI Convegno Internazionale di Studi sul Cinema: I cinque sensi del cinema/The Five Senses of Cinema*, ed. Alice Autelitano, Veronica Innocenti and Valentina Re (Udine, Italy: Forum, 2005), 161–173; Phil Wagner, "'An America Not Quite Mechanized': Fanchon and Marco, Inc. Perform Modernity," *Film History* 23.3 (2011): 251–267.
7. Stephen Heath, "Screen Images, Film Memory," *Edinburgh Magazine* 1 (1976): 33–42.
8. *Motion Picture News*, 30 January 1926: 580.
9. *Motion Picture News*, 8 November 1919: 3435.

10. *Motion Picture News*, 28 October 1922: 2793.

11. *Motion Picture News*, 6 February 1926: 689.

12. *The New York Times*, 8 June 1924: X2.

13. *New York Tribune*, 24 May 1920: 18.

14. "Tumulty Letter in Press Agent Inquiry," *The New York Times*, 30 July 1920: 8.

15. *Motion Picture News* 26: 24, 9 December 1922: 2989.

16. *Exhibitors' Herald*, 12 January 1924: 36.

17. *Motion Picture News*, 2 September 1922: 1141.

18. *Motion Picture World*, 19 April 1919. It would seem fairly obvious that organizing a fake Bolshevik riot in the midst of an American city in 1919 is an idea that is promised, indeed, to "boomerang." And so it did: alarmed by this advice and its potential for "riotous demonstration," Labor Secretary William B. Wilson immediately asked U.S. General Prosecutor A. Mitchell Palmer to contemplate bringing the magazine, *The Motion Picture World*, to justice ("Raps 'Bolshevist' Movie," *The New York Times*, 19 April 1919: 6.

19. Harold Franklin, *Motion Picture Theater Management* (New York: Doran, 1927), 250.

20. Laura Kent Mason, "The Movies Outdo Barnum," *Motion Picture Magazine* 27.5, June 1924: 78.

21. Anne Cronin, "Publics and Publicity: Outdoor Advertising and Urban Space," in *Public Space, Media Space*, eds. Chris Berry, Janet Harbord, and Rachel Moore (London: Palgrave Macmillan, 2013), 272–275.

22. Cheryl Campanella Bracken and Paul D. Skalski, eds., *Immersed in Media: Telepresence in Everyday Life* (New York: Routledge, 2010), xvii.

23. *Motion Picture News*, 22 November 1919.

24. *Motion Picture News*, 26 August 1922.

25. Harry Reichenbach and David Freedman, *Phantom Fame: The Anatomy of Ballyhoo* (New York: Simon & Schuster, 1931), 106.

26. *The New York Tribune*, 8 March 1920.

27. The *New York Tribune* reveals the whole story on 27 July 1920. Possibly boosted by such publicity, the film plays for two whole weeks.

28. "Swann to Run Down Publicity Fakers," *The New York Times*, 30 July 1920, 8.

29. "*Blind Bargain* Victim Brings Space in Newspapers," *Motion Picture News*, 23 December 1922, 3196. The film, a variation on the Frankenstein story, has an author, Robert Sandell, agreeing to a test that will change him *back* into a monkey, thus allowing the mad doctor, Dr. Lamb, to prove the theory of evolution. It thus offers another fascinating point of contact between fiction and reality, by tapping into a contemporary debate that will come to the surface in the Scopes Monkey Trial of 1925 in Tennessee.

30. I am here using the notion proposed by Daniel Boorstin, *The Image: A Guide to Pseudo-Events in America* (New York: Harper & Row, 1964).

31. "Lion, Here to See Sights, Is Guest in Broadway Hotel," *The New York Tribune* 24 May 1920: 18.

32. *Paramount—Your Contract for Paramount Pictures*, August 1922–January 1923.

33. "Police Stunts Used on *I Am the Law* at Gadsden, Ala.," *Motion Picture News* 7 October 1922: 1754.

34. "Kansas City Police to Aid *In the Name of the Law*," *Motion Picture News* 21 October 1922: 2027.

35. On Barnum's "operational aesthetics," see Neil Harris, *Humbug: The Art of P.T. Barnum* (Chicago: University of Chicago Press, 1973).
36. *The Film Year Book of 1927*, published in 1928 by John W. Alicoate, offers some twenty pages of "Practical Showmanship Ideas" where most of the stunts in use in the early 1920s may still be found (482–504).
37. *Motion Picture News*, 2 January 1926: 79.
38. Bryan Alexander has proposed that "literary hoaxes," which he sees as behind the origin of modern ARGs, are "bimodal, as they create two castes of readers: Those who see through the text to expose the joke and those who take the text at face value." Bryan Alexander, "Antecedents to Alternate Reality Games," in *Alternate Reality Games White Paper*, eds. A. Martin, B. Thompson and T. Chatfield (International Game Developers Association, 2006), 61.
39. "*Blood and Sand* Is Billed as Bull-Fight at Mattoon," *Motion Picture News*, 28 October 1922: 2168.
40. Michael Leja, *Looking Askance: Skepticism and American Art from Eakins to Duchamp* (Berkeley: University of California Press, 2004), 1.
41. For an informal exposé of advertising stunts in 1950s American B cinema, see Mark Thomas McGee, *Beyond Ballyhoo: Motion Picture Promotion and Gimmicks* (Jefferson, NC: McFarland, 1989).
42. This is the term used to designate a tendency shared across cultures and civilization to put reality in play, according to Markus Montola, Jaako Stenros, and Annika Waern, *Pervasive Games: Theory and Design* (Amsterdam: Elsevier/ Morgan Kaufmann, 2009), xix.
43. Markus Montola et al., *Pervasive Games*, 206.
44. Jane McGonigal, "This Might Be a Game: Ubiquitous Play and Performance at the Turn of the Twenty-First Century" (Ph.D. dissertation, University of California, 2006).
45. "Sony Spools West Village Coffee Shop with 'Carrie' Mind Control Stunt," *New York Daily News*, 8 October 2013, accessed 15 September 2014, *http:// www.nydailynews.com/entertainment/tv-movies/sony-spooks-west-village-cafe- customers-carrie-mind-control-stunt-article-1.1479485*.
46. This prank was staged by New York ad agency Thinkmodo, which was also responsible for the *Carrie* stunt. "Why Terrifying Pranks Make the Best Advertising," *Bloomberg Businessweek*, 1 November 2013, accessed 15 September 2014, *http:// www.businessweek.com/articles/2013-11-01/why-terrifying-pranks-make-the- best-advertising*.
47. "LG's Shock Ad Raises Questions about 'Prankvertising'," *ABC News*, 6 September 2013, accessed 15 September 2014. *http://abcnews.go.com/blogs/ business/2013/09/lgs-shock-ad-raises-questions-about-prankvertising*.

References

Alexander, Bryan, "Antecedents to Alternate Reality Games." In *Alternate Reality Games White Paper*. eds. Adam Martin, Brooke Thompson, and Tom Chatfield, 8–15. International Game Developers Association, 2006.
Alicoate, John W. *The Film Year Book of 1927*, New York: The Film Daily, 1928.
Anonymous. "Raps 'Bolshevist' Movie." *The New York Times*, 19 April 1919.
Anonymous. "Lion, Here to See Sights, Is Guest in Broadway Hotel." *The New York Tribune*, 24 May 1920.

Anonymous. "Swann to Run Down Publicity Fakers." *The New York Times*, 30 July 1920.

Anonymous. "Tumulty Letter in Press Agent Inquiry." *The New York Times*, 30 July 1920.

Anonymous. "Police Stunts Used on *I Am the Law* at Gadsden, Ala." *Motion Picture News*, 7 October 1922.

Anonymous. "Kansas City Police to Aid *In the Name of the Law*." *Motion Picture News*, 21 October 1922.

Anonymous. "*Blood and Sand* Is Billed as Bull-Fight at Mattoon." *Motion Picture News*, 28 October 1922.

Anonymous. "*Blind Bargain* Victim Brings Space in Newspapers." *Motion Picture News*, 23 December 1922. Anonymous. "LG's Shock Ad Raises Questions about 'Prankvertising.'" *ABC News*, 6 September 2013. Accessed 15 September 2014. *http://abcnews.go.com/blogs/business/2013/09/lgs-shock-ad-raises-questions-about-prankvertising.*

Boorstin, Daniel. *The Image: A Guide to Pseudo-Events in America*. New York: Harper & Row, 1964.

Burgin, Victor. *The Remembered Film*. London: Reaktion, 2004.

Campanella Bracken, Cheryl, and Paul D. Skalski, eds. *Immersed in Media: Telepresence in Everyday Life*. New York: Routledge, 2010.

Caulfield, Philip. "Sony Spools West Village Coffee Shop with 'Carrie' Mind Control Stunt." *New York Daily News*, 8 October 2013. Accessed 15 September 2014. *http://www.nydailynews.com/entertainment/tv-movies/sony-spooks-west-village-cafe-customers-carrie-mind-control-stunt-article-1.1479485.*

Cronin, Anne. "Publics and Publicity: Outdoor Advertising and Urban Space." In *Public Space, Media Space*, eds. Chris Berry, Janet Harbord, and Rachel Moore, 265–277. London: Palgrave Macmillan, 2013.

Franklin, Harold. *Motion Picture Theater Management*. New York: Doran, 1927.

Genette, Gérard. *Seuils*. Paris: éditions du Seuil, 1987.

Gray, Jonathan. *Show Sold Separately: Promos, Spoilers, and Other Media Paratexts*. New York: New York University Press, 2010.

Harris, Neil. *Humbug: The Art of P.T. Barnum*. Chicago: University of Chicago Press, 1973.

Heath, Stephen. "Screen Images, Film Memory." *Edinburgh Magazine* 1 (1976), 33–42.

Hediger, Vinzenz. "'Putting the Spectators in a Receptive Mood.'" In *Limina/Le soglie del film/Film's Thresholds/X Convegno internazionale di studi sul cinema/X International Film Studies Conference, University of Udine*, eds. Veronica Innocenti and Valentina Re, 291–309. Udine, Italy: Forum, 2004.

Klinger, Barbara. "Digressions at the Cinema: Reception and Mass Culture." *Cinema Journal* 28.4 (1989): 3–19.

Leja, Michael. *Looking Askance: Skepticism and American Art from Eakins to Duchamp*. Berkeley: University of California Press, 2004.

Mason, Laura Kent. "The Movies Outdo Barnum." *Motion Picture Magazine* 27.5 (1924): 51–52, 78.

McGee, Mark Thomas. *Beyond Ballyhoo: Motion Picture Promotion and Gimmicks*. Jefferson, NC: McFarland, 1989.

McGonigal, Jane E. *This Might Be a Game: Ubiquitous Play and Performance at the Turn of the Twenty-First Century*. Ph.D. Dissertation (Berkeley: University of California, 2006).

Montola, Markus, Jaako Stenros, and Annika Waern. *Pervasive Games: Theory and Design*. Amsterdam: Elsevier/Morgan Kaufmann, 2009.

Reichenbach, Harry, and David Freedman. *Phantom Fame: The Anatomy of Ballyhoo*. New York: Simon & Schuster, 1931.

Suddath, Claire. "Why Terrifying Pranks Make the Best Advertising." *Bloomberg Businessweek*, 01 November 2013. Accessed 15 September 2014. *http://www. businessweek.com/articles/2013-11-01/why-terrifying-pranks-make-the-best-advertising*.

Wagner, Phil. "'An America Not Quite Mechanized': Fanchon and Marco, Inc. Perform Modernity." *Film History* 23.3 (2011): 251–267.

Waltz, Gwendolyn. "Confounding! Sense Deception and 'Film to Life' Effects." *XI Convegno Internazionale di Studi sul Cinema: I cinque sensi del cinema/The Five Senses of Cinema*, eds. Alice Autelitano, Veronica Innocenti and Valentina Re, 161–173. Udine, Italy: Forum, 2005.

Wasson, Haidee. "Electric Homes! Automatic Movies! Efficient Entertainment!: 16mm and Cinema's Domestication in the 1920s." *Cinema Journal* 48.4 (Summer 2009): 1–21.

Wickham, Phil. "Scrapbooks, Soap Dishes and Screen Dreams: Ephemera, Everyday Life and Cinema History." *New Review of Film and Television Studies* 8.3 (2010): 313–330.

8 Sound Memories

"Talker Remakes," Paratexts, and the Cinematic Past

Kathleen Loock

Movies had a short shelf life during the early years of Hollywood's golden age, before television reruns and the emergence of information storage technologies like VHS and DVD ensured their re-watchability. They were ephemeral commodities whose lifespan depended on prolonged first-runs, rereleases and—especially after the film industry's transition to sound between 1927 and 1931—on remakes. This chapter argues that the so-called "talker remakes" of the 1930s and the paratexts surrounding them helped to construct and communicate a cinematic past and archive. They anticipated the ways in which originals and remakes are being consumed and understood today, where television channels, online platforms, DVD special editions, and bonus features are specifically designed for a digital media culture that thrives on remembering, storing, and archiving Hollywood's past and present.

Historical perspectives on Hollywood's remaking practices are still largely absent from the research done in remake studies. The field tends to focus on definitions and taxonomies, on more contemporary case studies, and on cross-cultural circulations of films and television series. "Talker remakes" have received very little attention so far, even though their analysis promises to yield valuable insights into the cultural work of remaking—understood as a historically evolving practice of innovative reproduction that has taken on various meanings in changing cinematic contexts.[1] Drawing on film-historical studies that examine the transition from silent to sound cinema and often refer to the 1930s wave of "talker remakes," this chapter engages in what Jonathan Gray has termed "off-screen studies"[2] in order to explore a very specific moment in film history from a remake studies perspective and open it up for further investigation and debate.

In keeping with Gray's conception that paratexts play a "constitutive role in creating textuality,"[3] I will focus on the ways in which industry news items, film reviews, fan letters, contests, movie quizzes, and commentaries on the silent-to-sound remaking practice published in trade papers and fan magazines produced meaning. I argue that these different paratexts provided interpretive frameworks for understanding the sound innovation and its impact on Hollywood cinema, both on the level of individual films and within a larger film-historical context. They kept the memory of silent film versions alive, thereby highlighting, making visible, and structuring the historic development of cinema as a technological medium. These paratexts, in other words, served archival and mnemonic functions that contributed to Hollywood's processes of self-historicizing by remembering silent films as something of the past and by framing the transition to sound as a narrative of cinema's technological progress.

"Talker Remakes" and the Transition to Sound: Paratextual Framing in Trade Papers and Fan Magazines

"Hollywood has gone Talking Picture crazy," Martin Martin began her "Chatter from Hollywood" column in the 1928 October issue of the fan magazine *Screenland*. Later, she observed that "[i]t is fashionable to remake the stories that were successes."[4] Remaking box office hits had been an established practice in Hollywood by then,[5] but it was gaining a new level of prominence with the transition to sound and throughout the 1930s. Cinema attendance decisively increased, with between 80 and 90 million Americans going to see double features every week in theaters that remained open all year long,[6] and Hollywood produced 400 to 800 films each year to meet the public demand for talking pictures.[7] Recycling old properties was both a way to "[feed] the maw of exhibition"[8] when studios found it difficult to find fresh stories for the talkies and to encourage return visits with tried and proven material from cinema's recent past.

Under the headline "Old Films Offer Suitable Fodder for Talkies," the trade journal *Motion Picture News* reported on 16 February 1929 that many past successes were being "exhumed" by the studios.[9] A year later, in 1930, playwright and screenwriter Robert E. Sherwood wrote that he was "surprised that there have not been more [remakes of old silent pictures in talking form]."[10] In this Bell Syndicate opinion piece, printed in the leading industry publication *The Film Daily*, Sherwood further explained that "[i]n view of the widely advertised shortage of stories in Hollywood ... it would seem to be logical to go through the files and resurrect all the acknowledged triumphs of earlier days."[11] The same argument was brought forth in other news items, where it was often cast in a similar language. Articles spoke of "box office successes of former days [that] are to be reborn,"[12] for instance, and producers who were "digging deep"[13]—either to find a lost gem in "the veritable Treasure Chest [studio production had accumulated in the past two decades]"[14] or to "Rattl[e] the Skeleton" and "unearth old material for talkers."[15] The word choice evokes vivid images of zombie-like resurrections from the dead, and of tomb raiding and adventurous treasure hunts in the studios' archival vaults. Furthermore, it is indicative of the transient nature of Hollywood movies, which were quickly outdated and forgotten.

In the introduction to his edited collection *Ephemeral Media*, Paul Grainge has drawn attention to the ephemeral properties of film at the time.

He explains that even though "motion pictures achieve[d] greater solidity in their length, circulation and status as material property" as the Hollywood studio system began to operate and prosper, "film remained a time-specific and place-bound encounter."[16] Audiences could see a feature film while it played at a theater near them, but once it was taken off the bill, it would (most likely) never return. During the silent era, it was common that major productions like Cecil B. DeMille's original *The Ten Commandments* (1923) ran for up to 62 weeks,[17] yet opportunities for repeat viewing associated with such long first-run exhibition practices dwindled when the U.S. film industry converted to sound. Movies became cinema's main attraction, the lavish stage shows that had accompanied the screenings disappeared altogether, and first-run engagements were reduced to only a few weeks or days.[18]

The major studios MGM, Paramount, RKO, Warner Bros., and Twentieth Century Fox (known as the "Big Five") organized their film production and distribution according to the run-zone-clearance system, which "favored rapid turnovers" and was "almost fully geared to novelty."[19] Vinzenz Hediger has observed that "[o]ld films held little value in this system," adding that rereleases or reissues, which offered another opportunity to re-watch a favorite movie or finally enjoy it if one had missed it the first time around, "were usually limited to a few major films, particularly to those that had been box-office successes during their original release."[20] However, the transition to sound complicated matters. Although silent films such as *The Phantom of the Opera* (Rupert Julian, 1925), *The Birth of a Nation* (D. W. Griffith, 1915), *Ben-Hur* (Fred Niblo, 1925), and *The Big Parade* (King Vidor, 1925) attracted large audiences when they were rereleased with new synchronized music scores, sound effects, and added dialogue sequences in the early sound years, the exhibition of silent films decreased throughout the 1930s and was extremely rare by the end of the decade.[21] The best chance silent films had for an afterlife was to be remade, not "as pepped-up reissues," as *Motion Picture News* put it, but as "made-over, new material," featuring new stars, and with "the story ... changed entirely in many cases."[22]

As mentioned earlier, trade journals were concerned with the perceived shortage of suitable talkie material and printed news items about the studios' search for remakable properties in their vaults. I argue that these publications were crucial agents in analyzing and making sense of the remake boom that was set in motion by the sound innovation. They constituted a paratextual framework that actively negotiated the meanings and implications of talking picture for the U.S. film business. By 1930, trade papers provided long lists of the remakes studios had scheduled on their annual production slates, published production news about individual remakes as well as rumors about future projects, and printed interviews with leading industry figures.

Thus, Universal boss Carl Laemmle Jr. told *Motion Picture News* in January 1930 that "silent successes of other years, remade with sound and dialogue, are registering heavily at the box-office," adding that "[s]hortage of talker story material, which producers are reported as viewing with concern, can be and is being overcome, to a large extent, by the remaking of pictures upon which the public has put its stamp of emphatic approval in other years."[23] Such authorizing statements notwithstanding, it was obvious that the film industry had difficulties fathoming in which direction it was heading. With a "minimum of 70 Remakes" scheduled for the 1929–1930 season, *Motion Picture News* expected a lineup of more than 125 remakes for the next season[24] but had to revise its projection by the end of the year. On 22 November 1930, another headline announced: "Remake Question Still Puzzling Studio Chiefs."[25]

Audience reaction was unpredictable, and "talker remakes" quickly turned out to be anything but a safe bet for regularizing audiences and encouraging return visits to the theaters, even if the original silent film had been a hit. *Motion Picture News* stated that some remakes "have made money at the box office," some "have not grossed any great amount, but are out of the red," and "others have not measured up to the standards of good pictures and have suffered accordingly."[26] These different outcomes confused producers and studio bosses, who considered remaking a strategy to manage risk in times of uncertainty (at that point many of them still thought that the silent film would continue to exist alongside the sound film). While they were convinced that "any good picture will register at the box-office regardless of whether or not it has been made previously,"[27] the remake trend stalled temporarily, with only seventeen and nine scheduled for the following two seasons. As industry insiders grappled with the "Remake Question," moviegoers eagerly responded to the "talker remakes," offering their own analyses and paratextual commentaries in popular fan magazines.

The late 1920s had seen a proliferation of fan magazines that catered to what Donald Crafton has called "Americans' movie craziness."[28] These publications claimed to speak for their audiences (who were mostly female readers under 25) and cultivated fan response.[29] This is why Crafton has described fan magazines "as mediators of a complex web of exchange between the industry, the commercial world, and the consumer … [and] as filters through which ideas about the movies emerged."[30] The magazines offered fan-oriented coverage about what was happening in Hollywood, on the set and behind-the-scenes. They also suggested that fans might have some degree of control over the direction in which the film business would develop. This concerned their favorite star's fate during the transition to sound, for instance, as fan magazines weaved elaborate narratives around the question of whether or not the star would be able to master the microphone and encouraged their readers to express their opinions and take part in the star's triumphs or hardships.[31]

In its 1930 September issue, *Screenland* held a contest that centered on the career of Mexican American actor Ramon Novarro. In order to win Novarro's autographed guitar, readers were asked to send a letter to the magazine, answering the following question: "Which of the following Ramon Novarro silent screen successes would you like to have him remake into talking pictures: *The Prisoner of Zenda* [Rex Ingram, 1922], *Scaramouche* [Rex Ingram, 1924], *Ben Hur* [Fred Niblo, 1925], *The Student Prince* [Ernst Lubitsch, 1928]?"[32] The contest took up a double page in the magazine issue and everything about it—the prize question, the gift guitar, several photos showing Novarro with the musical instrument, and the accompanying texts—advertised the actor's singing and speaking voice, thereby constructing a narrative around the star-persona in which his outstanding vocal qualities would enable Novarro to make a smooth transition. The contest may not have advanced his acting career (all four films were eventually remade, yet none of them starred Novarro), but it illustrates how *Screenland* engaged its readers by suggesting that they could actively participate in Hollywood's transition to sound.

The Novarro contest further implied that fans were in a position to influence the studios' decisions concerning which silent films to remake as talkies. Fan magazines usually printed letters that contained specific suggestions for movies their readers wanted to see remade and for which they would return to the theaters. Published letters were often awarded small prizes, so there is no assurance as to their authenticity.[33] They might have been written by staff members or freelance authors with an eye on the prize;[34] after all, leading fan magazines like *Photoplay* paid up to $10 prize money each month for the best letter published in full. Then again, Hollywood was desperate to learn more about audience tastes and moviegoing habits. Donald Crafton notes that, especially in the period between 1928 and 1931 when sound was gradually introduced, "films [were] more like tests than texts," and that the industry was eager to engage "with active but unpredictable consumers."[35] Talking trailers addressed cinemagoers directly, for example, and asked them to share their preferences with the theater manager who would then pass them on to the studios.[36] *Photoplay*'s competitor, *Modern Screen*, had a "Between You and Me" department (with the telling subheading "Where Readers Become Authors"), in which the editor reminded fans that they did have a say in the movie business:

> Dear Friends: Right now Hollywood is making more effort to win your approval than ever before. … Hollywood is ripe for new ideas. … Perhaps you have hit on the type of picture which would be a tremendous success and which you would like above all others. It may be a new type of story. Or a new treatment of an old type of story. Whatever it is, I'd be glad to have your ideas. Come on, now, drop me a line and pour out your ideas.[37]

Reader suggestions for "talker remakes" that were printed in the letter columns were usually not connected to a particular Hollywood star. Rather, they promoted a good story that would benefit from a talkie treatment. In the

July 1933 issue of *The New Movie Magazine,* Jack Kleinman from Chicago thought that "a lot of fans will flock to the box office to see ... new pictures made from the best pictures before the talkies."[38] "Talker remakes" of *The Lost World* (Harry O. Hoyt, 1925) and *The Volga Boatman* (DeMille, 1926), Kleinman was convinced, "would be a great help to the box-office in these days of depression."[39] Mrs. Effie Myers from Williamsport, Indiana, in contrast, hoped to see a sound version of *Ben-Hur*. "I hardly think it needs to be remade," she wrote in her letter to *The New Movie Magazine*, "(in my opinion the acting and filming couldn't be improved upon), but with the addition of sound it would be superb—what a thrill seeing [this picture] again would bring!"[40]

While many fans embraced "talker remakes" of their favorite movies, they also used the space of the fan magazines to air their discontent with individual films and, more generally, Hollywood's silent-to-sound remaking practice.[41] Toward the end of the 1930s and into the early 1940s, there seemed to have been an important shift in opinion, as Mrs. Frank Kurlick's letter in *Photoplay*'s "Speak for Yourself" column indicates. "Something must be done about the new evil perpetrated by the movie moguls," she demanded, referring to "remakes of pictures that movie-goers have not yet forgotten."[42] Mrs. Kurlick wondered: "Why should I pay to see a story ... that I know beforehand?"[43] A couple of months later, Sue Anna from Lexington, Kentucky, asked the same question in a letter that won *Photoplay*'s $10 prize. "Doesn't Hollywood have any original stories left?" she wanted to know.[44] Interestingly, Sue Anna did not condemn Hollywood's remaking practice as such but was against "remakes of pictures [that are] still easily remembered by movie-goers." She even suggested that studios "go a little further into the years," in order to find "something worth reviving" that "has been forgotten by all but a few and would be something new to the present generation."[45] Prizewinning or not—these opinions were contested, and the remake debate in *Photoplay*'s letter column took a different turn when Clarence Thornbey and other readers set out to defend the practice. Thornbey wrote:

> In "Speak for Yourself" and other various columns I have read articles that start out "Why all the remakes of old pictures? Aren't there any new stories in Hollywood?" etc. Don't those people that write that stuff ever realize that the younger generation likes to go to shows too? They like to see famous stories on the screen no matter how old they are, just so they're entertaining.[46]

Contrary to one contemporary critic's opinion that remakes lose their appeal because "themes grow old and tastes are changeful"[47]—a view that perfectly encapsulated Hollywood's obsessive fear of being outdated—many movie fans clung to the stories, (sometimes) regardless of stars, and appreciated the fact that remakes preserved the repertoire of popular narratives for themselves and for younger generations. It is in this sense that cinematic paratexts surrounding the "talker remakes" of the 1930s fulfilled more than a communicative function that enabled producers and fans to make sense of the transition to sound. They also cast these films as sites of memory, cultural archives, and catalysts for processes of media-generational identity formations.

"Talker Remakes" as Sites of Film-Historical Memory: Paratextual Constructions of a Cinematic Past

When Cecil B. DeMille remade *The Squaw Man* as a talkie in 1931, editor Frederick James Smith wrote in *The New Movie Magazine*:

> This is Mr. De Mille's [*sic*] third production of *The Squaw Man*. It was the first film he ever made, back in 1912 [sic]. Dustin Farnum played the title role then. In 1919 he made it again, with Elliott Dexter as the Englishman who married an Indian girl. Both these versions of the old Edwin Milton Royle melodrama were silent films, of course. Now, in 1931, comes *The Squaw Man* as a talkie.[48]

In his short review, Smith listed key dates and facts about *The Squaw Man*, chronologically following the three different cinematic incarnations of the movie, all of which can (quite curiously) be traced back to the same director and his sentimental attachment to the movie with which he started his Hollywood career. What changed, then, were the actors starring in each version, and, of course, the fact that the latest *Squaw Man* was a "talker remake." Strictly speaking, however, Smith did not say anything about DeMille's new picture in these lines, which constituted no less than half of the entire review. Instead, he distinguished himself as a connoisseur of the cinematic past with ample knowledge about actors and directors of twenty years ago, and he passed this knowledge on to the readers of *The New Movie Magazine*.

If Donald Crafton states that fan magazines "'fanned' consumers' desires to learn more about movies and to become 'fanatic' about their screen favorites,"[49] one can add that they also fostered film-historical knowledge about those favorites, especially when "talker remakes" were involved. Such practices of knowledge transfer counteracted the ephemeral nature of film (as described above), and transformed the remakes and their paratexts into agents of remembrance work. Toward the mid-1930s and the end of the decade, remembering what had quickly been labeled the "silent era" became, in fact, a regular feature of fan magazines, as I will illustrate with the following two examples from *Modern Screen* and *Photoplay*.

In the February 1936 issue of the popular fan magazine *Modern Screen*, readers found a double page with the heading "Yesterday—Today." The serif typeface used for "Yesterday," printed at the top of the left page, lent a vintage appearance to the word and stressed its semiotic relationship to a time already past. On the right page, the word "Today" was printed in a modern-looking Art Deco typeface, whose sans-serif letters consisted of stylized and geometric shapes. The opposition between past and present expressed by the words and fonts was further emphasized on the left and right margins, where decorative drawings of two female figures dressed in different fashion styles embellished the double page. The woman on the left wore a long, heavily draped, corseted outfit of the late Victorian era, finished with a broad feathered hat and an umbrella. Her counterpart on the right margin had a much simpler and streamlined silhouette, wearing a fashionable 1930s clutch coat with wide shoulders and a narrow waist. It reached below the knee and was trimmed with a stylish fur collar and cuffs. Her look was complete with a small hat, gloves, and a dog on a leash. Heading and illustrations created the context in which the photos printed in the center were supposed to be consumed by the readers. "Remember these great scenes in silent films?" they could read under the drawing on the left; "And now each finds voice in a modern version," on the right.[50]

In the middle, twelve film stills from altogether six pictures (the silent originals and their remakes) were juxtaposed, prominently featuring the stars of each movie.[51] Short captions accompanied the photos and provided the film title, actors' names, and the year of the original. Under the influence of the temporal binary established by the suggestive typefaces and illustrations, the poses the stars assumed in these stills instantly exposed them as belonging to the past or the present because they stood in for a particular fashion, acting style, and film aesthetic that could be associated with either the silent or the sound cinema. *Modern Screen* did not explicitly spell out these connotations, but they were nonetheless foregrounded through the content and layout of the double page.

By asking readers to remember these silent films and by contrasting them with their modern sound versions, the fan magazine raised interest in a recent cinematic past and prompted its readers to recognize themselves as a media generation, existing in a sound film present that was clearly distinct from the silent era. Remakes made the differences between past and present visible, thereby enabling such media generational identifications among moviegoers. As *Modern Screen*'s double page suggests, however, feelings of belonging to this or that era required film-historical knowledge about originals that were no longer accessible to most contemporary viewers.[52] By the mid-1930s, only a few silent films still circulated in the free market; some were forever lost to nitrate fires, and others were intentionally destroyed by the studios to free up storage space for new films and reduce the risk of fires.[53] As fan magazines printed cinematic paratexts that were concerned with "talker remakes" and the silent originals from which they derived (just like *Modern Screen*'s "Yesterday–Today" item), they bestowed permanence on ephemeral silent pictures.

A couple of years later, in its 1938 November issue, *Photoplay* even set out to test its readers' film-historical knowledge with a movie quiz entitled "Match Them If You Can." Twenty film stills from silent pictures of the late 1910s and early 1920s and their contemporary "talker remakes" (which were all released around the time of publication, i.e., 1937 and 1938) had been arranged on a double page, surrounding a short text with instructions for taking the quiz. Readers were supposed to match scenes from the old films with scenes from the new ones, and had to fill in blank spaces with the film titles as well as the names of the actors for both the silent and the sound versions. Before providing the rules for the quiz *Photoplay* addressed the nature and life-prolonging effects of the remake: "In addition to the 'flash in the pan' film, which is seen by many audiences and then consigned to oblivion," the magazine explained, "there are those perennial classics that live forever in the form of 'remakes'—new versions of old films that are often remade two or three times."[54]

Despite this explanation, *Photoplay* obviously expected its readers to be already familiar with Hollywood's practice of remaking former box office hits. After all, at least 75 percent of the answers had to be correct in order to pass the test. Anyone who knew 85 percent of the answers, one could read in the instructions, was on a par with the magazine's movie experts. "If you're better than that, you won't need the answers found on page 83."[55] *Photoplay* elegantly packaged this hint on where to look for the correct matches and answers in the issue, before going into detail about the grading procedure that held special rewards for knowledge about the silent films. One could score a total of ten points for each question: five points for the film title that the original and remake shared, three points for the names of the actors in the old film, and two points for the names of the actors in the new version.[56]

Like *Modern Screen*'s "Yesterday–Today," "Match Them If You Can" illustrates the extent to which cinematic paratexts did remembrance work and encouraged fans to do the same. Once more, the transition to sound was presented as a momentous innovation that had a lasting impact on filmmaking and film aesthetics. Hollywood's conversion to sound was foregrounded and framed as a narrative of technological progress. Both in the layout of the double page and in the answers section, the remakes figured more prominently than their distant originals, and *Photoplay* clearly endorsed identifications with the updated versions of the sound era that replaced the silent pictures and that readers still had a chance to go and see in the theaters. Yet, the fan magazine was also invested in collectively constructing and preserving the cinematic past with this quiz, and it becomes apparent how paratexts like this one contributed to the ways in which Hollywood imagined itself and wrote its own history in and with "talker remakes."[57]

"Talker remakes" were assigned to the sound age, while their precursors belonged to another time, the silent era. The new labels caught on quickly during the transition to sound, and the films associated with each functioned as structuring devices, marking different stages in a teleologically progressing film history that depended on technological innovation. Along these lines, talkies were generally considered to represent cinema's evolution toward a mature art. In the late 1920s, such views were embedded in prevalent discourses of scientific progress as Donald Crafton has shown. "Like other electrical technologies," he notes, "sound film was on the cusp of modernity."[58]

Against this background, the paratextual framing of "talker remakes" as film historical structuring devices is consistent with Hollywood's self-descriptions following the conversion to sound. As Shelley Stamp has argued in her work on Lois Weber, Hollywood showed "interest in chronicling its own past ..., beginning [by the late 1920s] to mark anniversaries and milestones, the discourse surrounding which crafted a particular story about Hollywood's past in which an older generation of Hollywood denizens was distanced from a new, modern generation."[59] If such anniversaries and milestones "[had] come to perform canonical and commemorative functions, inscribing passing ephemera into the permanence of history,"[60] "talker remakes" and the different paratexts surrounding them in trade papers and fan magazines also participated in Hollywood's processes of self-historicizing. In fact, the remakes themselves ultimately served paratextual functions since they operated as frames and filters (in Jonathan Gray's sense) through which audiences could experience cinema's progress.

By the mid-1930s and toward the end of the decade, as the novelty of the talking picture started to fade and the last silent films disappeared from the market, "talker remakes" had begun to do more than merely replace old films from another era: they helped preserve an otherwise ephemeral cinematic past. Paratexts underscored the remakes' mnemonic and archival functions, and within the interpretive framework constructed by news items, film reviews, fan letters, contests, and movie quizzes, these films documented cinema's technological development and became sites of film-historical memory that were closely tied to a specific media generation.

Conclusion

Many decades later, in today's digital age, "talker remakes" are themselves part of the cinematic past. Hollywood has remade these films time and again for new media generations, bringing them up to date with the latest technological innovations such as color film, wide screen, special effects, CGI (computer-generated imagery), and 3-D. Meanwhile, the early mnemonic and archival functions I have described for the "talker remakes" are radically changing in contemporary "home film cultures"[61] whose playback technologies extend the lifespan of old Hollywood movies so that they coexist alongside their latest remake. If chances to re-watch a favorite film once depended entirely on prolonged first-runs, reissues, remakes, or, later, on inflexible television program schedules, VHS and DVD have lifted all external temporal constraints and created individualized possibilities for film consumption and repeat viewing. These new technologies have made the cinematic past increasingly more accessible and ultimately enabled viewers to become film collectors and cultural archaeologists.[62]

In the 1980s and 1990s, three cable channels devoted to classic film exhibition were launched in the United States (American Movie Classics [AMC], Turner Classic Movies [TCM], and Movies from Fox [FXM]), and "while profit-motivated, ... have achieved the status of central archives of the past, promoting viewers' awareness of film history, selecting films that will be remembered by future generations, and helping to prevent film illiteracy."[63] The channels' programming combines movies from the major studio libraries with original documentaries and programs framing the showcased Hollywood fare.[64] More paratexts are available on the channels' websites, which make up only three among numerous online platforms and forums dedicated to keeping the cinematic past alive. As far as the remake is concerned, however, the DVD has proven to be the medium that continues and remediates the format's film historical remembrance work in the digital age.

When it became apparent in the early 1990s that the theatrical success of remakes such as *Robin Hood: Prince of Thieves* (Kevin Reynolds, 1991), *Cape Fear* (Martin Scorsese, 1991), and *Father of the Bride* (Charles Shyer, 1991) stirred VHS sales and rentals of earlier versions, marketing strategies were adapted to accommodate viewer interest in the classics.[65] Soon, the release of new remakes coincided with the repackaging of older titles. Such "piggybacking" became gradually more sophisticated in the following years,[66] especially with the rise of the DVD, which quickly turned into the digital format of choice for home exhibition after it was introduced in 1997. DVD's larger storage capacity has made possible the inclusion of numerous extra features, including trailers, outtakes, commentary tracks, interviews, and making-of documentaries. This additional material explicitly invites the viewers' active engagement with a particular film, and—if that film is a remake—with the cinematic past.

In the case of contemporary Hollywood remakes like *King Kong* (Peter Jackson, 2005), for instance, the property's long history is discussed extensively in the DVD bonus features. This was, after all, the third cinematic incarnation of *King Kong*, after Merian C. Cooper's 1933 original and John Guillermin's remake from 1976. The *King Kong* Deluxe Extended DVD Edition, released in 2006, boasts over six hours of bonus material, including "King Kong Homage" on disc one—a featurette that explains all the remake's references to the 1933 original and juxtaposes several scenes from both movies for direct comparison. In fact, one entire disc of the three-disc set provides nothing but documentaries from what has been labeled "The King Kong Archives." These extras last over three hours and cover Peter Jackson's personal investment in *King Kong* as well as the origins of the project and the production of the film. Throughout, the 1933 original is presented as the reference point for the new *King Kong*, framing the remake as tribute to a milestone in film history. Jackson even claims in an interview: "I wanted our version of *Kong* to be like a thank you to the original film and to the people who worked on the original movie."[67] His statement is underscored by documentary sequences about filmmaking in the 1930s, the first *King Kong*'s groundbreaking stop-motion animation, the look of Skull Island in the 1933 film, and Peter Jackson and Naomi Watts visit with old-time actress Fay Wray.

While remakes and their cinematic paratexts in the digital age no longer need to save old films from sinking into oblivion, as their talkie counterparts once did during the 1930s, examples like *King Kong* demonstrate that they are still concerned with imparting film-historical knowledge. The much-maligned remake of the present day derives its own cultural value from connections to beloved film classics and celebrated landmarks of Hollywood cinema. Its paratexts—DVDs in particular—foreground these connections and enable viewers to engage with the intertextual relationship between original and remake. In doing so, paratexts add both aesthetic and historical value to the new version and encourage a mode of reception that promotes cultural archeology into a once ephemeral and now largely accessible cinematic past.

Notes

1. A larger project investigating Hollywood remaking, with the working title "Retrospective Serialization: Remaking as a Method of Cinematic Self-Historicizing," is currently being conducted by Frank Kelleter and myself within the Popular Seriality Research Unit at Freie Universität Berlin. See Frank Kelleter and Kathleen Loock, "Hollywood Remaking as Second-Order Serialization," in *Media of Serial Narrative*, ed. Frank Kelleter (Columbus: Ohio State University Press, 2016).
2. Johnathan Gray, *Show Sold Separately: Promos, Spoilers and Other Media Paratexts* (New York: New York University Press, 2010), 4, 7.
3. Ibid., 7.
4. Martin Martin, "Chatter from Hollywood," *Screenland* (October 1928): 68, 70.
5. Jennifer Forrest and Leonard R. Koos, "Reviewing Remakes: An Introduction," in *Dead Ringers: The Remake in Theory and Practice*, eds. Jennifer Forrest and Leonard R. Koos (Albany, NY: State University of New York Press, 2002), 2.
6. John Belton, *American Cinema/American Culture* (New York: McGraw-Hill, 1994), 3. Donald Crafton, *The Talkies: American Cinema's Transition to Sound, 1926–1931* (New York: Charles Scribner's Sons, 1997), 262.
7. Vinzenz Hediger, "'You Haven't Seen It Unless You Have Seen It at Least Twice': Film Spectatorship and the Discipline of Repeat Viewing," *Cinéma and Cie 5* (2004): 26.
8. Tino Balio, "Feeding the Maw of Exhibition," in *Grand Design: Hollywood as a Modern Business Enterprise, 1930–1939*, eds. Tino Balio (Berkeley: University of California Press, 1995), 73. See also Forrest and Koos, "Reviewing Remakes," 4.
9. "Old Silent Hits Offering a Solution for Shortage of Good Sound Material," *Motion Picture News*, 25 January 1930: 33.

10. Robert E. Sherwood, "Silent Successes Adaptable for Talkies," *The Film Daily*, 2 October 1930: 4.
11. Ibid.
12. "Hits to Be Made Again as Dialogue Pictures," *The Film Daily*, 10 April 1929: 6.
13. "'U' Digging into Files for Sound Remakes of Silents," *Motion Picture News*, 25 January 1930: 33.
14. Phil M. Daly, "Along the Rialto," *The Film Daily*, 31 October 1935: 3.
15. "Rattlin' the Skeleton," *Motion Picture News*, 25 January 1930: 33.
16. Paul Grainge, "Introduction: Ephemeral Media," in *Ephemeral Media: Transitory Screen Culture from Television to YouTube*, ed. Paul Grainge (London: BFI and Palgrave Macmillan, 2011), 5.
17. Hediger, "'You Haven't Seen It,'" 27.
18. Ibid.
19. Ibid., 26. Hediger explains: "An average film took two years to descend the ladder of the distribution system, from urban first run in prestigious palaces to lower-run and rural theaters. After their two-year distribution period most films were withdrawn and disappeared into the vaults of the studio" (26).
20. Ibid.
21. William M. Drew, *The Last Silent Picture Show: Silent Films on American Screens in the 1930s* (Lanham, MD: Scarecrow Press, 2010), 37–62; Eric Hoyt, *Hollywood Vault: Film Libraries Before Home Video* (Berkeley: University of California Press, 2014), 86–87, 101.
22. "Old Silent Hits," 33.
23. Laemmle Jr., quoted in "Sound Bringing Remakes into B. O.?" *Motion Picture News*, 25 January 1930: 33.
24. "Old Silent Hits," 33.
25. "Remake Question Still Puzzling Studio Chiefs," *Motion Picture News*, 22 November 1930: 47.
26. Ibid.
27. Ibid.
28. Crafton, *The Talkies*, 480.
29. Ibid., 480, 482.
30. Ibid., 485.
31. Ibid., 15.
32. "A Gift from Ramon Novarro," *Screenland* 21.5 (September 1930): 61.
33. Crafton, *The Talkies*, 482.
34. Ibid.
35. Ibid., 6.
36. For the transcript of such a Vitaphone trailer from 1928 and a detailed discussion, see Crafton, *The Talkies*, 121–126.
37. "Between You and Me," *Modern Screen* 4.5 (October 1932): 80.
38. Jack Kleinman, "Remakes," *The New Movie Magazine* (July 1933): 70.
39. Ibid.
40. Mrs. Effie Meyers, "Remakes in Sound," *The New Movie Magazine* (January 1934): 68.
41. See also Crafton, *The Talkies*, 485–489.
42. Mrs. Frank Kurlick, Letter, *Photoplay* (May 1941): 23.
43. Ibid.
44. Sue Anna, "A Boo for an Encore," *Photoplay* (December 1941): 6.
45. Ibid.

46. Clarence Thornbey, Letter, *Photoplay* (May 1942): 74.
47. "The White Sister (M-G-M)," *The New Movie Magazine* (April 1933): 58.
48. Frederick James Smith, "Reviews," *The New Movie Magazine* (August 1931): 74.
49. Crafton, *The Talkies*, 482.
50. "Yesterday–Today," *Modern Screen* 12.3 (February 1936): 44–45.
51. These six films were: *A Tale of Two Cities* (Frank Lloyd, 1917; Jack Conway, 1935), *Love/Anna Karenina* (Edmund Goulding, 1927; Clarence Brown, 1935), *Captain Blood* (David Smith, 1924; Michael Curtiz, 1935), *The Three Musketeers* (Fred Niblo, 1921; Rowland V. Lee, 1935), *Rose Marie* (Lucien Hubbard, 1928; W. S. Van Dyke, 1936), and *Dark Angel* (George Fitzmaurice, 1925; Sidney Franklin, 1935).
52. On 16 mm distribution in the 1930s, see Hoyt, *Hollywood Vault*, 96–98.
53. See ibid., 100–105.
54. "Match Them If You Can," *Photoplay* (November 1938): 42.
55. Ibid. These films were *Maytime* (Louis Gasnier, 1923; Robert Z. Leonard, 1937), *If I Were King* (J. Gordon Edwards, 1920; Frank Lloyd, 1938), *Stella Dallas* (Henry King, 1925; King Vidor, 1937), *Sally, Irene and Mary* (Edmund Goulding, 1925; William A. Seiter, 1938), *Robin Hood* (Allan Dwan, 1923; Michael Curtiz, 1938), *Prisoner of Zenda* (Rex Ingram, 1922; John Cromwell, 1937), *Tom Sawyer* (William D. Taylor, 1917; Norman Taurog, 1938), *Holiday* (Edward H. Griffith, 1930; George Cukor, 1938), and *Camille* (Ray C. Smallwood, 1921; George Cukor, 1937).
56. Ibid.
57. More generally on this idea, see Kelleter and Loock, "Hollywood Remaking."
58. Crafton, *The Talkies*, 21.
59. Shelley Stamp, "'Exit Flapper, Enter Woman,' or Lois Weber in Jazz Age Hollywood," *Framework: The Journal of Cinema and Media* 51.2 (2010): 376–377.
60. Hoyt, *Hollywood Vault*, 65.
61. Barbara Klinger, *Beyond the Multiplex: Cinema, New Technologies, and the Home* (Berkeley: University of California Press, 2006), 11–14.
62. Cf. Kelleter and Loock, "Hollywood Remaking."
63. Klinger, *Beyond the Multiplex*, 93. See also Stephen Henderson, "Teaching New Generations the Joys of Old Movies," *The New York Times*, 8 June 1997: 29–30.
64. On AMC in particular, see 91–134.
65. Richard Natale, "Classics on Video Get Jolt from Hot Remakes," *Variety*, 9 December 1991: 3.
66. Ibid.
67. "Recreating the Eighth Wonder: The Making of King Kong." Disc 3. *King Kong*, deluxe extended ed. DVD. Directed by Peter Jackson (2005; Universal City, CA: Universal Studios, 2006).

References

"A Gift from Ramon Novarro." *Screenland* 21.5 (September 1930): 60–61.
Balio, Tino. "Feeding the Maw of Exhibition." In *Grand Design: Hollywood as a Modern Business Enterprise, 1930–1939*, ed. Tino Balio, 73–105. 1993. Vol. 4 of *History of American Cinema*. Berkeley: University of California Press, 1995.
Belton, John. *American Cinema/American Culture*. New York: McGraw-Hill, 1994.
"Between You and Me." *Modern Screen* 4.5 (October 1932): 80–81, 111.
Crafton, Donald. *The Talkies: American Cinema's Transition to Sound, 1926–1931*. Vol. 3 of *History of American Cinema*. General Editor Charles Harpole. New York: Charles Scribner's Sons, 1997.

Daly, Phil M. "Along the Rialto." *The Film Daily*, 31 October 1935: 3.

Forrest, Jennifer, and Leonard R. Koos, "Reviewing Remakes: An Introduction." In *Dead Ringers: The Remake in Theory and Practice*, eds. Jennifer Forrest and Leonard R. Koos, 1–36. Albany, NY: State University of New York Press, 2002.

Grainge, Paul. "Introduction: Ephemeral Media." In *Ephemeral Media: Transitory Screen Culture from Television to YouTube*, ed. by Paul Grainge, 1–19. London: BFI and Palgrave Macmillan, 2011.

Gray, Johnathan. *Show Sold Separately: Promos, Spoilers and Other Media Paratexts*. New York: New York University Press, 2010.

Hediger, Vinzenz. "'You Haven't Seen It Unless You Have Seen It at Least Twice': Film Spectatorship and the Discipline of Repeat Viewing." *Cinéma and Cie 5* (2004): 24–42.

Henderson, Stephen. "Teaching New Generations the Joys of Old Movies." *New York Times*, 8 June 1997: 29–30.

"Hits to Be Made Again as Dialogue Pictures." *The Film Daily*, 10 April 1929: 6.

Hoyt, Eric. *Hollywood Vault: Film Libraries Before Home Video*. Berkeley: University of California Press, 2014.

Kelleter, Frank, and Kathleen Loock. "Hollywood Remaking as Second-Order Serialization." In *Media of Serial Narrative*, ed. Frank Kelleter. Columbus: Ohio State University Press, 2016 (forthcoming).

Kleinman, Jack. "Remakes." *The New Movie Magazine* (July 1933): 70.

Klinger, Barbara. *Beyond the Multiplex: Cinema, New Technologies, and the Home*. Berkeley: University of California Press, 2006.

Kurlick, Mrs. Frank. Letter. *Photoplay* (May 1941): 23.

Martin, Martin. "Chatter from Hollywood." *Screenland* (October 1928): 68–71.

"Match Them If You Can." *Photoplay* (November 1938): 42–43, 83.

Meyers, Mrs. Effie. "Remakes in Sound." *The New Movie Magazine* (January 1934): 68.

Natale, Richard. "Classics on Video Get Jolt from Hot Remakes." *Variety*, 9 December 1991: 3, 8.

"Old Silent Hits Offering a Solution for Shortage of Good Sound Material." *Motion Picture News*, 25 January 1930: 33.

"Rattlin' the Skeleton." *Motion Picture News*, 25 January 1930: 33.

"Recreating the Eighth Wonder: The Making of King Kong." Disc 3. *King Kong*, deluxe extended ed. DVD. Directed by Peter Jackson. 2005. Universal City, CA: Universal Studios, 2006.

"Remake Question Still Puzzling Studio Chiefs." *Motion Picture News*, 22 November 1930: 47.

Sherwood, Robert E. "Silent Successes Adaptable for Talkies." *The Film Daily*, 2 October 1930: 4.

Smith, Frederick James. "Reviews." *The New Movie Magazine* (August 1931): 74.

"Sound Bringing Remakes into B. O.?" *Motion Picture News*, 25 January 1930: 33.

Sue Anna. "A Boo for an Encore." *Photoplay* (December 1941): 6.

"The White Sister (M-G-M)." *The New Movie Magazine* (April 1933): 58.

Thornbey, Clarence. Letter. *Photoplay* (May 1942): 74.

"'U' Digging into Files for Sound Remakes of Silents." *Motion Picture News*, 25 January 1930: 33.

"Yesterday–Today." *Modern Screen* 12.3 (February 1936): 44–45.

9 Paratexts from Cinephilia to Mediaphilia (through Ludification Culture)

Roy Menarini and Lucia Tralli

According to the most influential dictionaries, "-philia" is—among other things—"a positive feeling of liking, the experiencing of affective and emotional states," "a feeling of affection for a person or an institution," "or for an art expression." But also: "a feeling of unusual or abnormal (mainly sexual) desire for someone or something."[1]

Basically, all "-philias" convey the idea of closeness and assiduity with the object of one's affection, something that can often degenerate into excess and exaggeration (necrophilia, dendrophilia, and other pathological behaviors). Do media pose the same threat? They do, according to some recent theories on the relationship between media and quality of life. These theories also bring up the concept of "media obesity,"[2] which should be fought by following special "media diets." This is not a new topic for those involved in cinema studies, and it came up before any concerns over the risks of hyperexposure to the media—something existing even without the occurrence of a "-philia." Therefore, we will try to contextualize the problem. First, the course of cinephilia in time has to be illustrated.

As a community, cinephiles have been long considered to be rather conservative, even fetishistic lovers of old cinema or art-house movies. Books about the history of cinephilia (it is imperative to mention Antoine de Baecque's *La cinéphilie*[3] and Dudley Andrew's *André Bazin*[4]) show a massive resurgence of interest in Bazin among critics, scholars, and students. Neo-bazinian studies, most of which are carried out in French or French-oriented departments of English or American universities, have in a way capitalized upon the idea of cinephilia as a timeless relationship among spectators, critics, and movies set in a special period of film experience.

In the past few years, however, the so-called new cinephilia[5] developed another kind of relationship with new media and web culture, thanks to strategies such as social networking, which somehow manage to give a different, more progressive meaning to cinephilia. This is currently practiced by a new generation of equally devoted cinephiles who display and develop new modes of engagement with the overabundance of cinematic material widely available through advanced technology.

As Melis Behlil wrote in her article "Cinephilia, Internet, and Online Film Communities":

> Being a cinephile involved traveling to distant theaters to track down obscure art films and discussing them with fellow cinephiles, either in ciné-clubs or in respectable film journals. In the late 1970s and early 1980s, the boom in home-viewing technologies and the decline in the number of art house theaters changed things. And with the popularization of the internet in the 1990s, the cinephile world became a whole different scene. For some, like Susan Sontag, David Denby, and David Thomson, this marked the death of cinema and cinephilia. For others, it was merely a new beginning. In *The Decay of Cinema* Susan Sontag lamented the death of cinephilia.[6]

In the same book in which Behlil's article appeared (*Cinephilia, Movies, Love and Memory*), Marjike de Valck and Malte Hagener wrote:

> A large part of the public debate that followed Sontag's obituary to cinephilia in fact concentrated on the impact of new technologies. The online journal *Senses of Cinema* dedicated a dossier to this discussion entitled *Permanent Ghosts: Cinephilia in the Age of the Internet and Video* in 1999. One of the main oppositions that is played out in the debate is "going out" versus "staying in". Value judgements differ with regard to the question of which specific examples qualify as cinephile practice. The younger generation tends to defend the technology of their home video and internet education as a democratizing tool that not only allows a global, non-metropolitan public access to cinema culture, but also gives them control over their beloved films.[7]

It is clear that this quote from 1999 is even more useful for understanding contemporary practices of cinephilia. The past few years have witnessed a multifaceted institutionalization of digital cinephilia, which is often confined to a space of questionable legality, as the widespread problem of media piracy shows. An interesting example comes from the website MUBI (*https://mubi.com*): for the past eight years, this international platform has been offering a considerable number of auteur movies, many of them often barely known or with no distribution at all in several countries, which the platform makes available for streaming at a fairly reasonable price. Their catalogue includes experimental films, avant-garde authors, B-movie classics, contemporary award-winning short films, and restored masterpieces from the past. The cinephile viewer can interact with other subscribers in the standard forms of social networking, therefore exchanging ideas, experiences, lists, and opinions, both within and around this apparently isolated mode of film consumption. MUBI generally encourages this kind of critical evaluation and review of movies by offering a selection of in-depth analyses, critical reviews, essays, and articles on the history of cinema on its website.

Furthermore, new cinephiles, along with old but dynamic critics (such as Jonathan Rosenbaum or J. Hoberman), have come to terms with the importance of sharing movies over the Internet. All sides of cinephilia are involved. Cinema festivals, a popular topic of study within contemporary cinematographic culture, also provide an interesting example. In this domain, one could expect to see the very opposite of web culture prevail. Movies are watched on screen, in a cinema theater, next to other people, while works and auteurs are often discussed while queuing for each screening. Festival organizers also emphasize the social and collective side of movie events in order to gain public funding and legitimize their existence as part of a city's artistic life or within a project of urban redevelopment. However, new media are able to complete the offer: a perfect example is provided by *Festivalscope.com*, a portal where it is possible to legally stream some of the movies that are being screened at cinema festivals around the globe. *Festivalscope.com* targets mainly the movie industry but includes numerous members from other fields of cinema, including several critics. Previously, cinephilia had a very strong link with film showing, and the film festival system has been involved in a hybridization process with some patterns of French (and, later, American) cinephilia.[8]

At present, the "new cinephilia" continues to exist within the festival system, but it no longer seems to be interested in movie institutions or institutionalization. Film showing is increasingly moving to collective web channels and social media. For example, the Italian website *Mymovies.it* allows its users not only to watch movies online but also to discuss them collectively via chat during the viewing. After all, this is also an era of massive transformation in the use of TV and in the collection of data on audience flows: investors and advertisers often base their sponsorship strategies on a show's Twitter traffic, instead of on traditional surveys.[9]

Moreover, TV has popularized the *live tweet* form, which means that people who are watching a specific TV show or program comment on it on Twitter using a predetermined hashtag during its airing. Consequently, we are witnessing several experiments of live tweeting of movies that somehow mirror the form of film consumption typical of cinema festivals. For instance, the popular community-based social networking website *reddit* offers a subthread called *LiveTweetingOldMovies* (*http://www.reddit.com/r/LiveTweetingOldMovies*) where reddit users gather to watch and live-tweet old movies as a group ("old" is usually applied to a broad definition of "cult" movies, from Luc Besson's *The Fifth Element* to Rob Reiner's *The Princess Bride*). Similarly, the popular Italian web magazine *I 400 calci*, which focuses on action and horror movies, has been organizing collective and participated live-tweets among its readers since 2012, based on the shared hashtag "#400tv," which focuses on their core selection of movies (*http://www.i400calci.com/2012/06/400tv-la-rassegna*). These cases exemplify a widespread trend in contemporary media culture in which cinephilia, new cinephilia, and participatory culture's practices and spaces are entangled and progressively overlap.

We can also ask ourselves if—for example—some ultra-cinephile YouTube channels (e.g., full-length kung-fu movies or B-movie collections) are part of this, or if they are just the free initiatives of some exploitation cinema devotees. But how can one find the difference between the more organized communities of cinephiles and this kind of instinctive, genuine construction of film archives and film genre subcommunities through movie showing and movie sharing? Drawing the line is rather difficult and perhaps not even necessary since the hybridization of these two forms of cinephilia has already produced interesting examples.

Mark Cousins, author of the most discussed and controversial audiovisual history of cinema of the moment (the 15-hour long *Story of Film* that is now a cult movie itself), decided to add a series of quizzes on the history of cinema to the documentary's official website.[10] Similarly, in the summer of 2012, the latest movie-of-the-year chart from the magazine *Sight and Sound*[11] was one of the most discussed, shared and "replayed" topics on the Internet (with a plethora of cinephiles and critics compiling counter-lists and flaunting them on their Internet profiles). The same practices of reappropriation of films, through online mash-ups, parodies, or reenactment, belong to a realm where irony blends with cinephilia.

While some happily welcome the renaissance of cinephilia under the umbrella of participatory culture, others might question the quality and reliability of its audience-driven practices. Many such practices are undoubtedly recreational, but there is much more than meets the eye, and many common lusory activities express a high degree of cinephilia and strong viewing and appropriation skills. For example, fandom culture studies have often underlined a persistent trend of curatorial practices among fans that could be linked to more traditional cinephile curatorial endeavors. Not only do media fan practitioners have a long history of preserving their own culture (with fanzine collections stored in public libraries, online archives for fanfictions, and a wiki dedicated to stories and data from the last thirty years of fandom life)[12] but fan communities also function as hubs for trend-setting practices about new products and texts, based on a shared trust between their members.

That is to say, they belong to what has been referred to as ludification culture,[13] that is, the emergence of playful elements and attitudes not only in entertainment or leisure activities, but also in domains traditionally considered as "serious," such as education. As Frissen et al., the editors of *Playful Identities*, illustrate, the past century has been witnessing a moment of progressive ludification of personal and cultural identities in which media and technology play a significant role. Building on Huizinga's famous study of the "play-element in culture," the authors use his definition of "play" as a starting point to discuss the current "playful" state of digital media culture:

The ubiquitous presence of digital media in our everyday life is implicitly prefiguring our experiences and actions in a playful way. For instance, this is happening when our daily tasks, travels, and communications are being aestheticized by fancy apps on our smartphones and tablets, or when we are invited to rank a sportsman, actress, or politician on a fan site, share casual tweets or mobile camera images during our daily interactions with others, or get engaged in the erotic play of seduction when exchanging text messages. In a world full of playful technologies, we are constantly seduced to become more receptive to the ludic dimensions of life.[14]

The traditional networks of cinephilia continue to embrace *auteur* politics, overly refined writing, and appreciation of any movie that appears to be marginalized, over the top, or visionary. Yet when they merge with the rules of social media, such as "likes," shares, and lists, *ludification* reaches full bloom. The mantra for this community is still "to share," and it is time to start mixing up the studies on new cinephilia with those on fandom and subcultural communities.

Moreover, as Huizinga pointed out in his definition of "play," there is a specific community-centered principle in the *ludification* process, entailed by the fact that play "promotes the formation of social groupings which tend to surround themselves with secrecy and to stress their difference from the common world by disguise or other means."[15] We can easily witness a community forming pattern in both fandom and cinephile communities.

As Frances Morgan observes in *Of Cinephilia(s) and Fandom*:

The obsession that drives fandom is not so different from that which drives cinephilia—to commit to either requires passion, amassed knowledge, long hours spent in an alternate world; increasingly it also inspires production: debate, DIY theory, formulation of ideas fresh from viewing, instant connections with others' opinions.[16]

To the eyes of the uninitiated, these practices always seem to pertain to an exclusively recreational kind, yet in fandom communities irony and sarcasm are usually mixed with what Kristina Busse calls "affective aesthetics." Fandom productions function in a "quite complex interrelation between love and critique, aesthetic distance and affect [because] fans have long been trailblazing not just remixes but the ability to interrogate and criticize and culturally resist without dismissing the text and their relationship to it or ironically distancing themselves."[17]

We can trace this constant back-and-forth motion between criticism and affection, causticness and enthusiasm, which is typical of fandom, in many practices that pertain to new cinephilia paratextual productions. For example, this is evident in a very popular genre of mash-up, the *recut trailer*, which "take[s] source footage from one or more texts and recuts it, either to displace the film's original genre or to create a new film that will never exist."[18] There are many well-known examples of this kind of work, from *Scary Mary* (Chris Rule, 2007) to *The Shining Recut* (Robert Ryang, 2005), but, as Williams (2012) points out, there are two subcategories to this genre, *fake trailers* and *fan trailers*. While fake trailers "create a film that will never exist and often include footage shot specifically for the trailer," fan trailers "are made for actual movies, use original footage less often, and evoke fan traditions of vidding. Such traditions often involve uncovering a slash story line, giving a trailer a new soundtrack, or ... creating trailers for a film before the official trailer has been disseminated to demonstrate the fans' anticipation for the film."[19] The two types of trailers are similar in form but quite different in both context and intentions, and can briefly give a glimpse into the layered complexities that this kind of work entails. Both *fake* and *fan trailers*, though, are part of the broader category of paratexts and, as Jonathan Gray points out (in one of the most comprehensive accounts of paratexts' functions in the contemporary media ecosystem), in audience-produced paratexts: "Each style will simultaneously provide evidence about how any given community or individual watches the show in question, and it will serve as a paratext that encourages others to watch in a similar manner."[20]

Now, the question is whether this ludification of cinematographic culture and heritage is something entirely new or whether it originates from a latent traditional cinephile culture—the latter appearing to be the most fitting theory. If cinephilia is a complex matter, it is much easier to point out the phylogenesis from the recreational side of movie critique to contemporary ludification. It is a known fact that film criticism (also intended as film paratext) has always traded its cultural and social legitimization with a sort of utilitarian connection toward readers. It is as if both publishers and the public stated: "Fine, thank you for your meditations over the movie, but should I actually watch it or not?" Hence, we have the traditional proliferation of dots, stars, votes, and other numerical ways of indicating the supposed artistic value of a film. So what is new? The quantification culture. For example, on the website Rotten Tomatoes (*www.rottentomatoes.com*) you can not only read hundreds of reviews in English for any internationally distributed film, but you will also find a ratio of all of the evaluations, conveyed in a percentage of positive and negative that sums up all of the opinions, often antithetic, that are present. Another example comes from YouTube, where you can easily find some "fan criticism," the social media version of blogs and vlogs, where video reviews are often presented in informal and playful ways, which are nonetheless tied to the same values of personal reputation, and status legitimization that we can see at work in the more institutionalized critics.

If we consider some of the most influential *youtubers* in the realm of movie and media criticism in the Anglophone scenario, some common characteristics rapidly emerge. The above-mentioned utilitarian connection with the viewers is usually explicitly stated in the "about" section of their channels, often in the form of an allusion to an overabundant media offer that needs some sort of external intervention to be tamed: "In a world full of movies and television, only one channel is keeping them honest—SCREEN JUNKIES!"[21] "There's a lot of crap out there that wants to suck away your precious time; The Super Critics—Nostalgia Critic, Nostalgia Chick, Cinema Snob, and Todd in the Shadows—help guide you through the jungle of mediocrity and find the true gems in pop culture."[22] Although the overall playfulness of the channels' productions is adamant,[23] the amount of critical commentaries and reviews, annotated trailers, and even parodies and playful takes on movies and media products, which often have a daily scheduling, display the underlying "seriousness" of the channels' owners, who usually build careers out of their initially playful and *fannish* or *amateurish* endeavors. The connection between "old" and "new" critical practices can be retrieved not only in the channels revolving around a name-critic but also in those that produce only craftily edited compilations of scenes with an audio commentary, such as *Cinema Sins*[24] or *Screen Junkies*[25]—which host the popular *Honest Trailers* series.[26] The shows hosted on these channels, which seem aesthetically more akin to mash-ups and video-remixes than to actual movie reviews, are indeed a new way of showing deep and profound knowledge about movies and movie production, narrative structures and tropes, cinema history, and many more details that also clearly pertain to the realm of cinephilia, with a more evident preference for cult and mainstream products.

We can further explore these issues through the story of the YouTube channel *League of Super Critics*,[27] which opened in 2012 and distributes the video reviews of three critics: the Cinema Snob (Brad Jones), Nostalgia Chick (Lindsay Ellis), and Nostalgia Critic (Doug Walker). The three critics started their own shows between 2007 and 2008 and only recently joined together in a single channel. From their chosen *nom de guerre*, their willingness to play with "traditional" and "classic" cinephilic qualities is clear. They have elaborated their own characters around what the general audience identifies with core "critical" values such as pretentiousness, ostentatious encyclopaedic knowledge of minute and obscure details, parading an all-encompassing familiarity with abstruse cult media products, and so on. Although the playful (and ostensibly parodic) ways in which all three "characters" impersonate their critic persona (from mimicry to language) are indeed quite entertaining, in the end their videos do provide useful insights on their chosen topics: rare cult horror or pornographic movies from the 1960s to the 1990s in the case of the Cinema Snob or "nerd" favorites such as the *X-men saga* or *Batman* in the case of the other two. This proves their playful critical practices do not prohibit a more complex and deep analysis of a given media product.

The history of this channel can provide useful insights on the contemporary functioning of media production tied to critic and mediaphilic activities, especially around YouTube. The original channels of both the

Cinema Snob and Nostalgia Critic were threatened by copyright infringement allegations (probably triggered by their usage of movie scenes in their reviews), and as a result, they were compelled to create their own websites to host their original productions. In 2008, Doug Walker moved his show to another video-streaming hosting website (*Blip.tv*) and then joined the newly launched *That Guy with the Glasses* website (owned by online media company Channel Awesome)[28] hosting what would become their flagship show, and also producing four other series. In 2009, Brad Jones created his own website, *TheCinemaSnob.com*, and later joined Channel Awesome in 2010. The series he created has gathered a cult audience through the years, which prompted Jones to write a movie adaptation of the series *The Cinema Snob Movie* (Ryan Mitchelle), released on DVD in 2012. He has since returned on YouTube through the Blip-run YouTube channel *League of Super Critics*.

Meanwhile, Lindsay Ellis, who had her own show as Nostalgia Chick, created as a companion to the Nostalgia Critic one on the *That Guy With the Glasses* website in late 2008, announced in 2015 that she was ending her show but that she would continue to produce reviews for the *League* channel as Lindsay Ellis.[29] Apart from some recent controversies surrounding the *Channel Awesome* website,[30] and the evident complexities tied to building a business on the web, the story behind this channel and this website is clearly one of success: Doug Walker was selected as Entrepreneur of the Year in the Mashable Awards in 2010,[31] and they reached 120,000 subscribers and tens of thousands of monthly viewers. Through ad revenues from the video-hosting websites and a carefully crafted business, Walker has managed to build himself a career based on his activities as a movie and media reviewer, which clearly compel a broader reasoning around the new ways in which critics and critical activities can institutionalize themselves in this new media environment.

These few examples are all manifestations of a ludification culture that should not be diminished or relegated to the fringe of cinema discussion. There is obviously a price to pay, the fee being the slow and inevitable loss of the charisma of institutional criticism, where one person—the most erudite of the community—used to talk to many others. But beware: this is not some inflexible dynamic, according to which democratizing and ludic criticism and cinephilia would leave behind (like in a dialogue of matter and antimatter) holes of emptied and inverted forms where negotiability is out of the question. There are actually several single, occasionally charismatic competences that identify specific communities of recipients within the sometimes strict, sometimes varied media diet and that are proceeding obliquely, and often independently from the media outlet where they originally appeared, within contemporary media ecosystems.

This is probably just the beginning of a much bigger transformation toward redefining the *film experience* within the sphere of participatory culture, fans' playful practices, and ludification culture. Cinematographic culture is moving—or relocating—conversations and tastes of the tradition into new media and common practices, completely autonomously, and without any pressure from the outside. These are strategies of adaptation, spontaneous tactics of survival and surprising forms of ludification of the cinematographic heritage—all things we will continue to discuss for a long time.

Other forms of contemporary critical paratexts about online film culture contribute to this scenario: video reviews, film polls, and new forms of criticism (video essays, tweets, micro-reviews on Twitter, online journals, anthologies of scenes on Youtube, mash-ups, Facebook's "likes," comments, and debates) bring together fan culture and academic analysis. This kind of paratext around films is well known and definitely not new. Something that is new in this decade, however, and that is overtaking and exceeding debates in the late 1990s and early 2000s debates is the connection and fusion between movie watching and film criticism or discourse. Using the example of new cinephilia on social media, can we consider new participative communities as a paratextual context of contemporary film consumption in the digital era? How can we classify new cinephilia in order to rethink contemporary media paratexts? It is time to ask ourselves if these texts are becoming something different. Is watching and sharing movies the goal for the community of cinephiles, or is the ecosystem/mediasphere itself to become the primary focus of the participants?

For example, as in video-essays, a long-existing form in the realm of experimental cinema, we are witnessing a new, interesting academic development in the so-called videographic film and moving image studies, notably in the work of Catherine Grant. Grant is the curator of *Audiovisualcy*,[32] a platform for video-essays with a critical and analytical perspective on audiovisual media that in four years of activity has collected nearly 650 videos. As Grant states: "practitioners of these forms … explore the ways in which digital technologies afford a new mode of carrying out and presenting their research. The full range of digital technologies now enables film and media scholars to write using the very materials that constitute their objects of study: moving images and sounds."[33] From the exploration of an author's filmography to the in-depth analysis of specific scenes, from the study of film tropes to the tribute to cult film genres, these video-essays' range of inquiry into audiovisual culture is truly all-encompassing. These kinds of work bear witness to a significant shift in the ways different cinema and audiovisual practices, cinephilia, fandom culture, and academic culture are merging to engender a new grassroots approach to film culture.

Moreover, we are considering the existence of a growing paratext, originated from old cinephilia and driven to new cinephilia, consisting of reviews, journals, social media practices, lists, new standards, debates, forums, and so forth, that is strongly intermingled with film showing. As we know, there are two oppositional attitudes, and two very different behaviors: some try to liberate film culture from its artistic or institutional status (cutting it into small pieces on the web and mixing it up using all the different practices of online appropriation), while others try to homogenize the fragmented nature of today's film consumption. The second tendency is more conservative, in terms of policy of culture and in every possible sense that can be given to the philosophy of art. Our argument is that new cinephilia is reconstructing itself thanks to the possibilities offered by social media and that it is potentially exploiting the possibility to consider both film paratexts and movies as primary sources, with the routine of movie watching and the practice of movie discussing cohabiting in time and space. This comes at the end of a long history ranging from the *Cahiers du Cinéma* to the *nouvelle vague* and back, from filmmaking to film criticism. On the one hand, new cinephilia tries to convert its tradition to social media and to share culture through an emphasis on ludification; on the other hand, this project aims at multiplying paratextual discourses and dignifying the scattered world of cinema aesthetics. The whole experience (a frequent topic of discussion for movie forums around the web) is changing, but new cinephilia, with its contradictions and even its conflicting practices between the demolition of an experience and the reconstruction of that same one, is looking for new forms of aestheticization of media culture.

The feeling that emerges is that of a system in which the primary texts serve as collectors of opposing forces: through both traditional and multimedia paratexts, media culture seems to force a certain type of consumption of the text, steering it through "ephemeral media" and structuring it from above. Thanks to the strategies of spreadable media identified by Henry Jenkins[34] in the opposite direction, the "user contents" date back through numerous counter-paratexts to the main content. Despite the complexity, or maybe the little use in distinguishing mainstream paratexts and grassroots paratexts, the fact remains that in ecosystems and media narrative, a great use of paratext is imposed. In addition, in inclusive societies and the consumption complex of this age, the very concept of the paratext undergoes important transformations, starting with the fact that many of them are arranged in the same horizon of the consumption of the text itself. In the case of the film, this is exemplified in the trailer, criticism, comment, evaluation, and the like.

These opposing forces converge toward what we can call *mediaphilia*. As Dale Hudson and Patricia Zimmerman wrote:

> The theorizations of cinephilia that articulate a psychoanalytic model (Jane Gaines, Paul Willemen) of an eternal quest for what has been lost and can never again be found. This insatiable, fetishistic desire for an unassailable object is now rerouted by technofilia, which purport to offer each generation of cinephiles new and enhanced access to lost "masterpieces" and "contemporary classics" in remastered DVD transfers, special boxed editions, and extra features.[35]

We might also add—online unlimited availability. If there are no more lost movies, or lost experiences, or anything lost at all, there is only one possibility left: dignifying movie culture through the fusion of paratext and text, and developing a large-scale criticism able to turn every media product into an artistic work: TV series, webseries, mash-ups, trailers, spoofs, cross-media documents, found footage, and every single practice with or without an artistic intent.

The relationship with the past, in the context of this (sometimes exasperated) mediaphilia, contains contradictory connotations to say the least. Forms of storage, indexing, and canonization promise not to leave anything to chance (e.g., Wikipedia makes a tremendous work of the periodization and chronological cataloguing of universal knowledge); at the same time, the crushing to the present leads us to think that the primary texts and the preexisting media objects are disposed on a horizontal axis. New platforms, from Spotify to Netflix, push the aestheticization of media products themselves and develop a sort of desire for individual texts (the classic film, the cult TV series; the old, dusty long-playing record; the legendary accessory etc., in the context of what is known as "retroculture"). So the relationship with the culture of the past, already challenged by the "ironic" report with the time by postmodern culture, is today a further acceleration of the uncontrolled media diet.

Notes

1. "Philia," The Free Dictionary, *http://www.thefreedictionary.com/philia<https:// www.google.com/url?q=http://www.thefreedictionary.com/philia&sa=D&ust= 1445881878761000&usg=AFQjCNGIFihq-ZIZa3qwIQH8Kt6xeiXlHg>;* "Philia", *Vocabulary.com, http://www.vocabulary.com/dictionary/philia<https:// www.google.com/url?q=http://www.vocabulary.com/dictionary/philia&sa=D& ust=1445881878762000&usg=AFQjCNFzeviJ2SaAgxr6Qj_ggDFMz0Mu4Q>;* "-philia," Merriam Webster Dictionary, *http://www.merriam-webster.com/ dictionary/ philiahttps://www.google.com/url?q=http://www.merriam-webster. com/dictionary-philia&sa=D&ust=1445881878762000&usg=AFQjCNFudG CPqDidWlm-jFVFhOgl1HbBPg,* accessed 24 October 2015.
2. Clay A. Johnson, *The Information Diet: A Case for Conscious Consumption* (Farnham, UK: O'Reilly, 2012); Marco Gui, *A dieta di media: Comunicazione e qualità della vita* (Bologna: Il Mulino, 2014).
3. Antoine de Baecque, *La cinéphili:. Invention d'un regard, histoire d'une culture, 1944–1968* (Paris: Fayard, 2003).
4. Dudley Andrew, *André Bazin* (New York: Oxford University Press, 1978).
5. James Quandt, "Everyone I Know Is Stayin' Home: The New Cinephilia," *Framework. The Journal of Cinema and Media* 50.1–2 (2009): 206–209.
6. Miles Behill, "Cinephilia, Internet, and Online Film Communities," in *Cinephilia: Movies, Love and Memory*, eds. Malte Hagener and Marijke De Valck (Amsterdam: Amsterdam University Press, 2005), 117.
7. Hagener and De Valck, *Cinephilia: Movies, Love and Memory*, 13.
8. See Dina Iordanova, ed. *The Film Festival Reader* (St. Andrews: St Andrews Film Studies, 2013).
9. In July 2013, U.S. TV-Ratings Measurement Agency Nielsen launched a new tool dedicated solely to Twitter activity connected with TV shows and

programs, in order to provide insights on audience engagement through the popular social network (cf. *http://www.nielsensocial.com/product/nielsen-twitter-tv-ratings*, 24 October 2015).

10. We refer to Mark Cousins, *The Story of Films* (London: Pavilion, 2013) and to the documentary film *The Story of Film: An Odyssey* (Mark Cousins, 2012).
11. "The Top 50 Greatest Films of All Time," *Sight and Sound* 22.9 (2012).
12. In the United States, there are several fanzine collection. Two of the biggest are the "Zine and Amateur Press Collections," deposited at the University of Iowa, and the "Sandy Hereld Memorial Digitized Media Fanzine Collection," deposited at the Texas A&M University Libraries. The biggest online fanfiction archive, run by the fan-based Organization for Transformative Works (OTW), is the *Archive of our Own—A03* (*http://archiveofourown.org*, accessed 17 September 2015). OTW volounteers also run *Fanlore* (*http://fanlore.org*, accessed 17 September 2015), a wiki entirely dedicated to the history of fandom, as told by the fans themselves.
13 See Peppino Ortoleva, "Homo ludicus. The ubiquity of play and its roles in present society," *G.A.M.E. – The Italian Journal of Game Studies* 1 (2012), accessed 20 January 2015, *http://www.gamejournal.it/homo-ludicus-the-ubiquity-and-roles-of-play-in-present-society/#.VL5T5Y3wvIU*.
14. Valerie Frissen, Sybille Lammes, Michiel De Lange, Jos de Mul, and Joost Raessens, "Introduction," in *Playful Identities. The Ludification of Digital Media Cultures*, ed. Frissen et al. (Amsterdam: Amsterdam University Press, 2015), 36.
15. Johan Huizinga, *Homo ludens: A Study of the Play-Element in Culture* (Boston: Beacon, 1955), 13.
16. Frances Morgan, "Of Cinephilia(s) and Fandom," *Online Roundtable 1, Project: New Cinephilia*, 31 May 2011, accessed 17 September 2015, *http://projectcinephilia.mubi.com/2011/05/25/of-cinephilias-and-fandom*.
17. Kristina Busse, "[META] Affective Aesthetics," *Fanhackers*, 23 November 2010, accessed 17 September 2015, *http://fanhackers.transformativeworks.org/2010/11/affective-aesthetics*.
18. Kathleen Amy Williams, "Fake and Fan Film Trailers as Incarnations of Audience Anticipation and Desire," *Transformative Works and Cultures* 9 (2012), accessed 17 September 2015, *http://journal.transformativeworks.org/index.php/twc/article/view/360/284*.
19. Ibid.
20. Jonathan Gray, *Show Sold Separately: Promos, Spoilers, and Other Media Paratexts* (New York: New York University Press, 2010), 162.
21. *Screen Junkies* YouTube Channel description, accessed 17 September 2015, *https://www.youtube.com/user/screenjunkies/about*.
22. *League of Super Critics* YouTube channel description, accessed 17 September 2015, *https://www.youtube.com/user/LeagueOfSuperCritics/about*.
23. For example: "A show of movie reviews and comedy. If I make you laugh, then I've done my job." *Jeremy Jahns* YouTube channel description, accessed 17 September 2015, *https://www.youtube.com/user/JeremyJahns/about*. See also "Quick, Funny Reviews of Movies and Games, New and Old," *Chris Stuckmann* YouTube channel description, accessed 17 September 2015. *https://www.youtube.com/user/ChrisStuckmann/about*.
24. *https://www.youtube.com/user/CinemaSins*, accessed 17 September 2015.
25. *https://www.youtube.com/user/screenjunkies*, accessed 17 September 2015.

26. *https://www.youtube.com/playlist?list=PL86F4D497FD3CACCE,* accessed 17 September 2015.
27. *https://www.youtube.com/user/LeagueOfSuperCritics/about,* accessed 17 September 2015.
28. In the end of 2014, the website was rebranded as *ChannelAwesome.com.*
29. Lindsay Ellis, "Farewell, Channel Awesome, and a Pre-emptive FAQ," *Real Name Brand Lindsay,* 10 January 2015, accessed 17 September 2015, *http://namebrandlindsay.com/2015/01/10/farewell-channel-awesome-and-a-pre-emptive-faq.*
30. At the beginning of 2015, some of the long-time producers left the website, accusing the site management of misconduct. See Obscurus_Lupa, "Bye, CA!," *Obscurus Lupa Tumblr,* 13 January 2015, accessed 17 September 2015, *http://obscuruslupa.tumblr.com/post/108008749157/bye-ca.*
31. "Mashable Awards 2010: Announcing the Winners," *Mashable,* 7 January 2011, accessed 17 September 2015, *http://mashable.com/2011/01/06/mashable-awards-2010-announcing-the-winners.*
32. *http://vimeo.com/groups/audiovisualcy,* accessed 17 September 2015.
33. Catherine Grant, "[in]Transition: Editors' Introduction," *[In]transition,* 4 March 2014, accessed 17 September 2015, *http://mediacommons.futureofthebook.org/intransition/2014/03/04/intransition-editors-introduction.*
34. Henry Jenkins, Sam Ford, and Joshua Green, *Spreadable Media: Creating Value and Meaning in a Networked Culture* (New York: New York University Press, 2013).
35. Dale Hudson and Patricia Zimmerman, "Cinephilia, Technophilia and Collaborative Remix Zones," *Screen* 50.1 (2009): 135–136.

References

Andrew, Dudley. *André Bazin.* New York: Oxford University Press, 1978.
Behlil, Melis. "Cinephilia, Internet, and Online Film Communities." In *Cinephilia: Movies, Love and Memory,* eds. Malte Hagener and Marijke De Valck, 111–123. Amsterdam: Amsterdam University Press, 2005.
Busse, Kristina. "[META] Affective Aesthetics." *Fanhackers,* 23 November 2010. Accessed 20 January 2015. *http://fanhackers.transformativeworks.org/2010/11/affective-aesthetics.*
Cousins, Mark. *The Story of Films.* London: Pavilion, 2013.
de Baecque, Antoine. *La cinéphilie: Invention d'un regard, histoire d'une culture, 1944–1968.* Paris: Fayard, 2003.
de Valck, Marijke, and Malte Hagener. "Down with Cinephilia? Long Live Cinephilia? And Other Videosyncratic Pleasures." In *Cinephilia: Movies, Love and Memory,* eds. Marijke de Valck and Malte Hagener, 13–24. Amsterdam: Amsterdam University Press, 2005.
Ellis, Lindsay. "Farewell, Channel Awesome, and a Pre-emptive FAQ." *Real Name Brand Lindsay,* 10 January 2015. Accessed 20 January 2015. *http://namebrandlindsay.com/2015/01/10/farewell-channel-awesome-and-a-pre-emptive-faq.*
Frissen, Valerie, et al., eds. "Homo ludens 2.0: Play, Media, and Udentity." In *Playful Identities. The Ludification of Digital Media Cultures,* eds. Valerie Frissen et al., 9–50. Amsterdam: Amsterdam University Press, 2015.

Grant, Catherine. "[In]Transition: Editors' Introduction." *[In]transition*, 4 March 2014. Accessed 20 January 2015. *http://mediacommons.futureofthebook.org/intransition/2014/03/04/intransition-editors-introduction*.

Gray, Jonathan. *Show Sold Separately: Promos, Spoilers, and Other Media Paratexts*. New York: New York University Press, 2010.

"The Greatest Films of All Time." *Sight and Sound* 22.9 (2012): 39–42, 44–60, 62–71.

Gui, Marco. *A dieta di media: Comunicazione e qualità della vita*. Bologna: Il Mulino 2014.

Hudson, Dale, and Patricia Zimmerman. "Cinephilia, Technophilia and Collaborative Remix Zones." *Screen* 50.1 (2009): 135–146.

Huizinga, Johan. *Homo ludens: A Study of the Play-Element in Culture*. Boston: Beacon, 1955.

Iordanova, Dina, ed. *The Film Festival Reader*. St. Andrews: St Andrews Film Studies, 2013.

Jenkins, Henry, Sam Ford, and Joshua Green. *Spreadable Media: Creating Value and Meaning in a Networked Culture*. New York: New York University Press, 2013.

Johnson, Clay A. *The Information Diet: A Case for Conscious Consumption*. Farnham, UK: O'Reilly, 2012.

"Mashable Awards 2010: Announcing The Winners," *Mashable*, 7 January 2011. Accessed 20 January 2015. *http://mashable.com/2011/01/06/mashable-awards-2010-announcing-the-winners*.

Morgan, Frances. "Of Cinephilia(s) and Fandom." *Online Roundtable 1, Project: New Cinephilia*, 31 May 2011. Accessed 20 January 2015. *http://projectcinephilia.mubi.com/2011/05/25/of-cinephilias-and-fandom*.

Obscurus_Lupa. "Bye, CA!" *Obscurus Lupa Tumblr*, 13 January 2015. Accessed 20 January 2015. *http://obscuruslupa.tumblr.com/post/108008749157/bye-ca*.

Ortoleva, Peppino. "Homo ludicus. The Ubiquity of Play and Its Roles in Present Society." *G.A.M.E.—The Italian Journal of Game Studies* 1.1 (2012). Accessed 20 January 2015. *http://www.gamejournal.it/homo-ludicus-the-ubiquity-and-roles-of-play-in-present-society/#.VL5T5Y3wvIU*.

Quandt, James. "Everyone I Know Is Stayin' Home: The New Cinephilia." *Framework. The Journal of Cinema and Media* 50.1–2 (2009): 206–209.

Williams, Kathleen Amy. "Fake and Fan Film Trailers as Incarnations of Audience Anticipation and Desire." *Transformative Works and Cultures* 9 (2012). Accessed 20 January 2015. *http://journal.transformativeworks.org/index.php/twc/article/view/360/284*.

Part III

Mutant Paratexts

Interactivity, Promotion,
Gameplay, Fandom

10 Interactivity and the Modalities of Textual-Hacking

From the Bible to Algorithmically Generated Stories

William Uricchio

Interactivity seems a familiar condition in today's digital media as we click, speak, and swipe our way through games, phone applications and e-books. These behaviors have encouraged new thinking about the nature of the text (a fixed constellation of signs or one's meandering path through that constellation? an author-defined artifact or reader-enabled experience?) They have empowered the reader, enabling her to go beyond interpretation and to collaborate in the act of textual construction. They have upset the long-standing borders between text and paratext. But these developments, exciting and challenging as they are, also encourage us to rethink some of our old certainties, to reconsider assumptions about our stable textual past and perhaps find precedent for what today seems so radical and new. As we enter an era of personalized algorithmic textual construction, these precedents are crucial if we seek to put interactivity in context.

Interactivity and the Enacted Text

'Interactivity' is a charged term for those of us who have witnessed the emergence of 'active audiences' from a media studies world dominated by textually extrapolated readings and grand theory, and a mass communications world dominated by effects theories. Reception theory and the cascade of research it inspired showed that media audiences actively construct meanings and use their encounters in quite different ways. The interpretive process, it seems, is not only ephemeral but highly inventive, as Umberto Eco's (1932–2016) notion of the 'open' text and Roland Barthes's (1915–1980) 'writerly' text showed. Studies on soap opera viewers, fan communities, and the complex and shifting terrain that constitutes media use demonstrated eloquently just how creative the people once deemed 'passive' could be. A decade or two later, just as these insights settled into taken-for-grantedness, the media industry found itself struggling to maintain analogue business models in an increasingly digital world, and media academics found themselves struggling to distinguish audience activity from interactivity.

'Isn't every textual encounter interactive?' one might ask; a meeting of the intertextually positioned reader with the intertextually produced text, as Tony Bennett once put it? Or is the notion of interactivity bound to a specific technological order, in particular, the computer and uses that have come in its wake? These questions have been answered in any number of ways.[1] For the purposes of this chapter, I would like to draw the following distinction: *active* readers encounter texts, interpret them, and make meanings; *interactive* readers also co-create texts, entering textual environments and assembling disparate textual elements into new wholes. One might say that they are textual hackers: transgressing upon the sanctity of the initial author's *urtext*, exploring, recombining, and making their own texts—in addition to their own interpretations—from it. So, for example, active audiences read a mystery novel and, armed with an interpretive stance, puzzle their way through it; interactive audiences stray across the author's organization of the novel, perhaps starting with the conclusion or reading other elements out of sequence, in the process creating their own composite text and textual experience.[2] They may also make use of textual elements provided on the back of the book or from reviews (what Gérard Genette would call paratexts if we respect the normal textual distinction), incorporating and recombining them with the text in unintended ways, emerging as co-authors of new textual configurations (and going beyond Barthes's notion of a 'writerly' text, which is still essentially interpretive).

I would like to include this kind of textual production, easily written off as aberrant behavior and textual abuse on the part of the reader, in the domain of interactivity. The term 'active' in both words underscores the importance of meaning-making as part of 'interactivity'; after all, decisions about which textual elements to draw together into a new whole, a new collaboratively authored text, usually turn on a process of desire and comprehension.

Academics have spent a lot of time with texts and active audience interpretations, but the text-enacting or text-hacking activities of the interactive user, the creative collaborations that result in new and variant texts, have remained on the sidelines (with the great exception of fan studies). One of the main reasons regards the widely held view of the text as a stable entity: the utterances of an author fixed and bound to a particular medium, confronting the reader as a given even if open to interpretation. As suggested, armed with the hindsight of today's interactive computational forms, I see the text differently: as the particular path taken by a reader through the possibilities provided by an author. It may be the path urged as the only appropriate one by the author, a path reinforced by the structural affordances of a given medium (the beginning-to-end sequence of images in a film or words in novel); or it may be the new path taken by the meandering reader, deviating from the official marked pathway to create one of his own, a path that, seen in hindsight, constitutes the text as experienced (and co-authored) by a particular reader. This is something akin to what Eco calls a 'work in movement'[3] in reference to the viewer's interaction with Calder's mobiles, except expanded to include the reader's relationship to traditionally fixed textual forms like novels and television shows. It is a notion of the text that necessarily relativizes and blurs the intended distinctions between text and paratext, producing a text that is experiential and ephemeral rather than objective and fixed.

The example taken from the mystery novel suggests that 'interactivity' precedes the digital era, even though the digital has made interactivity much easier and even, as many computer games attest, requires it as a textual condition. Then again, so do *all* games, both digital and analogue. No interaction? No activation of choice within the system's textual possibilities? Nothing happens. As with Calder's mobile, there is certainly an element of media specificity at play. But games also help us to think in terms of *textual environments* (as opposed to our usual unit of analysis—texts) and to consider that even those texts we consider fixed have interactive potentials: it is a question of whether or not they give users the opportunity to reformulate them. Admittedly, quite a range of textual possibilities come into play with a definition this broad, from works like Julio Cortázar's *Hopscotch* that cater explicitly to this behavior to something like Genette's notion of the paratext, where an array of textual elements adjacent to the core text can be selectively activated, reconfiguring the textual experience in various ways.[4] The computer game series *Grand Theft Auto* (Rockstar Games, 1997–2015) offers an example: the game can be played as an author-constructed narrative, but it can also be played by the user on her own terms without engaging any of the emplotted elements. However, the game's paratexts 'call out' certain elements, imbuing them with authorial intent and establishing them as a preferred text, in the process relegating free-form textual engagements to a negotiated or oppositional status.

Interactivity, as I use it in this chapter, goes beyond interpretation and turns on the idea of a text that the user has helped to construct, a process that may be as simple as creating one's own path through an existing (multi-) textual environment; or as profound as contributing user-generated content to the new textual ensemble. It is bound to neither a particular technology nor a technological effect, but rather it exists as a condition of use, something that readers and viewers and gamers do together with an originating author's work that results in a collaborative textual act. Interactivity can be ephemeral, an experience that results from a user's unique decisions about how to operate within a textual environment and that leaves no physical trace. Or it might leave a trace behind, a textual residue … a path that might, in turn, be taken or interacted with by some other user. In this latter case, interaction generates a new collaborative text that is persistent, not ephemeral. But whether ephemeral or not, interaction is an act that goes beyond meaning-making to a particular form of textual construction that builds from an initially authored text or texts.

I begin with this long prelude because I would like to both locate and problematize our notion of interactive in media. We tend, in part because of our late embrace of the term 'interactivity,' to use the term to focus on things like computers and videogames, environments bound by formal or informal rules and larded with textual elements that we can patch together, navigate through, and otherwise interact with. With this notion in mind, I intend to start by focusing in part on a category of objects that can, with little controversy, be deemed 'interactive': participatory and interactive documentaries. But I would also like to step back and consider earlier instances of interactivity, arguing that they have been with us as textual conditions from the start (at least in the West).

This recursive move has several advantages. First, it can put the 'new' to work, helping us to not simply look ahead and dream about what is next, but to discover new patterns in our past, revealing something unexpected of our relationship with it. Henry Jenkins did this, for example, when he revisited his earlier work on fans as active readers, redefining those parts of their activity that resulted in collective creations such as mash-ups, zines, parodies, and the rest as the work of 'interactive audiences.'[5]

Second, by revealing new patterns in the past, a recursive move of this kind can illustrate the specifically historical character of interactive works, helping us better to attend to variations in textual form over time and space that we often encounter retrospectively as fixed and stable. Interactivity has a relationship to a textual system's underlying media platform, helping us better to assess some of our current adventures in this ephemeral—and sometimes not so ephemeral—domain.

Finally, by thinking about the ephemeral's inconsistent relationship to interactivity in digital as well as analogue media forms, I hope to complicate the term in ways that might be productive as we move into the domain of algorithmically generated personalized textual systems that can be highly ephemeral and interactive, despite their apparent lack of what we have come to understand as interactive features.

Interactive and Participatory Documentary

As evidenced by the activities of the International Documentary Festival, Amsterdam's DocLab, Sundance's New Frontiers, Tribeca's Interactive Festival, and MIT's Open Documentary Lab, something happened to the form of reality-based storytelling known as the documentary over the past few years. Long understood as an authorial viewpoint, an argument steeped in knowledge and experience, a carefully crafted rhetorical utterance designed to inform or activate, the documentary's value was bound up in its point of view, the credibility of its attribution, and the persuasiveness and efficacy of its structure. But newly enabled forms of interactivity and participation have changed the terms of engagement. New documentary strategies have emerged partly as a response to environmental factors such as connectivity, ubiquitous production equipment (video camera-equipped smartphones, for instance), and widespread participation;[6] informed by developments in Interactive Fiction, game design, dynamic data visualization, and app-culture;

and shaped by an emergent set of textual expectations particularly evident in young users.

Documentary makers, like their counterparts in other once-fixed, linear forms, are exploring new ways of collaborating with their audiences, of enabling choice, of giving users data blocks with which they can build their own texts and experiences. The web-based documentaries that have emerged take many forms, one of the most common being databases in which textual elements (provided by the project's makers as well as, in some cases, members of the public) can be accessed through radically different metaphorical as well as technical interfaces (games, data visualizations, scrapbooks, maps, timelines, 'virtual worlds,' and 3D environments).[7] Users selectively call upon and assemble these authored data and textual elements into their own personalized sequences, producing textual pathways that in retrospect exist as new co-authored texts. But there is a price: ephemerality. As individual users design their own experiential paths, they engage in acts of textual creation through performance. At best, the issue of textual permanence shifts to the larger, originally authored data environment rather than the myriad co-authored paths taken through it.[8]

For some in the documentary world (as well as in the digital journalistic community, where these forms also thrive), this development poses problems. In the pursuit of interactively inclined users and at the cost of engaging these users by permitting them to follow their own interests within a given data space, the traditional values of the form are being compromised in the opinion of some skeptics. The author-as-expert, the well-crafted argument, the text-that-can-be-shared and discussed as part of a cultural moment—all of these elements are sacrificed for something more ephemeral, even if more engaging. Indeed, the more radical the notion of interactivity, and the more populous the content contributions from user-participants, the greater the distance from the old certainties that the documentary tradition has embraced for so long. Yet, in this moment of widespread change, one might argue that in most cases (except perhaps those generated with live streaming data), authorship has not been abandoned or ceded to the user. Rather, a new partnership has emerged, and with that partnership between the initiator (the conceptualizer, designer, data aggregator, etc.) and the user, there is also substance, a definable 'there' there. The database, the interface, and the rule sets that structure user activity, all enjoy relative stability, even if countless texts and experiences can be generated by the individuals who use them.

As with most computer games, an identifiable body of materials, affordances, and constraints ultimately gives its users a distinguishable (and highly marketable) experience. Does the same hold true for the well-honed argument long at the heart of many documentaries? Perhaps that is asking the wrong question. These new documentary spaces encourage user exploration of the issues portrayed, leading—one hopes—to greater engagement and knowledge. But the terms of the trade-off distinguishes them: on one hand, the classic documentary's communication of a carefully crafted argument is available-for-all-comers, and, on the other, an interactive documentary's invitation for users to explore and follow their own interests is inherently individualistic. In place of the stability of a one-size-fits-all text, an engaging-if-ephemeral opportunity to explore a carefully structured environment and rule set awaits. Why engaging? Because decisions about which textual elements to assemble are driven by the individual's interests and questions from the terrain and possibilities assembled by the interactive documentary's author. The text emerges from personal exploration. Why ephemeral? Because the path taken by the user through the textual environment (data set, interface, etc.) serves as an enactment of a possible text that is both performative in nature and transient in character. It exists as a complete text only retrospectively, as the user looks back over the trajectory she has followed. Of course, one could sidestep the ephemeral by recording the text produced by one's journey through an authored textual environment. The recording, much like a recorded computer game 'walkthrough,' would then stand as an embodied text, a tangible manifestation of the text as performed.[9]

I have intentionally overstated the differences between these two paths, one fixed and available to all readers and the other ephemeral and individual, and thus not drawn on specific examples. The truth, as always, is more complicated. But this turn in documentary production—a turn for which one can find parallels in most other digital textual systems—illustrates the core challenges of our current notions of interactivity if we use as a frame of reference the active reader's encounter with the stable text so long at the center of the scholarly gaze.

In the Beginning Was the Word ... (John 1:1)

And the word was subject to change. The mutability of the Bible, whether Old Testament or New, tends to stay on the periphery of our consciousness. For nearly two and a half thousand years, we have been too preoccupied with the project of interpretation to spend much time challenging the status of the underlying text. Besides, for much of its history, the Bible came backed up by institutional authorities: challenging the nature of the text, whether by questioning authorship, contesting passages, or adding or deleting particular texts, could result in imprisonment, death, or the birth of a new religion. Yet, despite its apparent fixity, the Bible (or at least the text by that name that each of its adherents takes to be the true and only version) exists in countless variations. Decisions regarding which texts to accrete and include and in which sequence, and in which translations have rippled across cultures and time in ways that would seem fundamentally to destabilize those who believe in the literal truth of the Bible's words.

Yet the Bible as a historical reference in Judeo-Christian cultures has been invoked as the basis for state power, has provided the authority and knowledge at the core of many religious organizations, and has enjoyed a taken-for-grantedness unparalleled by other texts. It is nevertheless malleable. We know that various parts of what is now commonly received as the Pentateuch enjoyed the ephemeralities of orality in the millennium before they were codified as scrolls (ca. the fourth century BC).[10] Divine inspiration doubtless takes many forms, but even so, oral transmission is notoriously difficult to verify or compare, especially over the long haul. Whether scroll or codex, handwritten manuscripts brought their own problems (slight variations and textual corruptions), control protocols (exemplars, emendations), and logics (in particular, the logic of scarcity). These medium-specific challenges compounded the already existing editorial undulations in biblical texts, but they were also largely contained by the supervening institutions whose task included the safekeeping of the word. Gutenberg's Bible and the printed versions that followed in its wake greatly enhanced both access to the text and the potential for textual stability, although paradoxically, greater access seems to have contributed to institutional destabilization in the form of the Reformation and the acceleration of new textual variants.

Considered over thousands of years, the Bible was formed and reformed countless times by myriad communities. Its apparent fixity is a matter of our frame of reference, just as glaciers are taken as so stable that they appear on our maps, despite the fact that, viewed over centuries, they constantly move, shift, and transform. In the case of the Bible, we might see this constant transformation as a process of collective interactivity, with particular communities shaping and re-shaping the text. At any given moment, the text seems stable enough, glacier-like in magnificence and authority; but in fact, it is constantly in flux, even if morphing at too slow a pace for us to notice. Interactive? The historical record clearly supports this view. And better, the Bible's textual undulations over time point to the affordances of various media platforms in shaping the nature of that interactivity as it moves across the spoken word, the manuscript and the printed page. These undulations also underscore the importance of institutional context. While this text's first thousand years as an oral tradition are indeed ephemeral and difficult to document, its manuscript years seem to have enjoyed the relative stability that comes with scarcity and institutional control. The printing press enabled a break from that control. As Adrian Johns argued against Elizabeth Eisenstein's notion that the printing press stabilized and helped spread the word, it also allowed for the amplification of noise and opened the door for nonauthorized, alternate uses and in the case of the Bible, revisions.[11] The Bible in its many textual variations also illustrate that interactivity and ephemerality are not bound to one another.

Johns and Eisenstein both remind us that the printed word is bound up in social practices, and despite what we may assume about the printed word's stabilities, those practices at times seem particularly prone to interactive relations with their readers. The Bible offers a *longue durée* example; but we might also look to the serialized publication practices of a nineteenth-century author like Wilkie Collins (1824–1889) for a different kind of interactivity. Like Charles Dickens (1812–1870), Eugène Sue (1804–1857), and Alexandre Dumas (1802–1870), Collins published most of his major works in piecemeal fashion. Appearing in weekly or monthly episodes, the individual chapters would be aggregated into a book near the end of the run. Collins designed his fictional worlds to make the most of this release structure, endowing them with complex and overlapping narratives, and giving each chapter something of a cliff-hanger ending to build interest for the next episode. Like today's television serials, this strategy stimulated readerly activity, as Collins's audiences speculated and debated about what was likely to happen with the next episode's appearance. Unlike today's television productions, in which the entire season is produced before the first episode airs, Collins usually wrote 'in real time,' gauging the public's response to each episode and, on occasion, modifying his planned narrative trajectory in ways he thought would better attract an audience.

While seriality stimulated reader activity, interactivity played out behind the scenes as authors like Collins tracked the ebb and flow of audience interest and, on occasion, responded to the readers' suggestions. The Preface to the 1860 edition of *The Woman in White* gives some sense of Collins's interactions with his readers.

> I remember gratefully that 'Miriam' and 'Laura' made such warm friends in many quarters, that I was peremptorily cautioned at a serious crisis in the story, to be careful how I treated them—that Mr. Fairlie found sympathetic fellow-sufferers, who remonstrated with me for not making Christian allowance for the estate of his nerves.[12]

And indeed, we know that he was not alone; Dickens, for example, responded to the pressure of friends and public alike in reassessing the fate of Little Nell. However Collins, unlike Dickens, often altered already published episodes while in the final stages of preparing the book edition, correcting inconsistencies noted by his readers and 'planting' details to accommodate changes in plot that developed along the way.

As with the example of the Bible, we tend to mistake the frozen novel that finally emerged and circulates today in canonized form as being the same as the dynamic and socially interactive process experienced by the texts' authors and first readerships. True, the variants of the Bible, like Collins's stories, enjoyed 'fixed' textual status and were bound to a medium (the book) that is generally not ephemeral, but the process of their creation attests to a creative interaction between 'author' and 'reader' in ways that resulted in multiple and competing textual variants that both drew from and differed from the author's initial text. The permanence and stability that we associate with these texts is more a matter of our frame of reference, our scale of historical analysis, and our institutional interventions than any inherent textual or medial features. We may today—in an era of instantaneous computer-enabled interactivity—read these texts as stable, fixed, and only open to interpretation, but the history of their production suggests a far more dynamic and interactive creative process.

These two examples—one spanning the history of the written word and the other from nineteenth-century publishing history—can be complemented with other public text-transforming practices such as censorship, translation, and synopsizing. The slow pace of change and the hard work of bibliographic studies notwithstanding, these practices attest to individual and collective forms of textual interactivity that we have tended to gloss over in favor of pinning down a particular authorized interaction that we today take as given. This is all to say that we have rendered a history of textual variations ephemeral, reducing those variations to developmental steps on the way to a teleological end and marginalizing a counternarrative of interactivity thanks to our preference for the authorized and stable. Moreover, we have done so in a way that is easy to mistake as media essentialism, since the apparent stability of the book would seem to make it a poor contender for the interactivity we understand best from digital media.

Back to the Future: Appearances and Deception

These historical examples are relevant as we consider 'next-generation' interactive texts, if we can call them that, especially those that rely on personalized algorithmic authoring. As we can already see from the world of print, companies like Narrative Science are capable of generating unique on-the-fly stories for individuals, producing fixed texts even though they are dynamically generated and personalized from a database of possibilities.[13] For example, Narrative Science has been exploring the niche market of reporting on Little League Baseball, a sport for children that rarely receives press coverage and yet has millions of proud parents who are eager to share news of their offspring's success. An authoring algorithm can produce a barrage of stories that rework the basic information of a particular game to fit the needs of its individual players and their parents: the same basic events, but told differently for each potential customer. As with readers of the many competing versions of the Bible, each parent believes fully that he has *the* definitive news story of the game. Better, no parent had to intervene, bribe, or otherwise pressure the reporter to write a story favorable about her child. No overt interaction was needed—the algorithm simply offered the parents of each player an appropriately different path through the data set. If the millennia-long interactivity of the Bible is too slow to notice, then the instant interactivity of Narrative Science's algorithm, which comes to the reader in the form of an already-selected-set-of-options, is too fast. Like the Bible, we don't *seem* to interact—we simply receive a fixed text; but as in the case of the Bible, appearances can be deceiving.

This example of on-the-fly personalized text production represents a relatively new direction in our relationship with media. The text is configured *for* us, on the basis of information *about* us, but without our active intervention (and sometimes, despite our active intervention!). One might describe this as a *responsive text* since the ordering of textual elements is dynamic and corresponds to the system's notion of our preferences. Yet it appears to us a stable, fixed text. The question is, can we consider this an example of inter-action? This chapter opened with a comparison of the active audience with the interactive audience as a way of clarifying the meaning of interactive texts, that is, texts that take form thanks to the combined inputs of their authors and their users. With algorithmic authoring, the user need not do anything—she is simply offered a text that feels familiar in its old-school solidity and fixity (no clicking or navigation needed!). 'Interactivity' occurs at the program level, where the text is constructed from preexisting textual elements and organized on the basis of information gleaned about the user; and where the process of interactivity is 'hidden' from view and rendered into an 'automatic' process.

In a way, we experience something similar when we perform a Google search or see the advertisements that appear on the pages of our digital newspapers. Links calculated as having high relevance based on our profiles and past web behaviors seamlessly interpenetrate whatever texts we have set out to explore. Unless we take active steps to mask our identity, we do not usually have to ask Google to give us results in the language we speak or that relate to our geographical location, nor for suggestions that echo our interest in buying a car or baby clothes or whatever it was that we last searched for. If we think of Google's search page as a composite text, and with it, the digital newspaper page studded with 'relevant' advertisements, then we can see this notion of 'responsive text' in action. Interaction, as an act of human agency, is not required (although active agency *is* required if one wishes to circumvent these new deployments).

Instead, the basis for the construction of a unique textual composite derives from tracking the human subject's behaviours, together with the transformation of the resulting data into instructions. This 'automatic' extrapolation of our behaviors and anticipation of our desires is increasingly evident: consider the predictive capacities of Pandora with music, Amazon with book recommendations, and Netflix with film and television programs.

Is this interactivity? The astute reader might already have guessed that for the purposes of this chapter, it is—just as those long-term, collectivized interactions with texts such as the Bible and some nineteenth-century seri-als that resulted in multiple and competing textual versions also qualify as interactive. To the extent that our definition privileges the text-generating interaction between the user and the preauthored textual environment, then the historical examples help to show that this is a long-standing practice. One might argue that this is a semantic game: other terms could be deployed with equal or better effect to describe these user–text relationships. But use of the term 'interactivity' helps to underscore a common set of behaviors binding today's 'point-and-click' notion of digital interactivity to both ear-lier and emergent forms of interactivity.

Interactivity in our current generation of computer games, or as discussed earlier, interactive documentaries, relies on real-time behaviors of the one-to-one variety. Each use of the control interface results in a textual change. But if we take the term to refer to a condition of user-generated textual change and textual multiplicity, then we can challenge the relevance of several of the characteristics we today also seem to associate with interactivity. Consider temporality: the real time 'cause–effect' notion of interactivity, I have suggested, can be complemented with temporalities of textual production that are glacially slow (the Bible, etc.) and quicker than our fingers can click (algorithmic generators). Consider agency: the individual pointing-and-clicking subject can be complemented by the creative intervention of collectivities (from religious interpretive communities to reading publics) and by the work of algorithms (informed by the data passively generated or actively collected by logging on to the computer). If we challenge and strip away the constrained ideas of temporality and agency that have accompanied contemporary uses of interactivity, we can discover a long history (and vibrant future) for a textual practice that we would otherwise ignore.

The axis of ephemerality and permanence works differently than agency and temporality, since the issue of storage so closely bound up with permanence plays out differently across media platforms. In most of today's digital environments, interactivity leads to textual encounters that tend to be ephemeral and fleeting, although they have textual consequences (a score in a game, the 'completion' of a documentary) and are capable of being forensically recovered or even recorded in some way. However, the environments from which users carve texts tend to be much more permanent; for example, the data set and interface design that constitute a particular version of a game are fixed as intellectual property and are distinctly persistent relative to the text-producing interactions that one has while playing it. Genette's notion of the paratext has an enhanced value in these settings, offering a way to delineate the initial author's (or reviewer's) ideas and preferred route through the data set … the author's text. Paratexts also help to frame our experience of traditional texts in media such as books and film as well. But as the earlier example of the game *Grand Theft Auto* suggests, some forms of interactivity—particularly those that require the user to navigate through a textual environment—can be particularly dependent upon them.

In many cases, like games or interactive documentaries but also like reading practices (shall I start reading at the beginning of the mystery or with its end?), the new texts that arise from interaction are articulated as such only *after* the experience. Where we went, what we experienced, how we worked our way across texts to construct a new coherence, all benefit from post-facto description. Not so the examples that we have seen from the Bible or Collins's serialized novels. Although these can of course be restructured interactively (the way a reader might make a new text out of newspaper stories or mysteries), I have argued that the work of collectives over time tends to result in textual variants that exist in the world (the *New Jerusalem*

Bible vs. the *Christian Community Bible*, for example; or Collins's published serials vs. the novels that ensued). These texts are, generally speaking, permanent, even if we have rendered the process of their users' interactions with other versions of the text ephemeral. Their process of 'becoming' is forgotten and largely rendered invisible. Similarly, if we turn our attention to algorithmically generated interactive texts, we tend to ignore the process of 'becoming.' The ways in which information about the user is gleaned, feeds back into, and interacts with the textual production process are too quick, too ephemeral, to understand. Instead, we look to the texts that are generated, texts that may, as suggested with the Narrative Science example, exist (permanently) in the world in the form of reports; or that may be as fleeting and ephemeral as today's point-and-click routines.

Conclusion

The new offers fresh ways to see the old. Today's highly visible regime of interactivity serves as an incentive to think about what the term means. Is it a media affordance, uniquely bound to a particular technological constellation? Or can its visibility in the present help us to tease out interactivity's components and look for their traces both in the past and as our media technologies continue to change? It turns out that elements such as an authored environment containing textual elements, rule sets, a particular interface, and a well-developed frame are not unique to the digital age. Yes, interactive documentaries and computer games make explicit use of these elements. And yes, today's interactive media embody distinctive notions of agency and temporality. But these specificities, I have argued, are not so much limit cases for interactivity as they are the particular flavor of our media age, a testament to medium-specific affordances of the computer as opposed to the book or film.

We inhabit a moment when, for some of our new media such as interactive documentaries and games, interaction is a textual requirement. The 'read-only' option is impossible, and this also seems to set these forms apart from earlier textual systems (the Bible, the newspaper, or television) where we can simply sit back and take in a preexisting text. The presence of this option seems to confuse us. If 'read-only' is possible, then the question quickly moves on to, what is the definitive version of the text to be read? And aren't the conditions that I have alluded to—multiple and variant texts and textual collaborations—simply the awkward developmental stages of a text's emergence to a state of finality? It is a question with implication, particularly for those texts like the Bible that continue to morph ever so slowly, but also for emerging algorithmic or responsive texts, that seem at first glance to exist in 'read-only' fixed form, even though they are in fact dynamically produced.

I do not mean to dismiss the utility of privileging an 'urtext' and the importance of the scholarly work involved in documenting an originating authorial gesture. Much of our cultural history reveals a deep and abiding concern with establishing authorial lineage and textual permanence. And yet, a closer look at certain texts, genres, and uses suggests that there is much more to be gained in some cases by exploring textual multiplicity, modification, and what we might today call textual hacking as *generative and interactive* practices in their own right rather than as mere developmental steps or worse, corruptions of an idealized end-state.[14] I have pointed to several examples of readers and communities of readers working with authored texts to create new textual variations. Tracing and understanding these generative practices has yet to be a major scholarly concern. Besides, we inhabit a moment when the advances of networked digital technologies, aided and abetted by the vagaries of widespread participation (as opposed to the certainties of authorship), require a critical, productive, and historically grounded response.

Disaggregating the concept of interactivity from exclusive association with the contemporary technoculture helps us in several ways. As argued, it benefits our understanding of the past, where we can better consider long marginalized forms of textual hacking. But it also benefits our understanding of the present. Acknowledging the *longue durée* of interactivity's defining components permits us to focus on what is distinctive about our latest media iteration. The algorithmic repositioning of the subject and with her, the notion of agency, is a far more distinctive development than the requirement for interaction that distinguishes interactive documentaries from earlier generations of hackable texts. As noted earlier, interactive games and documentaries require interaction as a textual condition. But as currently configured, that interaction generally requires the subject to make choices, to take control. The emerging algorithmic systems that I alluded to preempt that control, both 'reading' the user as a set of preferences and 'writing' the text accordingly. The user simply sees a uniquely constructed text thanks to a form of interactivity that precludes the active role of the subject it alleges to interact with. This development is far more profound than a claim for distinction that turns on interactivity as a required condition. One key implication of this development suggests that we consider expanding the definition of paratext to take account of the information that drives authoring algorithms, or else come up with a new concept to describe this mix of data regarding the reader, genre conventions, the textual environment, and the larger information set of previous reader behaviours, all of which bear directly upon the construction of the text.

Interactivity is too useful a concept to be confined to the early days of digital media. We have tended to conflate the term with a number of conditions specific to the current state of media, obscuring its utility as a concept in other settings where unwitting (and probably unwanted) collaborations between authors and their readers have generated new texts and textual variants. Those alternate texts may take the form of collectively constructed and ever-changing public artifacts like the Bible; or the many competing 'versions' of texts that we have inherited in one particular canonized form or another; or simply, as is often the case with some of today's digital media, individual texts produced by users who have assembled textual building blocks and paratextual elements in ways that address their interests. And as we look ahead, we can see that a relevant new textual class is on the rise: texts generated by algorithmic interaction with selectively gathered and processed information about the reader, in which various (and variously authored) textual elements are aggregated into uniquely designed wholes.

The term 'interactivity' offers a way to think about the long-term dynamics that conjoin authors and their readers in the *pas-de-deux* of modification, transformation, and creation of texts emanating from an initial authorial act. At the same time, it offers a way to clarify the dynamics of our media present, helping us to attend to that which is truly defining and transformative rather than reinventing the wheel.

Notes

1. To the extent that the *Oxford English Dictionary* gives an insight into word use, it seems that, although the term 'interactive' comes into robust use in the late 1960s and afterward particularly with regard to computers, it was already in use at the start of the nineteenth century with regard to causes and, later, atoms.
2. William Uricchio, "TV as Time Machine: Television's Changing Heterochronic Regimes and the Production of History," *Relocating Television: Television in the Digital Context*, ed. Jostein Gripsrud (London: Routledge, 2010).
3. Calder's mobiles yield ever-changing compositions depending on how the viewer interacts with them. Eco goes on to distinguish these 'works in movement' from traditional paintings, fixed works but still 'open' in the sense of encouraging divergent engagements. Umberto Eco, *Opera Aperta* (Cambridge, MA: Harvard University Press, 1989), 86.
4. Gérard Genette, *Paratexts: Thresholds of Interpretation* (Cambridge, UK: Cambridge University Press, 1997).
5. Jenkins uses the term 'interactive' with characteristic robustness. "Rather than talking about interactive technologies, we should document the interactions that occur amongst media consumers, between media consumers and media texts, and between media consumers and media producers." See Jenkins, "Interactive Audiences," in *The New Media Book*, ed. Dan Harries (London: British Film Institute, 2002), 157–170.
6. As of this writing, over 300 hours of video are uploaded to YouTube every minute.
7. For a good sense of what is happening in this sector, see MIT Open Documentary Lab's *Docubase*, an annotated database of developments in the sector. *http://docubase.mit.edu*, accessed 4 October 2015.
8. This is not uniformly the case; some interactive documentaries are occasionally performed for collective audiences and occasionally leave behind traces or even artifacts of a particular user's route.
9. Whitney Trettien's *Computers, Cut-Ups and Combinatory Volvelles: An Archaeology of Text Generating Mechanisms* offers an example (Master's Thesis, MIT Comparative Media Studies, 2009), *http://www.whitneyannetrettien.com/thesis*,

accessed 4 October 2015. Its interactive structure requires the reader to repeatedly choose among four quadrants of prose in order to progress through the material. The process of textual construction can be purely experiential and thus ephemeral; but each choice made also accumulates into a linear form, standing as a tangible, printable text at the end of one's encounter.

10. For a detailed look at this process, see Michael Fishbane, *Text and Texture: Studies in Biblical Literature* (New York: Schocken Books, 1979). I benefited greatly from conversations on things biblical with Nathaniel Levtow at the American Academy in Berlin where we were both fellows.

11. Adrian Johns, *The Nature of the Book: Print and Knowledge in the Making* (Chicago: University of Chicago Press, 1998); Elizabeth Eisenstein, *The Printing Press as an Agent of Change: Communications and Cultural Transformations in Early Modern Europe* (Cambridge, UK: Cambridge University Press, 1979).

12. Cited in Lyn Pykett, *Wilkie Collins (Authors in Context)* (Oxford, UK: Oxford University Press, 2005), 79.

13. According to the *New York Times*, some one billion algorithmically generated stories were in print as of early 2015. "Did a Human or a Computer Write This?" *The New York Times*, 7 March 2015.

14. Northeastern University's *Viral Texts Project*, for example, tracks the reprinting and recirculation of textual elements in nineteenth-century newspapers and magazines, demonstrating how recontextualization effectively generates new texts and meanings.

References

"Did a Human or a Computer Write This?" *The New York Times*, 7 March 2015. Accessed 1 August 2015. *http://www.nytimes.com/interactive/2015/03/08/opinion/sunday/algorithm-human-quiz.html?_r=0*.

Eco, Umberto. *The Open Work*. Trans. Anna Cancogni. Cambridge, MA: Harvard University Press, 1989.

Eisenstein, Elizabeth. *The Printing Press as an Agent of Change: Communications and Cultural Transformations in Early Modern Europe*. Cambridge, UK: Cambridge University Press, 1979.

Fishbane, Michael. *Text and Texture: Studies in Biblical Literature*. New York: Schocken Books, 1979.

Genette, Gérard. *Paratexts: Thresholds of Interpretation*. Trans. Jane E. Lewin. Cambridge,UK: Cambridge University Press, 1997.

Jenkins, Henry. "Interactive Audiences." In *The New Media Book*, ed. Dan Harries, 157–170. London: British Film Institute, 2002.

Johns, Adrian. *The Nature of the Book: Print and Knowledge in the Making*. Chicago: University of Chicago Press, 1998.

Pykett, Lyn. *Wilkie Collins (Authors in Context)*. Oxford, UK: Oxford University Press, 2005.

Trettien, Whitney. *Computers, Cut-Ups and Combinatory Volvelles: An Archaeology of Text Generating Mechanisms*. Master's Thesis. MIT Comparative Media Studies, 2009. *http://www.whitneyannetrettien.com/thesis*.

Uricchio, William. "TV as Time Machine: Television's Changing Heterochronic Regimes and the Production of History." In *Relocating Television: Television in the Digital Context*, ed. Jostein Gripsrud, 27–40. London: Routledge, 2010.

11 One Does Not Simply Walk Away from the Past. The Van Der Memes and the Dynamics of Memory and Spreadability

Paola Brembilla

Introduction

This chapter discusses the case of the *Van Der Memes*, Internet memes based on close-ups of actor James Van Der Beek (hereafter, JVDB) expressing feelings that, born as user-generated content, end up working as marketing tools for a rebranding campaign of the actor. This case study is used as a prism for understanding the dynamics of transformations of media objects in contemporary media culture, where an idea can evolve and take different forms according to specific technological, cultural, institutional and economic contingencies, ultimately blurring the boundaries between binaries like past and present, ephemerality and permanence, replication and creation of meaning, bottom/up practices and top/down strategies. I therefore propose an examination that, in trying to untangle a complex wave of heterogeneous cross-platforms and cross-spaces practices, ultimately accounts for the transformations of meaning and values, across time and contexts, of the media objects, texts, and presonalities involved. Given all these considerations, I will finally argue that, given certain conditions, a past cultural phenomenon could turn into a contingent memory of itself, shaped by and retrofitted to a new cultural context in order to make it valuable and (hopefully) profitable again.

"You have to walk away from your past in slow motion, as it explodes behind you like in a John Woo movie": this is what Chloe (Kirsten Ritter) suggests JVDB should do with his burdensome *Dawson's Creek* legacy. This line is taken from "A Reunion ...", an episode from the short-lived TV series *Don't Trust the B---- in Apartment 23* (ABC, 2012–2013, Episode no. 8, 2012), in which JVDB plays a fictionalized version of himself. The episode revolves around his willingness to set up a reunion of the actors from the well-known teenage drama, only to be rejected by each cast member. After a heartfelt talk with another fallen star, Mark-Paul Gosselaar from *Saved by the Bell* (NBC, 1989–1993), JVDB resolves he cannot be the "Beek from the Creek" anymore and sets out to leave *Dawson's Creek* in the past and move forward with his professional life.

In reality, that might also have been the case for his *actual* professional life. After the cancellation of *Apartment 23*, the actor seemed to have definitely detached himself from the show that made originally him popular, as proven by his casting in the latest installment of the *CSI* franchise, *CSI: Cyber* (CBS, 2015–). Nevertheless, *Apartment 23* marked a turning point in JVDB's carreer, since it stood as the peak of a reboot and rebranding campaign of his image that relied precisely on that *Dawson's Creek* legacy he wanted to discard in "A Reunion…". This all started with an Internet meme.

The so-called *Crying Dawson* is both an animated Graphics Interchange Format (GIF) and a macro image that has been circulating over the Internet since roughly 2007. Taken from the *Dawson's Creek* episode "True Love" (The WB, Episode no. 58, 2000), it is a close-up of the leading character, Dawson (JVDB), crying after yet another break-up with Joey (Katie Holmes). In short, the GIF became a reaction face meme that was reworked, repurposed, and shared, spreading virally over the Internet and rapidly gaining a great deal of popularity. Taking advantage of this renewed recognition, JVDB partnered with the website *Funny or Die* (hereafter *FoD*) to create *Jamesvandermemes. com*, a space that gathered a new series of reaction faces acted out by JVDB specifically for the venture. In 2012, *Apartment 23* put JVDB in the television spotlight again, having him play a skewed version of himself inspired by the parodic image that the meme and the *FoD* parodies contributed to (re)designing.

Figure 11.1 The original Crying Dawson.

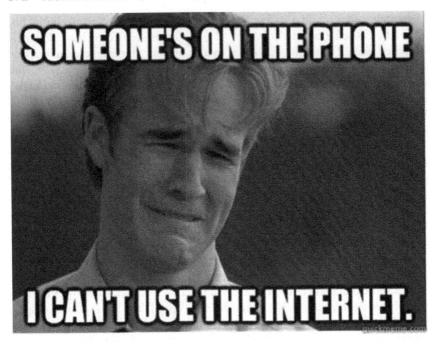

Figure 11.2 An example of "1990s Problems" meme.

Set in the range of possibilities offered by the contemporary mediascape, this case proves particularly interesting as it raises questions about the temporality of digital media objects, the role of audience memory in retrobranding practices, and the relations between user-generated content and corporate branding strategies. All of these processes ultimately contribute to the reactivation of a seemingly closed text. What is the role of the user's memory in these processes? How is this same memory exploited by the industry? How do both users and the industry create different meanings and values by retrofitting a media text to the contingencies of the present? This chapter tries to answer these questions through a phenomenological analysis of the *Van Der Memes* cultural and commercial paths, tracing the steps of the meme's evolution from user-generated GIF to the center of an industrial rebranding campaign. To this end, the first section centers on how the open and participatory nature of the original Internet meme, the *Crying Dawson*, impacts its future forms. A particular emphasis is put on the role of technology and networked memory of the primary text in fostering and shaping a new parodic image of JVDB and Dawson.

The second section deals with the incorporation of the *Crying Dawson* into a rebranding campaign for JVDB himself, which is intended to function as a reboot of his public image. Focusing on the collaboration with *FoD*, this part highlights the evolution of the meme from a by-product of contemporary participatory and remix culture to a marketing tool.

The third section examines the shift from the Internet to television, when the new JVDB image, suggested by the meme and consolidated through the *Van Der Memes*, is "institutionalized" into a network TV series. Here, matters of meanings and value in both the online and TV environment are examined and questioned. Ultimately, this structure leads to a few main points of final discussion regarding the contrast between ephemerality and permanence in the digital environment; the relationship between cultural memory and meaning in the contemporary mediascape; and the value of media objects in both participatory culture and industrial settings.

The theoretical framework of the analysis draws on cultural and media studies, particularly on the dynamics of cultural memory in the context of spreadable media. With regard to the dynamics of cultural memory, I take up Astrid Erll and Ann Rigney's argument that "the shift from 'sites' to 'dynamics' within memory studies runs parallel to a larger shift of attention within cultural studies from products to processes, from a focus on discrete cultural artefacts to an interest in the way those artefacts circulate and interact with their environment."[1] To better understand how this environment works, I also turn to the definition of spreadability by Henry Jenkins, Sam Ford, and Joshua Green, which "assumes a world where mass content is continually repositioned as it enters different niche communities. ... As material spreads, it gets remade: either literally, through various forms of sampling and remixing, or figuratively, via its insertion into ongoing conversations and across various platforms."[2] Framing the study in terms of the shift from site to dynamics and from products to processes, inserted into a paradigm that values the repurposing of content as it enters different contexts and media spaces, allows us to account for the complex interplay among the different cultural, social, economic, and technological factors that ultimately contribute to shaping the phenomenon in all its stages and forms.

The Crying Dawson

When the *Crying Dawson* GIF started spreading, it had two basic functions: (1) the GIF became a reaction face, that is, a meme that can be used on online discussion threads in order to portray a specific emotion; and (2) it made fun of JVDB's poor acting in that particular scene from *Dawson's Creek*. It is hard to say what came first, the reaction face or the mockery, but we can certainly argue that knowing where the clip comes from boosts the hilarious effects of the reaction face. In fact, it is this ironic aspect that survives and thrives despite the supposed ephemerality of Internet memes, giving birth to a discursive and cultural phenomenon that relies on the production of "different copies" of the same object.

This contradiction in terms of fidelity of form is the basis of the meme's spreadability. According to Patrick Davison, a meme is indeed

> perfectly replicable. Copy and paste functions (or their equivalents) are ubiquitous, expected parts of software platforms. However, a piece of digital media in the modern landscape of robust and varied

manipulation software renders it also perfectly malleable. Individual sections of a piece of digital media can be lifted, manipulated, and reapplied with little effort.[3]

We should keep in mind that, in the digital environment, the concept of *replicability* is necessarily combined with the idea of *constant updating*. This means that content, like open-source software, is open to implementation, extension, and renewal by both producers and users.[4] Most importantly, as Yochai Benkler puts it, "technology creates feasibility spaces for social practices."[5]

Once it started spreading, the *Crying Dawson* was no longer the original GIF. Not only did it assume different communication functions according to the context it was inserted into, it actually turned into something formally different, as happens with so-called image macros (captioned images consisting of a picture and a witty message or a catchphrase). Using basic image editor software or online platforms as *Memegenerator.net*, it is fairly easy for users to make their own version of the *Crying Dawson* and then, of course, to spread it. This is why, in light of contemporary participatory culture and the spreadable media model, replication of the same material should be associated with practices of reuse, rework, and remix that do not simply lead to the creation of *derivative works*, but above all to *discursive productions* involving the active participation and work of different agents. Henry Jenkins, in discussing Internet memes, takes up Richard Dawkins's well-known definition of a meme[6] in order to adjust the idea of direct self-replication. He argues that a meme can no longer be defined as an object that perpetually self-replicates without any alteration. The phenomenon is rather about dynamic processes of appropriation, reworking and repurposing of the original text by a wide variety of users. Jenkins therefore emphasizes the role of the users, rather than the singular objects or texts, stressing the shift from the mechanical creation of copies to the active creation of meaning.[7] As Limor Shifman suggests, "memes may best be understood as cultural information that passes along from person to person, yet gradually scales into a shared social phenomenon."[8]

As the *Crying Dawson* is constantly reworked, repurposed, and shared, what endures is a reliance on humor and playfulness that, as David Gurney observes about viral videos, is often the main "hook with which to pull in new viewers and to subsequently encourage those viewers to further disseminate the content ... sometimes even allowing viewers to take part in the formation of the text by comically modifying it and/or responding to it through direct video re-editing or versioning."[9] This is exactly how the *Crying Dawson* meme works as, from one user to another, it gradually becomes a parody of both its original source (*Dawson's Creek*) and even the era it belongs to, exemplified by the *1990s-Problems* image macros. Over the years after its cancellation, *Dawson's Creek* was often associated with a 1990s imaginary and nostalgia. So, "what better star for an image macro about the struggles of a 1990s youth than the crying face of someone from the quintessential

90s teen show?"[10] Here, the creation of meaning is taken one step further in combining a particular time and one of the texts that time produced. The result is a series of inside jokes that capitalize on the memories of people who shared and now remember both those cultural and textual experiences, amplified by the *Crying Dawson* macro. Examples include: "I wanna get on the internet, but my mom is waiting on an important call," or "I wanna call this girl from school, but I'm afraid her dad will answer the phone."[11]

In this context, we can consider other seemingly contrasting binaries that become increasingly blurred. As Andrew Hoskins argues, "the distinctions between the totalizing and the contextual, the permanent and the ephemeral, the archive and narrative, are less effectual when memory is embedded in networks that blur these characteristics."[12] As we have seen, those networks rely on the possibilities offered by contemporary technogical and cultural scenarios, which can alter the traditional role and functions of "old" media:

> Although television has been characterized as possessing an embedded 'liveness' as a property of the medium itself (i.e. television is always 'on') the internet is itself a temporally dynamic networked archival infrastructure which makes it a qualitatively different mechanism of memory. … Despite its archival promise, the Web does not merely produce an interweaving of past and present, but a new networked 'coevalness', of connectivity and data transfer.[13]

It is this "networked coevalness" of the Internet, combined with its constant updating possibilities, that allows users to turn old media objects into acts of discursive creation. Through the *Crying Dawson*, we can see how users may reactivate sleeping content, retrofitting it to their communication needs and to the contours of contemporary networked culture. Furthermore, new meanings, can even lead to the creation of new texts.

The Van Der Memes

This is not the first time memes have been associated with marketing practices. In their extensive study on Internet memes, Michele Knobel and Colin Lankshear argue that "marketing strategies from the late nineteenth century can be described retrospectively in terms of selling memes to consumers."[14] Here memes are intended as catchy and compelling promotional tools that are made to replicate and propagate, carrying with them a well-defined media agenda. In order to be successful, these promotional messages need to be subsequently incorporated by the targeted consumers. Knobel and Lankshear also stress the idea of memes becoming *social*, rather than just *commercial* phenomena, emphasizing their relational aspects and social configurations.[15] However, this case study seems to reverse this process, as the audience creates and spreads the meme, which subsequently gets incorporated by the industry. In other words, by the time it becomes part of a promotional campaign, the meme is already a social phenomenon.

As JVDB states, he discovered the *Crying Dawson* when he started using Twitter: "People would tweet stuff like 'classic @vanderjames!' and I'd expect it to be, like, something heroic from *Varsity Blues* (Brian Robbins, 1999) or a cool shot from *Rules of Attraction* (Roger Avary, 2002). But inevitably, it was always the crying GIF. It would happen quite often, and I'd always fall for it. And I'd always laugh."[16] In January 2011, the comedy website *FoD* launched the *Van Der Week*, seven days devoted to comedy videos starring JVDB, all centering on the actor making fun of himself and the character he played ten years previously in *Dawson's Creek*. For instance, in the clip from the episode *Asshole for Hire*, he apologizes for being such a "good guy" in *Dawson's Creek* and makes it up to men by becoming their personal "asshole for hire." JVDB attempts to help the guys' girlfriends understand how great they really are—while demonstrating how Dawson is no longer that "good guy."[17] In another clip, he acknowledges the popularity of the *Crying Dawson* and launches the *Jamesvandermemes.com* project because he claims he has realized what the Internet really needs: more intense close-ups on his face. The website gathers a whole new batch of reaction face GIFs, from "happiness" to "eye roll," from "mild sadness" to "super-sad sobbing," and even a "ten year anniversary crying edition." The aim is clear: "Share your own *Van Der Feeling*."[18]

The *Van Der Memes*, along with *Van Der Week*, are part of the rebranding of the actor's public image that peaks with a new TV series. At this point, the meme had already turned into a marketing tool that found its basis precisely in the main strength of the *Crying Dawson*: an appeal to the audience's memory through mockery and parody. In fact, the memes' playful and viral cultural value, transpired to be the residual value of *Dawson's Creek*, that is, "the value that remains in an object once its useful life has ended."[19] Picking up on this unexpected long tail, what we might call the *Van Der Brand Operation* turns a by-product (the meme) into a selling element, thus capitalizing on the "social phenomena" that Knobel and Laknshear mark as fundamental to making a promotional meme effective.

From a broader business point of view, we could say that this process falls into the practices of retrobranding and retromarketing. As Robert V. Kozinets argues, "old brands retain value simply by being old: the value of nostalgia, the so-called retro appeal. There is also value in the communal or cultural relationships that the brand has built over its lifetime. Finally, there are values on an individual level that relate to the former two other values."[20] Past images and meanings, already reactivated and reworked by contemporary users, take on a value that can also be shaped and managed by the industry, hopefully appealing to the same audience that made it circulate in the first place.

The Van Der Brand

According to Jonathan Gray, just like trailers and previews, a star is his or her own generic signifier and intertext, which can be used differently according to filming needs, fostering certain interpretive strategies and expectations over others.[21] At this point in the process we are examining, JVDB had already come to embody an intertextual signifier that allowed him to reach a level of (online) stardom where he was more famous for being himself making fun of himself, rather than for being Dawson. Just like the memes, his rebranding campaign relied on parody and self-deprecation, combining it with the possibilities of circulation offered by the web. This image was finally put to use in 2012, when broadcast network ABC aired the new series *Don't Trust the B---- in Apartment 23.* As JVDB stated: "The people who created *Apartment 23* saw the *Funny Or Die* videos and said, 'This is perfect; we want him on the show doing this kind of comedy.' ... Now they're creating this whole character that has my basic résumé on it but the rest is completely made up."[22] The show follows June Colburn (Dreama Walker) as she moves from Indiana to New York City and ends up moving in with the worst roommate ever, Chloe (Kirsten Ritter), whose best friend happens to be the fallen TV star James Van Der Beek. Here JVDB plays a skewed version of himself who, throughout the twenty-six produced episodes, ventures into a series of absurd efforts in order to reboot his career.

Though he was not the leading character, right from its launch, the series relied heavily on meta discourses about JVDB and *Dawson's Creek*. The promo aired during the 2012 Academy Awards ceremony: a set of traumatized people recalling their worst moments living with Chloe. JVDB, perfectly relaxed as if conducting a TV interview, recalls: "Here I am, a twenty-year-old auditioning to play this 15-year-old named Dawson." Suddenly he realizes he is not supposed to talk about that, but, just to be sure, he then asks: "Are you sure you don't want to talk about me? I like talking about me. Nobody is better at talking about me than me." When, at the end of the promo, Chloe, June, and James are presented together, JVDB closes the clip, saying: "Are you sure this isn't about me?"[23] The series follows this path, constantly leaning on Van Der Beek's character for the most funny (and shareable) sketches. A cursory search on YouTube is enough to see that most of the clips from *Apartment 23* center on JVDB spoofing himself and the craft of acting, although, as TV critic Tim Goodman notes, "if you've never seen *Dawson's Creek*, a whole lot of jokes will go over your head."[24] Indeed, as parody itself works as a form of "critical intertextuality," aiming to bump a text or genre's meaning-making process off its self-declared trajectory,[25] *Apartment 23* works on different levels to disrupt and making new sense of our cultural memory. A past textual experience is definitely required to get the jokes and therefore make the entire operation effective.

The series achieves its goal in incorporating a web phenomenon into a sitcom-shaped TV text. However, it does not succeed in institutionalizing it for good. In terms of Nielsen results, arguably the real currency of television, the ratings dropped episode after episode, until the network announced the cancellation of the series at the beginning of season two.[26] This case would surely deserve a dedicated and in-depth study on detrimental scheduling and ratings policies. However, it is clear that, since Nielsen ratings draw on a sample representing a mass audience that does not take into consideration subsegments and niches, an audiovisual product could work online in terms of popularity and circulation, but not in broadcasting terms of coveted demo and eyeballs sold to advertisers. That "surplus audience" that can activate or reactivate the circulation of content on the Web, that can start or revamp a career in terms of buzz and affective economy, is not yet a proper and direct source of profit for the "traditional" TV industry, which still has to find a way to capitalize upon it.[27]

Conclusions

The case of the *Van Der Memes* allows us to examine a process of circulation, repurpose, and creation of meanings that calls into question some of the contradictions of the contemporary mediascape, as well as issues connected to cultural memory in digital networks.

First, consider the contrast between ephemerality and permanence in the digital media environment. The uses and circulation of the *Crying Dawson* memes underline the centrality of technology in turning ephemerality into permanence, embedding both of them in remix culture and spreadable media logics and practices. Platforms such as YouTube, Netflix, and even Torrents aggregators help turn fleeting content like TV programs, traditionally associated with the transitory status of the flow, into files stocked in digital archives; users can continuously draw on these archives. In this specific case, the content (*Dawson's Creek*) is no longer ephemeral; it is permanent as it can be found in a wide range of digital spaces. However, the permanence of the file simultaneously allows for the ephemerality of its meaning and value, since that same content can, more than ten years after its "industrial" closure, be reworked and repurposed by Internet users according to new needs and in relation to new contexts. As a basic law of the spreadable media model, "whatever the audience's motivations, they may discover new markets, generate new meanings, renew once-faded franchises ... or disrupt and reshape the operations of contemporary culture in the process. In some cases, the outcomes are the direct goal of participatory culture; in others, they are a byproduct."[28]

This lead us to a second argument, regarding the active role of users in re-shaping memories and meanings. As we have seen, memes soon become a by-product of contemporary culture as they embody a reinterpretation, or rather, a second reading of the past according to new perspectives. *Dawson's Creek*, as an already closed TV series, has clearly not changed over the decades. But its audience and the cultural context around it have, finally causing the text itself to collapse and shift meanings. For instance, given the ongoing enhancement in television production values, contemporary audiences can retrospectively see the *Crying Dawson* clip as an example of bad acting and poor productive judgment.[29] This detachment from the past, combined with the technical possibilities offered by the web, allows the spread of ironic attitudes toward that content that soon turns into a parodic production. As this production increasingly circulates under new shapes and formats, it becomes a standard image of how the original text is recalled, a decade later, by its now grown-up, digitally networked audience. Turning again to Errls and Rigney's argument about memory dynamics and processes, the users who ironically reworked and spread the *Crying Dawson* GIF were not only recollecting a part of their cultural past; they were, above all, actively allowing that past to circulate again and interact with a multi-faceted contemporary environment.

Finally, in its "marketing tool" phase, our case study raises questions of the monetary value of such media in contemporary media industries. As the "Dawson Case" was reopened, JVDB benefited from this unexpected popularity and, appealing to the same audience that revived his fame, focused on what seemed to be the winning element of the phenomen: parody. However, while the operation seemed to work in the online world, where value can come from affective economies that boost the popularity of a text, the move to television did not produce the same outcome. The business model of network television proved unable to capitalize on this online phenomenon and to turn Internet value into actual profit, even though a revamped stardom based on self-parody seemed to work perfectly in terms of reputation economy.[30] Thus, the outcomes of an operation like the *Van Der Memes* rely on two types of activities: unpredictable horizontal practices of the audience and strategically planned vertical industrial strategies. Although they can certainly influence each other, the unpredictable horizontal practices seem to be much more of a driver for dynamic meaning-creation than strategically planned vertical industrial strategies, as they stand at the crossroad of personal memories, experiences, and an ever-evolving cultural environment. As we have seen, in a media environment that fosters network coevalness, blurring the boundaries between temporal and spatial binaries, a past cultural phenomenon could turn into a contingent memory of itself, retrofitted to a new cultural context by unexpected forces. But as cultural value does not always equal monetary profit, the common currency for all the involved players is yet to be determined.

Notes

1. Astrid Errl and Ann Rigney, "Introduction: Cultural Memory and Its Dynamics," in *Mediation, Remediation, and the Dynamics of Cultural Memory*, eds. Astrid Errl and Ann Rigney (Berlin: Walter de Gruyter, 2009), 3.
2. Henry Jenkins, Sam Ford, and Joshua Green, *Spreadable Media. Creating Value and Meaning in a Networked Culture* (New York: New York University Press, 2013), 27.
3. Patrick Davison, "The Language of Internet Memes," in *The Social Media Reader*, ed. Michael Mandiberg (New York: New York University Press, 2012), 122–123.
4. On software culture, see Lev Manovich, *Software Culture* (Milan: Olivares, 2010).

5. Yochai Benkler, *The Wealth of Networks: How Social Production Transforms Markets and Freedom* (New Haven, CT: Yale University Press, 2006), 31.
6. Richard Dawkins, *The Selfish Gene* (Oxford, UK: Oxford University Press, 1976). Describing how rumours, catchphrases, melodies, and fashion trends replicate through a population, Richard Dawkins defines memes as cultural versions of the human genes: they self-create, they carry replicable codes, and they are therefore able to produce endless copies of themselves.
7. Henry Jenkins, "If It Doesn't Spread, It's Dead (Part One)," *Confessions of an Aca-Fan* (2009), accessed 18 November 2014, *http://henryjenkins.org/2009/02/if_it_doesnt_spread_its_dead_p.html*.
8. Limor Shifman, "Memes in a Digital World: Reconciling with a Conceptual Troublemaker," *Journal of Computer-Mediated Communication* 18 (2013): 364–365.
9. David Gurney, "'It's Just Like a Mini Mall'. Textuality and Paraticipatory Culture on YouTube," in *Flow TV: Television in the Age of Media Convergence*, eds. Michael Kackman et al. (New York: Routledge, 2011), 30.
10. Christine Friar, "1990s Problems Meme: 13 of Our Favorites," *The Huffington Post*, 9 July 2012, accessed 18 November 2014, *http://www.huffingtonpost.com/2012/07/09/1990s-problems-meme-pictures_n_1658560.html*.
11. More *1990s-Problems* macros can be found at *http://www.quickmeme.com/1990s-Problems/*, accessed 18 November 2014.
12. Andrew Hoskins, "Digital Network Memory," in *Mediation, Remediation, and the Dynamics of Cultural Memory*, eds. Astrid Errl and Ann Rigney (Berlin: Walter de Gruyter, 2009), 92.
13. Ibid., 98–100.
14. Michele Knobel and Colin Lankshear, "Online Memes, Affinities and Cultural Production," in *A New Literacies Sampler*, eds. Michele Knobel and Colin Lankshear (New York: Peter Lang, 2007), 201.
15. Ibid., 207–210.
16. Margaret Lyons, "James Van Der Beek: I Was Aware of 'Crying Dawson'," *Entertainment Weekly*, 5 January 2011, accessed 18 November 2014, *http://popwatch.ew.com/2011/01/05/james-van-der-beek-crying-dawson*.
17. The James Van Der Beek video on *FoD* can be found at *http://www.funnyordie.com/james_van_der_beek.*, accessed 18 November 2014.
18. The video is available at *http://www.youtube.com/watch?v=tLHAoYtxrt8*, accessed 18 November 2014.
19. Jenkins, Ford, and Green, *Spreadable Media*, 100–104.
20. Robert V. Kozinets, "Retrobrands and Retromarketing," *Spreadablemedia.org*, accessed 18 November 2014, *http://spreadablemedia.org/essays/kozinets/#.VDgJ877GoVo*.
21. Jonathan Gray, *Shows Sold Separately. Promos, Spoilers, and Other Media Paratexts* (New York: New York University Press, 2010), 51.
22. Leslie Goldberg, "James Van Der Beek: 'No Dawson-Con This Year,'" *The Hollywood Reporter*, 10 July 2011, accessed 18 November 2014, *http://www.hollywoodreporter.com/live-feed/james-van-der-beek-no-209528*.
23. The promo can be watched on YouTube at *https://www.youtube.com/watch?v=h3SD_oBOx7g*, accessed 14 November 2014.
24. Tim Goodman, "*Don't Trust the B---- in Apartment 23*: TV Review," *The Hollywood Reporter*, 10 April 2012, accessed 18 November 2014, *http://www.*

hollywoodreporter.com/review/dont-trust-b-apartment-23-krysten-ritter-james-van-der-beek-310286.

25. Gray, *Show Sold Separately*, 34.

26. According to Nielsen, the first season of *Apartment 23*, a midseason replacement that aired between 11 April and 23 May 2012, averaged roughly 6 million viewers. The second season premiered on 23 October 2012 and hit a low of 2.73 million on 15 January. A week later, on 22 January, ABC announced that it was pulling the show from its schedule immedialtey. The remaining, never-aired eight episodes are now available on Netflix, Hulu, and iTunes. In 2014, they were also acquired and aired by digital cable and satellite channel Logo TV.

27. Jenkins, Ford, and Green, *Spreadable Media*, 13–14.

28. Ibid., 35.

29. See, for instance, the discourses around *narrative complexity* on the one hand, and *quality television* on the other: Jason Mittell, *Complex TV. The Poetics of Contemporary Television Storytelling* (Media Commons Press, 2014), accessed 18 November 2014, *http://mcpress.media-commons.org/complextelevision*; Kim Akass and Janet McCabe, ed., *Quality TV: Contemporary American Television and Beyond* (London: IB Tauris, 2007).

30. Gwyneth Watkins, "James Van Der Beek on Putting Dawson Behind Him and *Don't Trust the B*'s Hulu Finale," *Vulture*, 22 May 2013, accessed 18 November 2014, *http://www.vulture.com/2013/05/james-van-der-beek-dont-trust-the-b-interview.html.* JVDB might in fact have had no control over the online spread of the new image, but he certainly did benefit from it in terms of popularity. In fact, when asked whether playing *Fake James* (with all the constant *Dawson's Creek* references) felt like putting Dawson behind him, he answered: "It absolutely, I think, took me out of one mold that I'd been in for a while. It's tough to compete with something that was the cultural phenomenon that *Dawson's Creek* was. … I feel like walking down the street, I do get called "Dawson" a lot less these days. So maybe that's a measure of what the show did. Now when people mock me on the street, they use my real name." JVDB's smart move therefore consisted of jumping on the parody bandwagon and casting the light on himself, taking advantage of an already ongoing social and cultural phenomenon. It might be dangerous, however, to do the opposite. On 10 November 2014, actor and comedian Bill Cosby tweeted to his followers: "Go ahead, meme me!", attaching a link to a meme generator where users could choose one photo, type their own text, and then submit the meme for approval. However, the operation backfired quickly as users started to tweet their own screenshots under the hashtag #CosbyMeme, solely focusing on the recent reports of his historic rape allegations spanning 20 years. This was certainly not a positive promotion for the actor. Rather than benefiting his public image, the memes simply brought further attention to allegations against Cosby, prompting even more negative publicity.

References

Akass, Kim, and Janet McCabe, eds. *Quality TV: Contemporary American Television and Beyond.* London: I. B. Tauris, 2007.

Benkler, Yochai. *The Wealth of Networks: How Social Production Transforms Markets and Freedom.* New Haven, CT: Yale University Press, 2006.

Davison, Patrick. "The Language of Internet Memes." In *The Social Media Reader*, ed. Michael Mandiberg, 120–134. New York: New York University Press, 2012.

Dawkins, Richard. *The Selfish Gene*, Oxford, UK: Oxford University Press, 1976.

Erll, Astrid, and Ann Rigney. "Introduction: Cultural Memory and Its Dynamics." In *Mediation, Remediation, and the Dynamics of Cultural Memory*, eds. Astrid Erll and Ann Rigney, 1–11. Berlin: Walter de Gruyter, 2009.

Friar, Christine. "1990s Problems Meme: 13 of Our Favorites." *The Huffington Post*, 9 July 2012. Accessed 18 November 2014. *http://www.huffingtonpost.com/2012/07/09/1990s-problems-meme-pictures_n_1658560.html*.

Goldberg, Leslie. "James Van Der Beek: 'No Dawson-Con This Year.'" *The Hollywood Reporter*, 10 July 2011. Accessed 18 November 2014. *http://www.hollywood reporter.com/live-feed/james-van-der-beek-no-209528*.

Goodman, Tim. "*Don't Trust the B---- in Apartment 23*: TV Review." *The Hollywood Reporter*, 10 April 2012. Accessed 18 November 2014. *http://www.hollywood reporter.com/review/dont-trust-b-apartment-23-krysten-ritter-james-van-der-beek-310286*.

Gray, Jonathan. *Shows Sold Separately. Promos, Spoilers, and Other Media Paratexts*. New York: New York University Press, 2010.

Gurney, David. "'It's Just Like a Mini Mall'. Textuality and Paraticipatory Culture on YouTube." In *Flow TV. Television in the Age of Media Convergence*, ed. Michael Kackman et al., 30–45. New York: Routledge, 2011.

Hoskins, Andrew, "Digital Network Memory." In *Mediation, Remediation, and the Dynamics of Cultural Memory*, eds. Astrid Erll and Ann Rigney, 91–106. Berlin: Walter de Gruyter, 2009.

Jenkins, Henry. "If It Doesn't Spread, It's Dead (Part One)." Accessed 18 November 2014. *http://henryjenkins.org/2009/02/if_it_doesnt_spread_its_dead_p.html*.

———, Sam Ford, and Joshua Green. *Spreadable Media: Creating Value and Meaning in a Networked Culture*. New York: New York University Press, 2013.

Knobel, Michael, and Colin Lankshear. "Online Memes, Affinities and Cultural Production." In *A New Literacies Sampler*, eds. Micheal Knobel and Colin Lankshear, 199–227. New York: Peter Lang, 2007.

Kozinets, Robert V. "Retrobrands and Retromarketing." Accessed 18 November 2014. *http://spreadablemedia.org/essays/kozinets/#.VDgJ877GoVo*.

Lyons, Margaret. "James Van Der Beek: I Was Aware of 'Crying Dawson.'" *Entertainment Weekly*, 5 January 2011. Accessed 18 November 2014. *http://popwatch.ew.com/2011/01/05/james-van-der-beek-crying-dawson*.

Manovich, Lev. *Software Culture*. Milan: Olivares, 2010.

Mittell, Jason. *Complex TV. The Poetics of Contemporary Television Storytelling*. Media Commons Press, 2014. Accessed 18 November 2014. *http://mcpress.media-commons.org/complextelevision*.

Shifman, Limor, "Memes in a Digital World: Reconciling with a Conceptual Troublemaker." *Journal of Computer-Mediated Communication* 18 (2013): 364–365.

Watkins, Gwineth. "James Van Der Beek on Putting Dawson Behind Him and *Don't Trust the B*'s Hulu Finale." *Vulture*, 22 May 2013. Accessed 18 November 2014. *http://www.vulture.com/2013/05/james-van-der-beek-dont-trust-the-b-interview.html*.

12 "You Had to Be There"

Alternate Reality Games and Multiple Durational Temporalities

Stephanie Janes

Alternate reality games (ARGs) are commonly misconceived as videogame tie-ins for films, virtual worlds like *Second Life* (Linden Lab, 2003) or online role-playing games like *World of Warcraft* (Blizzard Entertainment, 2004). They are none of these things, but their precise definition is hard to pin down. A good definition is provided by designer Andrea Phillips:

> In these games a cohesive narrative is revealed through a series of websites, emails, phone calls, IM, live and in-person events. Players often earn new information to further the plot by cracking puzzles ... players of these games typically organize themselves into communities to share information and speculate on what it all means and where it's all going.[1]

Promotional ARGs create buzz around a film but may also provide opportunities for deeper engagement with the filmic world. As a transmedia paratext, they often extend the film's narrative across other media platforms, and in some cases the games are structured in such a way that to finish the game, players have to see the film. This is particularly true of *Cloverfield* (Matt Reeves, 2008) and *Super 8* (JJ Abrams, 2011) where the ARGs offered clues leading to the films' revelation of a monster.

The first ARG used to promote a film was part of the marketing strategy for A.I. *Artificial Intelligence* (Steven Spielberg, 2001). Named *The Beast* by its Microsoft creators, it lasted three months prior to the film's release and attracted large numbers of players, around 7,000 of whom formed the online player community known as the Cloudmakers. *The Beast* was a piece of experimental marketing developed by a small team at Microsoft Games. Three members (including Lead Writer Sean Stewart and Lead Designer Elan Lee) went on to found specialist firm 42 Entertainment, who developed similar campaigns over the following decade, including *Why So Serious* for *The Dark Knight* (Christopher Nolan, 2008) and *Flynn Lives* for *Tron: Legacy* (Joseph Kosinski, 2010). In contrast to their larger corporate clients, these are small, creative, and technical teams often referred to as Puppetmasters or PMs by player communities.

This chapter refers primarily to three promotional ARGS: *The Beast*, *Why So Serious*, and Super8. The years following *Super 8*'s release in 2011 have seen a steady decline in the use of large-scale promotional ARGs. *Super 8*'s ARG was a decidedly smaller scale affair, involving none of the live events for which *Why So Serious* and *Flynn Lives* were so highly praised. The reasons for this require further detailed research, but there may be several contributing factors. The games are labor intensive, requiring a committed team to work long hours to respond adequately to player movements. In addition, the return on investment (ROI) on a promotional ARG is difficult to discern, which is offputting in the current economic climate. There is also something of a limit to their reach. Core player communities might number in the thousands, but even with the potential for this group to spread influential word of mouth, many promotional ARGs will not reach the audience numbers demanded for Hollywood blockbusters.

In contrast, less complex viral campaigns offer reduced (but not completely removed) levels of interactivity, which also reduces logistical and financial risk. The increased integration of established social networks such as Facebook and Twitter allows engagement data to be more measurable and quantifiable using existing industry metrics. This makes them more reportable, and it becomes a little easier to argue for positive ROI. This strategy also allows the virals to access large audience segments in spaces which are semipersonal but do not necessarily encroach on dedicated fan spaces like forums or fan-created websites. Such social networks are occupied by fans and nonfans, allowing word of mouth to spread more efficiently to wider audiences, rather than being confined to the player community. All these adjustments make the games infinitely more accessible to broader audience demographics.

Current academic literature often discusses ARGs in terms of narrative extension or in their role as paratext in relation to a primary text.[2] In less text-focused analyses, they are discussed as sites for participatory culture and consumer empowerment.[3] Jenkins discusses ARGs in terms of affective economics and brand awareness but emphasizes that "for the most hardcore players, these games can be so much more."[4] Quoting games designer Jane McGonigal, he argues that ARGs can impact upon the way people think and behave in their everyday lives.[5] McGonigal herself goes as far as to suggest that the strategies and techniques of such collaborative play can prompt players to attempt real-world problem solving. She argues that such acts of "collective intelligence" can make a serious impact on social, political, and personal life.[6]

Rarely does the focus turn to the temporal dimensions of this unique piece of promotional material, despite the fact that real-time gameplay is one of the genre's defining features and a fundamental part of the experience. This chapter will therefore consider ARGs from a temporal perspective, looking at the different durational temporalities that coexist within these promotional paratexts. After outlining both their ephemeral and persistent elements, it will consider the implications of these temporalities for film marketers, as they attempt to win over consumers in a perceived "attention economy."[7] Finally, it asks how this may affect the ways ARG audiences construct and maintain mediated memories of such experiences in a contemporary media environment.[8]

Between the "Hyper-Ephemeral" and the "Anti-Ephemeral"

Several scholars have noted a tension between the ephemeral and the persistent in contemporary short-form media. Paul Grainge argues for "a dual movement towards speed and storage, immediacy and archiving," exemplified in YouTube.[9] While some scholars such as Steven Schneider and Kirsten Foot have identified this as a tension inherent in the web itself,[10] Mary Ann Doane traces this back to the emergence of film and photography, which offered new ways to capture and store the present moment.[11] Doane describes the result as a "tension between a desire for instaneity and an archival aspiration."[12]

Elizabeth Evans locates a similar tension in web dramas, describing them as involving "modes of engagement that are both anti-ephemeral and hyper ephemeral."[13] These can be used as a framework to discuss elements of ARGs, which may also fit into these two categories. However, rather than resulting in tension, the two appear to coexist comfortably, each offering different advantages for media producers and marketers trying to survive in a perceived "attention economy."[14] Furthermore, they offer users different opportunities for creating and maintaining mediated memories of these experiences.

Elements of the "hyper-ephemeral" are often the most easily identifiable forms of temporality in an ARG and contribute strongly to their appeal. The duration of the game itself is always restricted. A promotional ARG can last anywhere between three (*The Beast*) and eighteen months (*Flynn Lives*) before release. It is not, in this sense, a short-form text like a trailer or viral video; indeed, something that runs in months rather than minutes could be construed as a very lengthy experience. However, its duration is commercially restricted by its status as a piece of marketing. The ARG exists predominantly to promote another media text and ends with the release of that primary text, meaning the game comes out of circulation as soon as the film comes into circulation. In this sense, its temporality is strictly defined by commercial imperatives. Few other paratexts are this dependent on their primary text in dictating their shelf life.

However, what has the most impact on ARG players is the real-time nature of gameplay. Evans points out that web dramas "create a permanent media object that can be watched whenever the viewer chooses, but also privilege engagement with a particular moment that can never be replicated."[15] ARGs privilege that present moment even more profoundly in that they are not at all replayable since updates to websites and puzzles occur in real time. In addition, they make extensive use of live offline events like scavenger hunts or flashmobs, for which you literally have to be there. The collaborative nature of the games also means that unless players are ready and waiting for the next update, puzzles are likely to have been solved before they get there. Updates are scheduled at regular intervals, depending on the timescale of the campaign. Players are not formally made aware of this schedule; they have to anticipate it themselves. Cloudmakers therefore came to refer to "Update Tuesdays," when they would gather in forums to chat and await the next release of information. These regular updates reinforce a duality that Schneider and Foot suggest is an inherent characteristic of the web itself, "which is a unique mixture of the ephemeral and the permanent."[16]

Players tend to grow impatient for new, more challenging content, which resonates with what Jon Dovey refers to as "upgrade culture," wherein the new itself has intrinsic value.[17] Producers often cite the timing and volume of content delivery as a major issue with ARGs, as despite the most thorough preparations, players still collectively have the ability to solve content faster than producers can write it. During *The Beast*, PMs had prepared a timeline of content to last the three-month duration of the game. Cloudmakers solved all the content in twenty-four hours and were waiting expectantly for more.[18] Having set a high bar for response rates, designers were understandably concerned about the implications of "upgrade culture" in such a fast paced, real-time gaming situation. In future ARGs, attempts were made to provide more content further in advance. Unfortunately, players reacted negatively, having expected an increased amount of live interactions.[19] Over time, these expectations have been negotiated, but players continue to desire games that are responsive and play out, as much as possible, in the present.

In addition, both live events and online updates privilege the present moment in a manner similar to the "media event" described by Dayan and Katz.[20] Evans notes that although this model is applied specifically to factual programming, the key implication is "an emphasis on hyper-ephemerality and sharing a 'moment.'"[21] ARGs could certainly fall into this category, and the regular scheduling of 'update Tuesdays' could allow comparisons to be drawn with the ephemeral traditions of broadcast media. Many players describe the games in terms of an unrepeatable experience, but also of a shared experience. Some players report the pleasurable feelings of community play; of being part of something "greater than ourselves."[22] Such an experience effectively belongs to that community, partly because it cannot be experienced by anyone else again.

Finally, ARGs lean even further toward the hyper-ephemeral in that, unlike web dramas, they do not leave behind a permanent media object. This is partially due to their numerous components and delivery channels. However, the real-time nature of the games also means that, more often than not, game websites are only accessible in their final, solved state, if they can be found at all. One example from *Why So Serious* is the Joker's page, *ibelieveinharveydentoo.com*. The initial page (*ibelieveinharveydent.com*) was released on 17 May 2007. It was designed as a campaign poster featuring an image of Harvey Dent (played by Aaron Eckhart) against a background of a United States flag. Featuring the slogan "I Believe in Harvey Dent," it encouraged players to sign up for alerts on Dent's political campaign. However, on *ibelieveinharverydenttoo.com*, the same poster appeared to have been defaced, with maniacal black circles around Eckhart's eyes and a red, clown-like smile hashed across his face. At the end of the slogan, someone had scrawled the word "too." As on the original site, viewers signed up with names and email addresses, causing pixels in the vandalized image to be gradually replaced and revealing the first official image of Heath Ledger as the Joker. On 23 May 2007, the image was replaced with a black screen and a red error message "Page not found," which appeared when the Ledger image was completed. Highlighting the black background uncovered a secret message from the Joker, warning players that more games were afoot.

The site has remained in this state since that date, rendering the initial two images of Eckhart and Ledger inaccessible. Such documents cannot be stored or archived in the same way as other promotional paratexts, such as posters, trailers, or viral videos, because the content itself is in a constant state of flux. This is partially the nature of the Internet, where any upgrades of pages are not rigorously archived. Without tools like the Web Archive, it is extremely difficult to retrace these games as they happened, and even these processes cannot guarantee to capture the updates at precisely the time they were made.[23]

Since both their real-time nature and status as marketing are so fundamental to promotional ARGs, they seem to lean more toward the 'hyper ephemeral' rather than the 'anti-ephemeral.' In addition, this tendency may appear to be driven by commercial imperatives, in some cases, out of the control of players. However, despite its apparently short, commercially determined shelf life, an ARG also displays elements of permanence, some of which lie in the hands of players (and therefore media consumers) rather than producers.

The term 'ephemeral' is often used to discuss more material media 'detritus,' but ARGs leave behind a trail of *digital* flotsam and jetsam.[24] The games may not create a singular media object proper, but leave in their wake a series of websites or partial websites. Some links will be removed, some fail over time, but many linger and may be accessible via services like Web Archive. Many sites from *The Beast* are now only accessible in this manner. The games also produce physical detritus in the form of merchandise that is offered up as prizes for completing tasks. During *Why So Serious*, players received official merchandise in the form of Joker t-shirts but also received in-game items that were unavailable anywhere else. Examples included copies of the in-game newspaper *The Gotham Times* as well as Harvey Dent campaign flyers, bumper stickers, and buttons.

During the ARG for *Super 8*, players were divided into teams to play a number of flash games that earned them points for their team or 'fleet.'

Individual players with the highest scores received a limited edition replica of an 'Argus' cube, a piece of alien technology that featured prominently in the film. During the sign-up process, some players also received certificates or letters through the post, which were deemed more interesting and valuable than those that were emailed in a digital document. These items (known on forums as 'swag') function as more permanent, physical remnants of the gaming experience.

The continued existence of the player community itself is also a permanent legacy of an ARG. While it often begins with an existing fan community (e.g., *Batman* fans or *Tron* fans), an individual community grows around each game, sometimes across a number of forums.[25] Players check in on forums at differing rates, but a core team usually updates the group at least daily, if not more frequently. As with any other online community, their interactions and conversations (in-, or out of game) are recorded on the forums and some, like *unfiction.com*, are publicly viewable.

Gameplay may also involve player-created media objects. For example, during *The Beast*, players created two documents. The first was the Trail, which details every site discovered during the game.[26] The second document, the Guide, is a thorough, chronological walkthrough that describes every inch of the game as it played out, authored by player Adrian Hon.[27] Players also frequently create accompanying wiki pages to record the progress of games.[28] Because these documents are actively curated by players, they are less likely to degenerate over time than in-game "official" websites and they form more permanent web-based artifacts.

However, it is the archival tendency of these communities that displays a more active negotiation of the temporal tensions in ARGs and that contributes to their anti-ephemerality. Players are aware of the fleeting nature of the games to which they are so passionately committed and are driven in an attempt to make a permanent record of their experience. This helps newcomers familiarize themselves with the game's progression, but also provides a more permanent record of the game's existence and of player experience. Such an active involvement in curating as well as playing the games leads to a strong and long-lasting affective impact for many players. Almost 60 percent of survey respondents agreed that ARGs could be accurately described as "an intensely felt, emotionally affective experience."[29]

A number of moderators and administrators from the Cloudmakers player group went on to be key figures in transmedia and interactive game design. These include Steve Peters (Founder/CCO of No Mimes Media), Andrea Phillips (freelance transmedia writer, game designer, and author), and Adrian Hon (Founder/CCO of Six to Start). For some, the games prompted a drastic career change. Game designers even recall being invited to the weddings of couples who met through an ARG.[30] As with many other online communities, players create strong bonds of friendship and often meet up offline. The collaborative nature of ARGs makes them highly social and emotional experiences, which often stay with players long after the games have ended and which also drive the desire to archive those experiences as comprehensively as possible.

Finally, the game narrative may also continue to circulate long after the ARG has finished. Speculation as to what could have happened and positing of alternative endings continue on the boards for some time after the conclusion of an ARG. This is more noticeable when a game narrative has been particularly difficult or confusing to unravel, or when the ending has not been definitive enough for the community. In some instances, this might be tactical on the part of producers, particularly for games linked to producer JJ Abrams, for whom withholding narrative information is something of a signature move.

The ARG for *Cloverfield* led players to believe the film's monster may have emerged from the ocean, linked to a reported drilling accident at the fictional oil firm, Tagruato. Yet it offered no definitive answers. Players were then prompted to see the film, which showed them what the monster looked like and documented its attack on Manhattan, but could not answer questions surrounding its origin. However, the film did offer more clues. Something could be seen in the final scenes, falling from the sky into the sea. Suddenly a new possibility emerged—the creature came from the sky, not the sea. Players returned to the ARG to continue the search, and ensuing speculation kept the narrative in circulation far beyond the release date of the film. It should be noted, however, that this is not typical of promotional ARGs, which, as previously mentioned, tend to end their narratives with the release of the film being promoted.

Multiple Temporalities in an "Attention Economy"

Most of the energy devoted to archiving the games comes from players, keen to preserve an experience they have often invested in emotionally. In contrast, Hollywood film-marketing campaigns are focused on the present moment, with a heavy emphasis on opening weekend box-office figures. The ephemerality of ARGs provides high levels of marketing buzz and a sense of exclusivity. The games often drive players to see the film as soon as possible in order to conclude the narrative and avoid spoilers. However, the importance of a more sustained level of attention is not lost on producers. A huge amount of revenue lies in longer term purchases such as DVD and merchandise sales, so it has become crucial not only to grab audience attention immediately, but to sustain that level of interest and buzz beyond opening weekend. The varying durational temporalities of ARGs might therefore be seen to work toward this end in a number of ways.

First, the cyclical viewing pattern noted previously sustains that continued interest. From a creative perspective the circulation of narratives promotes further participation and audience engagement. A more commercial take on this is that it promotes repeat viewings and DVD purchases. It allows players to further analyze the film for clues that might relate back to the game. The game then continues to pose unanswered questions, so players are more likely to return to the film again to see if they missed something the first time around.[31]

Second, the ephemeral nature of the games offers a sense of exclusivity that the product itself simply cannot provide. Once the film is released, anyone can see it, but only a select few can say they were part of the ARG, part of a wider experience that gives them cultural capital over those who were not there and often a higher authority to speak about the film. They know the backstory to *Cloverfield*. They know what happened to Harvey Dent before he became Gotham's DA, and they have the t-shirt and the bumper sticker to prove it.

This exclusivity also creates strong 'buzz.' Goldhaber's notion of an 'attention economy' suggests the apparently fleeting nature of the contemporary audience's attention span This audience is now so media saturated that it requires more than a 30-second TV spot to capture their attention in the first place, let alone sustain it.[32] Whether consumer attention spans are in fact shrinking is not for this chapter to ponder; what is evident is the increasing amount of media competing for that attention. Whether we describe this as 'saturation' or a 'glut' of information, media producers are desperate to reach consumers who are perpetually surrounded by media, to break through the noise. "Attention" as resource is considered so scarce that it may take on a higher perceived value than actual monetary capital. As the implications of this theory, Dovey suggests that "if you focus enough attention on your brand, you will make money even if there is no actual cash flow."[33] To this end, ARGs can create the buzz and column inches in the trade press that Dovey claims are "as valuable to the brands concerned as a rise in sales."[34] They have the potential to confer event status on a marketing campaign in a way traditional strategies cannot. Although the format is becoming increasingly familiar to audiences, they retain a novelty that allows them to keep up with the aforementioned "upgrade culture."[35]

Dovey also suggests that previous methods for measuring viewer engagement, particularly TV ratings, were more concerned with the quantity rather than the quality of engagement.[36] However, increased competition for that attention means quality is becoming increasingly important. This concern is reflected by immersive marketing agency 42 Entertainment's conceptualization of their target audience. In an early version of their website, 42 Entertainment identified its audience structure in the form of an inverted triangle. Elan Lee, Lead Designer on *The Beast*,explains this structure clearly:

> The largest broad part at the top is the very very casual player. There are more of them than anyone else. So we try to make sure there is at least some easy way into every game we create—a two-ten minute experience that is rewarding and fun and will hopefully encourage you to come back.

The middle part is not nearly as populated as the top. Those guys are going to maybe check in every week, every two weeks. We try to make sure they have plenty to do whenever they want to experience it.

And then the very tip of the triangle. Those are the crazy guys—the hardcore guys. ... And the cool thing about this pyramid is there's a really lovely side effect where the bottom part entertains the top parts. ... And that's just as entertaining ... but in order for any one of our experiences to be successful we have to have some mechanism to allow all three of those kinds of players.[37]

The ephemeral qualities of an ARG might create buzz and draw people to the games simply to see what all the fuss is about. Those who 'lurk' on forums but do not participate in puzzle solving or live events hugely outnumber the more active players, offering a high volume of low-quality engagement. *Unfiction.com* suggests the ratio of lurkers to active players can range from 5–1 to 20–1, depending on the scale and nature of the game.[38] More committed players, distinctly smaller in number, will engage on a much higher level. This means ARGs have the potential to attract both a high quantity of low-quality engagement and a low quantity of high-quality engagement at the same time. Getting the balance of content right to suit all levels of audience participation is difficult but not necessarily impossible.

Finally, the lingering affective impact of such a high level of engagement can also work in favor of marketers. Jenkins refers to "affective economics," a media marketing theory that "seeks to understand the emotional underpinnings of consumer decision-making as a driving force behind viewing and purchasing decisions."[39] Once they understand those emotional attachments, marketers can attempt to shape them, getting people emotionally involved with brands or products. Kevin Roberts (former CEO of Saatchi and Saatchi) developed this into a marketing concept, dubbing such brands "lovemarks."[40] It might be argued that by using ARGs as promotional materials, marketers are encouraging consumers to associate these strong emotional attachments with a film they have not seen yet, encouraging a longer term investment in the property.

Multiple Temporalities and Mediated Memories

These varying temporalities may seem more productive for media producers than for consumers. Players may experience more tension between them, as they enjoy the pleasures of the ephemeral, but they also display a strong archival tendency in their meticulous documenting of the games. The archive is often used as a metaphor for human memory, yet Ernst argues that it does not function in terms of narrative memory but merely as a storage facility. Narrative remembrance is then imposed from without and is "external to the archive."[41] For Ernst, the dynamic temporality of the Internet means digital or online archives shift from being spatial to temporal entities: "Within the digital regime, all data become subject to real-time processing. Under data processing conditions in real-time, the past itself becomes a delusion; the residual time delay of archival information shrinks to null."[42]

This flattening of time and a perpetual sense of present due to real-time processing resonates with the experience of an ARG. Players' archival tendencies may represent an attempt to retain control and make sense of the slippery temporalities associated with such experiences, suggesting a struggle to reclaim memory in the face of a digital media environment that privileges the ephemeral so strongly. Hyper-ephemerality therefore prompts an archival tendency that is even more pronounced in a digital era which simultaneously offers "archival promise" and yet possesses a shifting temporality that is "emergent and continuous," a "continuous networked present."[43] As communities collectively reconstruct their experiences of the games, they negotiate their experiences within what Hoskins describes as "digital network memory," wherein data is highly transferable and accessible but also eminently erasable.[44] ARGs can therefore be seen as a site where this tension between temporalities is actively negotiated by media consumers as they work to create memory objects to which they can repeatedly return.

This might seem something of a burden for players, but this same fluid temporality has its advantages. Ernst argues that digital archives are interactive, with digitally networked documents being "time-critical to user feedback."[45] The classical, spatial archive, removed from its attachment to state bureaucracies becomes fluid instead of static. Rather than being organized space and memory, this digital archive is in constant flux, continually being reorganized and redrawn. The ability to perpetually redraw, reorganize, and redefine confers a certain amount of power on those users. Ernst suggests that the power of the archive resides in its silence; its function as mechanical media storage rather than its ability to tell a story.[46] It is organized, calculating memory, not social or narrative memory that is imagined and projected onto it. The dynamism of the digital archive means traditional power structures are no longer relevant and users may arguably become as influential as any state institution (or indeed media organization) in the organizing of mediated memory. As Ernst notes, one need not possess archival information, but merely the means to access it in order to control it.[47]

Indeed, players need not own ARG content to access and manipulate it. Such archiving has also historically been the remit of players rather than game designers or the corporate media clients who contract them to create the games. The closest "official" records of ARG activities exist as videos on company websites promoting the work. These videos are usually edited to be short and informative rather than really delving into the complexity some of these games can offer.[48] It is players who construct the more residual online memory of their gaming experiences. Speculation similarly allows for the construction of alternative narratives, which means players may tell their own stories in a way that reflects their personal experience of the games, not necessarily the ones PMs intended to tell.

Van Dijck also points to the importance of what she calls "mediated memory objects" in the construction of cultural memory.[49] Such objects are defined as "the activities and objects we produce and appropriate by means of media technologies, for creating and re-creating a sense of past, present, and future of ourselves in relation to others."[50]

The entire game itself, with its amalgam of player and PM-produced content, could be described as a mediated memory object, although that object is often somewhat fragmented and distributed across various online spaces. These fragments could also be individually described as mediated memory objects, particularly those created by players, such as the wiki pages, or tribute websites, such as *whysoseriousredux.com*. An ARG focuses strongly on the ephemeral and the fleeting but at the same time provides some more permanent media objects that form strong sites of remembrance, particularly for those players for whom the games become an emotionally affecting experience. For some, these can even form a locus for identity formation, making them even more relevant to Van Dijck's definition: "At a fundamental level my identity as a player reflects who I am and what I believe." (UF)

It also provides material memorabilia such as swag. Possession of swag becomes not only a more permanent reminder of the games, free from the prospect of digital deletion, but also a form of cultural capital amongst players. It is possible that, as Hoskins suggests, the ephemerality of the digital side of ARGs affords the "material objects ... of cultural memory ... greater significance."[51] Ernst similarly notes that "the more cultural data are processed in electronic, fugitive form, the more the traditional archive gains authority from the very materiality of its artefacts (parchment, paper, tapes)—an archival retro effect."[52]

Many of the comments from players suggest that these material objects form an important part of remembering and reminiscing about a game experience that is otherwise difficult to document:

> *It represents all this time I spent going nutso over something and I can always look at it and be like, 'Oh yeah ... that was pretty awesome.'* (SHH)

> *I plan on passing it along to my son when he gets old enough.* (SHH)

While this chapter has dealt primarily with the impact of the temporalities present in an ARG, there is scope for further research into the relationship between ARGs and cultural memory construction. In particular, the collective experience of the games and the ensuing collective speculations and constructions of game content reflect Van Dijck's position on the mutual interdependence of collective and individual cultural memory.[53] The two are often separated in scholarly work in memory studies but are quite explicitly intertwined in a media experience that requires collective as well as individual work for it to succeed.

ARGs, like many online media texts, can be seen to incorporate both ephemeral and permanent elements. However, while it might look like they lean more toward the "hyper-ephemeral" than the "anti-ephemeral," they have the potential to make a far longer lasting impact on audiences, which is reflected in the passionate and committed player responses to the games. This could be extremely valuable for marketers and producers in their continuing struggle to survive in a perceived 'attention economy.'[54] They also involve mechanisms that allow players to construct mediated memory objects, provided either by the game itself (e.g., swag) or by players (e.g., wikis and tribute sites). Many scholars have noted the fears surrounding media technology and the erasure or disintegration of memory.[55] The ephemeral nature of these games and their focus on present-ness might contribute to this perception. However, these varying temporalities also allow for players to have a sense of control over how they remember and recount the stories of their experiences between themselves and to others.

Notes

1. Andrea Phillips, "Soapbox: ARGs and How to Appeal to Female Gamers" *Gamasutra.com*, 29 November (2005), accessed 20 January 2014, *http://www. gamasutra.com/features/20051129/phillips_01.shtml*.
2. Jonathan Gray, *Show Sold Separately: Promos, Spoilers, and Other Media Paratexts* (New York: New York University Press, 2010); Henrik Örnebring, "Alternate Reality Gaming and Convergence Culture," *International Journal of Cultural Studies* 10:4 (2007).
3. Henry Jenkins, *Convergence Culture: Where Old and New Media Collide* (New York: New York University Press, 2006).
4. Ibid., 130.
5. Ibid., 131.
6. Jane McGonigal, "Why I Love Bees: A Case Study in Collective Intelligence Gaming," in *The Ecology of Games: Connecting Youth, Games, and Learning*, ed. Katie Salen (Cambridge, MA: MIT Press, 2008), 199–228.
7. Michael Goldhaber, "The Attention Economy and the Net," *First Monday* 2.4 (1997), accessed 6 February 2015, *http://firstmonday.org/article/view/519/440*.
8. Data for this chapter was taken from interviews with Sean Stewart and a small player survey, the answers to which provided a structure for analyzing the vast quantities of player forum discussion available online. The online survey involved around thirty core ARG players (most of whom were based at *ARG forum unfiction.com*) which asked them to provide details of their gaming experiences. Participants were selected from this forum, as it forms the largest and most well-established hub of active ARG players (34,246 registered users as of December 2014). Results of the survey were then used to structure a more in-depth analysis of online discussions on player forums at both *unfiction.com* (UF) and *superherohype.com* (SHH), which provided the central player hub for *Why So Serious*. All survey responses are anonymous, and no users have been identified either by name or by their forum handles. All forums are publicly accessible and do not require registration or membership to view.

9. Paul Grainge, ed., *Ephemeral Media: Transitory Screen Culture from Television to YouTube* (London: BFI and Palgrave, 2011), 3.
10. Steven M. Schneider and Kirsten A. Foot, "The Web as an Object of Study," *New Media and Society* 6.1 (2004).
11. Mary Ann Doane, *The Emergence of Cinematic Time: Modernity, Contingency, The Archive* (Cambridge, MA: Harvard University Press, 2002).
12. Ibid., 29.
13. Elizabeth Evans, "Carnaby Street, 10am': Kate Modern and the Ephemeralization of Online Drama," in *Ephemeral Media: Transitory Screen Culture from Television to YouTube*, ed. Paul Grainge (London: BFI and Palgrave, 2011), 156.
14. Goldhaber, "The Attention Economy and the Net," accessed 6 February 2015, *http://firstmonday.org/article/view/519/440*.
15. Evans, "Carnaby Street, 10am,'" 156.
16. Steven M. Schneider and Kirsten A. Foot, "The Web as an Object of Study," *New Media and Society* 6.1 (2004): 115.
17. Jon Dovey, "Time Slice: Web Drama and the Attention Economy," in *Ephemeral Media: Transitory Screen Culture from Television to YouTube*, ed. Paul Grainge (London: BFI and Palgrave, 2011), 142.
18. Elan Lee, *This Is Not a Game: A Discussion of the Creation of the AI Web Experience*, paper presented at Game Developers Conference, San Jose California, accessed 6 February 2015, *https://groups.yahoo.com/neo/groups/cloudmakers/files*.
19. Sean Stewart, Interview by author, London (9 December 2012).
20. Daniel Dayan and Elihu Katz, *Media Events: The Live Broadcasting of History* (Cambridge, MA: Harvard University Press, 1992).
21. Evans, "Carnaby Street, 10am,'" 163.
22. Cloudmaker quoted in Jenkins, *Convergence Culture: Where Old and New Media Collide*, 131.
23. See *http://archive.org/web*, accessed 6 February 2015.
24. Amelie Hastie, "Detritus and the Moving Image: Ephemera, Materiality, History," *Journal of Visual Culture* 6.2 (2007): 171–174; Charles Acland, ed., *Residual Media* (Minneapolis: University of Minnesota Press, 2007).
25. *Why So Serious* was played on *unfiction.com* but also on the broader fan site *superherohype.com*.
26. *www.cloudmakers.org/trail*, accessed 5 February 2015.
27. *www.cloudmakers.org/journey*, accessed 5 February 2015.
28. *Why So Serious* wiki—*http://batman.wikibruce.com/Home*, accessed 5 February 2015. *Super 8* wiki—*http://super8.wikibruce.com/Home*, accessed 5 February 2015.
29. Player Survey conducted by author, 2012.
30. Stewart, Interview by author, London, UK.
31. A commercial advantage also noted in Stephanie Janes, "1-18-08—Viral Marketing Strategies in Hollywood Cinema," in *Besides the Screen: Moving Images through Distribution, Promotion and Curation*, eds. Virginia Crisp and Gabriel Menotti Gonring (London: Palgrave Macmillan, 2015).
32. Goldhaber, "The Attention Economy and the Net," accessed 6 February 2015, *http://firstmonday.org/article/view/519/440*.
33. Dovey, "Time Slice: Web Drama and the Attention Economy," 151.
34. Ibid., 150.

35. Ibid., 139.
36. Ibid., 42.
37. Elan Lee quoted in Mary Jane Irwin, "Q&A with Alternate Reality Games Director Elan Lee," *Wired Magazine* 16.6 (17 May 2007), accessed 5 January 2015, *https://web.archive.org/web/20130614215450/http://www.wired.com/gaming/virtualworlds/magazine/15-06/st_arg3*.
38. *www.unfiction.com/glossary*, accessed 5 February 2015.
39. Jenkins, *Convergence Culture*, 62.
40. Kevin Roberts, *Lovemarks: The Future Beyond Brands* (New York: Power House Books, 2004), 43.
41. Wolfgang Ernst, "The Archival Metaphor: From Archival Space to Archival Time," in *Open* 7 (2004): 29.
42. Ibid., 51.
43. Andrew Hoskins, "Digital Network Memory," in *Mediation, Remediation, and the Dynamics of Cultural Memory*, eds. Astrid Erll and Ann Rigney (Berlin: De Gruyter, 2012), 100.
44. Ibid.
45. Ernst, "The Archival Metaphor," 50.
46. Ibid., 48.
47. Ibid., 50–1.
48. For examples see *www.42entertainment.com/work*, accessed 5 February 2015.
49. José Van Dijck, *Mediated Memories in the Digital Age* (Stanford, CA: Stanford University Press, 2007).
50. Ibid., 21.
51. Hoskins, "Digital Network Memory," 103.
52. Ernst, "The Archival Metaphor," 48.
53. Van Dijck, *Mediated Memories in the Digital Age*.
54. Goldhaber, "The Attention Economy and the Net," accessed 6 February 2015, *http://firstmonday.org/article/view/519/440*.
55. See Hoskins, "Digital Network Memory"; Van Dijck, *Mediated Memories in the Digital Age*; Martin Zierold, "Memory and Media Cultures," in *A Companion to Cultural Memory Studies*, eds. Astrid Erll and Ansgar Nünning (Berlin: De Gruyter, 2010), 399–207.

References

Acland, Charles, ed. *Residual Media*. Minneapolis: University of Minnesota Press, 2007.
Dayan, Daniel, and Elihu Katz. *Media Events: The Live Broadcasting of History*. Cambridge, MA: Harvard University Press, 1992.
Doane, Mary Ann. *The Emergence of Cinematic Time: Modernity, Contingency, The Archive*. Cambridge, MA: Harvard University Press, 2002.
Dovey, Jon. "Time Slice: Web Drama and the Attention Economy." In *Ephemeral Media: Transitory Screen Culture from Television to YouTube*, ed. Paul Grainge, 138–155. London: BFI and Palgrave Macmillan, 2011.
Ernst, Wolfgang. "The Archival Metaphor: From Archival Space to Archival Time." In *Open* 7 (2004): 46–53.
Evans, Elizabeth. "'Carnaby Street, 10am': Kate Modern and the Ephemeralization of Online Drama." In *Ephemeral Media: Transitory Screen Culture from*

Television to YouTube, ed. Paul Grainge, 105–121. London: BFI and Palgrave Macmillan, 2011.

Goldhaber, Michael H. "The Attention Economy and the Net." *First Monday* 2.4 (1997). Accessed 6 February 2015. *http://firstmonday.org/article/view/519/440*.

Grainge, Paul, ed. *Ephemeral Media: Transitory Screen Culture from Television to YouTube*. London: BFI andPalgrave Macmillan, 2011.

Gray, Jonathan. *Show Sold Separately: Promos, Spoilers, and Other Media Paratexts*. New York: New York University Press, 2010.

Hastie, Amelie. "Detritus and the Moving Image: Ephemera, Materiality, History." *Journal of Visual Culture* 6.2 (2007): 171–174.

Hoskins, Andrew. "Digital Network Memory." In *Mediation, Remediation, and the Dynamics of Cultural Memory*, eds. Astrid Erll and Ann Rigney, 91–106. Berlin: De Gruyter, 2012.

Irwin, Mary Jane. "Q&A with Alternate Reality Games Director Elan Lee." *Wired Magazine* 16.6 (17 May 2007). Accessed 5 January 2015. *https://web.archive. org/web/20130614215450/http://www.wired.com/gaming/virtualworlds/ magazine/15-06/st_arg3*.

Janes, Stephanie. "1-18-08 – Viral Marketing Strategies in Hollywood Cinema." In *Besides the Screen: Moving Images through Distribution, Promotion and Curation*, eds. Virginia Crisp and Gabriel Menotti Gonring, 87–104. London: Palgrave Macmillan, 2015.

Jenkins, Henry. *Convergence Culture: Where Old and New Media Collide*. New York: New York University Press, 2006.

Lanham, Richard. A. *The Economics of Attention: Style and Substance in the Age of Information*. Chicago: University of Chicago Press, 2006.

Lee, Elan. "This Is Not a Game: A Discussion of the Creation of the AI Web Experience." Paper presented at Game Developers Conference, San Jose, CA, 22 March 2002. Accessed 2 December 2014. *https://groups.yahoo.com/neo/groups/ cloudmakers/files*.

McGonigal, Jane. "Why I Love Bees: A Case Study in Collective Intelligence Gaming." In *The Ecology of Games: Connecting Youth, Games, and Learning*, ed. Katie Salen, 199–228. The John D. and Catherine T. Macarthur Foundation Series on Digital Media and Learning, Cambridge, MA: MIT Press, 2008.

Örnebring, H. "Alternate Reality Gaming and Convergence Culture." *International Journal of Cultural Studies* 10.4 (2007): 445–462.

Phillips, Andrea. "Soapbox: ARGs and How to Appeal to Female Gamers." *Gamasutra.com* (29 November 2005). Accessed 6 January 2015. *http://www. gamasutra.com/features/20051129/phillips_01.shtml*.

Roberts, Kevin. *Lovemarks: The Future Beyond Brands*. New York: Power House Books, 2004.

Schneider, Steven M., and Kirsten A. Foot. "The Web as an Object of Study." *New Media and Society* 6.1 (2004): 114–122.

Stewart, Sean. Interview by author. London, UK, 9 December, 2012.

van Dijck, José. *Mediated Memories in the Digital Age*. Stanford, CA: Stanford University Press, 2007.

Zierold, Martin. "Memory and Media Cultures." In *A Companion to Cultural Memory Studies*, eds. Astrid Erll and Ansgar Nünning, 399–407. Berlin: De Gruyter, 2010.

13 The TV Recap

Knowledge, Memory, and Complex Narrative Orientation

Claudio Bisoni

Introduction

Within media studies, both short and paratextual media forms and long-lasting serial narratives are often taken as significant sources for the study of audience agency. Brief YouTube parodies, home-made trailers, and mash-ups are assumed to privilege user empowerment much more than traditional broadcasting. We view them as elements of an audiovisual politics that contrasts the demands of large-scale media conglomerates insofar as they feed two of the typical characteristics of the digital age: autonomy and the fragmentation of traditional audiences.[1] The same thing has happened for particularly long, complex serial forms: multi-platform narratives function as temporally enduring media environments, within which the user's cognitive activity is constantly challenged, following the industry's encouragement.[2]

Certain media objects bridge the universes of long and short forms. These objects, which are often placed within the category of 'orienting paratexts' (online encyclopedias, maps, lists of characters, etc.), are narrative-content management tools that allow spectators to 'do things with long narratives.' One of these tools is the recap. In the following pages, I will provide an analysis of the recap, or the recapitulation in its unabbreviated name: those brief, autonomous, self-contained narrative segments that are posited at the beginning of single episodes of TV series. Generally, their duration will be anything between 20 and 90 seconds, though at times they last longer, as per certain episodes of *Game of Thrones* (HBO, 2011–), on which I will focus in greater depth below. Recaps provide a summary of what occurred in previous episodes of a series, often beginning with the standard expression "Previously on. ..."

My initial hypothesis is that these narrative devices mark a point of contact and coordination between short and long serial forms. The most evident point of contact is given by the fact that short, ephemeral forms and long, serial forms have different temporalities. Recaps, precisely by means of their short form, activate mnemonic and cognitive processes that allow users to recall the essential elements of long plots. Spectators often value vast narratives such as *Lost* (ABC, 2004–2010), *Breaking Bad* (AMC, 2008–2013), and *Game of Thrones* as important experiences in their entirety. These are shows that have contributed decisively to the formation of identity for many as consumers of TV series. Nevertheless, the way in which we recall very long series is inevitably selective: not all of the content remains in our minds with the same persistence. There are certain elements of these series that we take, more or less consciously, as superfluous; elements that did not engage us on an emotional or intellectual level therefore become ephemeral memories. Yet some of these elements may have an important role in fully explaining certain aspects of the narrative content, and therefore demand some kind of persistent and articulated recognition on behalf of the viewers. As we will see, it is possible to suggest that the primary function of the recap is to help the spectator sustain a persistent and an active memory of content that might otherwise be forgotten.

In the following paragraphs, I consider how the problem of the summary has been studied in relation to literature and what changes when such studies are instead applied to the context of serial television. In the third section, I identify three areas of study for the recap: its collocation within serial forms, its two principal types, and its most important functions. The fourth section is devoted to the mode in which the recap interacts with the viewer by managing sets of knowledge and recollection. The final section offers some conclusions, along two lines of thought: (1) I read the recap not only as a tool that summarizes narrative universes, but also as a map that allows us to orient ourselves within them; and (2) I consider the role of the recap in the construction and preservation of memories of long serial forms.

Summary, Seriality, Recapitulation

In the field of literary theory, Gérard Genette has studied the literary summary, identifying the possible modes of textual reduction and particularly focusing on the different forms of quantitative reductions: excision, concision, condensation, and so forth.[3] The principal criterion of Genette's classification is the way in which reduction relates to the hypotext, since to reduce a text necessarily means to alter it. In literature, according to Genette, the reduction practices of excision and concision sustain a constant and direct relationship with the hypotext (however, he specifies that concision abbreviates a text, rewriting it concisely and therefore producing a new text that might not contain a single word of the original). Condensation, in contrast, is based on the original text "only in an indirect way."[4] Entire sentences and details from the original are forgotten, and what remains is "the movement of the whole." This process, he writes, is what is otherwise called "digest, abridgement, résumé [or] summary."[5]

In summarizing certain, earlier parts of a narrative, recaps offer a sample of that narrative's past, in the same way that trailers offer a sample, a preview, of a film. Jonathan Gray has demonstrated the connection between the growing universe of paratexts and the fact that today we live in a climate of "saturation of everyday life with media."[6] "Surrounding texts," like trailers and spoilers (and also recaps) serve to direct the viewer's attention toward specific elements of a narrative universe, to guide the spectators in their choice or understanding of media texts, and elements of the environments from which they emerge and which they help to shape in turn.

Lisa Kernan has illustrated how trailers constitute a short textual form that unites promotional discourse with narrative pleasure. Within this relationship, it is possible to identify precisely how trailers constitute textual forms that reflect on spectatorship: "Trailers provide unique and specific rhetorical structures that fold visual and auditory evidence of the film production industry's assessment of its actual audience (as well as its desires for a potential audience) into a one- to three-minute cinematic experience."[7] Even though trailers and recaps therefore have different aims and functions, another shared trait that unites them (aside from the fact that they both offer a 'sample' of a larger text, and that they are both orientation tools for a mediascape characterized by an extremely abundant supply) is that they are strategic locations in which the production of a show or a story reflects and activates the cognitive work of the viewer.

Recaps are above all connected to the experience of seriality and to the narrative complexity that lies at the root of TV series. Narrative complexity in contemporary cinema has been studied from varied perspectives. For Allan Cameron, it is chiefly an account composed of "disarticulated narrative pieces." This complexity is connected to a database aesthetic, in which one can perceive a "modular conception of time," thereby making time decomposable and "subject to manipulation."[8] This highlights a link between the complexity and disarticulation of a narrative, to which I will return in the study of the recap's function.

Jason Mittell has outlined the connection between the narrative complexity of contemporary TV series and the problems of "accessibility" that this poses. Mittell similarly reads recaps as "orienting paratexts"—in other words, as elements that allow the spectator to manage the complexity of serial narratives.[9]

In what remains of this chapter, I will analyze recaps in relation to the work of two scholars in particular. I will first apply Mittell's model of analysis to the specific example of a recap. I will then seek to demonstrate the more general function of the recap with reference to several theoretical notions developed by Ruggero Eugeni, in the fields of the social semiotics of cinematographic texts and the semiotics of the media experience.[10] One of the foundational principles of social semiotics is that cinematographic (but also televisual) texts select and activate certain sets of knowledge that are communicated to the spectator. These processes of selection and activation "imply that sets of knowledge are translated in perceptible terms and, specifically, in terms of visibility."[11] Knowledge sets therefore become visible within the audiovisual text and can also vary in type: social or historical, but also textual, intertextual and metatextual knowledge (in other words, knowledge that transmits to the viewer a recognition of how the text itself is composed). What remains to be understood, then, is how recaps trigger the knowledge and recognition of the very TV series that they must summarize.

The majority of these knowledge sets, in the case of the recap, adhere to the narrative type. Eugeni has proposed several terms for the analysis of modular narratives, which I will make use of here. He describes the situations that appear on screen as stimuli that allow the spectators to update their situational map continually. A situational map is a kind of cognitive schema realized by the viewer, consisting of a rich array of information in synthetic form. It includes information describing specific places and moments at which the character's actions overlap with the emotive states in which they carried them out (Eugeni refers to the practical and emotive chrono-topological developments that take place in a certain situation).

The use of situational maps implies activity on behalf of the viewer: *retrospective activity*, where the spectator recalls the situational map employed up until that moment and prepares to modify its relevant details; *inspective activity*, where the spectator grasps differences and modifies the situational map; and *prospective activity*, where the spectator imagines and presupposes the transformations that are to follow shortly. Situational maps, moreover, operate in varying dimensions. There are reduced-scale maps that enable us to define overview situations; in other words, they allow us to record the fundamental events of an episode or the entire narrative arc of a series, or of a whole diegetic world. Then there are large-scale maps, which allow us to define standard situations—that is, contingent situations that have importance and relevance only in limited segments of the diegetic world or the narration.[12]

Collocation, Morphology, Functions

In this section, I will analyze the recap in relation to three principal characteristics: its collocation, its form, and its function.

Collocation (Location)

Recaps are "entryway paratexts."[13] Their position is generally paratextual; however, the relationship between the recap and the very episode that it has to introduce is ambiguous. The recap is a kind of threshold that is connected to other, more traditional thresholds, such as the opening credits, logo, or theme song. The theme song tends to fade or be absorbed into a position within single episodes, often following the first, inciting incident of the current installment: this occurs in series such as *Romanzo Criminale* (Sky Cinema 1, 2008–2010); *Boardwalk Empire* (HBO, 2010–2014); and *Six Feet Under* (HBO, 2001–2005). The recap, differently, usually appears before every other textual element, though at times with small variations. In *24* (FOX, 2001–2010/2014), for example, it appears after the logo, is announced with the text "Previously on *24*," and is followed by a further text that indicates the temporal coordinates of the events to come ("The following takes place between 9:00am and 10:00am") and by the opening credits that underlie the first moments of action. The second episode of the second season of *Utopia* (Channel 4, 2013–) begins with the opening credits over images of the first events; this continues for two and a half minutes and includes a standard situation (a dialogue in prison between a man and Jessica Hyde). The sequence is then interrupted by the logo of the series over a green–yellow background. Only after this do we see a comprehensive recap of the entire first season, which lasts exactly 60 seconds.

The recap, then, is always situated in the incipit zone of the text-episode to which it belongs; however, it can ultimately fall into different zones within the initial boundary of the text, borrowing Genette's terms, before or after the other "liminal devices and conventions" that constitute the peritext.[14] The collocation of the recap is dependent on a preliminary, if not presupposed, condition: essentially that it is included at all. In general, TV producers create one recap per episode aired. It is not a given, though, that it will appear at the beginning of every episode when it comes to the quotidian viewing experience of the spectator. TV audiences often make use of illegal downloading services, via torrents or software such as eMule, and frequently those who upload the illegal copy of the episode cut the initial recap. With the multiplication of the channels of media content delivery, then, in the empirical conditions of contemporary viewing it is common to find both video files of episodes equipped with the recap, and those 'corrupted' equivalents that go without. In the latter case, the recapitulatory function for the series is therefore omitted from the peritextual area and, in many cases, shifted to the epitext where it is entrusted to other resources, for the most part online (summaries on Wikipedia or on official websites, encyclopedias, books, forums).

For Mittell, TV series encompass three different types of time: story time, which is the timeframe of the diegesis and which follows a linear progression; discourse time, which refers to the duration of the narrative as it is presented in a given account; and screen time, which is the material time taken up by recounting a story (or having a story told to us) by means of a cinematic and televisual language. This final 'time' exists in literature and reading, too (narration time), and in that case it is variable insofar as it is controlled by the reader. In the case of cinema and TV, screen time, having long been controlled by the cinematic apparatus and by networks, is becoming increasingly something that the user can regulate thanks to personalization processes.

The recap is significant on the levels of story time and discourse time. However, it also has a key role in managing screen time. Screen time has been long neglected by scholars, and yet it is central in defining the experience of seriality today because, as Mittell notes, it is precisely what regulates the links between episodes and seasons. Above all at the beginning and end of each episode, there are formal markers—such as opening credits, theme song, and recaps—which delineate single episodes as discrete units (as indeed do chapter lists of episodes on the DVD menus of TV shows). The recap therefore helps to define the autonomy of every episode, while also introducing a ritual element, repeated at the beginning of each episode and underlining the serial nature of the viewing experience (in standard weekly programming, each episode is separated from the next by a serial gap). In this sense, the recap is a short form that collaborates in the organization of long-form serials, given that it marks each episode as separate from the preceding and subsequent ones.

The recap is an obstacle to the continued and uninterrupted viewing of a series as though it were a single, very long film. In fact, its summary function loses significance in practices such as binge watching or marathon viewing, where the spectator seeks a continued and uninterrupted playback and therefore has little need for memory cues that recall the essential elements of a plot (at that moment, all the information is still deposited in the viewer's short-term memory). The use and meaning of the recap are therefore closely tied to the viewing mode. However, since viewing modes today are much freer than they once were, and since spectators have an ever greater control of the screen time of a series, it is possible to perceive the recap as something useless and therefore expendable. This constitutes a principal characteristic of the recap in terms of its collocation: it is not only an ancillary textual form connected to the episode that it introduces, but also an ephemeral form. On one hand, when speaking of 'ephemeral media' generally, the emphasis tends to fall on an idea of 'ephemeral' as synonymous with 'temporary,' 'volatile,' and 'subject to extinction.' The recap, on the other hand, sheds light on another important aspect of ephemeral media. The recap is an ephemeral object insofar as it is superfluous: by nature, its presence is not certain; it is not guaranteed, nor always taken as systematically indispensable to the modification of empirical viewing conditions.

Morphology

In order to fulfill their primary, synoptic function, recaps have evolved according to two principal models: the summary recap and the modular recap. In the summary recap, the succession of images is primarily composed of audiovisual material from the immediately preceding episode, then secondarily of even older textual threads, and in some cases narrative material from earlier seasons. The images are accompanied by a soundtrack consisting almost entirely of a voice-over that orients and defines the story. The voice-over assumes the summary function and attempts to produce an organic reconstruction of the whole narrative.

The second model, the modular recap, is much more common. In this type, the images included are built of a succession of material that is very similar to that of the summary recap. However, the voice-over is often absent, or if included it rejects the pretense of an exhaustive or 'omni-comprehensive' recapitulation of past narrative material. The modular recap offers only a concentrated selection of events. In order to understand how it does this, it is necessary to examine more closely the function of the recap.

Functions

Let us consider a concrete example: the modular recap from the beginning of the fifth episode of the third season of *Game of Thrones* (HBO, episode no. 5, season no. 3, 2013). The recap falls at the beginning of the episode. It is preceded by the on-screen text stating "Previously on *Game of Thrones*" and is followed by the HBO logo and series theme music. The recap is divisible into ten narrative units; it lasts a total of 87 seconds, and it offers a brief summary of the subplots of which the series' narrative is composed, as follows. First and second narrative units: we observe two dialogues that take place in King's Landing, one between Cersei Lannister and her father (the first subplot), the other between Sansa Stark and Lady Margaery, regarding their respective future engagements (second subplot). Third narrative unit: we see Stannis Baratheon talking with Melisandre on Dragonstone (third subplot). Fourth narrative unit: Rob Stark faces Lord Karstark's vindictive intentions (fourth subplot). Fifth narrative unit: Jaime Lannister's attempted escape fails, and his captors threaten to cut off his left hand, too (fifth subplot). Sixth narrative unit: Rob Stark discusses the scarce possibility of killing the two youngest Lannisters, held captive, in revenge (fourth subplot again). Seventh narrative unit: Stannis Baratheon imprisons his advisor Davos Seaworthy, who had attempted to warn the former about Melisandre's intentions (third subplot again). Eighth narrative unit: we witness a dialogue between Eddard Stark and Robert Baratheon on the nature of the traitor Jorah Mormont. Ninth narrative unit: the character nicknamed The Hound is challenged to a duel (sixth subplot). Tenth narrative unit: Daenerys orders Astapor to free the slaves and have Kraznys, the king of the realm, incinerated by one of the dragons (seventh subplot).

This recap therefore presents the various subplots, highlighting the most significant events of each. The excerpts taken from each narrative unit use the dialogues in the clips to recall the names of places and characters, and to re-present events and situations. According to Mittell, contemporary TV series are increasingly inserted into a media landscape that provides orienting paratexts designed to help users adapt to complex narrative universes. These paratexts (encyclopedic wiki, character lists, chronologies, and location maps) provide mapping and orientation roles with regard to four macro areas: time, events, characters, and spaces. The recap considered here evidently plays this orientation role, and in fact it presents some of the main characters of the series, locating them in their respective spaces of action as they undertake significant acts.

On closer inspection of the same recap, however, one realizes that not all of the subplots are afforded the same space. Rather, on two occasions it lingers on two subplots (one with Rob Stark at the center, the other focusing on Stannis Baratheon and Melisandre). There are some series-long subplots that feature in the fifth episode and that are nevertheless absent in the recap (for example, the subplot with Jon Snow at the center or that with the protagonist Tyrion Lannister). Moreover, the eighth narrative unit presents us with material from the first season of the series, therefore covering material that has no temporal vicinity to the other contiguous narrative units, refreshing the memories of the viewers with details from an extremely long time ago, that moreover appear unrelated to what has so far happened in the third season. *Game of Thrones* has a complex narrative structure that is linear from a temporal point of view. Unlike *Lost*, *Heroes* (NBC, 2006–2010), *FlashForward* (ABC, 2009–2010), and *Damages* (FX, 2007–2012), it does not employ flashbacks or flashforwards.

The number of subplots is extremely consistent, however, and, over the course of the seasons in fact increases. As such, it happens that some subplots go untouched for entire episodes. Recaps are thus necessary above all to remind the spectator of events that might not have happened in the previous episode but will nonetheless have an important role in the successive ones. As such, recaps in *Game of Thrones*: (1) summarize only approximately the essential elements of the various subplots; and (2) do not do this in anything like a uniform way: they might dedicate more space to one subplot and entirely neglect another. In other words, recaps are not recapitulations of entire narrative universes but rather of *narrative modules*. Recaps carry out a choice between what needs to be shown and what is not relevant to a given moment of a narrative arc. But it does more than this: it places the material that is shown into a hierarchy so as to highlight significantly or subtly its potential for development in the narrative that immediately follows.

The Knowledge in Play

It is now time to investigate what kinds of knowledge the recap activates in the spectator. What I have outlined thus far can be summarized by reviewing the recap's engagement with the spectator in three phases of operation.

A first analeptic moment, which depicts parts of a diegetic world belonging to the past of an ongoing narrative. This triggers a 'recapitulative' role in the addressee—in other words, what Eugeni calls retrospective activity.[15] In this phase, the spectator is asked to recall a group of events (that will prove decisive in understanding the overall progression of the plot), like an anthology. The general recollection of what had taken place earlier allows the user to understand the plot correctly. It is in this moment that those key clarifying areas identified by Mittell—relating to time, space, events and characters—establish themselves.

A second, proleptic moment, in which an orienting impulse is introduced ("here is the information that might help you orient yourself here in the immediate future"). This triggers selective and pre-visional knowledge within the spectator, that is, that kind of activity that Eugeni labels prospective. The viewer must keep hold of the most relevant narrative elements in order to understand correctly what will happen in the future of the story. By observing the way in which recaps include certain narrative threads and not others, the spectators can advance hypotheses on what events will progress significantly in the episode that they are about to watch.

A third moment, in which the recap provides information indirectly concerning the structure of the macrotext that it seeks to navigate. This phenomenon is notable above all in the case of series with particularly complex narratives. In North American television, for example, networks and conglomerates have enabled distribution and production practices that manage to coordinate operation in different areas and sectors of the media system. High-concept series are narrative products that are filmed with a recognizable look and a characteristically complex structure.[16] In the era of convergence, these narratives often extend across the various media. They become media franchises that are expanding narrative universes. This kind of structure encourages active user participation and makes space for varied modes of consumption that can be personalized.[17]

In order to favor the process of content fragmentation and its consumption on varied platforms, the narratives of complex TV become constructed in blocks or modules (they are multi-strand narratives) that are only loosely connected to a general narrative universe. Indeed, this is one of the principal characteristics of complex TV. Some series are built around plots that have the typical properties of so-called vast narratives distributed in cross-media universes. The stories within these narratives have a clear combinatorial and procedural potential that is typical to certain videogames; they are stories that might develop secondary threads, alternative narratives, further information about certain characters and their pasts, and so on.[18] We are therefore dealing with narrations composed of blocks that can be moved around within the whole, that is, inserted at different points of a single narrative arc, or expanded and contracted according to the public's approval. Broadly autonomous sequence narratives and joined-up narrative modules at the same time relate single components to a whole and sanctify their relative individuality.

Recaps prove to some extent that narrative blocks can be moved and removed. The components of the source text that appear in the recap exhibit their own modular structure and separability. Put differently, recaps exemplify that modular quality that enables them in the first place and that lies at the foundation of the series they are summarizing. Here I use the term 'exemplify' as it is used by Nelson Goodman, when he considers exemplification as a symptom of the aesthetic and states that a sample swatch exemplifies some properties of a textile but not all of them.[19] I would like to suggest that the recap functions as a 'sample' of a specific property of complex TV series: specifically, their modularity. The recap "makes manifest, selects, focuses upon, exhibits, heightens in our consciousness"[20] the modular nature of the majority of contemporary series.

In this third moment of the recap, the meta-discursive competencies of the spectator are tested: by means of recaps, the viewer is prompted to note not only the what of the narrative, but also how it is constructed; to reflect on some of its characteristics, adopting a kind of aesthetic attention that is oriented to the form of a show, which Mittell calls the operational aesthetic (in this case, operational knowledge corresponds to the spectator's familiarity with some of the norms of storytelling).

In short: what prevails during the first stage is the summary function of a narrative world; during the second it is the process of selection and prevision; and in the third, the mapping function of the 'narrative playground.'

Conclusions: Space and Memory

The notion of the 'narrative playground' might rouse some perplexity. How can a story, which by definition is distributed across time, have spatial properties? This is a question that is found today in the notion of narrative architecture common in game studies.[21] Mittell insists that the accessibility of a complex TV series, aside from relating to time, events, and characters, also invests directly in space. The space of a TV series must be accessible to its users. According to Mittell, the majority of contemporary TV series have not yet explored the full potential of spatial storytelling: most programs follow the filmic procedures of classical continuity in order to orient their viewers within a diegetic space.

Often, however, the paratexts of TV series provide maps of the various settings of the action. In the case of *Game of Thrones*, for example, the function of spatial orientation is the responsibility of that peritextual threshold of the opening credits: they present a digital animation that introduces us to the places in the narrative universe (the various cities of the kingdoms involved in the series' cosmos). Different versions of the credits appear with each episode, according to a principle that privileges those places that are more relevant to the episode that will immediately follow.[22] More generally, the media industry today assumes not only that spectators will re-appropriate, re-elaborate, and commentate content, but also that they will know how to move within and around it; that they can orient themselves with ease. Knowing how to move within the spaces of a series becomes an essential part of a positive experience of consumption. Since narrative ecosystems are often built of complex architecture, whoever accesses their space requires several orientation points: an entrance, an exit, and footpaths to move along.

The authors of contemporary TV series must ask themselves the same question that has always faced the screenwriters of traditional soap operas: how to deal with those viewers who have not seen entire episodes of a show. In the past, one possible solution was to construct situations in which the same narrative information was (re-)presented at different points of a plot, through dialogues or other resources (what Mittell calls diegetic retelling). Even classical serials were designed for distracted spectators and unordered viewings. The writers of new TV series, however, have not only the problem of viewers who have missed some episodes of the show. They are also faced with a further dilemma since the consumption of new serials is experienced through processes of selective navigation inside an expansive and complex media space. For this reason, recaps do not limit themselves to facilitating the story's logic of succession, but rather offer tools for spatial orientation within a territory.

In recaps, experimentation and narrative complexity—both of which are capable of influencing much contemporary film and TV—are relocated to an orientation map, converted into space, and approximated to a cartographic representation. The recap is not the space of narrative virtuosity; rather, it is a map that helps us to *manage* narrative virtuosity. Managing this virtuosity is like managing an extremely large territory. Therefore, the recap works as an interface that permits the user to interact with a complex medial system from a defined access point. This idea—that of the shift from a conception of the recap in terms of summary or recapitulation to a notion of the recap as an interface—could make a small contribution to the geographic turn in which scholars of media ecosystems are investing today.[23]

One final question, on which I would like to pause, is that of memory. Recaps have a privileged and intuitive relationship with mnemonic functions: recapitulations are systems of memory activation. But to what kinds of memory are we referring here? Recaps relate in particular to 'practical' memory: a recollection that allows spectators to recover basic plot information at a certain point of a narrative universe, in order to understand a story and take pleasure in its narration. In contemporary media research, scholars have reflected at length on the relationship between memory, the archive, and digital technologies.[24] With regard to serial television of the past twenty years, it is clear that the cultural value of certain series is strictly connected to its duration and to the intensity of the social processes of reception that surrounded the series.[25] The question of the intensity and the duration of fandom phenomena have often been interweaved with attempts to understand how a stratified and complex social memory was created around media products.[26]

Mariagrazia Fanchi has recently recalled how one of the future challenges in media research will be to integrate, in an increasingly conscientious way, the work of memory (and its various functions and modes of access) into the study of the ways we experience the media.[27] Today it is already clear that the work of fan communities is significant in defining memories of media experiences and of the ways in which they circulate and remain alive. Here, one thinks of those cases in which a series that ended many years ago is kept alive in the practices of its fans and in the texts that they produce, so as to extend as much as possible the authenticity of that cultural experience.

Certain extremely common activities relating to user agency can be seen as contributors to social memory operating successfully around certain media products. Spin-offs, parodies, fake trailers, commentaries, encyclopedias, as well as practices that play on the relationship between online and offline generally, all feed the fan communities of certain media products, and therefore feed the memory of those very media products, too. Audiovisual archives such as YouTube collect 'reaction to' video series, which inscribe digital memories of emotional reactions to particular narrative passages of certain programs. Alongside those apparatuses that feed social memory, there are others that work on a more circumscribed level. This is the level on which we can situate recaps in relation to the problem of memory. Recaps assist what we might call a functional memory of TV series. Functional memory probably does not have a decisive role in the way we recall the TV series that we love best and therefore incorporate as authentic experiences, or those that we recall with emotional intensity within our media consumption. It nevertheless has a complex composition, and remains foundational to the users' successful content management.

Mittell has demonstrated how TV producers must address various types of spectators in relation to the "mechanics of serial memory."[28] There are spectators who will explore the various paratextual extensions of a series, for example, reading reviews or contributing to fan forums and other participatory cultural sites, which keep the narrative aspects of a series fresh in their minds. Others do not. Furthermore, when consumed over a period of months and years, it becomes difficult to manage what one ought to remember and what can be forgotten from a series. For this reason, Mittell writes, "the long arcs of complex television must balance the memory demands of a wide range of viewers and reception contexts."[29]

The recap—with its optional and uncertain presence, and its internal articulation that allows us to recuperate narrative segments from the past of a series' plot—is a 'retain and recall' apparatus that helps us to engage with mnemonic variables of consumption involved in the action of remembering a complex narrative universe. Specifically, the recap reactivates within our 'operative working memory' a local, contained selection of information that with the passing of time has slipped into long-term memories or into oblivion. The information contained by long-term memory as well as that within the operative working memory together constitute what I have called the functional memory of a series—that is, the prerequisite memory for an adequate and sufficient understanding of a narrative universe. Even if, as I have suggested, single recaps allow us to trace partial maps of the narrative playing field, all of the recaps of a series together can offer an easy-access foothold that helps to keep active the functional memory of the series as a whole. In other words, recaps collaborate in the process of maintaining functional relationships between memory and narrative comprehension at different levels (local and general). Mittell has clarified the extent to which narrative comprehension depends on functional memory operating correctly. What remains to be seen, and what is beyond the scope of this chapter, is whether there is, as one suspects, a connection between the narrative comprehension of a series and the ways in which it becomes an enduring memory in the lives of individuals, with a fixed place in the cultural memory of the public.

Recaps are a short form that maintain a kind of ancillarity with regard to the long narrative forms to which they are 'glued.' They offer a contained and modest orientation function to complex TV. However, the function of the recap has also evolved, providing it, as we have seen, with a more ample role than its traditional one of merely summarizing. The recap therefore responds to different needs today than those of the past, and as such it tells us much about how the new forms of contemporary serial TV think through the relationships between viewer agency, narrative complexity, the need for orientation inside this complexity, and the short- and long-term mnemonic processes that are necessary for precisely that orientation.

Notes

1. See Massimo Scaglioni, *TV di culto: La serialità televisiva americana e il suo fandom* (Milan: V&P, 2006); Pelle Snickars and Patrick Vonderau, ed., *The YouTube Reader* (Stockholm: National Library of Sweden, 2009); Thomas B. Ksiazek and James G. Webster, "The Dynamics of Audience Fragmentation: Public Attention in an Age of Digital Media," *Journal of Communication* 62.1 (February 2012): 39–56.
2. See Henry Jenkins, *Convergence Culture: Where Old and New Media Collide* (New York: New York University Press, 2006); Henry Jenkins, "Authoring and Exploring Vast Narratives: An Interview with Pat Harrigan and Noah Wardrip-Fruin" (2009), accessed 8 December 2014 *http://henryjenkins.org/2009/05/an_interview_with_pat_harrigan.html*.
3. Gérard Genette, *Palimpsests. Literature in the Second Degree*, trans. Channa Newman and Claude Doubinsky (Lincoln: University of Nebraska Press, 1997).
4. Ibid., 238.
5. Ibid.
6. Jonathan Gray, *Show Sold Separately. Promos, Spoilers, and Other Media Paratexts* (New York: New York University Press, 2010), 1.
7. Lisa Kernan, *Coming Attractions. Reading American Movie Trailers* (Austin: University of Texas Press, 2004), 3.
8. Allan Cameron, *Modular Narratives in Contemporary Cinema* (New York: Palgrave Macmillan, 2008), 1.
9. See Jason Mittell, *Complex TV: The Poetics of Contemporary Television Storytelling*, accessed 4 October 2015, *http://mcpress.media-commons.org/complextelevision*.
10. See Ruggero Eugeni, *Film, sapere, società: Per un'analisi sociosemiotica del testo cinematografico* (Milan: V&P, 1999); Ruggero Eugeni, *Semiotica dei media: Le forme dell'esperienza* (Rome: Carocci, 2010).
11. Ruggero Eugeni, *Film, sapere, società*, cit., 8 (translation my own).
12. See Eugeni, *Semiotica dei media*.
13. Gray, *Show Sold Separately*, 18.
14. Richard Macksey "Foreword," in Gérard Genette, *Paratexts: Thresholds of Interpretation*, trans. Jane E. Lewin (Cambridge, UK: Cambridge University Press, 1997), xviii.
15. See Eugeni, *Semiotica dei media*.
16. See Justin Wyatt, *High Concept: Movies and Marketing in Hollywood* (Austin: University of Texas Press, 1994).

17. See Paola Brembilla and Guglielmo Pescatore, "La serialità televisiva americana: produzione, consumo e tipologie di prodotto," in *America oggi. Cinema, media, narrazioni del nuovo secolo*, ed. Giulia Carluccio (Turin: Kaplan, 2014), 275–290.
18. See Pat Harrigan and Noah Wardrip-Fruin, ed., *Third person: Authoring and Exploring Vast Narratives* (Cambridge, MA: MIT Press, 2009).
19. See Nelson Goodman, *Ways of Worldmaking* (Hassocks, UK: Harvester Press, 1978).
20. Ibid., 65.
21. See Henry Jenkins, "Authoring and Exploring Vast Narratives: An Interview with Pat Harrigan and Noah Wardrip-Fruin" (2009), accessed 8 December 2014 *http://henryjenkins.org/2009/05/an_interview_with_pat_harrigan.html*.
22. Enrico Terrone and Luca Bandirali, "*Game of Thrones*. L'immagine-mappa," in *La costruzione dell'immaginario seriale contemporaneo: Eterotopie, personaggi, mondi*, ed. Sara Martin (Milan: Mimesis/Cinergie, 2014), 61–70.
23. The spatial nature of cultural production is at the center of cultural geography, and of that which has come to be called the "spatial turn." See Barney Warf and Santa Arias, eds., *The Spatial Turn* (London: Routledge, 2009).
24. See Temeruga Trifonova, "Archiving Time in the Post-Medium Condition," in *L'archivio/The Archive*, eds. Alessandro Bordina, Sonia Capanini, and Andrea Mariani (Udine. Italy: Forum, 2012), 233–242; Wolfang Ernst, *Digital Memory and the Archive* (Minneapolis: University of Minnesota Press, 2013).
25. See Elizabeth Evans, *Transmedia Television: Audiences, New Media, and Daily Life* (New York: Routledge, 2011).
26. See Mariagrazia Fanchi, *Identità mediatiche: televisione e cinema nelle storie di vita di due generazioni di spettatori* (Milan: Franco Angeli, 2002); Annette Kuhn, *An Everyday Magic. Cinema and Cultural Memory* (London: I. B. Tauris, 2002).
27. See Mariagrazia Fanchi, *L'audience* (Rome: Laterza, 2014).
28. Mittell, *Complex TV*, 'Comprehension,' paragraph 26.
29. Ibid., paragraph 27.

References

Brembilla, Paola, and Guglielmo Pescatore. "La serialità televisiva americana: produzione, consumo e tipologie di prodotto." In *America oggi. Cinema, media, narrazioni del nuovo secolo*, ed. Giulia Carluccio, 275–290. Turin: Kaplan, 2014.

Cameron, Allan. *Modular Narratives in Contemporary Cinema*. New York: Palgrave Macmillan, 2008.

Ernst, Wolfgang. *Digital Memory and the Archive*. Minneapolis: University of Minnesota Press, 2013.

Eugeni, Ruggero. *Film, sapere, società: Per un'analisi sociosemiotica del testo cinematografico*. Milan: V&P, 1999.

———. *Semiotica dei media: Le forme dell'esperienza*. Rome: Carocci, 2010.

Evans, Elisabeth. *Transmedia Television: Audiences, New Media, and Daily Life*. New York: Routledge, 2011.

Fanchi, Mariagrazia. *Identità mediatiche: televisione e cinema nelle storie di vita di due generazioni di spettatori*. Milan: Franco Angeli, 2002.

———. *L'audience*. Rome: Laterza, 2014.

Genette, Gérard. *Palimpsests. Literature in the Second Degree*. Trans. Channa Newman and Claude Doubinsky. Lincoln: University of Nebraska Press, 1997.

———. *Paratexts: thresholds of interpretation*. Trans. Jane E. Lewin. Cambridge, UK: Cambridge University Press, 1997.

Goodman, Nelson. *Ways of Worldmaking*. Hassocks, UK: Harvester Press, 1978.

Gray, Jonathan. *Show Sold Separately. Promos, Spoilers, and Other Media Paratexts*. New York: New York University Press, 2010.

Harrigan, Pat, and Noah Wardrip-Fruin, eds. *Third Person: Authoring and Exploring Vast Narratives*. Cambridge, MA: MIT Press, 2009.

Jenkins, Henry. *Convergence culture: Where Old and New Media Collide*. New York: New York University Press, 2006.

———. "Authoring and Exploring Vast Narratives: An Interview with Pat Harrigan and Noah Wardrip-Fruin." Accessed 8 December 2014. *http://henryjenkins.org/2009/05/an_interview_with_pat_harrigan.html*.

———. *Spreadable Media: Creating Value and Meaning in a Networked Culture*. New York: New York University Press, 2013.

Kernan, Lisa. *Coming Attractions: Reading American Movie Trailers*. Austin: University of Texas Press, 2004.

Ksiazek, Thomas B., and James G. Webster. "The Dynamics of Audience Fragmentation: Public Attention in an Age of Digital Media." *Journal of Communication* 62.1 (2012): 39–56.

Kuhn, Annette. *An Everyday Magic: Cinema and Cultural Memory*. London: I. B. Tauris, 2002.

Macksey, Richard. "Foreword." In Gérard Genette, *Paratexts: Thresholds of Interpretation*, Trans. Jane E. Lewin, xi–xxii. Cambridge, UK: Cambridge University Press, 1997.

Mittell, Jason. *Complex TV: The Poetics of Contemporary Television Storytelling*: *http://mcpr.media-commons.org/complextelevision*.

Scaglioni, Massimo. *TV di culto: La serialità televisiva americana e il suo fandom*. Milan: V&P, 2006.

Terrone, Enrico, and Luca Bandirali. "*Game of Thrones*. L'immagine-mappa." In *La costruzione dell'immaginario seriale contemporaneo. Eterotopie, personaggi, mondi*, ed. Sara Martin, 61–70. Milan: Mimesis/Cinergie, 2014.

Trifonova, Temenuga. "Archiving Time in the Post-Medium Condition." In *L'archivio/ The Archive*, eds. Alessandro Bordina, Sonia Capanini, and Andrea Mariani, 233–242. Udine, Italy: Forum, 2012.

Snickars, Pelle, and Patrick Vonderau, eds. *The YouTube Reader*. Stockholm: National Library of Sweden, 2009.

Warf, Barney, and Santa Arias, eds. *The Spatial Turn*. London: Routledge, 2009.

Wyatt, Justin. *High Concept: Movies and Marketing in Hollywood*. Austin: University of Texas Press, 1994.

14 *The Girl with the Dragon Tattoo*
Paratexts in a Flexible World

Marta Boni

This chapter seeks to stretch the notion of paratext while dealing with the galaxy of heterogeneous material that constitutes *The Girl with the Dragon Tattoo's* world. I will offer an explanation of the role of paratexts in terms of flexibility, fluidity, and complexity. The Genettian notion of paratext will be stretched, according to Jonathan Gray's reading, to include official paratexts, such as DVD covers and bonus material, trailers, and posters, as well as an alternate reality game, and grassroots paratexts, such as web parodies, homages, and fan art. Paratexts, designed to be mobile, short-lived, and *spreadable,* are spaces in which circulatory instances, characteristic of the current media panorama, are more visible. Instead of being thought of only in terms of ephemeral "thresholds" to textuality, they can be studied as key elements of a complex narrative ecosystem. This is especially the case when they are considered sites of negotiation of meaning and translation across worlds, parts of a semiotic process through which an ecosystem adapts to the environment during its lifetime.

Complex Paratextuality

The *Millennium Trilogy (Män som hatar kvinnor, Flickan som lekte med elden,* and *Luftslottet som sprängdes*), written by Stieg Larsson, was published between 2005 and 2008, quickly becoming a global success. The books tell the story of Lisbeth Salander, a 24-year-old computer hacker who assists the journalist Mikael Blomkvist in solving a complex detective story involving violence against women. The novels were immediately adapted into three Swedish movies (Niels Arden Oplev and Daniel Alfredson, 2009) and released in six parts, with added footage for Swedish television (2010). The trilogy was followed by *The Girl with the Dragon Tattoo* (David Fincher, 2011), an award-winning feature film.[1] The next three years saw the release of a graphic novel in two parts (Denise Mina, 2012–2014) and a radio drama (adapted by Sophie Bocquillon and directed by François Christophe for France Culture, 2011). Each version differs in rhythm, length, and detail.

The Girl with the Dragon Tattoo (hereafter *TGWTDT*) is generally seen by its critics and viewers as an edgy, hybrid product of popular culture that gives rise to polemics concerning feminism, the violence depicted, and the ambiguous body and sexuality of its protagonist. Controversial aspects of the main character's representation in the American movie have been raised in newspaper articles and on blogs.[2] Moreover, a contributive encyclopedia dedicated to Lisbeth Salander[3] appeared in the media sphere along with many fan blogs, fan fictions, parodies, Facebook pages, and Pinterest boards, proving her strength as an emblematic character in today's culture. Some fans pay tribute to her characteristics as a "female avenger." Other websites offer lists of tips instructing users on "how to be inspired by Lisbeth Salander."[4]

TGWTDT is a particularly interesting case study because of its striking ability to adapt—in evolutionary terms—to the current media panorama. Its internal characteristics, along with the temporal status of the multiple artifacts that constitute it, can be analyzed from a semiotic and cultural perspective. The impact of multiple scattered media fragments emerging before, during, and after the book publication and release of the films has to be measured from a cultural semiotic standpoint. An imaginary world such as *TGWTDT* can be compared to a space of discourse made of heterogeneous media objects: official texts, ancillary media, and derivative fan productions that all refer to the same fiction and, at the same time, contribute to anchoring it in a culture. We can think of such a fictional world as a semiosphere. According to Jurij Lotman, a semiosphere is a space of discourse that contains semiotic objects such as signs or languages that constitute meaning for a given culture.[5] Within this framework, interstitial and ephemeral fragments contribute toward a transmedia complexity and negotiate oppositions (physical/disembodied, ephemeral/persistent, local/global). This chapter will explore the relationship between a complex world or a transmedia system and the single, ephemeral forms of textuality that constitute it over time. This example will offer the opportunity to rethink the pertinence of terms such as 'permanent' and 'ephemeral' in defining paratextuality.

The study of the role of paratexts within and at the borders of a fictional world can be carried on through a systemic view, which is able to render transmedia complexity. We need to take into account the microscopic dimension by analyzing the format and the role of each paratext in a determined space–time configuration, and at the same time look at their interactions over time from a macroscopic point of view. The analysis of *TGWTDT* as a long-lived phenomenon can show that paratexts often function as active translation zones at the borders of the semiosphere, favoring links to other worlds, for example, in the case of crossovers in fan fictions.

Thresholds for Interpretation

Paratexts are situated in the space between the fiction and the reader's world: they present and embody the fictional universe. According to Gérard Genette, a text is always accompanied by productions that belong to the same world but have different verbal, spatial, temporal, substantial, pragmatic, and functional features and are found in different spaces.[6] Paratexts demonstrate that, especially today, media cannot be reduced to their textual dimension. On the contrary, a pragmatic approach, centered on real uses of media content, can reveal the ways a fictional world is explored by its consumers.

Trailers, book covers, DVDs, bonus material, iPhone apps, music, merchandising, and posters are paratexts that, over the years, have accompanied the growing flow of media adaptations of *TGWTDT*. This part of the chapter will apply a Genettian reading to see if we can talk of their function as thresholds for interpretation. In this section, paratexts will be studied as elements that relocate the experience in space and time, thus securing the flexibility of a media ecosystem in its various adaptations to different situations. Viewers use them for "validating the experience."[7] We can think of paratexts as stemming from a (textual) authority that aims at "orienting" the reading.[8]

If we literally "judge a book by its cover" and study *TGWTDT*'s "editorial peritext," we can see how it positions itself through intertextual discourses and strategies of meaning attribution that are grounded in common pictorial codes. Following brand strategies, the book trilogy is marketed in different countries following specific rules. The original Swedish version encourages the reader to form an interpretation in terms of the journalistic thriller, by using a magazine cover format that imitates Mikaël Blomkvist's magazine, *Millennium*. In the same way, the U.S. DVD design shows another play with a thematic feature of the world depicted in the fiction. The title looks hand-written, giving the buyer the impression of having purchased a bootleg copy instead of the original (playing on Lisbeth Salander's status as a computer hacker). As we will see, the blurring between reality and fiction is an important function of *TGWTDT*'s paratextuality that will also appear in other situations.

Conversely, Isabel Samaras and John John Jesse's creepy black and red covers for the French publisher Actes Sud evoke film, popular goth, and punk culture. Another example of the product's cultural adaptation can be found in the titles. In the U.S. version, the original *Män som hatar kvinnor* (*Men Who Hate Women*) is translated as *The Girl with the Dragon Tattoo*, possibly in order to lower the reference to gender violence and stress the "coolness" of the protagonist, a change that was possibly made to appeal to a broader readership.

Flexibility

Lisbeth Salander moves outside gender categories: her body is a writable text, characterized by flexibility. Some descriptions convey the idea that she is not fully a woman. In the novel, she is described as "doll-like," "childlike," and "anorexic looking"; yet, at the beginning of the second book, the reader discovers her breast-enhancement surgery, part of her transformation into an independent woman. Her clothes and make-up evoke a similar fluidity. In the Swedish film, during her first appearance at Dragan Armanski's office, she is dressed like a goth, the same extreme and almost parodic attire that she will use in her last appearance during the trial. She has a boyish look when she hikes to Bjurman's cabin in the woods, but at the end of the first book and film she dresses up as the more feminine, sophisticated Irene Nesser.

Some paratextual material encourages one particular reading of Lisbeth Salander, who emerges as a very flexible character.[9] According to the *Merriam Webster English Dictionary*, flexible means "characterized by a ready capability to adapt to new, different, or changing requirements." For example, some paratexts encourage the depiction of Salander in the icon of a fashionable female avenger. A theatrical movie poster shows Lisbeth topless and Blomkvist, completely dressed, putting his arm around her neck and shoulder, as if to protect or even restrain her. Daniel Craig, known for his recent incarnation of James Bond, rises as the star of the narrative. In addition, the narrative is restricted to the first book, thus becoming a detective story, centered mainly on the quest for the truth about the Vanger family.

Lisbeth is reduced to Blomkvist's "assistant" and occasional romance. She is not exactly the core of the plot. The pale and alien-like Rooney Mara adapts the description of Salander to the contemporary ideal of a good-looking woman: slender, childlike, flat-chested, and fragile (quite different from the strong and disturbing Noomi Rapace of the Swedish version). An article published during the shooting of the American film suggests that "Mara, who is 25, lithe, and petite, radiated an intriguing mix of menace and vulnerability."[10] Her body is transformed by an intense make-over, shown in DVD bonus material and interviews with the fashion designer: her hair is dyed black, her eyebrows are dyed white, and her ears, nipple, and eyebrows are pierced. She wears a series of fashionable accessories (black leather jacket, motorcycle pants and boots) that transform her into a punk-style rebel. Yet, she is a rebel without a cause. The film moves away from most of her troubling features, namely, her mental illness, queerness, and the "resistant" connotation of her hacking activities.

Significantly, her attempt to set her father on fire and her experience in mental institutions, described in the books and in the Swedish version, are erased in the American movie. This may be because the adaptations of the second and third books are still waiting for a new script-writer.[11] Moreover, it should be noted that the DVD cover shows a close-up of Blomkvist facing the viewer, whereas Lisbeth is shown in profile. Lisbeth's characteristics as an outcast are stylized. She becomes an iconic figure through a play on Fincher's authorial signature and the creation of a visual style.

This crystallization of meaning can be read as such only when considering a short temporality. In fact, within a specific time period, it is possible to identify a single emergent interpretation or a limited number of interpretations. The fictional world can then be compared to a polysystem or a cultural series: a system constituted by various units of signification, characterized by a constant interaction, a hierarchy, and whose center is represented by one single work that functions as a structuring principle. It is particularly interesting that the duration of a work's structuring role, according to Louis Francoeur, is linked to spatiotemporal coordinates.[12] The place and duration of paratexts are historically situated. Additionally, the cultural series of significations that contribute to building *TGWTDT* as a space of discourse is constantly evolving. When considering *TGWTDT* as a vast ecosystem, subject to transformations in a networked context, it appears that, along with flexibility, the term fluidity can be productive, especially for the analysis of single dynamic elements represented by converging and diverging interpretations.

Fluidity

Fictional worlds, typical phenomena of convergence culture, are designed to fill in every possible gap and meet any consumer's need. Therefore, it is increasingly difficult to conceive of paratext in terms of a straightforward correlation to a primary text. Paratexts should no longer be considered just "thresholds for the interpretation" (as in Genette's work): they have to be considered as separate mini-worlds building up a media 'ecosystem.' Within this framework, they can be conceived as media objects that may live separate lives and circulate, acting as bridges over different media incarnations of a narrative.

"Fluid" is defined as "having particles that easily move and change their relative position without a separation of the mass and that easily yield to pressure."[13] In this framework, paratexts can be studied as fragments circulating from the peripheral zones to the center of the polysystem, and back again, implying the emergence of decentered discourse, the production of meaning outside the official boundaries of a primary text, and possibly the influence of these meanings on the dominant interpretation. They are both a product and a seed planted in these zones (and as Derrida's work suggests, a seed—a *semen*—is also a *sema*, a meaning).[14]

A quite traditional, yet extremely illuminating, form of fluid paratextuality is represented by trailers, which play a key role due to their tendency to scatter through online networks. Some, like the trailer for *Män som hatar kvinnor* (Oplev, 2009),[15] encourage a reading in terms of the thriller genre, stressing the connotation of the "locked room crime" genre in both the Swedish and U.S. versions (a line from the trailer: "How close can you get to the truth before you become the target?") Everything is moving, slowly but incessantly: are the protagonists getting close to the truth, and what is at stake? In contrast, David Fincher's trailer promotes a reading in terms of a quality or "art" product.[16] The availability of a long (8 minutes, with a fast-edited conclusion)[17] and short (4 minutes)[18] version also encourages viewers to read these paratexts as forms of entertainment in themselves that can be chosen according to one's taste or time schedule.

This reading in terms of art product and the possibility of considering paratexts as forms of art per se, is reinforced by the opening credits of Fincher's film, which circulated broadly as a fragment on social networks, thanks to the haunting remix version of Led Zeppelin's "Immigrant Song" by Karen O, Trent Reznor, and Atticus Ross. The 2 minute and 25 second video is a sensual, arrhythmical fight of fire, water, air, and earth, and it sets the pace for the entire film, imposing Fincher's authorial style from the beginning. From the darkness of the image, some elements emerge, sometimes shaking spasmodically, including a computer keyboard and fragments of still bodies framed in close or extremely close shots. A dark fluid with a thick consistency—similar to ooze or blood—emerges from a woman's open mouth, then streams over a human head. Computer wires, moving like tentacles, reach a body still covered with liquid and intersect with several of the film's key motifs, such as fire and a dragon, offering a real depiction of fluidity. The U.S. teaser, fast-edited and rhythmic, is edited to the same *Immigrant Song* remix and centers on Salander's character and her 'difference.'[19]

Many fan-made trailers for other films, edited to the same music, circulate on YouTube: the *spreadable* trailer has the ability to infect other movies (such as *A Clockwork Orange*—Stanley Kubrick, 1971) or *Inception* (Christopher Nolan, 2010).[20] Here, paratexts may become the spaces where more than one world collide. Not only are paratexts an 'unsettled zone' (*zone indécise*) in which a social code meets the producer's code: they have to be studied as transitional and transactional spaces. They are also open doors that let one world (one space of discourse) flow into others: two or many different semiospheres meet in these interstitial media content zones.

Playing with the Viewer's Temporality: Blurring Boundaries

Often, transmedia phenomena include the blurring of boundaries between reality and fiction: this is the case for alternate reality games (ARGs). ARG specialists 42 Entertainment developed a participatory experience for David Fincher's film. The aim of the experience was to reinforce the fan's feeling of being part of the gloomy atmosphere of the Vanger family's mysteries. Tumblr and Twitter accounts ("Mouth Taped Shut" and "What Is Hidden in the Snow") delivered clues for earning collectibles from the film, encouraging immersion into the fictional world. Fans had to use clues from social networks to find film-based artifacts in American and European cities. The project also contained a behind-the-scenes production blog with pictures and videos.[21]

Particularly interesting were original "remediated" videos that the consumer could identify as footage coming from the diegetic world. One looked like a personal amateur archive from the 1960s because of the treatment of the image (scratched, fading colors, and showing cars from that time period). It consisted of one shot of the bridge that separates the Vangers' villa from the town of Hedeby right after the truck accident, the same day of Harriet's disappearance. The video gave clues on the girl's vanishing, if one tried to question the point of view of the camera.

Another remediated video was a faux, 9-minute *Hard Copy* episode with re-enactments of events and interviews with secondary characters (a caretaker, a police officer).[22] *Hard Copy*, a real American television show from the 1990s, centered on people's disappearances, thus making the video fragment part of a triple temporality involving the 1960s, the 1990s, and the present time. Interestingly, these ephemeral fragments that aim to create the situation for gameplay in which the consumer takes an active role also involve a play with temporalities, truly creating the feeling of giving access to secret archives and encouraging immersion into the fictional world. These videos can be considered as transmedia "bricks," since they give viewers complementary yet divergent viewpoints on the events, filling in gaps left by the film, thus encouraging the exploration of the world of *TGWTDT*. Along the same lines, the journalist Frank Rose, author of *The Art of Immersion*, collaborated in creating *Millennium* magazine's digital copies, which were downloadable from the official website.[23]

Simultaneously, these immersion-building paratexts are visible only for a small portion of viewers and for a limited time. ARGs target expert fans that are already used to explore real-world and online spaces and are willing to participate in collective puzzles. In response to such a complex playground, fans attempt to track down the most fleeting artifacts and re-create an impression of consistency of the transmedia world. For example, fans make accessible to other fans an archive of YouTube videos, lists of links that explain and map out *TGWTDT*'s complexity. Especially in the case of a "viral" campaign, some paratexts, like web links (or the unsuccessful and short-lived iPhone app "Chasing Salander") are no longer available after a few months. For the analyst, the act of mapping paratext-full digital worlds becomes essential to understand an ecosystem's complexity from a semiotic, pragmatic, but also aesthetic and economic point of view.

Grassroots Practices

Not only does paratextuality legitimize the study of traditionally marginalized objects (e.g., trailers, book covers, DVDs, bonus material, applications, music, merchandising, posters, and ARGs), but it also serves as the linchpin for an epistemological shift from a text-centered, intertextual approach to one based on appropriations. Paratextuality is a peripheral territory that welcomes and bolsters new material; therefore, studies should include not only official spaces, but also grassroots practices that contribute in expanding a fictional world's material.[24]

Grassroots appropriations are perhaps a more fluid territory than official paratexts, in terms of their temporality. For example, they are always at risk of cancellation for copyright infringement. In order to fully understand grassroots paratexts as a fluid territory, the circulation of *TGWTDT* as a phenomenon in popular culture must be explored.

A fictional world may expand through heterogeneous practices and simultaneously be used as raw material for remix and mash-up activities. For example, the American teaser is the starting point for playing with its fast editing as the user tries to put a word over each image.[25] It is also a basis for genre transformation, as genre is adjusted by adding special effects or music from another movie).[26] Taking into account the role of these often ephemeral artifacts in contributing to a polysystem's expansion requires the adoption of a complex approach (Morin, 2007). Within this framework, paratexts should be considered as spaces that favor emergences: meanings or forms that could not appear from the single text but from the interrelation of different parts. In the case of TGWTDT, emergences can be found in translation phenomena or in superimposition of meaning over time.

Parody, for example, has the virtue of betraying, but at the same time identifying, the main features of a text.[27] In many cases, content spreads via humor. Both the book and the cinematic adaptations are objects of parodies, authored both by well-known writers or producers and by ordinary fans. "The Girl Who Fixed the Umlaut," written by Nora Ephron for the *The New Yorker*,[28] is a parody of the system of typography, language, and punctuation of the book. Jim Henson's Muppets parody Fincher's film by adapting their film trailer into *The Girl with the Dragon Tattoo*'s teaser. The Funny or Die YouTube channel also produced the parodic "The Girl with the Tramp Stamp Tattoo.[29]

Some of the characteristics of Lisbeth's myth that crystallize over time in the social sphere and across all the different media adaptations can be highlighted by the analysis of a fan-made parody. Even though some of these products are meant only to belittle Salander, most of them aim at imitating, thus paying homage to her. To take a case in point, "Lisbeth Salander Explains the Internet"[30] is an episode of *BAMF Girls Club*, a fake reality show starring popular female heroines (Katniss Everdeen, Buffy the Vampire Slayer, Michonne from *The Walking Dead*, Hermione Granger, Bella Swan, and Lisbeth Salander). In this parody, Lisbeth is frustrated by the incompetence of her roommates regarding their use of computers, and she tries to lecture them. The parody brings some of her characteristics to the fore, such as the quickness and abruptness of her gestures, her edgy appearance, her ability to use technology, her inability to create positive emotional bonds with other people, as well as her rejection of excessive romanticism. The parody identifies Lisbeth as a geek, a person focused on a technical activity that other people do not understand, and who has no apparent practical usefulness or social interests. Unlike the other women, Lisbeth is almost rude and is dressed in her most extreme goth attire. Therefore, this parody exemplifies the media's difficulty in representing a woman with technological abilities without lessening her female normativity. Another parody compares Salander's detective genius with Sherlock Holmes (using images from the BBC series edited to the American trailer's music).[31]

When we focus specifically on Lisbeth Salander's character, it appears that her "producerly" feature (the element that grants the emergence of new interpretations) comes not only from the genre (crime fiction, the hacker theme) but also from her gender flexibility. Her body is reinvented in the different versions. In some cases, her feminine and romantic features are highlighted, such as in "Hidden Dimensions," a fan fiction that presents her as a mother.[32] In other instances, her androgynous attributes are placed at the core of the experience and can be seen through certain pieces of fan art.[33] Customized action figures are also available, showing the desire of fans to have a 3D version of Lisbeth that companies will probably never offer.[34]

These products both poke fun at and celebrate the phenomenon through complex pop culture crossovers. However, which Lisbeth Salander is the object of these practices? The referent is, in most cases, cross-medial: in Tumblr pages; for example, both Noomi Rapace's and Rooney Mara's Salander (and sometimes the "original" Salander from the book) are used for appropriations. Both American and Swedish films are fragmented into single images or GIFS and then regrouped within personal thematic boards.[35] GIFS have the characteristics of both the photo (the immobility of the shot) and the movie (the motion of the sequence they come from). Therefore, without focusing on narrative content, these paratexts fix Salander's unique gestures or "techniques of the body": looking up from the laptop, taking a drag off a cigarette, turning her head.[36] Single fragments, escaping the temporality of their original medium, become ephemeral and spreadable entities, destined to converge again, but in a semiosphere that has evolved over time, thanks to users' collective activity. Fragments like clothing accessories, not related to the original franchise, also converge in collaborative collections, such as Pinterest or Polyvore (websites proposing thematic boards of products that fans can buy in any store in order to imitate the character's style).[37]

Every fan's choice follows personal idiosyncrasies and tells us about an individual's affection. Yet, globally, the final image of the character is a collection of single views. The fictional world emerges from a collage of elements that build up Salander's character. A sense of shared interest and a broad connectivity replaces traditional hierarchies in the circulation of media content. Everyone has the potential to browse many different versions, to access both users' and producers' contents. Certainly, large companies still control the circulation and have more economic power than audiences. Nevertheless, similarly to the rhizome model, there is no need to define the position of an attribute, since each one can influence the others. Parodies, heuristic activities, tributes, fan fiction, and fan art follow a rhizomatic model. Meaning is produced in an indeterminate and generative way so that "any point ... can be connected to anything, and must be."[38]

Any of these productions can be considered from a paratextual framework. Without being entirely independent and original, they function as gateways to the fictional world for other users. They prepare and orient the viewing and expand it. Consider, for example, the different functions of discussions relating to the quality of the film, or playful remixes of images seen in parodies or tributes. *TGWTDT*'s semiosphere mutates and transforms thanks to these single, circulating fragments that can at any moment determine new interpretations in different contexts. Both narrative and non-narrative, created by either producers or users, paratexts are spaces for the growth of the fictional world. This is particularly true today. If building an "imaginary museum" was a common activity (already practiced by art lovers and film buffs), personal online collections of media content such as trailers, pictures on Tumblr or Pinterest allow fans to share their imaginary museums and collectively build a space of discourse. Paratexts are therefore a space in which the individual's cultural, ethical, and political relationship to media is reworked. Some meanings will emerge more clearly than others, stressing and consolidating one or more features of the characters (the characteristics of Fincher's Salander are either respected or altered in fans' drawings); and fixing a range of instructions for consumption and interpretation (the genre and the trailer are pervading elements that can potentially influence other trailers).

The meaning of a text, according to Derrida, comes from a *différance*, which is a "systematic play on differences" and the act of distinguishing? differentiating? one element from another.[39] In this sense, paratexts contribute to postponing the meaning of a text: every "text claims its exterior" ("*le texte affirme le dehors*"). The present article, though, suggests that the superimposition of experiences over time has a result: a fluid result that depends on contexts and situations, yet an ecosystemic result. Paratexts are flexible, fluid materials, contributing to the adaptability of an ecosystem. They serve its resilience, while also acting as spaces for translation, thus allowing transformations, mutations, and crossovers with other worlds. They constantly negotiate a world's coherence, forging relationships with internal elements and other systems. Paratexts thus participate in a double movement; they negotiate the relationship of a world to other worlds, and they are both permanent (within conglomerates) and fleeting (in networks). Most of the time they are short-lived (since they are made for a small community of users). Yet, their circulation in networks can ensure their persistence over time. A new level results from the multiplicity of single, scattered temporalities: a complex and stratified temporality.

Conclusions

Contemporary theories that attempt to explain today's media-saturated culture highlight the heterogeneity of communication experiences. They describe networks of ephemeral fragments circulating through multiple screens. On the one hand, the scattered and disembodied nature of media experiences, enhanced by digital devices, allows the emergence of circulatory phenomena. Temporality in media circulation is therefore defined using the terms 'flexibility' and 'fluidity.'

On the other hand, unifying tendencies, such as those observed in collaborative boards, can also be highlighted. Despite the fragmentation and multiplicity of screens, a media work is still a unifying experience that, be it for only a moment, stops the flow. Today, users get involved with media when they want, where they want, and how they want, but their choice is always comparable to the aggregation of scattered particles.

A larger phenomenon, from a semiotic perspective, is the emergence of complex systems, comparable to semiospheres. Circulation of ephemeral artifacts and aggregation of particles in big systemic phenomena are not contradictory concepts. On the contrary, different systems of temporality (short-lived ARGs, long-lived book covers or trailers), and different speeds (trailers require an engagement over a short time period; playing an ARG requires concentration and participation over months; and true fans wait for the release of the second part of Fincher's movie over years ...) have to be taken into account when studying a fictional world. Long-lived textual phenomena evolve over time and are made up of microscopic elements that are often ephemeral, constantly finding their balance with global social and cultural media contexts. This is only an apparent contradiction, if we think in terms of cultural semiotics. In fact, the persistence of an interpretation over time lives longer than the cultural artifacts that first supported it. Reading, conceived as a rewriting, gives life to new products that fill in the gaps of official texts, within a complex system. Therefore, when we compare imaginary worlds to ecosystems, it is necessary to highlight the coexistence of both persistence and ephemerality.

In this regard, paratexts are unique elements of shows that are "sold separately"; they are bricks converging into a world. Studying paratexts means focusing on a new semiotic entity made of marginalized elements (both users' productions and all forms of ancillary artifacts) that is comparable to an ecosystem. From this approach, we will be able to consider every single particle, be it industrially produced or user-generated, as a semiotic step that contributes to the building of an ecosystem's meaning and identity. Similar to the cinematographic apparatus, its unity is dynamic. The multiplicity that makes up this unity is not just a superimposition of undifferentiated elements. On the contrary, it creates a qualitatively different phenomenon.[40] From single, fixed elements, we get motion; and, from single ephemeral paratexts, we get a new whole, only visible over a long duration.

We can compare this image to a 'cultural series,' built through shared memories and interpretations over time. Some fragments will inevitably escape the viewer's experience because of their short-lived nature or simply because of cultural and geographical bias: one could not possibly be exposed, at the same time, to every single paratext, spread in different languages, in the world. Nevertheless, the ecosystem is built from the interaction, at a global level and in different spaces, of all its elements and the production of meaning created by all users.

Notes

1. The movie received five Academy Award nominations at the 84th Academy Awards, including: Best Actress for Rooney Mara, Best Cinematography, Best Sound, and Best Sound Mixing and won one award for Best Film Editing.
2. "How to Be Inspired by Lisbeth Salander," accessed 10 February 2015, *http://www.wikihow.com/Be-Inspired-by-Lisbeth-Salander*. Melissa Silverstein, "The Pornification of Lisbeth Salander," "Women and Hollywood," 8 June 2011, accessed 10 February 2015, *http://blogs.indiewire.com/womenandhollywood/the_pornification_of_lisbeth_salander*.
3. "Millennium Trilogy Wiki," accessed 10 February 2010, *http://millenniumtrilogy.wikia.com/wiki/Millennium_Trilogy_Wiki*.
4. Melissa Silverstein, "Book Excerpt—The Tattooed Girl: The Enigma of Stieg Larsson," "Women and Hollywood," accessed 10 February 2015, *http://blogs.indiewire.com/womenandhollywood/book_excerpt_the_tattooed_girl_the_enigma_of_stieg_larsson*.
5. Jurij Lotman, "On the Semiosphere," *Sign Systems Studies* 33.1 (2005): 5–23.
6. Gérard Genette, *Seuils* (Paris: Ed. Du Seuil, 1987), 1.
7. Jonathan Gray, *Show Sold Separately* (New York: New York University Press, 2010).
8. Jason Mittell, *Complex TV: The Poetics of Contemporary Television Storytelling*, pre-publication edition (New YorK: MediaCommons Press, 2012), 1–104.
9. In the books and in the movies, a constant reworking of her appearance can be read in relationship to post-feminist or neo-feminist culture, where the individual agency is the defining constituent of feminine identity, in a "largely indifferent, if not hostile, environment" of neoliberal culture. Moreover, her sexuality builds her identity as a third-wave feminist: "She did not give a damn about labels, did not see that it was anybody else's business who she spent her nights with. If she had to choose, she preferred guys. ... The only problem was finding a guy who was not a jerk, and who was good in bed—Mimmi was a sweet compromise." Stieg Larsson, *The Girl with the Dragon Tattoo*, 250. See also Hilary Radner, *Neo-Feminist Cinema: Girly Films, Chick Flicks, and Consumer Culture* (New York: Routledge, 2010).
10. Lynn Hirschberg, "David Fincher Gets the Girl," *http://www.wmagazine.com/people/celebrities/2011/02/rooney_mara_girl_with_the_dragon_tattoo_film*, accessed 12 February 2015.
11. As of January 2015, there is no official confirmation that books two and three will be adapted into English-language films.
12. Louis Francoeur, *Les signes s'envolent. Pour une sémiotique des actes de langage culturels* (Québec, Presses de l'Université Laval, 1985), 69–70.
13. Merriam Webster English Dictionary.
14. Jacques Derrida, *La dissémination* (Paris, Seuil, 1972).
15. *http://www.youtube.com/watch?v=RL8LI-h2WFc*, accessed 12 February 2015.
16. Reading supported by discourses in the media sphere, such as the following: "David Fincher's adaptation of the international best-seller is a triumph of craftsmanship over material" (Sachs "The Girl with the Dragon Tattoo," *The Chicago Reader*, 20 December 2011).
17. *http://www.youtube.com/watch?v=X7awaM0UmYI*, accessed 12 February 2015.
18. *http://www.youtube.com/watch?v=VK-sahH6lY0*, accessed 12 February 2015.
19. "She's one of the best, she's different" a character says in the teaser.

20. *https://www.youtube.com/watch?v=WBSWdhbpF0Q*, *https://www.youtube.com/watch?v=T964rvfHWes*, accessed 12 February 2015.
21. *http://mouth-taped-shut.tumblr.com*, accessed 1 March 2015.
22. It should be noted that this way of delivering information on the narrative by creating paratexts that unveil points of views or portions of the world that are absent from the main media is not new: see Hitchock's *Rope* trailer (1948).
23. *http://www.frankrose.com/millennium-magazine.html*, accessed 12 February 2015.
24. See, for example Carlos Alberto Scolari, "Transmedia Storytelling: Implicit Consumers, Narrative Worlds, and Branding in Contemporary Media Production," *International Journal of Communication*, 3 (2009): 586–606.
25. *http://www.youtube.com/watch?v=bH_lyn8MlOs*, accessed 12 February 2015.
26. *http://www.youtube.com/watch?v=LZpRr8qXgGM*, accessed 12 February 2015.
27. Linda Hutcheon, *Theory of Parody: The Teachings of Twentieth-Century Art Forms*, (Champaign: University of Illinois Press, 2001), 15.
28. Nora Ephron, "The Girl Who Fixed the Umlaut," *The New Yorker*, 5 July 2010, accessed 12 February 2015. *http://www.newyorker.com/humor/2010/07/05/100705sh_shouts_ephron*.
29. Mandi Bierly, "Emma Roberts Is 'The Girl with the Tramp Stamp Tattoo' (and Joe Manganiello Is Hot in a Cardigan)." *Entertainment Weekly*, accessed 12 February 2015, *http://popwatch.ew.com/2011/12/07/emma-roberts-girl-tramp-stamp-tattoo*.
30. *http://www.youtube.com/watch?v=wNvpiS1X-B4*, accessed 1 March 2015.
31. "The Man with a Cunning Mind," *http://www.youtube.com/watch?v=hNkLLwlnAU0*, or the fan fiction "The Criminal, The Hacker and The Detective," *http://archiveofourown.org/tags/Sherlock%20Holmes*s*Lisbeth%20Salander/works*, both accessed 1 March 2015.
32. *https://www.fanfiction.net/s/8560392/1/Hidden-Dimensions*, accessed 1 March 2015.
33. *https://i2.wp.com/farm8.staticflickr.com/7005/6669046475_c34ae89197_o.jpg*, accessed 1 March 2015.
34. *http://www.figurerealm.com/viewcustomfigure.php?FID=38054*, or *http://www.figurerealm.com/viewcustomfigure.php?FID=41363*, or *http://www.youtube.com/watch?v=elI8G6Z5e70*, accessed 1 March 2015.
35. *http://fuckyeahlisbethsalander.tumblr.com*, accessed 1 March 2015.
36. Marcel Mauss, *Les techniques du corps, Sociologie et anthropologie* (Paris: Presses Universitaires de France, 2004). First published in *Journal de Psychologie*, XXXII 3–4, 15 March–15 April (1936).
37. *http://www.polyvore.com/lisbeth_salander/set?id=39217302*, accessed 1 March 2015.
38. Gilles Deleuze and Félix Guattari, *A Thousand Plateaus: Capitalism and Schizophrenia* (Minneapolis: University of Minnesota Press, 1987), 7.
39. Jacques Derrida, "Semiology and Grammatology: Interview with Kristeva," in *The Communication Theory Reader,* ed. P. Cobley: 209–224, (New York: Psychology Press, 1996), 28. Also, "An element functions and signifies, takes on or conveys meaning, only by referring to another past or future element in an economy of traces. This economic aspect of *différance*, which brings into play a certain not conscious calculation in a field of forces, is inseparable from the more narrowly semiotic aspect of différance" (Ibid., 30).
40. André Gaudreault, "Du simple au multiple: le cinéma comme série de series." *Cinémas: revue d'études cinématographiques* 13.1–2 (2002): 39.

References

Certeau, Michel de. *L'invention du quotidien*, t.I, *Arts de faire*. Paris: Gallimard, 1990.

Deleuze, Gilles, and Félix Guattari. *A Thousand Plateaus: Capitalism and Schizophrenia*. Trans. Brian Massumi. Minneapolis: University of Minnesota Press, 1987.

Derrida, Jacques. *La Dissémination*. Paris: Seuil, 1972.

———. "Semiology and Grammatology: Interview with Kristeva." In *The Communication Theory Reader*, ed. Paul Cobley, 209–224. New York: Psychology Press, 1996.

Fiske, John. *Television Culture*. London: Methuen, 1987.

Francoeur, Louis. *Les signes s'envolent. Pour une sémiotique des actes de langage culturels*. Québec: Presses de l'Université Laval, 1985.

———. "La série culturelle, structure, valeur et fonction." *La culture inventée*, Québec, Institut Québécois de Recherche sur la Culture (1992): 61–85.

Gaudreault, André. "Du simple au multiple: le cinéma comme série de series." *Cinémas: revue d'études cinématographiques / Journal of Film Studies/Cinémas* 13.1–2 (2002): 33–47.

Genette, Gérard. *Palimpsestes: La littérature au second degré*. Paris: Éd. du Seuil, 1982.

———. *Seuils*. Paris: Ed. Du Seuil (Coll. Poétique), 1987.

Gray, Jonathan. *Show Sold Separately. Promos, Spoilers, and Other Media Paratexts*. New York: New York University Press, 2010.

Hills, Matt. *Fan Culture*. London: Routledge, 2002.

Hutcheon, Linda. *Theory of Parody: The Teachings of Twentieth-Century Art Forms*. Champaign: University of Illinois Press, 2001.

Innocenti, Veronica, and Guglielmo Pescatore. "Dalla cross-medialità all'ecosistema narrativo: L'architettura complessa del cinema hollywoodiano contemporaneo." In *Il cinema della convergenza: Industria, racconto, pubblico*, ed. Federico Zecca, 127–138. Milan: Mimesis, 2012.

Jenkins, Henry. *Textual Poachers: Television Fans and Participatory Culture*. New York: Routledge, 1992.

———, Sam Ford, and Joshua Green. *Spreadable Media, Creating Value and Meaning in a Networked Culture*. New York: New York University Press, 2013.

Larsson, Stieg. *The Girl with the Dragon Tattoo*. Trans. Reg Keeland. New York: Vintage, 2008.

———. *The Girl Who Played with Fire*. Trans. Reg Keeland. New York: Vintage, 2009.

———. *The Girl Who Kicked the Hornet's Nest*. Trans. Reg Keeland. New York: Vintage, 2009.

Lefebvre, Martin. *Psycho: de la figure au musée imaginaire. Théorie et pratique de l'acte de spectature*. Montréal: L'Harmattan, 1997.

Lotman, Jurij. "On the Semiosphere." *Sign Systems Studies* 33.1 (2005): 5–23.

Mauss, Marcel. *Les techniques du corps, Sociologie et anthropologie*. Paris: Presses Universitaires de France, 2004. First published in *Journal de Psychologie* 32.3–4, 15 March–15 April 1936.

Miller, Nancy. "Manifesto for a New Age." *Wired Magazine*, March 2007.

Mittell, Jason. *Complex TV: The Poetics of Contemporary Television Storytelling*, pre-publication edition. New York: MediaCommons Press, 2012.

Morin, Edgar. "Restricted Complexity, General Complexity." In *Worldviews, Science, and Us: Philosophy and Complexity,* eds. Carlos Gershenson, Diederik Aerts, and Bruce Edmonds, 5–29. New York: World Scientific Publishing, 2007.

Sachs, Ben. "The Girl with the Dragon Tattoo." *The Chicago Reader*, 20 December 2011. Accessed 22 April 2013. *http://www.chicagoreader.com/chicago/the-girl-with-the-dragon-tattoo/Film?oid=5004261.*

Scolari, Carlos Alberto. "Transmedia Storytelling: Implicit Consumers, Narrative Worlds, and Branding in Contemporary Media Production." *International Journal of Communication* 3 (2009): 586–606.

15 TV Series, Convergence Culture, and the Davy Crockett Hat

Veronica Innocenti and Guglielmo Pescatore

Introduction

This chapter will focus on the transition from ephemerality to persistence and vice versa. The contemporary mediascape is formed of short, audiovisual fragments that contribute to complex narrative worlds that we have elsewhere called "narrative ecosystems."[1] These fragments play an important role in defining our temporal experience of audiovisual products; they are also significant in shaping our use of the past.

This chapter will take for granted some relevant changes in the production and fruition models of TV serial narratives.[2] Such transformations have enforced a change of critical perspective, since contemporary narratives are an evolution of the "story": they are ongoing and intricately developed storylines with many characters and multiple settings, all of which are fundamental for the creation of vast narratives.[3] In the contemporary media environment, a vast narrative may often intersect with popular literature, comics, MMORPG (massively multiplayer online role-playing games), and TV series, the last-named of which are the main focus of our discussion. Contemporary TV series are no longer textual objects; instead, they are the result of an ecosystemic design where a general model is developed in advance as an evolutionary system with a high degree of consistency among all its components.[4] Vast narratives are less textual objects than open systems.

Within studies of intertextuality, it is common to consider the intertextual relation as a form of co-presence and as a reference to other textual objects and their cultural context (in the form of quotations, allusions, etc.).[5] This leads to a reading of the intertextual/intermedial link as rich and articulated, and capable of drawing together a dense network of texts and meanings. However, in the contemporary media context, intertextual relations are often the result of a dialectic between extraction and integration. We will later define these two processes as specific configurations of the convergence/divergence paradigm. A traditional intertextual view understands the integration process as taking place when we bring in textual elements and references. Contrary to this, we propose to consider the integration process as an operation that presumes a previous extraction and imposes a partial or total cancellation of the relations between the imported object and its referential cultural context.

The dialectic between extraction and integration also has an effect on the relationship between ephemerality and persistence, as well as on transformations from one to the other. Extraction processes tend to make the extracted object ephemeral, yet the following integration operation brings the object to a new life and condition. Thus, media memory processes (quotations and allusions, but also nostalgia, vintage, reconstructions, etc.) are the result of a process of re-creation (that might lead to the building of fake shared memories) rather than of intertextual integration.

The Convergence/Divergence Paradigm in the Contemporary Mediascape: An Overview

Media objects, especially TV serial narratives and their paratexts, are the result of a dialectic between project and use—in other words, between its official production plans and the way audiences acknowledge and use a product. These two polarities, the planning/production and the fruition of media objects, have undergone severe changes in the past few years, and therefore demand new theoretical and analytical tools.

Henry Jenkins first introduced his concept of transmedia storytelling in 2003[6] and later elaborated it in his book *Convergence Culture*.[7] In his book, Jenkins expanded upon several relevant concepts that he had begun to theorize in the early 2000s. In particular, he sought to differentiate technological convergence from cultural convergence, emphasizing that cultural convergence is the "explosion of new forms of creativity at the intersections of various media technologies, industries and consumers."[8] In the following years, Jenkins also refined the concept of convergence by reflecting on divergence as a part of the same process. In an online discussion with Al Ries, Jenkins states that the idea of convergence to which Ries refers requires "top-down coordination and systemic management of the technological infrastructure and would seemingly privilege some relationships between devices over others."[9] As this point indicates, Jenkins does not believe in technological convergence; rather, he is interested in reaffirming that convergence in a cultural sense is:

> occurring precisely because the public does not want a one-size-fits-all relationship to media content. Consumers want the media they want, where they want it and in the format they want. On the technological level, this does indeed involve divergence between technologies; on an economic level, this may involve fragmentation of the market. On the cultural level, though, this desire for a divergence of technology works to spread media content across every possible delivery system and insures that there will be multiple points of entry to many of the most successful media franchises.[10]

It is interesting and relevant to focus on instances of divergence in order to illustrate better the complex environment of audiovisual production. For a long time, media objects were designed and produced for a specific medium, whereas now they are produced for active audiences that can access content through a range of different devices. Divergence is also strongly linked to marketing, since divergent practices in the reception of audiovisual productions can contribute significantly to a product's increased spreadability. In the case of TV series, since we are no longer talking about single objects but rather are dealing with narrative universes that are dispersed over several different cross-media channels, industrial investments are highly concentrated on audiences. This is demonstrated by the notable increase of marketing expenses for the paratexts of audiovisual media productions.

The process of convergence can include a high rate of divergence, albeit this might take place at different levels. Fans and viewers use series, even more frequently than other TV shows, to define their own position and to negotiate their reputation inside consumption communities, following patterns and protocols of appropriation that diverge from the ones offered by broadcasters. Contemporary series cannot be equated to traditional narrative texts, not only because they branch across several media platforms, but also because they use unusual narrative forms (non-procedural, non-oriented, not governed by a principle of internal consistency) and thus create a strong asymmetry between the global and the local dimension. In other words, narrative processes, while still existing at the local level, produce not global narratives but rather environments within which users can literally live. Even if this kind of production is the result of a very intricate design, viewers often adopt and adapt them in unpredictable and irregular ways, sometimes demonstrating an interaction that goes far beyond the simple purpose of entertainment for which they had originally been produced.[11]

The successful and effective penetration of these products is not measured solely in terms of audience ratings, but also through their ability to engage with the audiences by eliciting their reactions. TV series can also stimulate audiences to react to production choices, as evidenced by the failure of the U.S. series *Firefly* (Fox, 2002–2003), created by Joss Whedon. Early cancellation of the series led its biggest fans to buy a page in *Variety* and launch a protest campaign against the broadcaster in an attempt to save their favorite series.

As Jenkins pointed out, there is a form of divergence that is triggered by the process of convergence, which engenders the fragmentation of markets as well as viewer use of different devices, but also (relatedly) a dynamic between industrial design and user fruition. In other words, on the one hand, there is a process of planning and design that relates to the industrial production and distribution of media products and paratexts in different markets and for different targets. On the other hand, there is a slice of unpredictability even in the most carefully planned project, which might create some misalignment between the aims of the media industry and the audience's use of the media object.

This misalignment might, for instance, affect interpersonal relationships, as in the case of the shipping phenomenon. Shipping (a diminutive of the word relationship) refers to the "desire by fans for two people, either real-life celebrities or fictional characters, to be in a relationship, romantic or otherwise."[12] This concept underlines fan involvement in the development of a relationship in a fictional universe and their desire to see two people paired. Such fan engagement might take the form of creative work, such as fan fiction and fan art, which is mostly made available to the fan community through the Internet. In this case, we are dealing with the two polarities mentioned before, desire and usage. Fans *desire* to see two people together as a couple, and they shape this desire in the form of fan fiction or fan art where they can see it realized through a direct *use* of the narrative material.

In terms of convergence and divergence mechanisms, this kind of misalignment produces two different possible outcomes. First, divergence can in fact be reabsorbed by the official production and can be, at least partially, reincorporated within the main storyline. This is the case for *Daria*, an animated series produced and aired by MTV between 1997 and 2002. The show was marked from its beginning by a debate run by shippers, who were strongly convinced that the protagonist Daria ought to have a relationship with a character named Trent. The writers of the show responded to these requests by letting Daria have a crush on Trent for several episodes until the third season's finale, when a new male character and love interest was introduced.

A second possible outcome for these fan solicitations is that the shipping proposed and supported by the audience is used as a what-if trigger for an alternative reality, which nevertheless lasts for only an episode or is used by fan fiction writers as one possibility among many others.[13] In essence, for viewers to engage with TV serial narratives, they need to relate not only to a recognizable emotional place, in which the product can live for a long time—much longer than its life on the TV channel—but also to adjust to the interferences and the frictions that occur between the fictional world and the real one.

An additional relevant issue involved in divergence is the presence of media niches. Although they can be external or peripheral compared to the traditional transmission and delivery of media content, media niches are also central to the circulation of media objects. For instance, fans contribute to the diffusion of products through the use and reappropriation of media content that is linked to specific gender practices and identities.[14] This extraction mechanism, paired with the multiplicity that is typically incorporated in contemporary audiovisual narratives, contributes to the creation of special fan-built universes that are aimed at restricted groups of consumers, characterized by very personal tastes. In this case, fans tend to extract a small part or a specific feature from the vast narrative ecosystem (be it a minor character, a narrative line, etc.) and make private use of it without sharing it with the greater audience. Within such niches, rather than the extraction of an object, we see processes of the extraction of environments. In fact, it is a form of subtraction rather than extraction inasmuch as it is meant to take a part of the narrative and to lock it within a niche, instead of (re-)using it to make a spreadable object.

In sum, slices of the narrative ecosystem can be taken away by the audience and put to unpredictable use. Paratexts as fan parallel productions are examples of subtraction, more than being transmedia extensions. The official, intricate design of plot and characters clashes with the often unexpected use viewers make of them. Industrial texts are frequently the result of a negotiation between production and consumption; nevertheless, the actions and reactions of the audiences are unpredictable and can drastically affect the balance of a narrative universe.

Radical Divergence: Extraction and Integration

The convergence/divergence process we have described can in some cases give birth to more radical forms of divergence that take the shape of extraction. Going back to Jenkins's position on transmedia storytelling and on the way transmedia operate, we can note that, Jenkins problematizes the idea of a "unified experience systematically developed across multiple texts."[15] Transmedia franchises push continuity to a new level. In this context, continuity becomes multiplicity, as in the case of Marvel and DC, whose superheroes are an interesting example of a kind of continuity structure that is widely appreciated by the fans, but where new phenomena are at stake. Jenkins makes the case for Spider-Man:

> So, for example, we can see Spider-Man as part of the mainstream continuity of the Marvel universe, but he also exists in the parallel continuity offered by the *Ultimate Spider-Man* franchise, and we can see a range of distinctly separate mini-franchises, such as *Spider-Man India* (which sets the story in Mumbai) or *Spider-Man Loves Mary Jane* (which stands alone as a romance comic series for young female readers). And indeed, some of these experiments—*Spider-Man India*, the DC Elseworlds series—use multiplicity—the possibility of alternative versions of the characters or parallel universe versions of the stories—as an alternative set of rewards for our mastery over the source material.[16]

Yet, the extraction process is not limited to the creation of other fragments of the narrative universe, but rather can take alternative directions. As Jenkins stresses, there is a constant dialectic between immersion, when consumers enter into the world of the story, and extractability, when "the fan takes aspects of the story away with them as resources they deploy in the spaces of their everyday life."[17] The viewer is an active subject who moves within a convergent and integrated environment. When the extraction process takes place, the consumer takes some fragments of a fictional universe and brings them with her. These fragments get completely detached from their source story.

This part of the process has been a main prerogative of the marketing strategies that are built around a media object, including all the licensing and merchandising operations that are typical of the media franchises. Nevertheless, these fragments do not seem to go toward any kind of recomposition; rather, they effectively remain as autonomous fragments of a story. An illustrative example would be those T-shirts that feature the face of Che Guevara, which no longer serve to tell the story of the Argentine revolutionary but rather exist just as a piece of a story that has been told for a long time, which may or may not be recognized by those who see the T-shirt image.

There are even some extraction operations that take elements from a narrative universe and diffuse them outside any specific context. But massive circulation makes the extracted objects (they might be images, as well as objects) subject to a quick obsolescence, since they tend to wear thin in a very short time. Thanks to their spreadability, some objects extracted (for instance from a serial narrative) can be seen and taken by a huge number of people. However, this undermines their durability, rendering them ephemeral objects. Nevertheless, their life might simply end with the extraction process, as instead they can be reintegrated within other media objects, for instance, through historical reconstructions. This kind of reintegration employs first a process of detachment that allows the reintegration to take place. In actual fact, in the media system, fragments that are extracted from a narration might ultimately prove to be persistent according to two different modalities.

In the first case, there might be a reintegration mechanism that allows a fragment to be adopted within a different universe. This is exemplified by the case of the Davy Crockett coonskin cap. In the 1950s, a fad became popular among young people who suddenly started to seek out the coonskin cap worn by Davy Crockett in the eponymous five-part Disney serial aired on ABC in one-hour episodes in 1954–1955. This kind of fad is a form of extraction that shares much with marketing strategies, which in turn can also help to guarantee the appropriate financing for the production of audiovisual products. In this specific case, the major success of the TV series, its hero and his cap (when re-edited, the first three episodes also found a theatrical release) led to a craze for the same cap in the United Stated and United Kingdom. A simplified version of the cap was marketed to young boys, together with a refined girl's version; at the peak of the fad, coonskin caps sold more or less five thousand pieces per day. But by the end of the 1950s, Crockett's popularity had waned and coonskin caps were left hidden in the back of the wardrobes. Nevertheless, the cap returned in numerous cultural references, the most important of which seems to have been the coonskin cap's presence as part of The Junior Woodchucks' uniform in Disney's Donald Duck comics.[18] The comic narration is in fact typically a "what-if" kind of narration, vast and without an ending, in which parallel universes and variations are welcome.

The other case is that of nostalgic recourse to vintage objects. These objects, taken from a vast narrative, are subjected to a comeback that is built through metonymy, as a part that stands for a whole. This is the case for the recent Italian TV series *1992* (Sky Italia, 2015) where the main character Leonardo Notte (played by Stefano Accorsi) wears a T-shirt saying "Ho ucciso io Laura Palmer" (I killed Laura Palmer). This T-shirt exists not only as a quotation of the David Lynch drama *Twin Peaks* (ABC, 1990–1991). Nor does the T-shirt mean to create any connection between *Twin Peaks* and *1992*. Instead, it is present because of its existence as an extracted fragment of a universe, taken away from where it belongs and reintegrated in a new fictional ecosystem. That T-shirt does not want the viewer to remember *Twin Peaks* and its narrative; instead, it wants the viewer to remember the fact that in 1992 in Italy, such a T-shirt was a must-have item, although nowadays it is nothing more than a prop in the scene. The T-shirt is now just a self-sufficient icon that persists with a very weak intertextual meaning.[19]

As mentioned, the extraction process has a lot in common with marketing strategies, which seek to encourage viewers to take pieces of the narration with them. Product placement strategies seek to do precisely this, for example, when sponsors pay to insert their products and brand into a fictional universe, hoping that these products will be extracted by the viewers and eventually purchased in the nonfictional world. This is the basic mechanism that lies behind the "as seen on TV" claim so frequently used in advertisements: the viewer buys something just because she has seen it on TV, regardless of whether this product maintains a relationship with the fictional world that generated it.

In sum, we consider the integration process as an operation that presumes a previous extraction, imposing a partial or total cancellation or even a substitution of the relations between the imported objects and its referential cultural context (e.g., when a fragment stands for a whole text, as in *1992*, when the Laura Palmer T-shirt stands for Italy in the 1990s rather than for *Twin Peaks*). The extraction process tends to make the extracted object ephemeral by being spreadable or viral in some cases and subject to a possible reintegration that would bring the object back to life under different conditions. As spreadable objects, the fragments extracted from a TV series are comparable to items of the world of fashion that suddenly are everywhere at a given time and are forgotten few weeks later, only to return again after ten years.

Memory and Permanence

Contemporary TV series display a particular sense of permanence. These products, through the integration of media offered by the big conglomerates, through franchising practices, and through the construction of high concepts, have been able to achieve exceptional duration (with some series lasting longer than ten years) and persistence among audiences. TV series are durable, furnished narrative universes, full of rich relationships between characters, the diegetic world, and the audience. In short, it is possible to inhabit those universes. TV series are extremely persistent, since they have been built on very long narratives and can survive various perturbations: both external ones, such as changes in programming slots, a decline in ratings, changing audiences or exceptional events, such as the 100-day writers' strike between 2007 and 2008; and internal ones, such as radical changes in the cast, the defection of actors, and spoiler phenomena.

With regards to the convergence/divergence paradigm and to the extraction and integration processes, we argue that memory and permanence, when they come to TV series, are not modes of convocation of textual mechanisms. In traditional narratives, we are able to remember a fragment precisely because it belongs to a larger text. This is the case of Count Ugolino, a character in Dante Alighieri's *Divine Comedy* but also a real person who lived in Italy in the 1200s. The way we recall this man and his story is entirely due to the persistence and efficiency of the text in which he features. Since the *Divine Comedy* is one of the world's greatest pieces of literature, we remember this part of the story because it comes from a very well-known and widely read book.

According to Jérôme Bourdon, "remembering television is not remembering a text with chapters, nor even a series of acts of viewing (as one might have expected): it is remembering contacts with a certain world 'out there,' which comes to exist through the television screen, but generates a variety of interactions that cannot be reduced to simple viewing."[20] Substantially, the ways in which the process of persistence is articulated in the contemporary media landscape make it clear that the existence of memories does not necessarily indicate the persistence of a text over the years. Rather, it indicates a dialectic of extraction/reintegration that, entirely unlike intertextual processes in traditional narratives, is produced by marketing, media systems, and production modes.

Thus, in the contemporary media system, memory and permanence[21] abstract from the text and are linked to the extraction/integration process. Permanence in this case is not due to the action of a subject that convenes a hypotext and reworks it, making it present again, but to a media and social practice that does not need the presence of a subject agent. It is an acephalous operation, situated more on the side of the marketing strategy than on that of quotation or allusion.

Conclusions

Starting from a very popular paradigm such as that of Jenkins's transmedia storytelling, we have sought to focus our attention on phenomena that Jenkins has not directly examined; instead, we concentrate on less evident features that are nonetheless helpful in discussions of intertextuality and memory.

This chapter studied intertextual relations, considering them to be the result of a dialectic between extraction and integration. This process can be explained as a form of the convergence/divergence paradigm, and we proposed reading extraction as an operation that often erases the relations between the extracted objects and their cultural context, therefore generating objects that are more the result of reconstruction than of an intertextual integration.

Fragments extracted from narratives can, moreover, attain persistence in media niches, where users free themselves from the constraints potentially imposed by the production project and take possession of the fragment, re-using it in oppositional ways and developing unusual reception and reappropriation practices. A media niche can be a very small environment, composed of relatively few fans, who are nevertheless extremely motivated with regard to the product, to such an extent that the value of such niches might be fairly high in terms of marketing strategies.

In the contemporary media system, the ways in which memory is built seem to be based more on the reintegration of extracted objects than on the transposition of the experience of a media past, as the aforementioned case of *1992* and *Twin Peaks* demonstrates. What is active here is mainly a showcase of objects, fragments, and paratexts that are reincorporated within a narrative, without any specific reference to the past media experience or to the memory of it.

Notes

1. With regard to narrative ecosystems, see Veronica Innocenti and Guglielmo Pescatore, "Information Architecture in Contemporary Television Series," *Journal of Information Architecture* 4, no. 1–2, Fall 2012, accessed 24 October 2015, *http://journalofia.org/volume4/issue2/05-pescatore*; Claudio Bisoni and Veronica Innocenti, eds. *Media mutations. Gli ecosistemi narrativi nello scenario mediale contemporaneo: spazi, modelli, usi sociali* (Modena: Mucchi, 2013).

2. See Veronica Innocenti and Guglielmo Pescatore, *Le nuove forme della serialità televisiva: Storia, linguaggio, temi* (Bologna: Archetipolibri, 2008), 29–53.

3. On vast narratives, see Pat Harrigan and Noah Wardrip-Fruin, eds., *Third Person: Authoring and Exploring Vast Narratives* (Cambridge, MA: MIT Press, 2009).

4. In reality, the development of ancillary texts and paratexts around a TV series can also originate in more spontaneous ways. This is the case, for instance, for the design mode of *derivation*, where the multistrand narrative structure of a series made the narrative content easily scalable, and therefore storylines could be easily broken down into modular packages. This was the case for products such as *ER* (NBC, 1994–2009) or *Buffy the Vampire Slayer* (The WB, UPN, 1997–2003), which generated videogames and novelizations in the wake of the success of the series. A further example, which is more dependent on the production project, is that of the *cross-media* parallel design mode, wherein

audiovisual products start with a narrative matrix and develop into a complex project whose completion necessitates several media, creating ad-hoc objects available for every kind of viewer.

5. On intertextuality, see Mikhail Mikhailovič Bakhtin, *The Dialogic Imagination: Four Essays*, ed. Michael Holquist, trans. Caryl Emerson and Michael Holquist (Austin: University of Texas Press, 1981); Julia Kristeva, *Semeiotiké: Recherches pour une sémanalyse* (Paris: Seuil, 1969); Gérard Genette, *Palimpsests: Literature in the Second Degree*, trans. Channa Newman and Claude Doubinsky (Lincoln: University of Nebraska Press, 1997). On intertextuality in cinema and media, see, among many others, Dan Harries ed., *The New Media Book* (London: BFI, 2002); Mikhail Iampolski, *The Memory of Tiresias: Intertextuality and Film*, trans. Harsha Ram (Berkeley: University of California Press, 1998) and, in Italian, Giovanni Guagnelini and Valentina Re, *Visioni di altre visioni: intertestualità e cinema* (Bologna: Archetipolibri, 2007); Guglielmo Pescatore, *L'ombra dell'autore. Teoria e storia dell'autore cinematografico* (Roma: Carocci, 2006), 107–128.

6. Henry Jenkins, "Transmedia Storytelling. Moving Characters from Books to Films to Video Games Can Make Them Stronger and More Compelling," *Technology Review*, 13 January 2003, accessed 24 October 2015, *http://www.technology review.com/news/401760/transmedia-storytelling*.

7. Henry Jenkins, *Convergence Culture. Where Old and New Media Collide* (New York: New York University Press, 2006).

8. Henry Jenkins, "Convergence? I Diverge," *Technology Review*, 1 June 2001, accessed 24 October 2015, *http://www.technologyreview.com/article/401042/convergence-i-diverge*.

9. Henry Jenkins, "Convergence and Divergence: Two Parts of the Same Process," 29 June 2006, *henryjenkins.org*, accessed 8 January 2016, *http://henryjenkins.org/2006/06/convergence_and_divergence_two.html*

10. Ibid.

11. On this concept of vast audiovisual narration and its complex ecosystem, built of ancillary and paratextual productions, and on the relations between convergence and divergence, see also Veronica Innocenti, Guglielmo Pescatore, and Luca Rosati, "Converging Universes and Media Niches in Serial Narratives: An Approach through Information Architecture," in Artur Lugmayr and Cinzia Dal Zotto, eds., *Media Convergence Handbook—Vol. 2 Firms and User Perspectives* (Springer, forthcoming).

12. "Shipping," Wikipedia, accessed 24 October 2015, *http://en.wikipedia.org/wiki/Shipping_(fandom)*.

13. In the contemporary media environment, multiplicity happens since media objects can be declined according to varied modalities and hypotheses, while in the traditional media context, this operation is difficult to achieve. Indeed, nowadays media objects can easily offer possibilities of alternative versions, "what-if" versions, and parallel universes, while this was far harder with traditional, closed texts.

14. On fan work and its link to specific practices and gender, see among others Francesca Coppa, "An Editing Room of One's Own: Vidding as Women's Work," *Camera Obscura: Feminism, Culture, and Media Studies* 26.2 (77), (September 2011): 123–130; Lucia Tralli, "Vidding as a Gendered Remix Practice," in "(En)Gendered Creativity. Actors Agencies Artifacts," Alice Cati, Mariagrazia Fanchi, and Rosanna Maule, eds., *Comunicazioni Sociali* 36.3 (2014): 406–416.

15. Henry Jenkins, "Revenge of the Origami Unicorn: The Remaining Four Principles of Transmedia Storytelling," 12 December 2009, *henryjenkins.org*, accessed 8 January 2016, *http://henryjenkins.org/2009/12/the_revenge_of_the_origami_uni.html*.
16. Ibid.
17. Ibid.
18. For further details on this story, see *http://en.wikipedia.org/wiki/Coonskin_cap*, accessed 24 October 2015.
19. A similar position on the presence of objects that emerge from our past media history in this TV series is proposed by Luca Barra, in "Ricomporre i frantumi," *La Rivista Il Mulino* website, 14 April 2015, accessed 24 October 2015, *http://www.rivistailmulino.it/news/newsitem/index/Item/News:NEWS_ITEM:2775*.
20. Jérôme Bourdon, "Some Sense of Time: Remembering Television," in *History and Memory* 15.2 (2003): 12–13.
21. On media and memory, see also Astrid Erll and Ansgar Nünning, eds., *A Companion to Cultural Memory Studies*, and in particular Section 6, *Media and Cultural Memory* (Berlin: De Gruyter, 2008); Motti Neiger, Oren Meyers, and Eyal Zandberg, eds., *On Media Memory: Collective Memory in a New Media Age* (Basingstoke, UK: Palgrave Macmillan, 2011).

References

Bakhtin, Mikhail M. *The Dialogic Imagination: Four Essays.* Trans. Caryl Emerson and Michael Holquist. Austin: University of Texas Press, 1981.
Bisoni, Claudio, and Veronica Innocenti, eds. *Media mutations: Gli ecosistemi narrativi nello scenario mediale contemporaneo: spazi, modelli, usi sociali.* Modena: Mucchi, 2013.
Bourdon, Jérôme. "Some Sense of Time: Remembering Television." *History and Memory* 15.2 (2003): 5–35.
"Coonskin cap," *http://en.wikipedia.org/wiki/Coonskin_cap*. Accessed 1 August 2015.
Coppa, Francesca. "An Editing Room of One's Own: Vidding as Women's Work." *Camera Obscura: Feminism, Culture, and Media Studies* 26.2 (2011): 123–130.
Erll, Astrid, and Ansgar Nünning, eds. *A Companion to Cultural Memory Studies.* Berlin: De Gruyter, 2008.
Innocenti, Veronica, and Guglielmo Pescatore. *Le nuove forme della serialità televisiva: Storia, linguaggio, temi.* Bologna: Archetipolibri, 2008.
———. "Information Architecture in Contemporary Television Series." *Journal of Information Architecture* 4.1–2 (2012): 57–72. Accessed 20 July 2015. *http://journalofia.org/volume4/issue2/05-pescatore*.
Innocenti, Veronica, Guglielmo Pescatore, and Luca Rosati. "Converging Universes and Media Niches in Serial Narratives. An Approach through Information Architecture." In *Media Convergence Handbook—Vol. 2: Firms and User Perspectives*, eds. Artur Lugmayr and Cinzia Dal Zotto. Berlin-Heidelberg: Springer, forthcoming.
Genette, Gérard. *Palimpsests: Literature in the Second Degree.* Trans. Channa Newman and Claude Doubinsky. Lincoln: University of Nebraska Press, 1997.
Guagnelini, Giovanni, and Valentina Re. *Visioni di altre visioni: intertestualità e cinema.* Bologna: Archetipolibri, 2007.

Harries, Dan, ed. *The New Media Book*. London: BFI, 2002.

Harrigan, Pat, and Noah Wardrip-Fruin, eds. *Third Person: Authoring and Exploring Vast Narratives*. Cambridge, MA: MIT Press, 2009.

Iampolski, Mikhail. *The Memory of Tiresias: Intertextuality and Film*. Trans. Harsha Ram. Berkeley: University of California Press, 1998.

Kristeva, Julia. *Semeiotiké : Recherches pour une sémanalyse*. Paris: Seuil, 1969.

Jenkins, Henry. "Convergence? I Diverge." *Technology Review*, 1 June 2001. Accessed 20 July 2015. *http://www.technologyreview.com/article/401042/convergence-i-diverge*.

———. "Transmedia Storytelling. Moving Characters from Books to Films to Video Games Can Make Them Stronger and More Compelling." *Technology Review*, 13 January 2003. Accessed 20 July 2015. *http://www.technologyreview.com/news/401760/transmedia-storytelling*.

———. *Convergence Culture. Where Old and New Media Collide*. New York: New York University Press, 2006.

———. "Convergence and Divergence: Two Parts of the Same Process." Accessed 20 July 2015. *http://henryjenkins.org/2006/06/convergence_and_divergence_two.html*.

———. "Revenge of the Origami Unicorn: The Remaining Four Principles of Transmedia Storytelling." Accessed 20 July 2015. *http://henryjenkins.org/2009/12/the_revenge_of_the_origami_uni.html*.

Neiger, Motti, Oren Meyers, and Eyal Zandberg, eds. *On Media Memory. Collective Memory in a New Media Age*. Basingstoke, UK: Palgrave Macmillan, 2011.

Pescatore, Guglielmo. *L'ombra dell'autore: Teoria e storia dell'autore cinematografico*. Rome: Carocci, 2006.

Ries, Al. "The Origins of Brands." Accessed 20 July 2015. *http://pr.harpercollins.com/author/microsite/readingguide.aspx?authorID=8182&isbn13=9780060570149&displayType=bookessay*.

"Shipping," Wikipedia, *http://en.wikipedia.org/wiki/Shipping_(fandom)*. Accessed 1 August 2015.

Tralli, Lucia. "Vidding as a Gendered Remix Practice." *Comunicazioni Sociali* 36.3 (2014): 406–416.

List of Contributors

Claudio Bisoni (University of Bologna) teaches courses on media reception and consumption, and the history and methodology of film criticism. His research focuses on the relationship between criticism, aesthetics, and modes of reception, as well as on North American and Italian cinema of the 1960s and 1970s. His publications include *Brian De Palma* (Recco, 2002); *La critica cinematografica. Metodo, storia e scrittura* (Bologna, 2006); *Gli anni affollati. La cultura cinematografica italiana (1970–1979)* (Roma, 2009); and *Elio Petri: Indagine su un cittadino al di sopra di ogni sospetto* (Torino, 2011). He has also worked on new media narrative forms and has edited (with Veronica Innocenti) the volume *Media Mutations: Gli ecosistemi narrativi nello scenario mediale contemporaneo. Spazi, modelli, usi sociali* (Modena, 2013). His essays and articles have appeared in various edited volumes and journals, including *La valle dell'Eden*, *Fotogenia*, *Close-up*, *Bianco e nero*, *Cinéma and Cie*, *Fata Morgana*, and *The Italianist*.

Marta Boni (University of Montreal) is Assistant Professor of Film and Television Studies. She works on television seriality, fan practices, and new media. Marta has published *Romanzo Criminale: Transmedia and Beyond* (Ca' Foscari University Press, 2013), co-edited *Networking Images* (Presses de la Sorbonne Nouvelle, 2013), and published various essays in international scientific journals. Her most recent accomplishment is the edited volume *World Building. Transmedia, Fans, Industries*, forthcoming (2016).

Paola Brembilla (University of Bologna) is a PhD candidate in Film and Media with a research project titled *American TV Series Between Aesthetics and Market*. Her research project, *American TV Series: How the Economic Network Shapes Content*, was published in the academic journal *Cinéma and Cie* (12:19, Fall 2012). In 2010, she was awarded a scholarship within the Overseas Exchange Program, and she attended the academic year 2010/2011 at the University of California—Berkeley as an EAP (Education Abroad Program) exchange student. Her research interests include the relationship between business strategies and narrative forms in U.S. TV series, along with media economics, narrative ecosystems, and economic networks in contemporary media industry. She has authored several other publications on the subject, including chapters and articles. She has also been a speaker at national and international conferences (Università di Bologna, Université Sorbonne Nouvell—Paris III, Universitat Ramon Llull—Facultat de Comunicaciò Blanquerna).

Jonathan Gray (University of Wisconsin-Madison) is Professor of Media and Cultural Studies. He is the author of *Television Studies* (with Amanda D. Lotz), *Show Sold Separately: Promos, Spoilers and Other Media Paratexts*, *Television Entertainment*, and *Watching with The Simpsons: Television, Parody, and Intertextuality*. He is also editor of *A Companion to Media Authorship* (with Derek Johnson), *Satire TV: Politics and Comedy in the Post-Network Era* (with Jeffrey P. Jones and Ethan Thompson), and *Fandom: Identities and Communities in a Mediated World* (with Cornel Sandvoss and C. Lee Harrington).

Veronica Innocenti (University of Bologna) is Assistant Professor and teaches History of Broadcasting and Film Marketing. She holds a PhD in Film Studies from the University of Bologna. She has been a speaker at several national and international conferences and the organizer of the conference Media Mutations 3 and 4, dedicated to narrative ecosystems (*www.mediamutations.org*). She is the author of several books, edited collections, and essays, including *Le nuove forme della serialità televisiva: Storia, linguaggio, temi* (Archetipo 2008, with Guglielmo Pescatore); *Factual, Reality, Makeover: Lo spettacolo della trasformazione nella televisione contemporanea* (Bulzoni 2013, co-edited with Marta Perrotta); and *Media Mutations: Gli ecosistemi narrativi nello scenario mediale contemporaneo. Spazi, modelli, usi sociali* (Mucchi 2013, co-edited with Claudio Bisoni).

Stephanie Janes (Royal Holloway, University of London) received her PhD in 2015. Her thesis focused on the production and reception of promotional alternate reality games in marketing campaigns for contemporary Hollywood cinema. Her broader research interests include promotional materials, digital media and digital cultures, audience research, and media fandoms. Recent publications include a chapter contribution to *Besides the Screen: The Distribution, Exhibition and Consumption of Moving Images* (ed. Virginia Crisp and Gabriel Menotti Gonring) and journal articles for *Arts and the Market* (October 2015) and *Participations: Journal of Audience and Reception Studies*.

Kathleen Loock (John F. Kennedy Institute for North American Studies, Freie Universität Berlin) is a postdoctoral research associate. As a member of the Research Unit "Popular Seriality: Aesthetics and Practice," she is writing a book that examines the cultural history of Hollywood remaking, from the transition to sound to the remakes, sequels, and prequels of the digital era. She is author of *Kolumbus in den USA: Vom*

Nationalhelden zur ethnischen Identifikationsfigur (2014), a study of the commemorative constructions and deconstructions of Christopher Columbus in nineteenth- and twentieth-century United States, and co-editor of the collections *Of Body Snatchers and Cyberpunks: Student Essays on American Science Fiction Film* (2011) and *Film Remakes, Adaptations, and Fan Productions: Remake | Remodel* (2012). She has also edited a special issue on serial narratives for the journal *Literatur in Wissenschaft und Unterricht* (2014) and is currently co-editing a special issue on film seriality for *Film Journal* (2017).

Giulio Lughi (University of Turin) is Associate Professor of Sociology of Cultural and Communicative Processes at the Interuniversity Department of Regional and Urban Studies and Planning. He teaches or has taught: Sociology of Media and Communication, Media Studies, New Media Culture, Multimedia Languages, Multimedia Publishing, and Multimedia Design. He mainly investigates the impact of information communication technology (ICT) in the humanities. he trained previously in literature, linguistics, and semiotics, has worked since the early 1990s on relations between culture and technology, new media, digital culture and creativity, interactivity, and narrative forms. He is currently president of the CISI (Interstructural Centre for Telematics and Information Services); director of NewMediaLab of University of Turin; member of the Scientific Council for Cultural Institutions and Processes Section of the Italian Association of Sociology; member of the Scientific and Educational Board of the Consortium ICON—Italian Culture on the Net; E-learning Activities Director of the University of Turin; and member of the Scientific Committee of the CSI Piemonte.

Fabrice Lyczba (University of Paris-Dauphine, France) is Associate Professor in American Studies. He defended his PhD dissertation in 2011 on "The Question of Realism in the Reception of Hollywood Silent Films, 1917–1927." His current research focuses on the circulation of media fiction in modern culture through cultural reception studies and ethnohistory. Among his recent publications are two articles dealing with 1920s American film reception: "Fictions of Intimacy and the Intimacy of Fiction: 'Going into People's Houses' and the Remediation of 1920s Film Reception" in David Roche ed., *Essays on Intimacy in English-Speaking Film* (McFarland, 2014, 46–60), and "Fictions incarnées: pratiques publicitaires du ballyhoo et regard spectatoriel dans le cinéma muet hollywoodien" (*1895: Revue de l'Association Française de Recherche sur l'Histoire du Cinéma*, 72 [Spring 2014]: 39–67).

Roy Menarini (University of Bologna, Rimini Campus) teaches Film and Cultural Industries and Fashion and Film Iconography. He has written several books on contemporary cinema, notably *Il cinema di David Lynch* (Alessandria, 2002), *William Friedkin* (Milano, 2003), and *Il cinema dopo il cinema* (Genova/Recco, 2011). He studied 1960s and 1970s italian popular cinema in *La parodia nel cinema italiano* (Bologna, 2002). He is currently working on the history and theory of cinephilia, and has edited *Le nuove forme della cultura cinematografica* (Milan/Udine, 2012). He also analyzes science fiction cinema: *Visibilità e catastrofi: Saggi di storia, teoria e critica della fantascienza* (Palermo, 2001) and *Cinema e fantascienza* (Bologna, 2012). He is programmer at the festival Cinema Ritrovato (Bologna), Premio Sergio Amidei (Gorizia), and director of the peer-reviewed online journal *Cinergie—Il cinema e le altre arti*.

Paolo Noto (University of Bologna) received his PhD in 2010 and now teaches and does research in the field of film history and new media. He is the co-organizer of the conference Media Mutations 6: *Modes of Productions and Narrative Forms in Contemporary TV Series* and Media Mutations 7: *Space Invaders. The Impact of Digital Games in the Contemporary Media Ecosystems.* Among his publications are *Il cinema neorealista*, a reader on Italian neorealism co-edited with Francesco Pitassio (Archetipolibri, 2010) and *Dal bozzetto ai generi: Il cinema italiano dei primi anni Cinquanta* (Kaplan, 2011), a monograph in which he challenged the most established examples of theory of film genres in light of Italian popular films of the 1950s. His most recent article, "'Che credeva, che fossi Cenerentola!': Changes of Clothes, Guest. Appearances, and Other Diva. Performances in 1950s Cinema," was published in *Italian Studies*, 70:3 (August 2015).

Roberta Pearson (University of Nottingham) is Professor of Film and Television Studies and Head of the Department of Culture, Film and Media. She is the author, co-author, editor, and co-editor of numerous books and articles. She has had a long-standing interest in popular cultural icons such as Batman and Sherlock Holmes. Among her recent publications are "Remembering Frank Sinatra: Celebrity Studies Meets Memory Studies" that discusses Sinatra's appropriation for heritage purposes in four American cities and "Good Old Index, or The Mystery of the Infinite Archive" that reflects on scholarly methods in the age of the Internet. She recently co-edited, with W. Brooker and W. Uricchio, *Many More Lives of the Batman* (BFI and Palgrave, 2015).

Guglielmo Pescatore (University of Bologna) is full Professor and teaches courses on Film and Media Semiotics as well as Theory and Techniques of New Media. His work has long focused on avant-garde and experimental cinema, topics on which he wrote several articles and essays published in journals and edited collections. Currently, his main interest is the impact of digital media on audiovisual communication, especially on new forms of authorship and new modes of fruition. He is the author of the books *L'ombra dell'autore: Teoria e storia dell'autore cinematografico* (Carocci, 2006) and *Le nuove forme della serialità televisiva* (Archetipo 2008, with Veronica Innocenti) and the editor of the collection of essays

Matrix. Uno studio di caso (Hybris, 2006). He is the coordinator of the PhD program in Visual, Performative and Media Arts of the University of Bologna.

Sara Pesce (University of Bologna) teaches Film History and Performance Studies and Media. Her research fields are: the historical and cultural roots of Hollywood industry, cultural memory and war representation in Italian and American cinema, memory and digital culture in the contemporary global context, acting, stardom and celebrity culture. On these topics she wrote articles published in journals and edited collections. She is the author of a few books: on Hollywood's Jewish founders (2005. *Dietro lo schermo: Gli immigrati ebrei che hanno inventato Hollywood. 1924–1946*); on World War II cultural memory and Italian cinema (2008. *Memoria e immaginario: La seconda guerra mondiale nel cinema italiano*); on the British actor Laurence Olivier's involvement in cinema and television (*Laurence Olivier nei film: Shakespeare, la star, il carattere*, Recco, Le Mani, 2012). She is editor and co-author of a book on film melodrama (2007. *Imitazioni della vita, il melodramma cinematografico*).

Valentina Re (Link Campus University, Rome) is Associate Professor. Her research focuses on film analysis methodologies, the relationships between film and media theories, literary theory and aesthetics, the relationship between cinema and the other languages, film consumption and circulation in the digital environment. In 2005, she obtained a PhD in Film Studies at the University of Bologna. From 2009 to 2014, she was Assistant Professor at Ca' Foscari University of Venice. She is a member of the editorial board of the journals *Cinéma and Cie* and *Cinergie*. Among her publications are the books, *L'innesto: Realtà e finzioni da Matrix a 1Q84* (2014, co-authored by A. Cinquegrani); *Cominciare dalla fine: Studi su Genette e il cinema* (2012); *Play the Movie: Il DVD e le nuove forme dell'esperienza audiovisiva* (2010, co-edited with L. Quaresima); *Visioni di altre visioni: intertestualità e cinema* (2007, co-authored by G. Guagnelini); and *Ai margini del film: Incipit e titoli di testa* (2006). In 2012, she edited the special issue of *Cinéma and Cie* titled *Nothing Is More Practical than a Good Theory: Genette Goes to the Movies/Rien n'est plus pratique qu'une bonne théorie: Genette va au cinéma*.

Lucia Tralli (University of Bologna) received her PhD in 2014 at the Visual, Performing, and Media Arts Department at the University of Bologna. Her main research focus is the reuse of media images in audiovisual productions. She received her MA with a thesis about the practice of found footage, and her doctoral dissertation, "Vidding Girls. Audiovisual Remix Practices in Contemporary Digital Culture," which focuses on fanvidding and gender-related issues in audiovisual remix practices. She has published papers on fandom, vidding, and gender in several Italian and international academic journals. She co-edited, with Monica Dall'Asta and Victoria Duckett, *Researching Women in Silent Cinema: New Findings and Perspectives* (2013).

William Uricchio (MIT and Utrecht University) is Professor of Comparative Media Studies at MIT in the United States as well as at Utrecht University in the Netherlands. He is principal investigator of the MIT Open Documentary Lab, which explores the frontiers of interactive and participatory reality-based storytelling. His work explores the frontiers of new media, at times by using a historical lens (old media when they were new, such as nineteenth-century television) and at times by working with interactive and algorithmically generated media forms (interactive documentaries and games in particular). Uricchio has been visiting professor at universities in Berlin (FU), Göttingen, Marburg, Stockholm and DREAM Professor in Denmark, as well as at the China University of Science and Technology. He has received numerous awards for his work, including Guggenheim, Humboldt, and Fulbright research fellowships and, most recently, the Berlin Prize. Uricchio has published widely, and his most recent book (with R. E. Pearson and W. Brooker) is *Many More Lives of the Batman* (BFI and Palgrave, 2015).

Kim Walden (University of Hertfordshire) is a Senior Lecturer in Film and TV Cultures at the School of Creative Arts, University of Hertfordshire, UK. She is currently completing research for her PhD. The thesis, titled "Transmedia: An Archaeology of Aesthetics," investigates the evolution of the transmedia in film culture. She is also researching and lecturing on film audience and the evolving relationship between films and the web, on the expanded texts of contemporary films, and on transmedia storytelling.

Index

Compiled by Stephanie Janes and Paolo Noto.